WALDEN

AND

CIVIL DISOBEDIENCE

Riverside Editions

RIVERSIDE EDITIONS

UNDER THE GENERAL EDITORSHIP OF

Gordon N. Ray

WALDEN

and

CIVIL DISOBEDIENCE

Henry David Thoreau

EDITED WITH AN INTRODUCTION AND NOTES BY

SHERMAN PAUL

THE UNIVERSITY OF ILLINOIS

HOUGHTON MIFFLIN COMPANY

Boston · 𝕿𝖍𝖊 𝕽𝖎𝖛𝖊𝖗𝖘𝖎𝖉𝖊 𝕻𝖗𝖊𝖘𝖘 𝕮𝖆𝖒𝖇𝖗𝖎𝖉𝖌𝖊

Henry David Thoreau: 1817–1862

WALDEN was first published in 1854
CIVIL DISOBEDIENCE was first published in 1849

CONTENTS

CONTENTS

INTRODUCTION

BY SHERMAN PAUL

I

LIFE — the "irrepressible satisfaction with the gift of life" — is the single theme of Thoreau's writing, all of which is biographical, the record of an aspiring soul's exploration of reality. "I . . . require of every writer," Thoreau said in explaining the "I," the subjective center of *Walden*, "a simple and sincere account of his own life. . . ." From first to last, all his work was devoted to telling not only how he had lived but how alive he had been, how much life he had got. But founded as it was on actual first-hand experience, it was never the immediate report of his experiment on life. Instead, it was the fruit of a slow growth, ripened by recollection, deeply colored by the hues of his mind, and "folded many times thick" by the seasons through which it matured. Place the day-to-day entries in his *Journals* against their final appropriation in his finished work, and the imaginative alchemy — the symbolization of his materials — becomes apparent. For he discovered early that "what is actually present and transpiring is commonly perceived by the common sense and understanding only, is bare and bald, without halo or the blue enamel of intervening air," but that "let it be past . . . and it is at once idealized." Then, he said, "it is a deed ripe and with the bloom on it. It is not simply the understanding now, but the imagination that takes cognizance of it."

Now, this is true of *Walden*, which, for all of its riches of common sense and actual things, was the "flower and fruit of a man," a deed ripe with the bloom on it, full of fragrance. According to Thoreau's intention, *Walden* was not to lead men to strict economies, not even to a life in the woods. In a letter to his "disciple" Harrison Blake, telling of his first encounter with Daniel Ricketson (a spiritual seeker who having read *Walden* turned to Thoreau for guidance), he reported that Ricketson wanted him, "having common sense," to "write in plain English always" in order to "*teach* men in detail how to live a simpler life. . . ." But, Thoreau told Blake, "I have no scheme about it, — no designs on men at all; and, if I had, my mode would be to tempt them with the fruit, and not with the manure." Give man, he added, changing the metaphor, "the bread of life compared with which *that* is bran," let him "only taste these loaves, and he becomes a skillful economist at once. He'll not waste much time in earning those." Unfortunately, like Ricketson, the reviewers and readers misunderstood Thoreau's intention: the symbolism — or *extra-vagant* expression, as he called it (page 221) — they thought only extravagance ("namby-pamby," "stuff," "mystical," Ricketson claimed); they did not see that "the words which express our faith and piety are not definite" but "significant and fragrant like frank-incense"; and even Thoreau's warning that words have several meanings, a "volatile truth," went unheeded. He did not intend, of course, to "level downward to our dullest perception always, and praise that as common sense"; and he had adopted symbolism because he had seen his universe symbolically and because it was the only way to truly communicate his valuable experiences, to speak "like a man in a waking moment, to men in their waking moments. . . ." If the "commonest sense is the sense of men asleep, which they express by snoring," nothing less would awaken them or cure their "brain-rot." Indeed, to get men to see their universe symbolically, to read beyond its lessons of matter-of-fact, was one of the most liberating things Thoreau had to offer.

Having misunderstood his method, however, these literalists of common sense also misunderstood what he had to say. They read *Walden* only as an account of Thoreau's life in the woods; they took the "residual statement," the factual record of his life at the pond, for the whole story, once more forgetting Thoreau's instructions — that the heavier element, the narrative fact, was required to float the lighter or spiritual fact. Seizing upon the dramatic act of his withdrawal from society, they thought him uncivil and, like Emerson who provided his Walden acres but did not approve of the experiment, branded him a hermit. As Holmes later remarked, giving the judgment of his generation, Thoreau was "the nullifier of civilization, who insisted on nibbling his asparagus at the wrong end. . . ." And perhaps to heal the sting of his remarks on economy, they saw in this simple means of dodging the pressures of society an end they considered worthless. Did this crank (and there were cranks aplenty in New England preaching the salvation of fresh air and water, of graham flour, of going without money) expect them, so happily satisfied with the luxurious benefits of civilization, to listen to his exultation over a needless belt-tightening? At best, as American society compounded the evils Thoreau had avoided, *Walden* was read as a social gospel — and *Walden* today is most often associated with his doctrine of simplicity, with escape from the burdens of complicated urban existence. That escape, however, is usually associated with the woods, with a return to a long-lost pastoralism; and even in Thoreau's time the identification of his experiment with the woods, as if only the woods promised fulfillment, forced him to clarify his intention by dropping the subtitle, *Life in the Woods*. If *Walden* needed any subtitle, it should have been *Life*; and to this end he offered, and continues to offer, not an escape, but the greatest discovery and gift: an open universe, forever novel, alive, and full of life, forever awaiting and sustaining the untried enterprises of man.

This was the discovery he had made when he went to Walden in the spring of 1845, a discovery that had certified the transcendental faith he had learned from Emerson and that, in the years of "decay" following Walden, he cherished and maintained by writing his book. Only after the fact, when he was powerless to perform the deed again, did he relive it in words, and then he more poignantly and fully realized its significance. With the trials and losses of these years, those glorious years of achievement climaxing the endeavors of his youth were subtly transformed into a testament of prospective hope, and *Walden* affirmed his faith in "the unquestionable ability of man to elevate his life by a conscious endeavor." The ecstasy of his former life in the Elysian fields — as he called Walden then — was magnificently reported because it was now colored by his resolution; and the season of joy was given its natural place among the other seasons he had known in such a way that joy was not only the gift of youth but the reward of a mature remaking of one's life.

That one does not readily separate these chronological strands, however, was due in part to Thoreau himself. He knew the artistic value of his narrative facts, that his "fable" had to have a firm foundation, and he minimized all that time had wrought by speaking of *Walden* as the record of his residence at the pond in 1845–47, claiming that only a few details had been added. And because he believed that the hero hides his struggles and that one should not communicate his dyspepsia but his joy, he did not "propose to write an ode to dejection, but to brag as lustily as chanticleer in the morning. . . ." His spiritual history, nevertheless, was woven into the texture of *Walden*. The resolute tone, if nothing else, proclaims it; and the chapter on "Higher

Laws," full of his later determination for discipline and purity, and indeed the very structure of the book, with its culmination in rebirth, disclose it. To read *Walden*, then, as the account of only the Walden years — and it has been read in this way because it has long been assumed that he wrote the book at the pond — is to miss the tremendous struggle that makes *Walden* so glorious. It is to overlook the obstacles and evils that transcendentalists, like all human kind, have known, to make the faith that Thoreau enacted easy, when he himself knew the abyss beneath unity and the horrors of spiritual emptiness, and confessed during the years he was writing *Walden* that "a ticket to Heaven must include tickets to Limbo, Purgatory and Hell." And it is to disregard the fact that the years at Walden yielded two books, that there he wrote *A Week on the Concord and Merrimack Rivers* and infused it with the new found joys of his adventure. For *Walden* was his second book and his second attempt to find a form that would express his life; it was primarily the spiritual history of the years from 1845 to 1854, just as the *Week* was the spiritual history of the years from 1839 to 1849. Companion volumes, they cover the course of his quest for an organic life in Nature, the easy, available communion of his youth and the hard-won, intellectual communion of his manhood; taken together, they are the American equivalent of Wordsworth's *Prelude*; they are the richest account we have of American transcendental experience.

II

ONE WOULD HAVE to know more of Thoreau's life than he provides in *Walden* in order to explain the "private business" he referred to when he said that "my purpose in going to Walden Pond was not to live cheaply nor to live dearly there, but to transact some private business with the fewest obstacles. . . ." For his private business was a concern of long standing, a matter long delayed that he preferred to speak of in whimsy and allegory. When he told of how he had desired to spend his life in years past, he said that he had been anxious "to stand on the meeting of two eternities, the past and the future, which is precisely the present moment," that he had been eager "to anticipate, not the sunrise and the dawn merely, but, if possible, Nature herself," and that he wanted "to hear what was in the wind, to hear and carry it express!" He told how in trying to achieve these ends — to live in the moment or eternal now, to know the laws of Nature so well that in her every phenomenon his mood would find its correspondence, and to participate in spirit and express it for all mankind — he had kept a journal "of no very wide circulation," had been the "self-appointed inspector" and warden of Nature and the wild, and had "woven a kind of basket of a delicate texture [the *Week*]" which no one would buy. His townsmen, he said, would not "make my place a sinecure with a moderate allowance," and his accounts — he punned — had never been "audited." And so he turned "more exclusively than ever to the woods" — for these reasons, and for other losses darkly hinted at in the hound, bay horse, and turtle-dove that he said he had lost long ago. Not one to postpone his life, he went to the pond, built a hut (his "small counting house"), and, entering the business without any capital but his own self-reliance, began his trade with the "Celestial Empire."

It was an unusual trade, and "a labor to task the faculties of a man" — certainly one that he had not been trained for at Harvard College, although there he had first been stirred by a nascent transcendentalism to follow it. Already dedicated to Truth and Principle, and hungry for the superiority and public influence he believed were the warrants of a devotion to Reason (as his college essays clearly show), he was one of those young men who illustrated, according to Henry James, the "queer search" of the New England character for "something to expend itself upon." He was one of the "young men of the fairest promise," whom Emerson addressed in "The American Scholar" on the occasion of the commencement of Thoreau's class: young men "who begin life upon our shores, inflated by the mountain winds, shined upon by all the stars of God" but who "find the earth below not in unison with these" and "are hindered from action by the disgust which the principles on which business is managed inspire. . . ." "The American Scholar" and the Emerson who represented him were, of course, a challenging alternative to the professions of expediency; especially since Emerson had wrapped about the scholar the mantle of greatness and had made his work "the study and the communication of principles" and "the conversion of the world" at the same time that he united this public end with individual fulfillment — with the "peculiar fruit . . . each man was created to bear. . . ." The scholar, he said at Dartmouth College in the following year, "is the favorite of Heaven and earth, the excellency of his country, the happiest of men. . . . His successes are occasions of the purest joy to all men."

The way to that vocation, however, was difficult because it required self-reliance — the repudiation of the traditional, social institu-

tions of culture — because one's vocation was unique, ultimately
one's own character, and even the calling Emerson had created for
himself would not afford, as both Alcott and Thoreau were to learn,
a sufficient model for others. Like many ideas Emerson announced
in his early years with the expectation of immediate enactment, that
of the scholar was slow in being fulfilled. Do what he would to instruct the youth who answered his summons, he found — and most
painfully in the case of his "brave Henry," in whom he saw the promise of an executive genius and the active powers to engineer for all
America that would complement his own passivity — that if the
young men "do not wish to go into trade" and "reject all the ways of
living of other men," as he told Carlyle in 1842, still they "have none
to offer in their stead."

The problem of vocation troubled Thoreau all his life — not that he
was without one, but that his was not covered by any respectable label.
It was not proper for a youth educated at Harvard, and at great sacrifice on the part of his family, to walk idly in the woods; and while all
his classmates were "choosing their profession, or eager to begin some
lucrative employment . . . it required rare decision," Emerson admitted in his funeral tribute, "to refuse all the accustomed paths and
keep his solitary freedom at the cost of disappointing the natural expectations of his family and friends. . . ." Disappoint them he did, even
Emerson who in "Self-Reliance" had approved of Thoreau's determination to follow his genius: "He walks abreast with his days and
feels no shame in not 'studying a profession,' for he does not postpone
his life, but lives already."

It was easier, perhaps, to walk abreast of the day in the years immediately following his graduation, when schoolteaching put off the
expectations of his friends and he was free to begin his apprenticeship
as a writer — for that was the vocation he had chosen. He could even
delay long enough to get the graduate training Emerson provided him
during his stay at the Emersons in 1841–43. Apprenticeships, however, have their term and even Emerson's benign help had its obliga-
tions: when Thoreau's lectures before the Concord Lyceum and his
poems and essays in *The Dial* (which he edited with Emerson) showed
that he was ready, Emerson shipped him off to Staten Island, to his
brother William, as a tutor, with the understanding that this scholar
and poet "as full of buds of promise as a young apple tree" should have
the time and place to continue his work, "pending the time when he
shall procure for himself literary labor from some quarter in New

York." Unfortunately, Thoreau did not carry his seige against the literary capital; he could not write "companionable" articles, and what he could and did write the Knickerbockers would not pay for. He returned home, having paid his debt to Emerson with failure, and having, meanwhile, acquired other debts, which he paid off in the following year in his father's pencil factory. Once more an Apollo enslaved to Admetus, as he frequently lamented his condition, he simply wrote in his biographical record of the year before he went to Walden Pond, "Made pencils in 1844."

Thoreau had chosen writing because to be socially useful the transcendental life had to be expressed and because writing permitted him to live the transcendental life that was "agreeable to his imagination." Success in the literary marketplace would have made this possible: then the very life he had chosen to live would have paid its way with its own fruit. But having failed to sell his "baskets," his vocation set him another problem, that of getting his living without losing his life, that of mingling in the world where "trade curses everything" without impoverishing those inspirations and perceptions for which he lived. "If we live truly," Emerson had posed the problem in "Self-Reliance," "we shall see truly." To be self-reliant was to live an organic life, to cut the bonds of artificial social life and remake one's relations according to the primary laws of Nature; it was self-culture, nothing less than making one's life one's vocation, tending it as one would a plant or as a poet shapes a poem. Thoreau never fully achieved this goal, though at the end of his life, as he recounted it in "Wild Apples," he was proud of his hardy, long-matured, and spicy fruit, sure that his determination to grow wild had been a good thing even though it had left him dwarfed and stunted and encrusted with thorns. That was the price he had paid to go his own way: the wild apple tree that "emulates man's independence and enterprise" had been browsed on by fate, by the coercions and importunities of society and friends, by the pencil-making and surveying which were, for the rest of his life, in spite of his continued efforts to succeed as a lecturer and writer, the servitudes by which he earned his freedom.

Even by the time he went to Walden, and especially afterwards, his problem was not so much finding a vocation as finding the conditions that would make the one he had never postponed possible; and then the success he sought became the moments of ecstatic communion with Nature, the perceptions and the insights that were *life* and that, by radiating him, vindicated his endeavor to live truly. Everything he wrote from the "Natural History of Massachusetts" to "Walking" was an attempt to define this vocation, from the sympathetic way of beholding "facts" by the "finer organization" of his senses, by an "Indian wisdom," to the sauntering that enabled him by long association with his environment to make the fact "flower in a truth." The bravery this life demanded, and which was one of its attractions for Thoreau, had been proclaimed as early as his lecture on "Society," in his youthful testament, *The Service: Qualities of the Recruit*, where the military imagery that figures in his work was first made explicit, and in "A Winter Walk"; and the leisure it required, and the richer experience it offered, which the pace and tone as well as the actual narrative of his writing always conveyed, were already in his earliest excursions, "A Winter Walk" and "A Walk to Wachusett."

In this early work, however, he defined his vocation only to announce it; from the *Week* on, with growing insistence, he defined it to defend it. For his vocation was defined or focused by the life he lived, by his deepening awareness of the struggle to wrest meaning from Nature and so make his life significant, and by a widening awareness of the uses of Nature. Indeed, the definition which took the final form of the saunterer — though walking had always been the mode of his life — was that of the student of environment. The loss of the private ecstasy of his youth, when his own delight in Nature had been sufficient, had transformed him into a student of human culture. Though life remained the heart of his vision, his vision had become public, scanning wide reaches of human history, even turning to close scientific scrutiny, that he might learn the essential lessons of man's interaction with the organic world. This was a greater "fruit" than the wild apple, simply because it opened to all men the possibility of self-culture that Thoreau's own life dramatized. And perhaps it was the greatest fruit of transcendentalism as well: for though the function of the organic environment in human culture no longer rests on the transcendental philosophy of Nature — as one sees in Benton Mac-Kaye's *The New Exploration*, a landmark in regional planning directly inspired by Thoreau, "the philosopher of environment" — the transcendental view had led Thoreau to the first American exploration of that relationship. Here, in fact, Thoreau had gone beyond Emerson's *Nature*, which had been the manual of his vocation and his introduction to the uses of Nature, and, unrecognized by his teacher, had engineered for all America.

Although Emerson's treatise, which Thoreau had read during his college years, had awakened him to the new vistas of a life in Nature, he did not at first associate this life with the woods. When he left college, Nature for him was a rather indefinite concept, a "prospect" of untried fields for heroism, a new way of seeing the possibilities of life. It answered his desire, as he wrote in his commencement part on "The Commercial Spirit," for a manly and independent life. Repudiating the "blind and unmanly love of wealth," he would be a "Lord of Creation" rather than a "slave of matter"; he would live in "this curious world which . . . is more wonderful than it is convenient; more beautiful than it is useful; . . . more to be admired and enjoyed than used." To do this, moreover, he would reverse the order of things — a promise he carried out in the *Week* and *Walden*, where vocation became vacation; for "the seventh should be man's day of toil," he said, "and the other six his Sabbath of the affections and the soul, — in which to range this widespread garden, and drink in the soft influences and sublime revelations of Nature."

Such was the life that was agreeable to his imagination, one that he felt was guaranteed by the stimulating assurances of Emerson's *Nature*. There he had learned not only that Nature was beneficent, that it supplied the needs of spirit as well as commodity, but that by means of the wonderful correspondence of man and Nature he could "enjoy an original relation to the universe" — share the currents of Being and thereby become a "creator in the finite." Armed with the idealistic philosophy Emerson had reclaimed for his generation, a philosophy in which ideas were sovereign, he felt that he could "walk even with the Builder of the Universe" and put the foundations under the castles he had built in the air. For Nature, Emerson had shown, was not mechanical but organic, the continuing handiwork of God; the life in Nature was the ever-present spirit of God, and her phenomena "the present expositor of the divine mind." Man, therefore, had "access to the entire mind of the Creator" because the ideas he had in his communion with Nature were Ideas, the constitutive Reality of the universe as well as the reality of his mind.

In this organically-spiritualized idealism, every fact of Nature answered to a fact of consciousness in the human mind, and because of this correspondence the life of consciousness could best be pursued in Nature. Everything in Nature, the entire external world, could be taken possession of by the mind: the brute fact transformed in this experience into value, fused with the inner and subjective and given its human-spiritual significance. Seized in this way the fact flowered in a truth; or rather projected in this way — since Emerson in going beyond "Idealism" to "Spirit" had internalized the whole process and had made Nature, the facts themselves, the issue of spirit — every mood of the mind found its objective expression. As Thoreau described his youthful confidence in this subjective idealism in "The Inward Morning,"

> Packed in my mind lie all the clothes
> Which outward nature wears,
> And in its fashion's hourly change
> It all things else repairs.

> In vain I look for change abroad,
> And can no difference find,
> Till some new ray of peace uncalled
> Illumes my inmost mind.

The inward morning, the wakefulness he sought later on, was, of course, the influx of inspiration without which Nature, as he found, was barren. Then his universe was indeed broken in two, the galvanic ecstasy gone. But rather than disown the faith in which he had invested his life, he accepted the implication of Emerson's statement that to see truly one must live truly: "The ruin or the blank that we see when we look at nature, is in our own eye." He found the fault, not in the Emersonian theory, but in his own unworthiness: he acknowledged the guilt of impurity. And where once, in his youth, he had all unconsciously had a perfect communion, he now determined, with a heroism he never dreamed he would be called on to show, to rebuild his universe and his faith. He tried to bring the poles of the Emersonian universe together by purifying the channels of perception, by living a disciplined and ascetic life, and by studying Nature more objectively. By the one he hoped to renew his worthiness, by the other to know Nature so intimately that he could anticipate her moods — together, he hoped, he would once more complete the circuit of inspiration. But if this conscious endeavor had its rewards in the richer symbolic readings of Nature of his mature writing, it did not bring with it the fullness of ecstasy, the flow of inspiration through him. "The unconsciousness of man," he said in the *Week*, where he criticized Goethe for being too consciously the artist, "is the consciousness of God." By conscious means he could not retrieve the unconsciousness of his youth, that glorious passivity he recalled in *Walden,* when he spent his life lavishly "dreaming awake," "floating over its [the pond's] surface as the zephyr willed...." This was the personal tragedy that humanized the youth who had had eternity in his eye; this rooted him and socialized his vision; but it was also the struggle that the hero tried to hide.

When he first read *Nature* he was hardly aware that the mountain by which he symbolized his transcendent aspirations would be so steep. He had been dazzled by the American scholar who had personally set him to work journalizing and who later sheltered him — the Emerson in whose world "every man would be a poet, Love would reign, Beauty would take place, Man and Nature harmonize." He had been stirred more deeply than anyone else in his generation by the power of Emersonian perception for the conduct of life, by the possibility of making life an art. For *Nature* affirmed that man was no longer the slave of matter but the shaper of the external circumstances of his life. These he could build around him with the same organic fitness with which the bark fits the tree, as a function of the idea that controlled his life, in the very way the Creator — the Supreme Artist — "put forth" the organic world as the expression of His Ideas. Man's life would grow out of him in the way a tree springs from the seed, puts forth leaves, flowers, and fruit, assimilating and transforming all that Nature provides for its nurture into a resplendent ripeness. Man would be the poem of his own creation, or the statue, as Thoreau said, that he would carve out of the elements about him. And even more grandly, he would make his own world, the landscape would radiate from him; he would have as Thoreau had at Walden, "my own sun and moon and stars, and a little world all to myself." This was the exhilarating prospect Emerson had opened: " 'Nature is not fixed but fluid,' " he said. " 'Spirit alters, moulds, makes it. The immobility or bruteness of nature is the absence of spirit; to pure spirit it is fluid, it is volatile, it is obedient. Every spirit builds itself a house, and beyond its house a world, and beyond its world a heaven. Know then that the world exists for you. For you is the phenomenon perfect. What we are, that only can we see.... Build therefore your own world. As fast as you conform your life to the pure idea in your mind, that will unfold its great proportions.' "

To conform one's life to the idea in one's mind, to live, as Thoreau wrote while he was composing *Walden,* "that you may the more completely realize and live in the idea which contains the reason of your life, that you may build yourself up to the height of your conceptions"

— this was to live greatly, to use one's life wisely. "The whole duty of life," Thoreau said in 1841, recognizing the problem of vocation, "is contained in the question how to respire and aspire both at once." Already discontented with the tame life he was living as a school-teacher, and with the fact that he was not marching to his own music, he proposed that he help himself by "withdrawing . . . [by] determining to meet myself face to face sooner or later." The solitary position in which he had pictured himself in his lecture on "Society" now became the "most positive life that history notices" — "a constant retiring out of life, a wiping one's hands of it seeing how mean it is, and having nothing to do with it." And farming, which he always felt was a noble vocation, first suggested itself as a solution. But before he could act on it, he went to the Emersons as handy-man, expecting in the adventure of friendship that "a great person . . . will constantly give you great opportunities to serve him. . . ."

Friendship was the supreme transcendental relationship, for without it, Thoreau learned, Nature ceased to be morally significant. He had gone to Emerson with high hopes that in their relationship the world would learn "what men can build each other up to be, when both master and pupil work in love." Their relationship, however, had its undercurrent of antagonism, if only because of Thoreau's ideal expectancies and Emerson's benevolent but patronizing attitude toward his superserviceable Henry. "We do [not] wish friends to feed and clothe our bodies — neighbors are kind enough for that," Thoreau complained, "but to do the like offices to ourselves. We wish to spread and publish ourselves, as the sun spreads its rays. . . ." Before long he found that "life in gardens and parlors" was unpalatable to him, that he was growing "savager and savager every day," that his wish, still unfulfilled, was to be "nature looking into nature," that from this recess he might "put forth sublime thoughts daily, as the plant puts forth leaves." "When any scorn your love," he wrote at this time, "let them see plainly that you serve not them but another. If these bars are up, go your way to other of God's pastures. . . . When your host shuts his door on you he incloses you in the dwelling of nature. . . . My foes restore me to my friends." Even at Emerson's, Nature became the refuge for his discontent, and before a year had passed, he wrote: "I want to go soon and live away by the pond, where I shall hear only the wind whispering among the reeds. It will be success if I shall have left myself behind. But my friends ask what I will do when I get there. Will it not be employment enough to watch the progress of the seasons?" And the next day he added: "I don't want to feel as if my life were a sojourn any longer. That philosophy cannot be true which so paints it. It is time now that I begin to live."

But he lingered because, with Emerson so much away lecturing, his services were indispensable, and because the deaths of his brother John and Emerson's son Waldo had united them in grief. Still the feeling of delay did not abate, but intensified in plaintiveness: "What . . . can I do to hasten that other time . . . [when] there will be no discords in my life? . . . My life, my life! why will you linger? . . . How often has long delay quenched my aspiration! Can God afford that I should forget him? Is he so indifferent to my career? Can heaven be postponed with no more ado?" And when he went to Staten Island it was with reluctance, the stigmata of which were an "unaccountable" bronchitis and a "skirmishing with drowsiness" that interfered with his literary projects. The city, moreover, unmanned him, for though he was always the most perceptive of travelers, he did not have a traveler's temperament; the strange surroundings and the multiplicity of sensations disturbed the tranquillity and stability, the pastoral routine, that he needed. The herds of people — "the pigs in the street" that he wrote of to Emerson — a great tide entering the Narrows and flowing West, all bent on progress, taught him, as he said in "Paradise (To Be) Regained," that "we must first succeed alone, that we may enjoy our success together."

But the most valuable thing his first — and longest — stay in the city taught him was his need for roots; it crystallized his longing and discontent into a hut beside a pond in Concord. When he wrote "The Landlord" for the *Democratic Review* he not only described a hut in a retired place but made it a symbol of his own sincerity and sociality — here was the open and hospitable hut, that one lofty room in which all the secrets of housekeeping were exposed, that he imagined in "House-Warming" in *Walden*; and in "A Winter Walk," which he also wrote at this time, he first canvassed the scenery of his life: Walden Pond, Fair Haven Cliffs and Bay, and the Concord River. Here, too, was a deserted woodman's hut that suggested the rude shelter he later built. And as he sat within it, he enjoyed "the friendship of the seasons" that he described in "Sounds" and "Solitude" in *Walden*, and felt the appeal of the life it would permit him to live. The pond, furthermore, first began to acquire the personal associations that he would explicitly develop in *Walden*, but the lesson it symbolized now was the Oriental wisdom in which the Staten Island interlude had schooled him: " 'sitting still at home is the heavenly way; the going out is the way of the world.' "

Staten Island, then, drove him back to Concord and to Nature. "Where nature ceases to be supernatural to a man what will he do then?" he had asked despairingly in this first crisis. "Of what worth is human life if its actions are no longer to have this sublime and unexplored scenery? Who will build a cottage and dwell in it with enthusiam if not in the Elysian fields?" His determination on Walden, however, even after the delay of a year in the pencil factory, was not made easy. His friends, understanding his proposal in theory — as one sees in Charles Lane's "Life in the Woods" in *The Dial* (see Appendix) — did not approve of the "simple, fibrous life" in practice; and when one considers that Thoreau's experiment was one of the most daring and dramatic of transcendental acts, their sullen silence during his years at the pond, as if he had gone out of the world, showed the strength of their disapproval. In fact, it was partly to get away from the ceaseless transcendental debates in Concord parlors that Thoreau wanted to go to the pond. To live in the woods was not only an economic expedient that would permit him the leisure to write; it would permit him to make his relations on his own terms, free from the expectations of his friends.

Once there, at last face to face with "the great facts of his existence," Thoreau was overwhelmed by a joy that was everything he had anticipated. This, he later realized, was the great occasion of his life — an adventure that mounts in excitement from day to day as one follows in the *Journal* his own sudden sense of release from bondage. At last, he said, he walked the fields "with unexpected expansion and long-missed content, as if there were a field worthy of me." The usual boundaries of his life were dispersed, and he learned, as he later dramatized his belief in the uncommitted life in his conversation with John Field (pages 140 ff.), that "your fetters are knocked off; you are really free." "Yes," he told himself, "roam far, grasp life and conquer it, learn much and live. . . . Dismiss prudence, fear, conformity. Remember only what is promised." Free "to adventure on life now, his vacation from humbler toil having commenced" and blest by his "hard and emphatic life" in the Elysian fields, his joy at the pond helped him transform his 1839 excursion on the Concord and Merrimack into the spiritual holiday of the *Week*. This book, in fact, with its confidence in Nature and its daily adventures in ecstasy, was a rhapsody to wakefulness, the record of his "morning work," a form for thought itself. And compared with *Walden*, which was the form for the growth of consciousness and the record of his wakening, it was more faithful in spirit to the life he had had at the pond.

There was nothing in this life, moreover, that justified the fears of his friends that he would lose himself in the solitudes of his own ecstasy. For as it had for Whitman, self-realization in Nature suffused him with love. Neither life nor love could be shared, he learned, until he had found his own center, the pride that rested on the security of his own self-reliance. Then, indeed, he could brag for mankind. And then he saw the representative value of his private reform; he even saw himself as a stock personality, better able to speak for common working men than Emerson because he had known and surmounted the conditions of their lives. His life in the woods had put in perspective the life of village and city, and counting his gains, he hoped that his example would begin the social redemption of New England. For unlike the many social experiments of his day (Alcott had gone to Fruitlands in 1843, and Brook Farm was in its Fourieristic phase when Thoreau lived at Walden) — unlike the ideal lives that Alcott had said "none of us were prepared to actualize practically," Thoreau's experiment had been successful. He had "reduced a fact of the imagination to be a fact to his understanding," as he said in *Walden*, in the hope "that all men will at length establish their lives on that basis."

He had not planned to live permanently at the pond, however, and the Walden experiment came to an end when Thoreau, at the bidding of Mrs. Emerson, returned to manage the household during Emerson's absence in England in 1847–48. In many respects, Thoreau took up his life where he had left it before going to Staten Island, with the advantages, however, of now being the master of the house and of having the manuscript of a publishable book in his possession. Walden had healed his defeat and restored his confidence, and he felt ready now for a life of successful authorship. He immediately set to work preparing lectures, and the reception of some of them seemed to promise success. But again he was thwarted by delay, this time by the refusal of publishers to print the *Week*, his bid for fame. Advised by Emerson to issue the book at his own expense, he finally published the *Week* in 1849, but the sale was so poor that Thoreau did not hazard another book until he had paid his debts. That delay, however, providing the background of new and more difficult obstacles, was the making of *Walden*.

For faced once more with the problem of economy in the years following Emerson's return, Thoreau had turned again, this time permanently, to the pencil factory — and had added to his chains those
of the surveyor.   This life, of course, was hardly satisfactory; it
robbed him of the time to work for and with his nobler faculties; it
was "trivial"; and surveying, which forced him "to live grossly or
inattentive to [his] diet," he felt, had made his life "prosaic, hard, and
coarse."   In "Life Without Principle," where the bitterness of these
years was distilled, leaving his gladness for *Walden*, he said that "a
man had better starve at once than lose his innocence in the process
of getting his bread."   Indeed, the despair of his later years, those
autumnal years of "decay" in which he was literally the " 'god in
ruins' " Emerson spoke of in *Nature* — the god who was once " 'per-
meated and dissolved by spirit,' " who " 'filled nature with his overflowing currents,' " and the laws of whose mind had " 'externized
themselves into day and night, into the year and the seasons' " — was
over his lost innocence.   This loss, this impurity, was measured by the
loss of communion with Nature, and his world, as Emerson said of the
fallen man, now lacked unity, and lay "broken and in heaps. . . ."
There were, of course, other contributory "stains": that bustling
nineteenth century that destroyed his repose, binding him to society
with the ligature of his own desire for social justice — Negro slavery
and Irish "slavery," the Mexican War, the Anthony Burns' affair,
and his own night in jail, all teaching him that "life itself being worthless, all things with it, that feed it, are worthless"; and more personally, the irreparable alienation from his friends, and his strenuous efforts to overcome the first advances of illness by an outdoor life,
which, intensified by the strain of the scientific attention he had given
to Nature in his attempt to find communion, became a permanent dis-
ability.   Moreover, from his arduous study of Nature — he had now
embarked on the staggering labor of finding in the seasons of Nature
the corresponding seasons of man — he learned that his pristine youth
or springtime was passed, that the "second spring" of autumn was not
a time of germination but of ripening, and that to achieve this seasoned
virtue, the sloth and sensuality and impurity of the hot summer of
of growth had to be overcome.   Summer was no longer the extended
spring it had been in his youth, but the season of his present manhood,
when "Pegasus," he confessed, "has lost his wings; he has turned a
reptile and gone on his belly."   The reptilian imagery of *Walden* (as
well as the imagery of carrion, stagnation, and slumber) were the re-

sult of these years when, living "this slimy, beastly kind of life," Thoreau felt that he had become "the very sewers, the cloacae of nature."

In his desire for purity, Thoreau transferred the values of spring to autumn, for autumn was a rejuvenescence, with its cooler days and purer atmosphere, its returning birds and late flowerings and running crystal streams. At the same time, however, he returned in memory to his youth. He longed again for "those youthful days!" He wished again to be a child. Nothing, he felt, was "comparable with the experiences of my boyhood. . . ." If the seasons of Nature taught him the inevitability of the seasons of man, and even assured him that harvest was superior to seedtime, still the "knowledge of ourselves" that came with manhood spoiled his satisfaction. In spite of (and because of) his discipline and asceticism, he could not win back the time when "nature developed as I developed, and grew up with me" and "my life was ecstasy." He could only remember that before his "losses" he had been "all alive, and inhabited my body with irrepressible satisfaction. . . ." As he wrote *Walden* in these years, he knew that his life had been one of obstacles; that once, at the pond, he had overcome them. The spring he now desired was the rebirth he hoped to earn by the purity of his manhood, a rebirth that he believed was possible because of his former victory, and guaranteed by a law of Nature as certain as that of the seasons — the law of renewal. With this double truth, he found that he could be true to the course of his life: to the seasons of life and to his faith in an eternal spring that would transcend the seasons themselves. In *Walden*, the fruit of his ripening year, he hoped to keep this faith alive by memorializing the period that had crowned his life. Still undaunted, he believed, as he once told Harrison Blake, that "what can be expressed in words can be expressed in life."

III

THE KNOWLEDGE of the seasons was the most important addition to Thoreau's thought after 1850. It made possible the metaphors of ripening and completion that give his last work a tone of acceptance and quiet satisfaction; and it also made possible the fable of the renewal of life in *Walden*. When "for convenience" Thoreau put the experience of his two years at the pond into one, when he saw that the narrative action might be related to the seasons, he had the "fable with a moral" with which to express the meaning he now gave to that period of his life. Unlike that of the *Week*, which made the day the unit of time and of inspiration, the fable of the seasons enabled Thoreau to be true to the trials, changes, and growth he had known — to actualize by means of his former life his present aspirations. "Some men's lives are but an aspiration, a yearning toward a higher state," he wrote in 1851, "and they are wholly misapprehended, until they are referred to, or traced through, all their metamorphoses." In the seasons of *Walden* he could trace his metamorphoses: the passage from servitude to liberation, and the self-transcendence of his transformation from impurity to purity — the rebirth of new life out of the old.

The day, of course, had its seasons; it was the epitome of the year: "The night is winter, the morning and evening are the spring and fall, and the noon is summer." The spiritual change from sleep to wakefulness — the prospect of the dawn that closes *Walden* — was proper to it; and the chapters nearest in fact to his ecstatic years employed it — "Where I Lived, and What I Lived For," with its morning philosophy, and "Sounds," with its account of his summer reverie, of a full day in Nature. He had used the day in the *Week* as the very possession of ecstasy, but now that he was earning it, he needed a longer cycle of time in order to participate in the organic processes of rebuilding and renewing his world. There had to be time to clear his land, build his hut, plant his seeds, and harvest his crop: time for that "something even in the lapse of time by which time recovers itself." Change, gradual transformation, now preoccupied him, and sleeping and waking, admirably fitted to the sudden advent of inspiration, were neither as adequate nor as rich in the details of change as the metaphors he now chose: ice-thaw-flux, seed-flower-fruit, grub-chrysalis-butterfly. These natural facts became the metaphors in terms of which he told of his desire to pass from a lower to a higher form of life, from fixity to fluidity (he would share again the "circulations" of Being), from the innocence of youth to the wisdom of maturity, from larval sensuality to aerial purity.

These transformations, moreover, were examples of change in obedience to the organic principle, by means of an inner expansion. In terms of Thoreau's personal life, their possibility was dramatized by his withdrawal from society to Nature, that is to say, from a condition fixed beyond growth (society for Thoreau was always a machine) to a condition permitting him to build his life from the inside out in obedience to his idea. "Our moulting season, like that of the fowls, must be the crisis of our lives," he explained. "The loon retires to solitary ponds to spend it. Thus also the snake casts its slough, and the caterpillar its wormy coat, by an internal industry and expansion. . ." In society, however, he remained his old "scurvy self," and society, as he now used it in *Walden* to enclose his experiment in renewal, was the sum of all the anxieties and constraints and failures he wished to leave behind. Not only because he was preaching self-reform, but because he wanted to show what he had surmounted, he began *Walden* with the long social analysis of "Economy," setting up the emphatic polarities and perspectives that would awaken his readers to see their — and his — condition absolutely, from a vantage outside of society. As Emerson had done in *Nature*, he began with commodity before turning to spirit. But more fully than Emerson, whose treatise had its point-by-point parallels in *Walden*, he employed history, anthropology, books (even Scripture), paradox, humor, irony, ridicule, scorn, philological puns, parables, dramatization, utopian prospects, and every variety of symbolic statement to establish the contrasting values of surface and depth (appearance and reality), transient and permanent, complex and simple, disease and health, tradition and the uncommitted life, desperation and joy, spiritual emptiness and spiritual fullness. From externality and circumstance, he turned to the inner dominion of self-reliance, from collective "humanitarian" reform to self-discovery, from a world broken and in heaps to the cosmos he had made. Indeed, in dramatizing these changes from society and commodity to spirit and self, *Walden* worked inward from the circumferential to the central life, from the external to the real self, from extrinsic to intrinsic success.

Thoreau also began with "Economy" because it was the aspect of his experiment that had aroused the most curiosity. The life of quiet desperation that he so brilliantly anatomized, however, had been (or was) his own, and the economic anxieties merely pointed to deeper anxieties — those of a life gone stale, without savor or animating purpose. The economy he proposed, therefore, was to the end of getting and spending one's life, an economy of spirit his readers little expected, one that denied the Puritan necessity of working with the sweat of the brow, one that made work itself a joy and a pastime rather than a duty. The irony of his economy, given to the fraction of a cent, was that on so little, he had got so much, that he did not carry a house on his back or possess a corner of the world, but had all the landscape for his own, and time (which Franklin said was money)

to read, to sit idle all day, to boat and fish, and to saunter at his ease
and enjoy those bounties of Nature that were reserved for a "Lord of
Creation." He had a self that he could hug, one that was not at
society's beck and call or twisted and thwarted by relations, which, he
had found by experiment, were customary rather than essential. And
if the simplicity of his economy seemed Franklinian, he was not
burning incense to the patron saint of State Street: the end of his
economy was enrichment, not denial, and he spent lavishly. "Give
me the poverty," he exclaimed when cursing Flint (pages 135 ff.),
"that enjoys true wealth." If anything, he was undermining the Franklinian virtues, replacing the *Autobiography* with a model for another
kind of success — utilizing the very terminology of business to raise
the uncomfortable question of whether possessions actually helped
one possess life. This was the purpose of his reductiveness in treating
the goods of the world, for the only good he wished to appropriate
(and here he added his voice to the swelling clamor of American literature) was experience, the quality or bloom of life. The burden of
"Economy," in fact, was that the way to wealth was not the way to
health, but to lives of quiet desperation. When he wrote Blake, who
was trying to use *Walden* as his guide, he said: "It is surprising how
contented one can be with nothing definite, — only a sense of existence. . . . O how I laugh when I think of my vague, indefinite riches.
No run on my bank can drain it, for my wealth is not possession but
enjoyment."

Standing in the way of this enjoyment, however, was the confusion
concerning the means and ends of life which Thoreau had tried to
clarify by reducing his life to its simplest terms; and, accordingly, the
central issue to those who either rejected or accepted his life was his
doctrine of simplicity. He had reduced the means of life, of course,
not because he wanted to prove that he could go without them, or to
disclaim their value in enriching life, but because they were usually
factitious — they robbed one of life itself. And though, like *Walden*,
the "shallow meaning" of this economy was "but too clear," the
meaning it had for him was not. His economy, like his withdrawal
to Nature, was not an ultimate abdication from social life; it was only
the means of the self-emancipation, which many, accepting social
bondage as the inevitable condition of life, did not find necessary.
Economy freed him from society, and Nature provided him the opportunity to share the recreative processes of life; but this life in Nature
was also a means, the goal being another, a "higher" and an organic

society, shaped by the same principles whose efficacy Thoreau had demonstrated. To this end, rather than to the renunciation of society, *Walden* was a social gospel.

He himself had adopted simplicity for many reasons. He believed, for example, that it would bring him nearer to those common influences in which Emerson had taught the poet to delight. And as a social critic, he believed that the only honest or absolute view required the detached prospect of "voluntary poverty." Considering his personal experiment, however, the most important reason was his need to clear away the obstacles that stood between him and the "grand fact" of life. For in order to front the fact and recover reality, he had to re-duce the problem of perception to its simplest terms — self and Nature. Simplicity, then, was a discipline and an ascetic, as necessary to his purification as the labor in the beanfield or the dietary practices of "Higher Laws," and he often hallowed it with religious associations by calling it "poverty." "By poverty, *i.e.* simplicity of life and few-ness of incidents," he wrote in 1857, bringing to the surface the sunken imagery of *Walden*, "I am solidified and crystallized, as a vapor or liquid by cold. It is a singular concentration of strength and energy and flavor. Chastity is perpetual acquaintance with the All [In "Higher Laws" he said that "Chastity is the flowering of man. . . . Man flows at once to God when the channel of purity is open."]. . . . You think that I am impoverishing myself by withdrawing from men, but in my solitude I have woven for myself a silken web or *chrysalis*, and nymph-like, shall ere long burst forth a more perfect creature, fitted for a higher society. By simplicity . . . my life is concentrated and so becomes organized, or a Κόσμος [cosmos], which before was inorganic and lumpish."

When simplicity, finally, was associated with his life in the woods and his hunger for the wild, it raised another issue — that of primitiv-ism *vs.* civilization. In espousing Nature, the transcendentalists, of course, had also glorified the primitive life. But having experienced the wilderness on his trips to the Maine woods in 1846 and 1853, Thoreau knew that his life at the pond and in Concord pastures was far from wild; and though he always maintained that the health of civilization needed the tonic of the wild, his experience had taught him that the pastoral landscape was the best setting for human life. On one level, in fact, he intended *Walden* for a modern epic of farming, and he had purposely begun his life from scratch in order to relive all history and test this mode of life against the achievements of civilization.

Had his problem been merely that of doing without society, it would have been easily solved; but his problem — the one that Lane had posed in *The Dial* — was what to do with it: how to join the values of urban and sylvan life. The paradox of civilization that Thoreau exploited (though it was hardly a paradox to one who recognized the enslavement to means) was that it did not civilize but barbarized most men, reducing them to a level of want below that of the savage. His own simple life, however, had been remarkably civil, and much of his satisfaction in it was due to the fact that it had provided the uncluttered and leisurely conditions of truly civilizing himself: savages, after all, did not read Homer or write books in the woods. His stance as a philosopher, moreover, made it clear that his demands on life were not simple or primitive, that only the self-sufficiency and adjustment of the Indians to the natural environment appealed to him — the style of their life rather than the "barren simplicity" of their elementary demands on it. "There are two kinds of simplicity," he had observed in the *Journal*, "one that is akin to foolishness, the other to wisdom. The philosopher's style of living is only outwardly simple, but inwardly complex. The savage's style is both outwardly and inwardly simple." The complex and refined life of society, however, did not necessarily yield a complex inner life. And when he proposed that the civilized man become a more experienced and wiser savage, he hoped that he would retain the physical simplicity of the one in order to achieve the complex goals of the other, that he would "spend as little time as possible in planting, weaving, building, etc." and devote his freedom to cultivating "the highest faculties." This could be done, he believed, as he had done it, not only by simplicity, but by making the organic communion of the sylvan the foundation of a higher life.

In showing the "positive hindrances" of civilization — that its means did not fit the ends of man — Thoreau used examples that also enabled him to develop the theory of organic functionalism so essential to his faith in the renewal of life. Everything — education, reform, clothing, shelter, and furniture — was tested by its fitness to living needs, by whether it answered to the inner necessities of man. Clothing, he found, for example, seldom fit the character of the wearer, in many cases did not even serve its basic function of preserving the "vital heat"; instead it was an outer covering worn in conformity to society. Houses, too, were "*exo*strious" [a pun on *indu*strious], a building from without, a more cumbersome clothing, indeed a "tomb" built by the "coffin-maker," as he called the carpenter, for the next

generation. Fine houses, like fashionable clothes, he said, were not
the expression or function of the indweller; they had not been built up
from the "foundation" of "beautiful housekeeping and beautiful living."
And furniture was *exuviae*, the cast skins of others, that cluttered the
house, the spider's web of tradition that trapped the "gay butterfly."
Accordingly, having by his withdrawal and simplicity divested himself of these impediments, he built his life from the inside out; and he
proposed that others build in the same "Orphean fashion," that they
"grow" their houses. "Let our houses first be lined with beauty," he
said, "where they come in contact with our lives, like the tenement of
the shellfish, and not overlaid with it." If he acknowledged that in
building his hut he had built too heedlessly to build well, still he recommended that others consider "what foundation a door, a window, a
cellar, a garret, have in the nature of man. . . ." For he knew that the
circumstances that man creates also shape him, that "this frame," as
he said of his hut, "was a sort of crystallization around me, and reacted
on the builder."

These principles, as well as the prospectus of his hopes and the
initial stages of his experiment, were placed in the intervals of the
social analysis of "Economy." The contrast they provided, however,
was immediately realized in "Where I Lived, and What I Lived For,"
for in his determination to adventure on life Thoreau was already reborn. When he went to the pond in March, 1845, he had already felt
the influence of "the spring of springs"; he had overcome his "tor-
pidity"; in the woods, as Emerson said in *Nature*, he had "cast off his
skin, as a snake his slough," and had again become "a child." Though
Thoreau buried this spring in "Economy," and deliberately began his
account with summer, with his going to the pond to live on Independence Day, the imagery of the melting pond, the returning birds, and
the stray goose were the same as in his second "Spring." This additional season, of course, made it possible for Thoreau to recapitulate
the entire history of his life from youth to maturity: the first spring,
the dewy, pure, auroral season of the Olympian life, was true to his
youth, and the subsequent seasons and the second spring were the
record of the growth of consciousness and of his conscious endeavor
to earn the new world of his springtime again.

Thoreau most patently dramatized this process of organic growth
and renewal by building his hut, the container of his vital heat and the
symbol of the self, to meet the developing seasons of man and consciousness. The seasons of man, of course, corresponded to the sea-

sons of Nature: summer representing the outdoor life, when man was
alive in all his senses and Nature supplied his vital heat; autumn, the
gathering of consciousness; and winter, the withdrawal inward to self-
reflection. This development, moreover, had its counterpart in the
seasons of history, for, as Emerson had noted, "The Greek was the
age of observation; the Middle Age, that of fact and thought; ours,
that of reflection and ideas." Thus, when Thoreau went to Walden,
he found that "both place and time were changed and I dwelt nearer
to those parts of the universe and to those eras in history which had
most attracted me." Spring was the Golden Age, that morning time
of heroic endeavor that he always associated with Greece; and this
explained why his first spring was so full of allusions to Greece, why
Homer was the proper scripture for his morning discipline, and why
the second spring recalled his reading in Ovid's *Metamorphoses* and
brought back the Golden Age. His year was the cycle of human history, and by renewing it he was trying to prove his proposition that
the joys of life were not exhausted, that the counsel of despair of his
elders, who believed that the whole ground of human life had already
been gone over, was untrue.

The frame and foundation of Thoreau's hut came from Nature, the
boards or outer covering from a shanty Thoreau purchased from James
Collins, an Irish laborer whose life, like his "dank, clammy, and
aquish" dwelling, was the very sum of quiet desperation. Dismantling
this hut, Thoreau bleached and warped the boards in the sun; he purified the materials of his life, as he did again the second-hand bricks he
used for his chimney; and with the stuff of the old, for he knew that
men must borrow from civilization, he built the new after an Orphean
fashion. When he first occupied his house in the summer, it was
"merely a defence against the rain, without plastering or chimney,"
with "wide chinks" between the boards, open, as he had been in the
summer, to the influence of Nature. "I did not need to go out doors to
take the air," he observed, "for the atmosphere within had lost none of
its freshness." This was the time of his rich communion with
Nature, when there were no barriers to the rapture he celebrated in
"Sounds," when his solitude (which he defined in terms of his nearness to God) was a satisfaction his friends never suspected. As long
as possible, therefore, he preferred to remain outdoors, warmed by
these genial influences; but, anticipating the bleaker seasons, toward
the end of summer he began to build his chimney and fireplace — "the
most vital part of the house." The foundation had already been laid

in the spring, and now in the cooler days of autumn, he carefully and slowly built his chimney a layer of bricks at a time. The chimney, of course, was his very self or "soul" — an "independent structure, standing on the ground and rising through the house to the heavens," and he built it deliberately because it "was calculated to endure for a long time." Finally, when the north wind came and the pond began to cool and he needed a fire to warm him, he first "inhabited" his house; he plastered and shingled, completely closing himself off from the elements — he internalized his life. "I withdrew yet farther into my shell," he wrote, "and endeavored to keep a bright fire both within my house and within my breast." In this season, as he told of it in "House-Warming," his chief employment was gathering wood for his fire: he was trying to keep alive, to maintain "a kind of summer in the midst of winter. . . ." For he found, during this "barren" season when he had only his heart to gnaw, that he began to grow torpid, that what he had gained in maturity by his self-confinement — by the change from outer to inner, from unconsciousness to consciousness — had brought with it an estrangement from Nature, the sense of "otherness" that bespoke his greatest loss.

If this development was true to Thoreau's life, so were the occupations or disciplines by which he hoped to burst the shell of his cocoon. His summer and morning work, for example, was cultivating beans, a discipline that was hardly consonant with the "fertile idleness" he had appropriately described in "Sounds" and "Solitude." During the Walden period he had, of course, hoed beans, but solely for the purpose of paying his way; from the vantage of his later years, however, this labor became the discipline by means of which he participated in the natural process and renewed his intimacy with Nature. "They attached me to the earth," he said of his beans, "and so I got strength like Antæus." The value of farming, or of any unspecialized vocation in Nature, he also found, was that it helped one catch Nature unaware, that it restored unconsciousness and permitted one to see out of the side of the eye. He advised the American scholar to live by this manual labor, moreover, not only because it was honest and because it rooted one in the native soil, but because it taught one how to reason from the hands to the head: here was the very creative process that would instruct him in the symbolic use of things, that would make the concrete object yield its truth, and that, accordingly, would remove the "palaver" from his style. In his own case, he had been "a plastic artist in the dewy and crumbling sand" in order that his work might bear the "instant and immeasurable crop" of "tropes and expression." And the expression it yielded was the parable of the chapter itself: how to plant the seeds of "sincerity, truth, simplicity, faith, innocence, and the like," how by constant vigilance to make the "germ of virtue" bear, how by redeeming the "lean and effete" soil of Massachusetts — the "dust of my ancestors" — the seed of one man might bear the harvest of "a new generation of men." Here was a parable of both individual and social reform, of the kind of moral reform that went to the root of things and that could not fail because, as Thoreau pointed out in the case of the word "seed," its root was "spica," "spe," and "gerendo" — hope-bearing.

The most important result of this discipline was that it helped him "clothe that fabulous landscape of my infant dreams. . . ." At the beginning of "The Bean-Field" he told how he had first been brought to the pond in his childhood, and in "The Ponds" he told how the wood-choppers had since laid waste its shores. These alterations in the shore, he now realized, were the evidence of his own coarsened, actual self. For the pond itself, he discovered, was "the same water which my youthful eyes fell on," that "all the change," as he confessed, "is in me." The pond, then, was his own pristine, eternal self, and by cultivating beans, by discipline, he was changing the aspect of its shore, making it more agreeable to his imagination. If in his "decay" he lamented that the poet could not sing because his groves were cut down, he was heartened now because, he said, "one of the results of my presence and influence is seen in these bean leaves, corn blades, and potato vines."

That the pond was his real or essential self and the shore his actual self was made clear in "The Ponds." "It is no dream of mine," he said of Walden. "I cannot come nearer to God and Heaven/Than I live to Walden even./I am its stony shore. . . ." In a variant of this verse, he wrote: "It is a part of me which I have not profaned/I live by the shore of me detained." And he even punned on its name — "*Walled-in* Pond." In "The Ponds," however, he did not linger over his shores, but lovingly related all the details of the "crystal well" that he had once been made. There he described the remarkable purity, depth, and transparency of the pond, its coolness and constancy, the cerulean color that made it a "Sky water," the "earth's eye," the very window of the soul. It was the "distiller of celestial dews" whose seasonal tides and daily evaporations kept it pure; it was alive with the motion imparted by the "spirit" of the air, and its surface was "a perfect forest mirror," reflecting all phenomena perfectly as an untarnished mind should. Even its bottom was "pure sand," with only the sediment of fallen leaves (Thoreau's autumnal decay); "a bright green weed," the token of life, could be found growing there in winter; and its fish — its "ascetic fish" — were "cleaner, handsomer, and firmer." Having in his *Journal* thanked God for making "this pond deep and pure for a symbol," Thoreau accounted for its creation with a "myth" of the "old settler," the same old settler he had used to explain why he was not lonely in "Solitude" and was to refer to again in "Former Inhabitants; and Winter Visitors" to explain his notion of society. "That ancient settler [God] . . . came here with his divining-rod [pun]," he wrote, "saw a thin vapor rising from the sward, and the hazel pointed steadily downward, and he concluded to dig a well here." Walden was " 'God's Drop.' " He also gave it Edenic associations, describing its immemorial breaking up in the imagery of his first and second springs, making the rebirth this signified Adamic. Finally, having told of the ecstasy of his youth upon its waters, he likened it to himself; for it was "the work of a brave man," it lived "reserved and austere, like a hermit in the woods," and like his life, which he had "deepened and clarified," it was "too pure to have a market value." And yet he "bequeathed it to Concord," hoping that it would serve society as an example of "greater steadfastness," that "this vision of serenity and purity" would "wash out State-street and the engine's soot."

"The Ponds" was a summer chapter, the record of the time when he floated on the bosom of Nature and even in the darkest night communicated with her by fishing her mysterious depths. Now, fishing, he explained in "Higher Laws," was the proper vocation of the Golden Age; with hunting, it was "the young man's introduction to the forest, and the most original part of himself." Following the inevitable cycle of the seasons, however, this youthful pursuit was soon over: "He goes thither at first as a hunter and fisher, until at last, if he has the seeds of a better life in him, he distinguishes his proper objects, as a poet or naturalist it may be. . . ." When unconscious communion was gone, showing him what his proper object was, the fisher angled instead (in "The Pond in Winter") for the pond itself, seeking the bottom or foundation "that will hold an anchor, that it may not drag."

But before this conscious exploration became necessary, Thoreau went afishing in the summer days. In "Baker Farm," he extolled the easy self-sufficiency of this uncommitted life in the wild and contrasted it with John Field's grubbing. Coming home with his string of fish, however, he turned to "Higher Laws," as if suddenly aware of the fact that in respect to diet at least he was as much in the larval condition as Field. Aware now that only discipline would help him continue his culture after manhood, that the instinct for the wild had been challenged by an instinct toward a higher or spiritual life, he repudiated his former mode of life and adopted the Oriental rituals of purification — bathing and diet and the conscious discipline of earnest labor. This resolution on purity, like the invocation to Hebe in "Solitude" and the martial vigilance of "The Bean-Field," betrayed an autumnal mood which Thoreau tried to dispel by the humorous dialogue that began "Brute Neighbors." There his going fishing was a breach of discipline that destroyed his "budding ecstasy"; but, having covered his loss by his self-protective humor, he nevertheless seriously explained the higher uses of Nature for which he was purifying himself. Nature, as Emerson said and as Thoreau first introduced this theme in "Sounds," was language. Thoreau's proper objects now were the correspondences of Nature; his brute neighbors were "beasts of burden . . . made to carry some portion of our thoughts." The partridge, for example, suggested "not merely the purity of infancy, but a wisdom clarified by experience." And the loon, whose return marked the advent of autumn, carried the heavy burden of his personal lapse. Enacting the play of inspiration by chasing this deep-diving bird, Thoreau told the story of his decay: consciously trying to pursue it — "While he was thinking one thing in his brain, I was endeavoring to divine his thought in mine" — he was balked; and even his passivity would no longer help him. Always the loon, he said, raised its "demoniac" laugh "in derision of my efforts. . . ." Finally, he wrote, the east wind came and "filled the whole air with misty rain, and I was impressed as if it were the prayer of the loon answered, and his god was angry with me. . . ." Like the "tumultuous surface" of the pond, here were the signs that the serene communion of summer was over.

The chapters that followed — "House-Warming," "Former Inhabitants; and Winter Visitors," "Winter Animals," "The Pond in Winter" — recapitulated the themes of the summer chapters, taking up solitude, the resources of the natural scene, sounds, and the pond. With the change to the season of inwardness, however, the mood had changed: now was the time of Thoreau's greatest solitude, a sleepy time when life was reduced to routine and staying alive was a problem, a time when he retreated to memory and held communion with the former inhabitants whose lives suggested the possibility of failure. Every image, from the pond whooping as it turned in its sleep to the fox "seeking expression" and "struggling for light," conveyed a sense of impoverishment and spiritual restlessness, and the need for bravery under duress. Now he longed for the "Visitor" who never came, and turned to the spiritual necessity of friendship, recalling those days when the faithful Alcott had come and their discourse had summoned the "old settler" and "expanded and racked my little house. . . ." But if "moral reform," as he said, "was the effort to throw off sleep," and "to be awake is to be alive," he found that, like the pond, he could not escape his dormant season. "Every winter," he observed, "the liquid and trembling surface of the pond, which was so sensitive to every breath, and reflected every light and shadow, becomes solid to the depth of a foot or a foot and a half. . . . it closes its eyelids and becomes dormant for three months or more. . . . After a cold and snowy night it needed a divining rod to find it."

In the midst of his winter of discontent, however, Thoreau began his intellectual search for faith. In "The Pond in Winter," he told of the question that he had tried to answer in his sleep, the question of "what — how — when — where?" which only dawning Nature, by her living presence, had answered for him. This awakening *to* life was the preparation for his rebirth, the beginning of the long process of conscious penetration to the law of the "spring of springs." This finally brought the rewards of "Spring," warranted his injunctions on self-exploration, and provided the testimony of his "Conclusion" — "Only that day dawns to which we are awake." Now his morning work was the "scientific" exploration of the bottom of the pond; for he "was desirous," he said, "to recover the long-lost bottom of Walden Pond," that "infinite" which its reputed bottomlessness suggested. In this survey he found that the fabulous pickerel (fish and fishing, as early as the *Week*, were symbols of thought and contemplation) still lived beneath the surface of the ice and that the "bright sanded floor" of the pond was "the same as in summer." And what was even more important for the foundation of his faith, he discovered and verified by accurate measurement the spiritual law of correspondences. The general regularity of the bottom — of the unseen — conformed to the shores: the correspondence was so perfect that "a distant promontory betrayed itself in the soundings quite across the pond, and its direction could be determined by observing the opposite shore." This universal law, which he applied to his own character, was also supported by the fact that "the line of greatest length intersected the line of greatest breadth *exactly* at the point of greatest depth. . . ." By these soundings he renewed his faith in the transcendental method; and reading his own life correspondentially, he found that the disciplines of his outer life indicated the purity of his inner life. Though winter was the barren season, it brought the compensation of "concentration"; in the purity of the Walden ice he could see the symbol of his steadfastness. He could meet the priest of Brahma at his well — and the pure Walden water could mingle with the sacred water of the Ganges — because he had observed the purificatory disciplines, had bathed his "intellect in the stupendous and cosmogonal philosophy of the Bhagvat Geeta. . . ."

At the bottom of the pond he also found the "bright green weed" that symbolized the everlasting life of organic Nature, the law of life to which even the frozen pond undulated in its sleep, to which it thundered "obedience . . . as surely as the buds expand in the spring." Its booming, accordingly, was the sign of its awakening, a morning phenomenon, when, responding to the sun, it "stretched itself and yawned like a waking man. . . ." It sounded the signal of spring, prefigured that irresistible thaw when "all things give way to the impulse of expression." Indeed, with the warmer weather, the snow and ice began to melt, the "circulations" began, and the blood of winter was purged. Once more Nature supplied her "vital heat" and, in the thawing clay of the railroad cut, gave way to the impulse of expression — to the impulse of life.

The most brilliant passage in "Spring," Thoreau's description of the thaw was a myth of creation as expression. This elaborate metaphor of the organic process that proceeds from the inside out, that creates and shapes by means of the Idea — the process of Nature, art, moral reform, and social reform — was also for Thoreau the metaphor of his purification and rebirth. Not only did the "bursting out" of the "insides of the earth" and the unfolding of "the piled-up history" of geology prove that there was nothing inorganic and that life provided fresh materials for the fictile arts of man, it showed that "Nature has some bowels, and . . . is mother of humanity. . . ." The frost coming out of the ground was Spring, a newly delivered child; and the flowing clay was an analogy of the development of the human body. The shapes and forms it took in its passage reminded him of "brains or

lungs or bowels, and excrements of all kinds," but, as he explained
this process in terms of "sand-foliage," the leaf-like character not
only appeared in liver and lungs, but in feathers and wings. This
evolution from excrementitious to aerial forms was a process of
purification: "You pass from the lumpish grub in the earth," he
wrote, "to the airy and fluttering butterfly. The very globe continually transcends and translates itself, and becomes winged in its
orbit."

If the thawing made him feel that he was "nearer to the vitals of the
globe," its leaf-like forms also reminded him that he was in the presence of "the Artist who made the world. . . ." The Creator was still
in his laboratory, "still at work, sporting on this bank, and with excess
of energy strewing his fresh designs about." In this analogy to the
creative process, the earth was laboring with "the idea inwardly" and
expressing itself "outwardly in leaves. . . ." For, as he had learned
from Goethe, the leaf was the unit-form of all creation, the simplest
form of which the most complex, even the world, was composed.
"This one hill side illustrated the principle of all the operations of
Nature," he explained. "The Maker of this earth but patented a leaf."
This process, of course, not only applied to art, but to all re-forming
and shaping. It illustrated Emerson's belief that "Nature is not fixed
but fluid. Spirit alters, moulds, makes it" — that not only poems and
individual lives, but institutions were "plastic like clay in the hands of
the potter." Hoeing beans, Thoreau had himself been a plastic artist
making the earth — that granary of seeds — express itself in leaves;
and of all the former inhabitants he had identified himself with Wyman
the potter, whose fictile art pleased him. Moreover, unknown to his
neighbors, he had practiced that fictile art himself — for himself and
society. He was not the reformer, however, who broke things, but
one whose method, like that of the thaw with its "gentle persuasion,"
melted things. By recasting his life he hoped that Nature again would
try, with him "for a first settler." For he was a "Champollion," de-
ciphering the hieroglyphics of Nature, that "we may turn over a new
leaf at last."

As a symbol of ecstasy, however, the thaw, even with its remarkable
suddenness, was spoiled by the intellectual purposes Thoreau made it
serve. Whatever ecstasy the passage conveyed was intellectual
rather than spontaneous or unconscious; it followed from his long
observation of Nature, and it showed that he had with his intellect
riven into the "secret of things." The faith he had earned by this

conscious endeavor, however, was rewarded, at least in the pages of
Walden, by his long-awaited ecstasy. This "memorable crisis" —
"seemingly instantaneous at last" — came with the melting of the
pond, when he saw its "bare face . . . full of glee and youth, as if it
spoke the joy of the fishes within it, and of the sands on its shore. . . ."
For in the sparkling water, he realized the contrast between winter
and spring: "Walden was dead," he said, "and is alive again." The
change he had awaited — "the change from storm and winter to
serene and mild weather, from dark and sluggish hours to bright and
elastic ones" — was at hand. "Suddenly," he wrote, "an influx of
light filled my house, though the evening was at hand, and the clouds of
winter still overhung it, and the eaves were dripping with sleety rain.
I looked out of my window, and lo! where yesterday was cold gray
ice there lay the transparent pond already calm and full of hope as in a
summer evening, reflecting a summer sky in its bosom, though none
was visible overhead, as if it had intelligence with some remote horizon.
I heard a robin in the distance, the first I had heard for many a thousand years . . . the same sweet and powerful song as of yore. . . . The
pitch-pines and shrub-oaks about my house, which had so long
drooped, suddenly resumed their several characters, looked brighter,
greener, and more erect and alive, as if effectually cleansed and restored by the rain. . . . As it grew darker, I was startled by the *honking*
of geese. . . . Standing at my door, I could hear the rush of their
wings. . . . they suddenly spied my light, and with hushed clamor
wheeled and settled in the pond. So I came in, and shut the door, and
passed my first spring night in the woods."

With the coming of spring, with renewal and rebirth, had come
"the creation of Cosmos out of Chaos and the realization of the
Golden Age." Like Ovid, Thoreau was ready to tell of bodies
changed by the gods into new forms, even glad, in the presence of
this alchemy, to accept the life in Nature — served though it was by
death — as the grand fact. Once again he lived in the eternal present,
reborn to innocence, with an overwhelming sense of freedom, release,
hope, and pardon. But even though he had regained the Golden Age
before the fall of man, his metamorphosis took the form of the hawk
rather than that of the butterfly; for having won his renewal by lonely
heroism, he saw his transcendence in the soaring, solitary hawk, the
bird he associated with nobleness and knightly courage. The hawk,
he wrote in his *Journal,* soared so loftily and circled so steadily and
without effort because it had "earned this power by faithfully creeping

on the ground as a reptile in a former state of existence." It symbolized his ultimate liberation, the emancipation from the senses. At
last, as he copied from *The Harivansa*, he was "free in this world, as
birds in the air, disengaged from every kind of chain."

As the logic of his metaphors demanded, however, Thoreau closed
his book with the fable of the beautiful bug that had come out of the
dry leaf of an old apple-wood table. This fable, of course, recapitulated his themes: "Who knows what beautiful and winged life, whose
egg has been buried for ages under many concentric layers of woodenness in the dead dry life of society, deposited at first in the alburnum
of the green and living tree, which has been gradually converted into
the semblance of its well-seasoned tomb . . . may unexpectedly come
forth from amidst society's most trivial and handselled furniture, to
enjoy its perfect summer life at last!" This was the fable of organic
renewal. But the fable of the creative enterprise that made it possible
— the transparent parable of his own life and vocation — was that
of the artist of the city of Kouroo. This artist, Thoreau wrote, "was
disposed to strive after perfection." Determined to make a staff, he
went to the woods to select the proper materials, rejecting stick after
stick, until "his friends gradually deserted him. . . ." In his striving,
however, he lived in the eternal now of inspiration which made the
passing of dynasties, even eras, an illusion. Finally, in fashioning his
staff, merely by minding his destiny and his art, he discovered that
he had "made a new system . . . a world with full and fair proportions.
. . ." And because "the material was pure, and his art was pure," the
result, Thoreau knew, could not be "other than wonderful." *Walden*
was that staff, that fuller and fairer and supremely organic world, because it was, by Thoreau's own test of sincerity, the form and expression of the life he had lived in the desire to live. But it was also — for
in it he had enacted the process of creating scripture — the kind of
heroic book that was worthy of morning discipline, a book so true "to
our condition" that reading it might date a new era in our lives.

A THOREAU CHRONOLOGY

1817   Born, July 12, Concord, Massachusetts.

1833   Enters Harvard College.

1837   Graduates Harvard College; teaches in the Concord school, but is dismissed for refusing to administer discipline; meets Emerson, and begins the *Journal*.

1838   Opens a private school with his brother John; lectures for the first time before the Concord Lyceum.

1839   August 31 — September 13, excursions on the Concord and Merrimack rivers with John: the narrative basis of the *Week*.

1840   Publishes a critical essay in the newly-launched *Dial*.

1841   Takes up residence at Emerson's home.

1842   Brother John dies.

1843   Leaves Emerson for Staten Island.

1844   Returns home; makes pencils.

1845   Begins Walden experience in March; begins his residence there on July 4.

1846   First excursion to the Maine woods.

1847   Leaves Walden on September 6; takes up second residence with the Emersons.

1849   Returns to his father's house; publishes *A Week on the Concord and Merrimack Rivers* and "Civil Disobedience"; first visit to Cape Cod.

1850   Second visit to Cape Cod; goes to Canada.

1853   Second trip to the Maine woods.

1854   Delivers "Slavery in Massachusetts"; publishes *Walden*.

1855   Third visit to Cape Cod.

1856   Meets Walt Whitman in New York.

1857   Fourth visit to Cape Cod; third excursion to the Maine woods; meets John Brown.

1859   Delivers "A Plea for John Brown."

1860   Last camping excursion to Monadnock.

1861   Goes to Minnesota for his health.

1862   May 6, dies of tuberculosis at Concord.

A NOTE ON THE COMPOSITION OF *WALDEN*

Walden grew out of Thoreau's daily record of his observations and thoughts, the "moments" that he stored in his *Journal*. His usual practice, like that of Alcott and Emerson, was to capture his insights as they spontaneously offered themselves, to let them gather helter-skelter (the fortuitous juxtapositions often suggesting new thoughts), to review this record of his "life," and, by indexing it, make it available for composition. This process not only revealed the growth of the mind; it permitted the germ of a thought to unfold: the fact to flower in a truth, the idea to accrete in a symbol. The *Journal* was thus a kind of memory, in which thoughts were hived against the time when, as Emerson said, these golden brothers joined hands: it helped the transcendentalist by showing him the consecutiveness of his thought. The value of the *Journal* for the reader, however, is just the reverse; for, by permitting the reader to work backwards, it enables him to find the original germ, to come at the moment in its original freshness — and then to follow out Thoreau's own method of getting his thoughts to cohere. For *Walden* specifically, it has another value: it helps one date the materials, to see them in their early experiential as well as later literary context. And it shows that *Walden* was more than the record of Thoreau's years at the pond, but, as Channing recognized, a "composite production," the work of a "constructing, combining talent," in which his earliest and last observations (up to the spring of 1854) were brilliantly unified.

Having used the *Journals* in this fashion myself, the Introduction will perhaps serve as an example of the growth of the root-metaphors that, along with the action, helped Thoreau to bind *Walden* together. As he proceeded to write his book, however, his awareness of symbolic as well as literary values prompted him to revise carefully. Of this process, the passage on the melting pond, which Thoreau used as his symbol of rebirth in *Walden* (pp. 212–213), is an instructive example. It was based on the actual Walden experience of March 26, 1846. This entry is more matter-of-fact, more reportorial. Not only did it need the context of *Walden* to raise it in intensity, it needed to be reworded and reordered: and this reconstruction of the experience (from sudden change to signs of purification and returning spring and serenity) required the symbolical awareness of each fact which the perspective of the later *Journals* provided. The original entry (*Journal, The Writings of Henry David Thoreau*, edited by Bradford Torrey and Francis H. Allen, Boston and New York, 1906, I, pp. 400–402) is as follows:

March 26, 1846. The change from foul weather to fair, from dark, sluggish hours to serene, elastic ones, is a memorable crisis which all things proclaim. The change from foulness to serenity is instantaneous. Suddenly an influx of light, though it was late, filled my room. I looked out and saw that the pond was already calm and full of hope, as on a summer evening, though the ice was dissolved but yesterday. There seemed to be some intelligence in the pond which responded to the unseen serenity in a distant horizon. I heard a robin in the distance, — the first I had heard this spring, — repeating the assurance. The green pitch [pine] suddenly looked brighter and more erect, as if now entirely washed and cleansed by the rain. I knew it would not rain any more. A serene summer-evening sky seemed darkly reflected in the pond, though the clear sky was nowhere visible overhead. It was no longer the end of a season, but the beginning. The pines and shrub oaks, which had before drooped and cowered the winter through with myself, now recovered their several characters and in the landscape revived the expression of an immortal beauty. Trees seemed all at once to be fitly grouped, to sustain new relations to men and to one another. There was somewhat cosmical in the arrangement of nature. O the evening robin, at the close of a New England day! If I could ever find the twig he sits upon! Where does the minstrel really roost? We perceive it is not the bird of the ornithologist that is heard, — the *Turdus migratorius*.

The signs of fair weather are seen in the bosom of ponds before they are recognized in the heavens. It is easy to tell by looking at any twig of the forest whether its winter is past or not.

[Three passages universalizing this experience in terms of the whole economy of Nature and socializing Thoreau's work at the pond follow. They were used in the last paragraph of "The Bean-Field."]

A flock of geese has just got in late, now in the dark flying low over the pond. They came on, indulging at last like weary travellers in complaint and consolation, or like some creaking evening mail late lumbering in with anserine clangor. I stood at my door and could hear their wings when they suddenly spied my light and, ceasing their noise, wheeled to the east and apparently settled in the pond.

The passage that sets up this sudden change and that Thoreau used to precede it in *Walden* was from *Journal*, V, pp. 28–29, March 20, 1853:

Walden is melting again. It has a canal two rods wide along the northerly side and the west end, wider at the east end, yet, after running round from west to east, it does not keep the south shore, but crosses in front of the deep cove in a broad crack to where it started, by the ice ground. It is glorious to behold the life and joy of this ribbon of water sparkling in the sun. The wind blows eastward over the opaque ice, unusually hard, owing to the recent severe though transient cold, all watered or waved like a tessellated floor, a figured carpet; yet dead, yet in vain, till it slides on to the living water surface, where it raises a myriad brilliant sparkles on the bare face of the pond, an expression of glee, of youth, of spring, as if it spoke the joy of the fishes within it and of the sands on its shore, a silvery sheen like the scales of a leuciscus, as if it were all one active fish in the spring. It is the contrast between life and death. There is the difference between winter and spring. The bared face of the pond sparkles with joy. How handsome the curves which the edge of the ice makes; answering somewhat to those of the shore, but more regular, sweeping entirely round the pond, as if defined by a vast, bold sweep!

The most significant phenomenon, of course, was the reflection of a summer sky in the bosom of the pond when none was visible overhead. On December 8, 1853 (*Journal*, VI, p. 14) Thoreau noted:

. . . now the sun is set, Walden (I am on the east side) is more light than the sky, — a whiteness as of silverplating, while the sky is yellowish in the horizon and a dusky blue above.

That this phenomenon was not merely optical but rather a luminosity from within the pond itself, Thoreau found might be corroborated by Humboldt's study of the sea. On May 4, 1853 (*Journal*, V, pp. 120–121) he recorded:

It is stated in the Life of Humboldt that he proved "that the expression, 'the ocean reflects the sky,' was a purely poetical, but not a scientifically correct one, as the sea is often blue when the sky is almost totally covered with light white clouds."

In any case, like the returning birds he used in both passages (he added the sparrow to the first, and the robin — with the wood-thrush, his favorite bird — was already a part of the second), this phenomenon became a certain sign of spring. "Birds are the truest heralds of the seasons," he wrote in his manuscript notebook, "since they appreciate a thousand delicate changes in the atmosphere which is their element, of which man cannot be aware." Obedient to the laws of Nature, the pond also responded to subtle changes. On June 26, 1852 (*Journal* IV, p. 147) Thoreau recalled:

The earliest water surfaces, as I remember, as soon as the ice is melted, present as fair and matured scenes, as soft and warm, reflecting the sky through the clear atmosphere, as in midsummer — far in advance of the earth. The earliest promise of the summer, — is it not in the smooth reflecting surface of woodland lakes in which the ice is just melted?

For a close examination of Thoreau's style as the requirement of his vision, consult F. O. Matthiessen, *American Renaissance*, New York, 1941.

BIBLIOGRAPHICAL NOTE

Although it is abundant, Thoreau scholarship has been generally appreciative and superficial: the man rather than the writer has been at the center of critical debate, the object of diatribe or effusive testimony; nothing comparable to the rich readings of Melville or Hawthorne has been given his work. The best sources for his life are still those written by his friends: William Ellery Channing, *Thoreau: the Poet-Naturalist*, Boston, 1873 (revised, 1902); F. B. Sanborn, *The Life of Henry David Thoreau*, Boston, 1917, especially valuable for Thoreau's college essays; *The Journals of Bronson Alcott*, edited by Odell Shepard, Boston, 1938; *Daniel Ricketson and His Friends*, edited by Anna and Walton Ricketson, Boston and New York, 1902; *The American Notebooks by Nathaniel Hawthorne*, edited by Randall Stewart, New Haven, 1932; *Journals of Ralph Waldo Emerson*, edited by E. W. Emerson and W. E. Forbes, Boston and New York, 1909–1914, 10 vols.; and *The Letters of Ralph Waldo Emerson*, edited by Ralph L. Rusk, New York, 1939, 6 vols. Of biographies, one of the best — an early one that furthered Thoreau's reputation in England — is Henry S. Salt, *The Life of Henry David Thoreau*, London, 1890 (revised, 1896); Henry Seidel Canby, *Thoreau*, Boston, 1939 is still the most complete; Joseph Wood Krutch, *Henry David Thoreau*, New York, 1948, is the most recent full-scale appraisal; George F. Whicher, *Walden Revisited*, Chicago, 1945, is a brief but valuable introductory study; and Ethel Seybold, *Thoreau: The Quest and the Classics*, New Haven, 1951, a monograph on his classical reading, furthers the much needed study of Thoreau's "inner" life.

The most significant essays in the shaping of Thoreau's reputation were those by Emerson, Lowell, and Robert Louis Stevenson. These can be conveniently found in *Thoreau: A Century of Criticism*, edited by Walter Harding, Dallas, 1954, along with the fairer estimate of Fannie Hardy Eckstorm, the suggestive essay of Stanley Edgar Hyman, and Philip and Kathryn Whitford's study of Thoreau as a pioneer ecologist. Bradford Torrey, "Thoreau," and "Thoreau's Demands on Nature," *Friends on the Shelf*, Boston, 1906, are still among the best.

For Thoreau the writer, the best study is F. O. Matthiessen, *American Renaissance*, New York, 1941, pp. 3–175.

The most convenient bibliography is *Literary History of the United States*, edited by Robert E. Spiller and others, New York, 1948, vol. III, pp. 742–746. An annotated bibliography up to 1934 can be found in *Henry David Thoreau, Representative Selections* . . . , edited by Bartholow V. Crawford, New York, 1934. For more recent studies, these should be supplemented by the current bibliographies in *American Literature*, published quarterly by the Duke University Press, Durham, North Carolina, and in *The Thoreau Society Bulletin*, a quarterly edited by Walter Harding at the University of Virginia.

The standard edition is *The Writings of Henry David Thoreau*, Boston, 1906, 20 vols. This includes a volume of letters and fourteen volumes of the *Journal*. F. B. Sanborn edited *Walden* for the Bibliophile Society, Boston, 1909. Though he rearranged the book, he included much of the material in the original manuscript that Thoreau excised. This manuscript is now the possession of the Henry E. Huntington Library. The text produced here, however, is that of the 1889 Riverside edition which first incorporated many of Thoreau's own corrections and revisions of the first edition. For descriptions of the various editions of *Walden*, see Walter Harding, *A Centennial Check-List of the Editions of Henry David Thoreau's Walden*, Charlottesville, Virginia, 1954.

WALDEN

I. ECONOMY

WHEN I wrote the following pages, or rather the bulk of them, I lived alone, in the woods, a mile from any neighbor, in a house which I had built myself, on the shore of Walden Pond, in Concord, Massachusetts, and earned my living by the labor of my hands only. I lived there two years and two months. At present I am a sojourner in civilized life again.

I should not obtrude my affairs so much on the notice of my readers if very particular inquiries had not been made by my townsmen concerning my mode of life, which some would call impertinent, though they do not appear to me at all impertinent, but, considering the circumstances, very natural and pertinent. Some have asked what I got to eat; if I did not feel lonesome; if I was not afraid; and the like. Others have been curious to learn what portion of my income I devoted to charitable purposes; and some, who have large families, how many poor children I maintained. I will therefore ask those of my readers who feel no particular interest in me to pardon me if I undertake to answer some of these questions in this book. In most books, the *I*, or first person, is omitted; in this it will be retained; that, in respect to egotism, is the main difference. We commonly do not remember that it is, after all, always the first person that is speaking. I should not talk so much about myself if there were anybody else whom I knew as well. Unfortunately, I am confined to this theme by the narrowness of my experience. Moreover, I, on my side, require of every writer, first or last, a simple and sincere account of his own life, and not merely what he has heard of other men's lives; some such account as he would send to his kindred from a distant land; for if he has lived sincerely, it must have been in a distant land to me. Perhaps these pages are more particularly addressed to poor students. As for the rest of my readers, they will accept such portions as apply to them. I trust that none will stretch the seams in putting on the coat, for it may do good service to him whom it fits.

I would fain say something, not so much concerning the Chinese and Sandwich Islanders as you who read these pages, who are said to live in New England; something about your condition, especially your outward condition or circumstances in this world, in this town,

1

what it is, whether it is necessary that it be as bad as it is, whether it cannot be improved as well as not. I have travelled a good deal in Concord; and everywhere, in shops, and offices, and fields, the inhabitants have appeared to me to be doing penance in a thousand remarkable ways. What I have heard of Bramins sitting exposed to four fires and looking in the face of the sun; or hanging suspended, with their heads downward, over flames; or looking at the heavens over their shoulders "until it becomes impossible for them to resume their natural position, while from the twist of the neck nothing but liquids can pass into the stomach;" or dwelling, chained for life, at the foot of a tree; or measuring with their bodies, like caterpillars, the breadth of vast empires; or standing on one leg on the tops of pillars, — even these forms of conscious penance are hardly more incredible and astonishing than the scenes which I daily witness. The twelve labors of Hercules were trifling in comparison with those which my neighbors have undertaken; for they were only twelve, and had an end; but I could never see that these men slew or captured any monster or finished any labor. They have no friend Iolas to burn with a hot iron the root of the hydra's head, but as soon as one head is crushed, two spring up.

I see young men, my townsmen, whose misfortune it is to have inherited farms, houses, barns, cattle, and farming tools; for these are more easily acquired than got rid of. Better if they had been born in the open pasture and suckled by a wolf, that they might have seen with clearer eyes what field they were called to labor in. Who made them serfs of the soil? Why should they eat their sixty acres, when man is condemned to eat only his peck of dirt? Why should they begin digging their graves as soon as they are born? They have got to live a man's life, pushing all these things before them, and get on as well as they can. How many a poor immortal soul have I met well nigh crushed and smothered under its load, creeping down the road of life, pushing before it a barn seventy-five feet by forty, its Augean stables never cleansed, and one hundred acres of land, tillage, mowing, pasture, and wood-lot! The portionless, who struggle with no such unnecessary inherited encumbrances, find it labor enough to subdue and cultivate a few cubic feet of flesh.

But men labor under a mistake. The better part of the man is soon ploughed into the soil for compost. By a seeming fate, commonly called necessity, they are employed, as it says in an old book, laying up treasures which moth and rust will corrupt and thieves break

through and steal. It is a fool's life, as they will find when they get
to the end of it, if not before. It is said that Deucalion and Pyrrha
created men by throwing stones over their heads behind them: —

Inde genus durum sumus, experiensque laborum,
Et documenta damus quâ simus origine nati.[1]

Or, as Raleigh rhymes it in his sonorous way, —

"From thence our kind hard-hearted is, enduring pain and care,
Approving that our bodies of a stony nature are."

So much for a blind obedience to a blundering oracle, throwing the
stones over their heads behind them, and not seeing where they
fell.

Most men, even in this comparatively free country, through mere
ignorance and mistake, are so occupied with the factitious cares and
superfluously coarse labors of life that its finer fruits cannot be
plucked by them. Their fingers, from excessive toil, are too clumsy
and tremble too much for that. Actually, the laboring man has not
leisure for a true integrity day by day; he cannot afford to sustain
the manliest relations to men; his labor would be depreciated in the
market. He has no time to be anything but a machine. How can he
remember well his ignorance — which his growth requires — who
has so often to use his knowledge? We should feed and clothe him
gratuitously sometimes, and recruit him with our cordials, before we
judge of him. The finest qualities of our nature, like the bloom on
fruits, can be preserved only by the most delicate handling. Yet we
do not treat ourselves nor one another thus tenderly.

Some of you, we all know, are poor, find it hard to live, are sometimes, as it were, gasping for breath. I have no doubt that some of
you who read this book are unable to pay for all the dinners which you
have actually eaten, or for the coats and shoes which are fast wearing
or are already worn out, and have come to this page to spend borrowed or stolen time, robbing your creditors of an hour. It is very
evident what mean and sneaking lives many of you live, for my sight
has been whetted by experience; always on the limits, trying to get
into business and trying to get out of debt, a very ancient slough,

[1] Many of Thoreau's audience had a sufficient classical training to appreciate his
quotations and his philological puns. By the time of *Walden*, however, he had
begun the practice of including translations. For the sources of his classical quotations, see Ethel Seybold, *Thoreau: The Quest and the Classics*, New Haven, 1951.

called by the Latins *æs alienum*, another's brass, for some of their coins were made of brass; still living, and dying, and buried by this other's brass; always promising to pay, promising to pay, to-morrow, and dying to-day, insolvent; seeking to curry favor, to get custom, by how many modes, only not state-prison offences; lying, flattering, voting, contracting yourselves into a nutshell of civility, or dilating into an atmosphere of thin and vaporous generosity, that you may persuade your neighbor to let you make his shoes, or his hat, or his coat, or his carriage, or import his groceries for him; making yourselves sick, that you may lay up something against a sick day, something to be tucked away in an old chest, or in a stocking behind the plastering, or, more safely, in the brick bank; no matter where, no matter how much or how little.

I sometimes wonder that we can be so frivolous, I may almost say, as to attend to the gross but somewhat foreign form of servitude called Negro Slavery, there are so many keen and subtle masters that enslave both North and South. It is hard to have a Southern overseer; it is worse to have a Northern one; but worst of all when you are the slave-driver of yourself. Talk of a divinity in man! Look at the teamster on the highway, wending to market by day or night; does any divinity stir within him? His highest duty to fodder and water his horses! What is his destiny to him compared with the shipping interests? Does not he drive for Squire Make-a-stir? How godlike, how immortal, is he? See how he cowers and sneaks, how vaguely all the day he fears, not being immortal nor divine, but the slave and prisoner of his own opinion of himself, a fame won by his own deeds. Public opinion is a weak tyrant compared with our own private opinion. What a man thinks of himself, that it is which determines, or rather indicates, his fate. Self-emancipation even in the West Indian provinces of the fancy and imagination, — what Wilberforce is there to bring that about? Think, also, of the ladies of the land weaving toilet cushions against the last day, not to betray oo green an interest in their fates! As if you could kill time without injuring eternity.

The mass of men lead lives of quiet desperation. What is called resignation is confirmed desperation. From the desperate city you go into the desperate country, and have to console yourself with the bravery of minks and muskrats. A stereotyped but unconscious despair is concealed even under what are called the games and amusements of mankind. There is no play in them, for this comes after work. But it is a characteristic of wisdom not to do desperate things.

When we consider what, to use the words of the catechism, is the chief end of man, and what are the true necessaries and means of life, it appears as if men had deliberately chosen the common mode of living because they preferred it to any other. Yet they honestly think there is no choice left. But alert and healthy natures remember that the sun rose clear. It is never too late to give up our prejudices. No way of thinking or doing, however ancient, can be trusted without proof. What everybody echoes or in silence passes by as true to-day may turn out to be falsehood to-morrow, mere smoke of opinion, which some had trusted for a cloud that would sprinkle fertilizing rain on their fields. What old people say you cannot do you try and find that you can. Old deeds for old people, and new deeds for new. Old people did not know enough once, perchance, to fetch fresh fuel to keep the fire a-going; new people put a little dry wood under a pot, and are whirled round the globe with the speed of birds, in a way to kill old people, as the phrase is. Age is no better, hardly so well, qualified for an instructor as youth, for it has not profited so much as it has lost. One may almost doubt if the wisest man has learned anything of absolute value by living. Practically, the old have no very important advice to give the young, their own experience has been so partial, and their lives have been such miserable failures, for private reasons, as they must believe; and it may be that they have some faith left which belies that experience, and they are only less young than they were. I have lived some thirty years on this planet, and I have yet to hear the first syllable of valuable or even earnest advice from my seniors. They have told me nothing, and probably cannot tell me anything to the purpose. Here is life, an experiment to a great extent untried by me; but it does not avail me that they have tried it. If I have any experience which I think valuable, I am sure to reflect that this my Mentors said nothing about.

One farmer says to me, "You cannot live on vegetable food solely, for it furnishes nothing to make bones with;" and so he religiously devotes a part of his day to supplying his system with the raw material of bones; walking all the while he talks behind his oxen, which, with vegetable-made bones, jerk him and his lumbering plough along in spite of every obstacle. Some things are really necessaries of life in some circles, the most helpless and diseased, which in others are luxuries merely, and in others still are entirely unknown.

The whole ground of human life seems to some to have been gone over by their predecessors, both the heights and the valleys, and all things to have been cared for. According to Evelyn, "the wise Solomon prescribed ordinances for the very distances of trees; and the Roman prætors have decided how often you may go into your neighbor's land to gather the acorns which fall on it without trespass, and what share belongs to that neighbor." Hippocrates has even left directions how we should cut our nails; that is, even with the ends of the fingers, neither shorter nor longer. Undoubtedly the very tedium and ennui which presume to have exhausted the variety and the joys of life are as old as Adam. But man's capacities have never been measured; nor are we to judge of what he can do by any precedents, so little has been tried. Whatever have been thy failures hitherto, "be not afflicted, my child, for who shall assign to thee what thou hast left undone?"

We might try our lives by a thousand simple tests; as, for instance, that the same sun which ripens my beans illumines at once a system of earths like ours. If I had remembered this it would have prevented some mistakes. This was not the light in which I hoed them. The stars are the apexes of what wonderful triangles! What distant and different beings in the various mansions of the universe are contemplating the same one at the same moment! Nature and human life are as various as our several constitutions. Who shall say what prospect life offers to another? Could a greater miracle take place than for us to look through each other's eyes for an instant? We should live in all the ages of the world in an hour; ay, in all the worlds of the ages. History, Poetry, Mythology! — I know of no reading of another's experience so startling and informing as this would be.

The greater part of what my neighbors call good I believe in my soul to be bad, and if I repent of anything, it is very likely to be my good behavior. What demon possessed me that I behaved so well? You may say the wisest thing you can, old man, — you who have lived seventy years, not without honor of a kind, — I hear an irresistible voice which invites me away from all that. One generation abandons the enterprises of another like stranded vessels.

I think that we may safely trust a good deal more than we do. We may waive just so much care of ourselves as we honestly bestow elsewhere. Nature is as well adapted to our weakness as to our strength. The incessant anxiety and strain of some is a well-nigh incurable form of disease. We are made to exaggerate the importance of what work we do; and yet how much is not done by us! or, what if we had been taken sick? How vigilant we are! determined not to live by faith if we can avoid it; all the day long on the alert, at night we unwillingly say our prayers and commit ourselves to uncertainties. So thoroughly and sincerely are we compelled to live, reverencing our life, and denying the possibility of change. This is the only way, we say; but there are as many ways as there can be drawn radii from one centre. All change is a miracle to contemplate; but it is a miracle which is taking place every instant. Confucius said, "To know that we know what we know, and that we do not know what we do not know, that is true knowledge." When one man has reduced a fact of the imagination to be a fact to his understanding, I foresee that all men will at length establish their lives on that basis.

Let us consider for a moment what most of the trouble and anxiety which I have referred to is about, and how much it is necessary that we be troubled, or at least careful. It would be some advantage to live a primitive and frontier life, though in the midst of an outward civilization, if only to learn what are the gross necessaries of life and what methods have been taken to obtain them; or even to look over the old day-books of the merchants, to see what it was that men most commonly bought at the stores, what they stored, that is, what are the grossest groceries. For the improvements of ages have had but little influence on the essential laws of man's existence: as our skeletons, probably, are not to be distinguished from those of our ancestors.

By the words, *necessary of life*, I mean whatever, of all that man obtains by his own exertions, has been from the first, or from long use has become, so important to human life that few, if any, whether from savageness, or poverty, or philosophy, ever attempt to do without it. To many creatures there is in this sense but one necessary of life, Food. To the bison of the prairie it is a few inches of palatable grass, with water to drink; unless he seeks the Shelter of the forest or the mountain's shadow. None of the brute creation requires more than Food and Shelter. The necessaries of life for man in this climate may, accurately enough, be distributed under the several heads of Food, Shelter, Clothing, and Fuel; for not till we have secured these are we prepared to entertain the true problems of life with freedom and a prospect of success. Man has invented, not only houses, but clothes and cooked food; and possibly from the accidental discovery of the warmth of fire, and the consequent use of it, at first a luxury, arose the present necessity to sit by it. We observe cats and dogs

acquiring the same second nature. By proper Shelter and Clothing
we legitimately retain our own internal heat; but with an excess of
these, or of Fuel, that is, with an external heat greater than our own
internal, may not cookery properly be said to begin? Darwin, the
naturalist, says of the inhabitants of Tierra del Fuego, that while his
own party, who were well clothed and sitting close to a fire, were far
from too warm, these naked savages, who were farther off, were observed, to his great surprise, "to be streaming with perspiration at
undergoing such a roasting." So, we are told, the New Hollander
goes naked with impunity, while the European shivers in his clothes.
Is it impossible to combine the hardiness of these savages with the
intellectualness of the civilized man? According to Liebig, man's
body is a stove, and food the fuel which keeps up the internal combustion in the lungs. In cold weather we eat more, in warm less.
The animal heat is the result of a slow combustion, and disease and
death take place when this is too rapid; or for want of fuel, or from
some defect in the draught, the fire goes out. Of course the vital
heat is not to be confounded with fire; but so much for analogy. It
appears, therefore, from the above list, that the expression, *animal
life*, is nearly synonymous with the expression, *animal heat;* for while
Food may be regarded as the Fuel which keeps up the fire within us,
— and Fuel serves only to prepare that Food or to increase the warmth
of our bodies by addition from without, — Shelter and Clothing also
serve only to retain the *heat* thus generated and absorbed.

The grand necessity, then, for our bodies, is to keep warm, to keep
the vital heat in us. What pains we accordingly take, not only with
our Food, and Clothing, and Shelter, but with our beds, which are our
night-clothes, robbing the nests and breasts of birds to prepare this
shelter within a shelter, as the mole has its bed of grass and leaves at
the end of its burrow! The poor man is wont to complain that this
is a cold world; and to cold, no less physical than social, we refer directly a great part of our ails. The summer, in some climates, makes
possible to man a sort of Elysian life. Fuel, except to cook his Food,
is then unnecessary; the sun is his fire, and many of the fruits are sufficiently cooked by its rays; while Food generally is more various, and
more easily obtained, and Clothing and Shelter are wholly or half
unnecessary. At the present day, and in this country, as I find by
my own experience, a few implements, a knife, an axe, a spade, a
wheelbarrow, etc., and for the studious, lamplight, stationery, and
access to a few books, rank next to necessaries, and can all be ob-

tained at a trifling cost. Yet some, not wise, go to the other side of
the globe, to barbarous and unhealthy regions, and devote themselves
to trade for ten or twenty years, in order that they may live, — that
is, keep comfortably warm, — and die in New England at last. The
luxuriously rich are not simply kept comfortably warm, but unnat-
urally hot; as I implied before, they are cooked, of course *à la mode*.

   Most of the luxuries, and many of the so-called comforts of life,
are not only not indispensable, but positive hindrances to the elevation
of mankind. With respect to luxuries and comforts, the wisest have
ever lived a more simple and meagre life than the poor. The ancient
philosophers, Chinese, Hindoo, Persian, and Greek, were a class than
which none has been poorer in outward riches, none so rich in inward.
We know not much about them. It is remarkable that *we* know so
much of them as we do. The same is true of the more modern reformers and benefactors of their race. None can be an impartial or
wise observer of human life but from the vantage ground of what *we*
should call voluntary poverty. Of a life of luxury the fruit is luxury,
whether in agriculture, or commerce, or literature, or art. There
are nowadays professors of philosophy, but not philosophers. Yet it
is admirable to profess because it was once admirable to live. To be
a philosopher is not merely to have subtle thoughts, nor even to found
a school, but so to love wisdom as to live according to its dictates, a
life of simplicity, independence, magnanimity, and trust. It is to
solve some of the problems of life, not only theoretically, but practically. The success of great scholars and thinkers is commonly a
courtier-like success, not kingly, not manly. They make shift to live
merely by conformity, practically as their fathers did, and are in no
sense the progenitors of a nobler race of men. But why do men degenerate ever? What makes families run out? What is the nature
of the luxury which enervates and destroys nations? Are we sure
that there is none of it in our own lives? The philosopher is in advance of his age even in the outward form of his life. He is not fed,
sheltered, clothed, warmed, like his contemporaries. How can a
man be a philosopher and not maintain his vital heat by better methods
than other men?

   When a man is warmed by the several modes which I have described, what does he want next? Surely not more warmth of the
same kind, as more and richer food, larger and more splendid houses,
finer and more abundant clothing, more numerous incessant and hotter
fires, and the like. When he has obtained those things which are

necessary to life, there is another alternative than to obtain the superfluities; and that is, to adventure on life now, his vacation from humbler toil having commenced. The soil, it appears, is suited to the
seed, for it has sent its radicle downward, and it may now send its
shoot upward also with confidence. Why has man rooted himself
thus firmly in the earth, but that he may rise in the same proportion
into the heavens above? — for the nobler plants are valued for the
fruit they bear at last in the air and light, far from the ground, and
are not treated like the humbler esculents, which, though they may
be biennials, are cultivated only till they have perfected their root,
and often cut down at top for this purpose, so that most would not
know them in their flowering season.

I do not mean to prescribe rules to strong and valiant natures, who
will mind their own affairs whether in heaven or hell, and perchance
build more magnificently and spend more lavishly than the richest,
without ever impoverishing themselves, not knowing how they live,
— if, indeed, there are any such, as has been dreamed; nor to those
who find their encouragement and inspiration in precisely the present
condition of things, and cherish it with the fondness and enthusiasm
of lovers, — and, to some extent, I reckon myself in this number; I
do not speak to those who are well employed, in whatever circumstances, and they know whether they are well employed or not; —
but mainly to the mass of men who are discontented, and idly com-
plaining of the hardness of their lot or of the times, when they might
improve them. There are some who complain most energetically
and inconsolably of any, because they are, as they say, doing their
duty. I also have in my mind that seemingly wealthy, but most ter-
ribly impoverished class of all, who have accumulated dross, but know
not how to use it, or get rid of it, and thus have forged their own golden
or silver fetters.

If I should attempt to tell how I have desired to spend my life in
years past, it would probably surprise those of my readers who are
somewhat acquainted with its actual history; it would certainly as-
tonish those who know nothing about it. I will only hint at some of
the enterprises which I have cherished.

In any weather, at any hour of the day or night, I have been anxious
to improve the nick of time, and notch it on my stick too; to stand on
the meeting of two eternities, the past and future, which is precisely
the present moment; to toe that line. You will pardon some obscuri-

ties, for there are more secrets in my trade than in most men's, and
yet not voluntarily kept, but inseparable from its very nature. I
would gladly tell all that I know about it, and never paint "No Ad-
mittance" on my gate.

I long ago lost a hound, a bay horse, and a turtle-dove, and am still
on their trail. Many are the travellers I have spoken concerning
them, describing their tracks and what calls they answered to. I have
met one or two who had heard the hound, and the tramp of the horse,
and even seen the dove disappear behind a cloud, and they seemed as
anxious to recover them as if they had lost them themselves.[1]

To anticipate, not the sunrise and the dawn merely, but, if possible,
Nature herself! [2] How many mornings, summer and winter, before
yet any neighbor was stirring about his business, have I been about
mine! No doubt, many of my townsmen have met me returning from
this enterprise, farmers starting for Boston in the twilight, or wood-
choppers going to their work. It is true, I never assisted the sun materially in his rising, but, doubt not, it was of the last importance only
to be present at it.

So many autumn, ay, and winter days, spent outside the town,
trying to hear what was in the wind, to hear and carry it express! I
well-nigh sunk all my capital in it, and lost my own breath into the
bargain, running in the face of it. If it had concerned either of the
political parties, depend upon it, it would have appeared in the Gazette
with the earliest intelligence. At other times watching from the
observatory of some cliff or tree, to telegraph any new arrival; or
waiting at evening on the hilltops for the sky to fall, that I might
catch something, though I never caught much, and that, manna-wise,
would dissolve again in the sun.

For a long time I was reporter to a journal, of no very wide circula-

---

[1] This passage has been the seed-bed of a considerable scholarship. Many have
tried to fix its meaning and find its sources. Even Emerson suggested that the hound
was the book Thoreau would have liked to have written, the bay horse his desire
for property, and the turtle-dove the wife of his dream. To one inquisitive correspondent, however, Thoreau explained that these animals *might* represent his
"losses," but that he had lost "a far finer and more ethereal treasure, which commonly no loss of . . . will symbolize." As for sources, the passage from Mencius
that Thoreau selected for *The Dial* might do better, say, than Voltaire or Dante:
"If a man lose his fowls or his dogs, he knows how to seek them. There are those
who lose their hearts and know not how to seek them. The duty of the student is
no other than to seek his lost heart." The heart, as Mencius' writing makes clear,
is man's natural goodness, despoiled — and lost — by his contact with the world.
[2] This was added to the original *Journal* entry of the Walden years, and expressed
the purpose of his scientific studies in his later years.

tion, whose editor has never yet seen fit to print the bulk of my contributions, and, as is too common with writers, I got only my labor for my pains. However, in this case my pains were their own reward.

For many years I was self-appointed inspector of snow storms and rain storms, and did my duty faithfully; surveyor, if not of highways, then of forest paths and all across-lot routes, keeping them open, and ravines bridged and passable at all seasons, where the public heel had testified to their utility.

I have looked after the wild stock of the town, which give a faithful herdsman a good deal of trouble by leaping fences; and I have had an eye to the unfrequented nooks and corners of the farm; though I did not always know whether Jonas or Solomon worked in a particular field to-day; that was none of my business. I have watered the red huckleberry, the sand cherry and the nettle tree, the red pine and the black ash, the white grape and the yellow violet, which might have withered else in dry seasons.

In short, I went on thus for a long time (I may say it without boasting), faithfully minding my business, till it became more and more evident that my townsmen would not after all admit me into the list of town officers, nor make my place a sinecure with a moderate allowance. My accounts, which I can swear to have kept faithfully, I have, indeed, never got audited, still less accepted, still less paid and settled. However, I have not set my heart on that.

Not long since, a strolling Indian went to sell baskets at the house of a well-known lawyer in my neighborhood. "Do you wish to buy any baskets?" he asked. "No, we do not want any," was the reply. "What!" exclaimed the Indian as he went out the gate, "do you mean to starve us?" Having seen his industrious white neighbors so well off, — that the lawyer had only to weave arguments, and by some magic wealth and standing followed, — he had said to himself: I will go into business; I will weave baskets; it is a thing which I can do. Thinking that when he had made the baskets he would have done his part, and then it would be the white man's to buy them. He had not discovered that it was necessary for him to make it worth the other's while to buy them, or at least make him think that it was so, or to make something else which it would be worth his while to buy. I too had woven a kind of basket of a delicate texture, but I had not made it worth any one's while to buy them. Yet not the less, in my case, did I think it worth my while to weave them, and instead of studying how to make it worth men's while to buy my baskets, I studied rather how to avoid the necessity of selling them. The life which men praise and regard as successful is but one kind. Why should we exaggerate any one kind at the expense of the others?

Finding that my fellow-citizens were not likely to offer me any room in the court house, or any curacy or living anywhere else, but I must shift for myself, I turned my face more exclusively than ever to the woods, where I was better known. I determined to go into business at once, and not wait to acquire the usual capital, using such slender means as I had already got. My purpose in going to Walden Pond was not to live cheaply nor to live dearly there, but to transact some private business with the fewest obstacles; to be hindered from accomplishing which for want of a little common sense, a little enterprise and business talent, appeared not so sad as foolish.

I have always endeavored to acquire strict business habits; they are indispensable to every man. If your trade is with the Celestial Empire, then some small counting house on the coast, in some Salem harbor, will be fixture enough. You will export such articles as the country affords, purely native products, much ice and pine timber and a little granite, always in native bottoms. These will be good ventures. To oversee all the details yourself in person; to be at once pilot and captain, and owner and underwriter; to buy and sell and keep the accounts; to read every letter received, and write or read every letter sent; to superintend the discharge of imports night and day; to be upon many parts of the coast almost at the same time, — often the richest freight will be discharged upon a Jersey shore; — to be your own telegraph, unweariedly sweeping the horizon, speaking all passing vessels bound coastwise; to keep up a steady despatch of commodities, for the supply of such a distant and exorbitant market; to keep yourself informed of the state of the markets, prospects of war and peace everywhere, and anticipate the tendencies of trade and civilization, — taking advantage of the results of all exploring expeditions, using new passages and all improvements in navigation; — charts to be studied, the position of reefs and new lights and buoys to be ascertained, and ever, and ever, the logarithmic tables to be corrected, for by the error of some calculator the vessel often splits upon a rock that should have reached a friendly pier, — there is the untold fate of La Perouse; — universal science to be kept pace with, studying the lives of all great discoverers and navigators, great adventurers and merchants, from Hanno and the Phœnicians down to our day; in fine, account of stock to be taken from time to time, to know how you stand. It is a labor to task the faculties of a man, — such problems of profit and loss, of interest, of tare and tret, and gauging of all kinds in it, as demand a universal knowledge.[1]

I have thought that Walden Pond would be a good place for business, not solely on account of the railroad and the ice trade; it offers advantages which it may not be good policy to divulge; it is a good post and a good foundation. No Neva marshes to be filled; though you must everywhere build on piles of your own driving. It is said that a flood-tide, with a westerly wind, and ice in the Neva, would sweep St. Petersburg from the face of the earth.

As this business was to be entered into without the usual capital, it may not be easy to conjecture where those means, that will still be indispensable to every such undertaking, were to be obtained. As for Clothing, to come at once to the practical part of the question, perhaps we are led oftener by the love of novelty and a regard for the opinions of men, in procuring it, then by a true utility. Let him who has work to do recollect that the object of clothing is, first, to retain the vital heat, and secondly, in this state of society, to cover nakedness, and he may judge how much of any necessary or important work may be accomplished without adding to his wardrobe. Kings and queens who wear a suit but once, though made by some tailor or dressmaker to their majesties, cannot know the comfort of wearing a suit that fits. They are no better than wooden horses to hang the clean clothes on. Every day our garments become more assimilated to ourselves, receiving the impress of the wearer's character, until we hesitate to lay them aside, without such delay and medical appliances and some such solemnity even as our bodies. No man ever stood the lower in my estimation for having a patch in his clothes; yet I am sure that there is greater anxiety, commonly, to have fashionable, or at least clean and unpatched clothes, than to have a sound conscience. But even if the rent is not mended, perhaps the worst vice betrayed is improvidence. I sometimes try my acquaintances by such tests as this, — Who could wear a patch, or two extra seams only, over the knee? Most behave

---

[1] The allegory is transparent. Thoreau used the contemporary China trade as the analogy of his own commerce. The images of commerce, discovery, and self-reliance, of course, served his purposes well; and the analogy enabled him to express other themes. The "purely native products . . . always in native bottoms" told of his belief in a native American literature; "to oversee all the details yourself in person" was an injunction to self-reliance and first-hand experience; "to anticipate the tendencies of trade and civilization" was to be a seer; to correct the charts and logarithmic tables described his own use and revision of history.

as if they believed that their prospects for life would be ruined if they should do it. It would be easier for them to hobble to town with a broken leg than with a broken pantaloon. Often if an accident happens to a gentleman's legs, they can be mended; but if a similar accident happens to the legs of his pantaloons, there is no help for it; for he considers, not what is truly respectable, but what is respected. We know but few men, a great many coats and breeches. Dress a scarecrow in your last shift, you standing shiftless by, who would not soonest salute the scarecrow? Passing a cornfield the other day, close by a hat and coat on a stake, I recognized the owner of the farm. He was only a little more weather-beaten than when I saw him last. I have heard of a dog that barked at every stranger who approached his master's premises with clothes on, but was easily quieted by a naked thief. It is an interesting question how far men would retain their relative rank if they were divested of their clothes. Could you, in such a case, tell surely of any company of civilized men which belonged to the most respected class? When Madam Pfeiffer, in her adventurous travels round the world, from east to west, had got so near home as Asiatic Russia, she says that she felt the necessity of wearing other than a travelling dress, when she went to meet the authorities, for she "was now in a civilized country, where . . . people are judged of by their clothes." Even in our democratic New England towns the accidental possession of wealth, and its manifestation in dress and equipage alone, obtain for the possessor almost universal respect. But they who yield such respect, numerous as they are, are so far heathen, and need to have a missionary sent to them. Beside, clothes introduced sewing, a kind of work which you may call endless; a woman's dress, at least, is never done.

A man who has at length found something to do will not need to get a new suit to do it in; for him the old will do, that has lain dusty in the garret for an indeterminate period. Old shoes will serve a hero longer than they have served his valet, — if a hero ever has a valet, — bare feet are older than shoes, and he can make them do. Only they who go to soirées and legislative halls must have new coats, coats to change as often as the man changes in them. But if my jacket and trousers, my hat and shoes, are fit to worship God in, they will do; will they not? Who ever saw his old clothes, — his old coat, actually worn out, resolved into its primitive elements, so that it was not a deed of charity to bestow it on some poor boy, by him perchance to be bestowed on some poorer still, or shall we say richer, who could do with less? I say, beware of all enterprises that require new clothes, and not rather a new wearer of clothes. If there is not a new man, how can the new clothes be made to fit? If you have any enterprise before you, try it in your old clothes. All men want, not something to *do with*, but something to *do*, or rather something to *be*. Perhaps we should never procure a new suit, however ragged or dirty the old, until we have so conducted, so enterprised or sailed in some way, that we feel like new men in the old, and that to retain it would be like keeping new wine in old bottles. Our moulting season, like that of the fowls, must be a crisis in our lives. The loon retires to solitary ponds to spend it. Thus also the snake casts its slough, and the caterpillar its wormy coat, by an internal industry and expansion; for clothes are but our outmost cuticle and mortal coil. Otherwise we shall be found sailing under false colors, and be inevitably cashiered at last by our own opinion, as well as that of mankind.

We don garment after garment, as if we grew like exogenous plants by addition without. Our outside and often thin and fanciful clothes are our epidermis, or false skin, which partakes not of our life, and may be stripped off here and there without fatal injury; our thicker garments, constantly worn, are our cellular integument, or cortex; but our shirts are our liber, or true bark, which cannot be removed without girdling and so destroying the man. I believe that all races at some seasons wear something equivalent to the shirt. It is desirable that a man be clad so simply that he can lay his hands on himself in the dark, and that he live in all respects so compactly and preparedly, that, if an enemy take the town, he can, like the old philosopher, walk out the gate empty-handed without anxiety. While one thick garment is, for most purposes, as good as three thin ones, and cheap clothing can be obtained at prices really to suit customers; while a thick coat can be bought for five dollars, which will last as many years, thick pantaloons for two dollars, cowhide boots for a dollar and a half a pair, a summer hat for a quarter of a dollar, and a winter cap for sixty-two and a half cents, or a better be made at home at a nominal cost, where is he so poor that, clad in such a suit, *of his own earning*, there will not be found wise men to do him reverence?

When I ask for a garment of a particular form, my tailoress tells me gravely, "They do not make them so now," not emphasizing the "They" at all, as if she quoted an authority as impersonal as the Fates, and I find it difficult to get made what I want, simply because she cannot believe that I mean what I say, that I am so rash. When I hear this oracular sentence, I am for a moment absorbed in thought, emphasizing to myself each word separately that I may come at the meaning of it, that I may find out by what degree of consanguinity *They* are related to *me*, and what authority they may have in an affair which affects me so nearly; and, finally, I am inclined to answer her with equal mystery, and without any more emphasis of the "they," — "It is true, they did not make them so recently, but they do now." Of what use this measuring of me if she does not measure my character, but only the breadth of my shoulders, as it were a peg to hang the coat on? We worship not the Graces, nor the Parcæ, but Fashion. She spins and weaves and cuts with full authority. The head monkey at Paris puts on a traveller's cap, and all the monkeys in America do the same. I sometimes despair of getting anything quite simple and honest done in this world by the help of men. They would have to be passed through a powerful press first, to squeeze their old notions out of them, so that they would not soon get upon their legs again; and then there would be some one in the company with a maggot in his head, hatched from an egg deposited there nobody knows when, for not even fire kills these things, and you would have lost your labor. Nevertheless, we will not forget that some Egyptian wheat was handed down to us by a mummy.

On the whole, I think that it cannot be maintained that dressing has in this or any country risen to the dignity of an art. At present men make shift to wear what they can get. Like shipwrecked sailors, they put on what they can find on the beach, and at a little distance, whether of space or time, laugh at each other's masquerade. Every generation laughs at the old fashions, but follows religiously the new. We are amused at beholding the costume of Henry VIII., or Queen Elizabeth, as much as if it was that of the King and Queen of the Cannibal Islands. All costume off a man is pitiful or grotesque. It is only the serious eye peering from and the sincere life passed within it which restrain laughter and consecrate the costume of any people. Let Harlequin be taken with a fit of the colic and his trappings will have to serve that mood too. When the soldier is hit by a cannon ball rags are as becoming as purple.

The childish and savage taste of men and women for new patterns keeps how many shaking and squinting through kaleidoscopes that they may discover the particular figure which this generation requires today. The manufacturers have learned that this taste is merely whimsical. Of two patterns which differ only by a few threads more or less of a particular color, the one will be sold readily, the other lie on the shelf, though it frequently happens that after the lapse of a season the latter becomes the most fashionable. Comparatively, tattooing is not the hideous custom which it is called. It is not barbarous merely because the printing is skin-deep and unalterable.

I cannot believe that our factory system is the best mode by which men may get clothing. The condition of the operatives is becoming every day more like that of the English; and it cannot be wondered at, since, as far as I have heard or observed, the principal object is, not that mankind may be well and honestly clad, but, unquestionably, that the corporations may be enriched. In the long run men hit only what they aim at. Therefore, though they should fail immediately, they had better aim at something high.

As for a Shelter, I will not deny that this is now a necessary of life, though there are instances of men having done without it for long periods in colder countries than this. Samuel Laing says that "the Laplander in his skin dress, and in a skin bag which he puts over his head and shoulders, will sleep night after night on the snow . . . in a degree of cold which would extinguish the life of one exposed to it in any woollen clothing." He had seen them asleep thus. Yet he adds, "They are not hardier than other people." But, probably, man did not live long on the earth without discovering the convenience which there is in a house, the domestic comforts, which phrase may have originally signified the satisfactions of the house more than of the family; though these must be extremely partial and occasional in those climates where the house is associated in our thoughts with winter or the rainy season chiefly, and two thirds of the year, except for a parasol, is unnecessary. In our climate, in the summer, it was formerly almost solely a covering at night. In the Indian gazettes a wigwam was the symbol of a day's march, and a row of them cut or painted on the bark of a tree signified that so many times they had camped. Man was not made so large limbed and robust but that he must seek to narrow his world, and wall in a space such as fitted him. He was at first bare and out of doors; but though this was pleasant enough in serene and warm weather, by daylight, the rainy season and the winter, to say nothing of the torrid sun, would perhaps have nipped his race in the bud if he had not made haste to clothe himself with the shelter of a house. Adam and Eve, according to the fable, wore the bower before other clothes. Man wanted a home, a place of warmth, or comfort, first of physical warmth, then the warmth of the affections.

We may imagine a time when, in the infancy of the human race, some enterprising mortal crept into a hollow in a rock for shelter. Every child begins the world again, to some extent, and loves to stay out doors, even in wet and cold. It plays house, as well as horse, having an instinct for it. Who does not remember the interest with which, when young, he looked at shelving rocks, or any approach to a cave? It was the natural yearning of that portion of our most primitive ancestor which still survived in us. From the cave we have advanced to roofs of palm leaves, of bark and boughs, of linen woven and stretched, of grass and straw, of boards and shingles, of stones and tiles. At last, we know not what it is to live in the open air, and our lives are domestic in more senses than we think. From the hearth the field is a great distance. It would be well, perhaps, if we were to spend more of our days and nights without any obstruction between us and the celestial bodies, if the poet did not speak so much from under a roof, or the saint dwell there so long. Birds do not sing in caves, nor do doves cherish their innocence in dovecots.

However, if one designs to construct a dwelling house, it behooves him to exercise a little Yankee shrewdness, lest after all he finds himself in a workhouse, a labyrinth without a clue, a museum, an almshouse, a prison, or a splendid mausoleum instead. Consider first how slight a shelter is absolutely necessary. I have seen Penobscot Indians, in this town, living in tents of thin cotton cloth, while the snow was nearly a foot deep around them, and I thought that they would be glad to have it deeper to keep out the wind. Formerly, when how to get my living honestly, with freedom left for my proper pursuits, was a question which vexed me even more than it does now, for unfortunately I am become somewhat callous, I used to see a large box by the railroad, six feet long by three wide, in which the laborers locked up their tools at night; and it suggested to me that every man who was hard pushed might get such a one for a dollar, and, having bored a few auger holes in it, to admit the air at least, get into it when it rained and at night, and hook down the lid, and so have freedom in his love, and in his soul be free. This did not appear the worst, nor by any means a despicable alternative. You could sit up as late as you pleased, and, whenever you got up, go abroad without any landlord or house-lord dogging you for rent. Many a man is harassed to death to pay the rent of a larger and more luxurious box who would not have frozen to death in such a box as this. I am far from jesting. Economy is a subject which admits of being treated with levity, but it cannot so be disposed of. A comfortable house for a rude and hardy race, that lived mostly out of doors, was once made here almost entirely of such materials as Nature furnished ready to their hands. Gookin, who was superintendent of the Indians subject to the Massachusetts Colony, writing in 1674, says, "The best of their houses are covered very neatly, tight and warm, with barks of trees, slipped from their bodies at those seasons when the sap is up, and made into great flakes, with pressure of weighty timber, when they are green. . . . The meaner sort are covered with mats which they make of a kind of bulrush, and are also indifferently tight and warm, but not so good as the former. . . . Some I have seen, sixty or a hundred feet long and thirty feet broad. . . . I have often lodged in their wigwams, and found them as warm as the best English houses." He adds that they were commonly carpeted and lined within with well-wrought embroidered mats, and were furnished with various utensils. The Indians had advanced so far as to regulate the effect of the wind by a mat suspended over the hole in the roof and moved by a string. Such a lodge was in the first instance constructed in a day or two at most, and taken down and put up in a few hours; and every family owned one, or its apartment in one.

In the savage state every family owns a shelter as good as the best, and sufficient for its coarser and simpler wants; but I think that I speak within bounds when I say that, though the birds of the air have their nests, and the foxes their holes, and the savages their wigwams, in modern civilized society not more than one half the families own a shelter. In the large towns and cities, where civilization especially prevails, the number of those who own a shelter is a very small fraction of the whole. The rest pay an annual tax for this outside garment of all, become indispensable summer and winter, which would buy a village of Indian wigwams, but now helps to keep them poor as long as they live. I do not mean to insist here on the disadvantage of hiring compared with owning, but it is evident that the savage owns his shelter because it costs so little, while the civilized man hires his commonly because he cannot afford to own it; nor can he, in the long run, any better afford to hire. But, answers one, by merely paying this tax the poor civilized man secures an abode which is a palace compared with the savage's. An annual rent of from twenty-five to a hundred dollars (these are the country rates) entitles him to the benefit of the improvements of centuries, spacious apartments, clean paint and paper, Rumford fireplace, back plastering, Venetian blinds, copper pump, spring lock, a commodious cellar, and many other things. But how happens it that he who is said to enjoy these things is so commonly a *poor* civilized man, while the savage, who has them not, is rich as a savage? If it is asserted that civilization is a real advance in the condition of man, — and I think that it is, though only the wise improve their advantages, — it must be shown that it has produced better dwellings without making them more costly; and the cost of a thing is the amount of what I will call life which is required to be exchanged for it, immediately or in the long run. An average house in this neighborhood costs perhaps eight hundred dollars, and to lay up this sum will take from ten to fifteen years of the laborer's life, even if he is not encumbered with a family, — estimating the pecuniary value of every man's labor at one dollar a day, for if some receive more, others receive less; — so that he must have spent more than half his life commonly before *his* wigwam will be earned. If we suppose him to pay a rent instead, this is but a doubtful choice of evils. Would the savage have been wise to exchange his wigwam for a palace on these terms?

It may be guessed that I reduce almost the whole advantage of holding this superfluous property as a fund in store against the future, so far as the individual is concerned, mainly to the defraying of funeral expenses. But perhaps a man is not required to bury himself. Nevertheless this points to an important distinction between the civilized man and the savage; and, no doubt, they have designs on us for our benefit, in making the life of a civilized people an *institution*, in which the life of the individual is to a great extent absorbed, in order to preserve and perfect that of the race. But I wish to show at what a sacrifice this advantage is at present obtained, and to suggest that we may possibly so live as to secure all the advantage without suffering any of the disadvantage. What mean ye by saying that the poor ye have always with you, or that the fathers have eaten sour grapes, and the children's teeth are set on edge?

"As I live, saith the Lord God, ye shall not have occasion any more to use this proverb in Israel."

"Behold all souls are mine; as the soul of the father, so also the soul of the son is mine: the soul that sinneth it shall die."

When I consider my neighbors, the farmers of Concord, who are at least as well off as the other classes, I find that for the most part they have been toiling twenty, thirty, or forty years, that they may become the real owners of their farms, which commonly they have inherited with encumbrances, or else bought with hired money, — and we may regard one third of that toil as the cost of their houses, — but commonly they have not paid for them yet.   It is true, the encumbrances sometimes outweigh the value of the farm, so that the farm itself becomes one great encumbrance, and still a man is found to inherit it, being well acquainted with it, as he says.   On applying to the assessors, I am surprised to learn that they cannot at once name a dozen in the town who own their farms free and clear.   If you would know the history of these homesteads, inquire at the bank where they are mortgaged.   The man who has actually paid for his farm with labor on it is so rare that every neighbor can point to him.   I doubt if there are three such men in Concord.   What has been said of the merchants, that a very large majority, even ninety-seven in a hundred, are sure to fail, is equally true of the farmers.   With regard to the merchants, however, one of them says pertinently that a great part of their failures are not genuine pecuniary failures, but merely failures to fulfil their engagements, because it is inconvenient; that is, it is the moral character that breaks down.   But this puts an infinitely worse face on the matter, and suggests, beside, that probably not even the other three succeed in saving their souls, but are perchance bankrupt in a worse sense than they who fail honestly.   Bankruptcy and repudiation are the springboards from which much of our civilization vaults and turns its somersets, but the savage stands on the unelastic plank of famine.   Yet the Middlesex Cattle Show goes off here with *éclat* annually, as if all the joints of the agricultural machine were suent.

The farmer is endeavoring to solve the problem of a livelihood by a formula more complicated than the problem itself.   To get his shoestrings he speculates in herds of cattle.   With consummate skill he has set his trap with a hair springe to catch comfort and independence, and then, as he turned away, got his own leg into it.   This is the reason he is poor; and for a similar reason we are all poor in respect to a thousand savage comforts, though surrounded by luxuries.   As Chapman sings, —

> "The false society of men —
> — for earthly greatness
> All heavenly comforts rarefies to air."

And when the farmer has got his house, he may not be the richer but the poorer for it, and it be the house that has got him.   As I understand it, that was a valid objection urged by Momus against the house which Minerva made, that she "had not made it movable, by which means a bad neighborhood might be avoided;" and it may still be urged, for our houses are such unwieldy property that we are often imprisoned rather than housed in them; and the bad neighborhood to be avoided is our own scurvy selves. I know one or two families, at least, in this town, who, for nearly a generation, have been wishing to sell their houses in the outskirts and move into the village, but have not been able to accomplish it, and only death will set them free.

Granted that the *majority* are able at last either to own or hire the modern house with all its improvements. While civilization has been improving our houses, it has not equally improved the men who are to inhabit them. It has created palaces, but it was not so easy to create noblemen and kings. And *if the civilized man's pursuits are no worthier than the savage's, if he is employed the greater part of his life in obtaining gross necessaries and comforts merely, why should he have a better dwelling than the former?*

But how do the poor *minority* fare? Perhaps it will be found that just in proportion as some have been placed in outward circumstances above the savage, others have been degraded below him. The luxury of one class is counterbalanced by the indigence of another. On the one side is the palace, on the other are the almshouse and "silent poor." The myriads who built the pyramids to be the tombs of the Pharaohs were fed on garlic, and it may be were not decently buried themselves. The mason who finishes the cornice of the palace returns at night perchance to a hut not so good as a wigwam. It is a mistake to suppose that, in a country where the usual evidences of civilization exist, the condition of a very large body of the inhabitants may not be as degraded as that of savages. I refer to the degraded poor, not now to the degraded rich. To know this I should not need to look farther than to the shanties which everywhere border our railroads, that last improvement in civilization; where I see in my daily walks human beings living in sties, and all winter with an open door, for the sake of light, without any visible, often imaginable, wood pile, and the forms of both old and young are permanently contracted by the long habit of shrinking from cold and misery, and the development of all their limbs and faculties is checked. It certainly is fair to look at that class by whose labor the works which distinguish this generation are accomplished. Such too, to a greater or less extent, is the condition of the operatives of every denomination in England, which is the great workhouse of the world. Or I could refer you to Ireland, which is marked as one of the white or enlightened spots on the map. Contrast the physical condition of the Irish with that of the North American Indian, or the South Sea Islander, or any other savage race before it was degraded by contact with the civilized man. Yet I have no doubt that that people's rulers are as wise as the average of civilized rulers. Their condition only proves what squalidness may consist with civilization. I hardly need refer now to the laborers in our Southern States who produce the staple exports of this country, and are themselves a staple production of the South. But to confine myself to those who are said to be in *moderate* circumstances.

Most men appear never to have considered what a house is, and are actually though needlessly poor all their lives because they think that they must have such a one as their neighbors have. As if one were to wear any sort of coat which the tailor might cut out for him, or, gradually leaving off palmleaf hat or cap of woodchuck skin, complain of hard times because he could not afford to buy him a crown! It is possible to invent a house still more convenient and luxurious than we have, which yet all would admit that man could not afford to pay for. Shall we always study to obtain more of these things, and not sometimes to be content with less? Shall the respectable citizen thus gravely teach, by precept and example, the necessity of the young man's providing a certain number of superfluous glow-shoes, and umbrellas, and empty guest chambers for empty guests, before he dies? Why should not our furniture be as simple as the Arab's or the Indian's? When I think of the benefactors of the race, whom we have apotheosized as messengers from heaven, bearers of divine gifts to man, I do not see in my mind any retinue at their heels, any car-load of fashionable furniture. Or what if I were to allow — would it not be a singular allowance? — that our furniture should be more complex than the Arab's, in proportion as we are morally and intellectually his superiors! At present our houses are cluttered and defiled with it, and a good housewife would sweep out the greater part into the dust hole, and not leave her morning's work undone. Morning work! By the blushes of Aurora and the music of Memnon, what should be man's *morning work* in this world? I had three pieces of limestone on my desk, but I was terrified to find that they required to be dusted daily, when the furniture of my mind was all undusted still, and I threw them out the window in disgust. How, then, could I have a furnished house? I would rather sit in the open air, for no dust gathers on the grass, unless where man has broken ground.

It is the luxurious and dissipated who set the fashions which the
herd so diligently follow. The traveller who stops at the best houses,
so called, soon discovers this, for the publicans presume him to be a
Sardanapalus, and if he resigned himself to their tender mercies he
would soon be completely emasculated. I think that in the railroad
car we are inclined to spend more on luxury than on safety and convenience, and it threatens without attaining these to become no better
than a modern drawing room, with its divans, and ottomans, and sun-
shades, and a hundred other oriental things, which we are taking west
with us, invented for the ladies of the harem and the effeminate natives
of the Celestial Empire, which Jonathan should be ashamed to know
the names of. I would rather sit on a pumpkin and have it all to myself
than be crowded on a velvet cushion. I would rather ride on earth in
an ox cart, with a free circulation, than go to heaven in the fancy car
of an excursion train and breathe a *malaria* all the way.

The very simplicity and nakedness of man's life in the primitive
ages imply this advantage, at least, that they left him still but a sojourner in nature. When he was refreshed with food and sleep he
contemplated his journey again. He dwelt, as it were, in a tent in this
world, and was either threading the valleys, or crossing the plains, or
climbing the mountain tops. But lo! men have become the tools of
their tools. The man who independently plucked the fruits when he
was hungry is become a farmer; and he who stood under a tree for
shelter, a housekeeper. We now no longer camp as for a night, but
have settled down on earth and forgotten heaven. We have adopted
Christianity merely as an improved method of *agri*-culture. We have
built for this world a family mansion, and for the next a family tomb.
The best works of art are the expression of man's struggle to free himself from this condition, but the effect of our art is merely to make this
low state comfortable and that higher state to be forgotten. There is
actually no place in this village for a work of *fine* art, if any had come
down to us, to stand, for our lives, our houses and streets, furnish no
proper pedestal for it. There is not a nail to hang a picture on, nor a
shelf to receive the bust of a hero or a saint. When I consider how
our houses are built and paid for, or not paid for, and their internal
economy managed and sustained, I wonder that the floor does not give
way under the visitor while he is admiring the gewgaws upon the
mantelpiece, and let him through into the cellar, to some solid and
honest though earthy foundation. I cannot but perceive that this
so-called rich and refined life is a thing jumped at, and I do not get on

in the enjoyment of the *fine* arts which adorn it, my attention being
wholly occupied with the jump; for I remember that the greatest genuine leap, due to human muscles alone, on record, is that of certain
wandering Arabs, who are said to have cleared twenty-five feet on
level ground.   Without factitious support, man is sure to come to
earth again beyond that distance.   The first question which I am
tempted to put to the proprietor of such great impropriety is, Who
bolsters you?   Are you one of the ninety-seven who fail, or the three
who succeed?   Answer me these questions, and then perhaps I may
look at your bawbles and find them ornamental.   The cart before the
horse is neither beautiful nor useful.   Before we can adorn our houses
with beautiful objects the walls must be stripped, and our lives must
be stripped, and beautiful housekeeping and beautiful living be laid for
a foundation: now, a taste for the beautiful is most cultivated out of
doors, where there is no house and no housekeeper.

Old Johnson, in his "Wonder-Working Providence," speaking of
the first settlers of this town, with whom he was contemporary, tells
us that "they burrow themselves in the earth for their first shelter under some hillside, and, casting the soil aloft upon timber, they make a
smoky fire against the earth, at the highest side."   They did not "provide them houses," says he, "till the earth, by the Lord's blessing,
brought forth bread to feed them," and the first year's crop was so
light that "they were forced to cut their bread very thin for a long
season."   The secretary of the Province of New Netherland, writing
in Dutch, in 1650, for the information of those who wished to take up
land there, states more particularly that "those in New Netherland,
and especially in New England, who have no means to build farm
houses at first according to their wishes, dig a square pit in the ground,
cellar fashion, six or seven feet deep, as long and as broad as they
think proper, case the earth inside with wood all round the wall, and
line the wood with the bark of trees or something else to prevent the
caving in of the earth; floor this cellar with plank, and wainscot it overhead for a ceiling, raise a roof of spars clear up, and cover the spars
with bark or green sods, so that they can live dry and warm in these
houses with their entire families for two, three, and four years, it being
understood that partitions are run through these cellars which are
adapted to the size of the family.   The wealthy and principal men in
New England, in the beginning of the colonies, commenced their first
dwelling houses in this fashion for two reasons: firstly, in order not to
waste time in building, and not to want food the next season; secondly,

in order not to discourage poor laboring people whom they brought over in numbers from Fatherland. In the course of three or four years, when the country became adapted to agriculture, they built themselves handsome houses, spending on them several thousands."

In this course which our ancestors took there was a show of prudence at least, as if their principle were to satisfy the more pressing wants first. But are the more pressing wants satisfied now? When I think of acquiring for myself one of our luxurious dwellings, I am deterred, for, so to speak, the country is not yet adapted to *human* culture, and we are still forced to cut our *spiritual* bread far thinner than our forefathers did their wheaten. Not that all architectural ornament is to be neglected even in the rudest periods; but let our houses first be lined with beauty, where they come in contact with our lives, like the tenement of the shell-fish, and not overlaid with it. But, alas! I have been inside one or two of them, and know what they are lined with.

Though we are not so degenerate but that we might possibly live in a cave or a wigwam or wear skins to-day, it certainly is better to accept the advantages, though so dearly bought, which the invention and industry of mankind offer. In such a neighborhood as this, boards and shingles, lime and bricks, are cheaper and more easily obtained than suitable caves, or whole logs, or bark in sufficient quantities, or even well-tempered clay or flat stones. I speak understandingly on this subject, for I have made myself acquainted with it both theoretically and practically. With a little more wit we might use these materials so as to become richer than the richest now are, and make our civilization a blessing. The civilized man is a more experienced and wiser savage. But to make haste to my own experiment.

Near the end of March, 1845, I borrowed an axe and went down to the woods by Walden Pond, nearest to where I intended to build my house, and began to cut down some tall arrowy white pines, still in their youth, for timber. It is difficult to begin without borrowing, but perhaps it is the most generous course thus to permit your fellow-men to have an interest in your enterprise. The owner of the axe, as he released his hold on it, said that it was the apple of his eye; but I returned it sharper than I received it. It was a pleasant hillside where I worked, covered with pine woods, through which I looked out on the pond, and a small open field in the woods where pines and hickories were springing up. The ice in the pond was not yet dissolved, though there were some open spaces, and it was all dark colored and saturated with water.   There were some slight flurries of snow during the days that I worked there; but for the most part when I came out on to the railroad, on my way home, its yellow sand heap stretched away gleaming in the hazy atmosphere, and the rails shone in the spring sun, and I heard the lark and pewee and other birds already come to commence another year with us.   They were pleasant spring days, in which the winter of man's discontent was thawing as well as the earth, and the life that had lain torpid began to stretch itself.   One day, when my axe had come off and I had cut a green hickory for a wedge, driving it with a stone, and had placed the whole to soak in a pond hole in order to swell the wood, I saw a striped snake run into the water, and he lay on the bottom, apparently without inconvenience, as long as I stayed there, or more than a quarter of an hour; perhaps because he had not yet fairly come out of the torpid state.   It appeared to me that for a like reason men remain in their present low and primitive condition; but if they should feel the influence of the spring of springs arousing them, they would of necessity rise to a higher and more ethereal life. I had previously seen the snakes in frosty mornings in my path with portions of their bodies still numb and inflexible, waiting for the sun to thaw them.   On the 1st of April it rained and melted the ice, and in the early part of the day, which was very foggy, I heard a stray goose groping about over the pond and cackling as if lost, or like the spirit of the fog.

So I went on for some days cutting and hewing timber, and also studs and rafters, all with my narrow axe, not having many communicable or scholar-like thoughts, singing to myself, —

> Men say they know many things;
> But lo! they have taken wings, —
> The arts and sciences,
> And a thousand appliances;
> The wind that blows
> Is all that anybody knows.

I hewed the main timbers six inches square, most of the studs on two sides only, and the rafters and floor timbers on one side, leaving the rest of the bark on, so that they were just as straight and much stronger than sawed ones.   Each stick was carefully mortised or tenoned by its stump, for I had borrowed other tools by this time.   My days in the woods were not very long ones; yet I usually carried my dinner of bread and butter, and read the newspaper in which it was wrapped, at noon, sitting amid the green pine boughs which I had cut off, and to my bread was imparted some of their fragrance, for my hands were covered with a thick coat of pitch. Before I had done I was more the friend than the foe of the pine tree, though I had cut down some of them, having become better acquainted with it. Sometimes a rambler in the wood was attracted by the sound of my axe, and we chatted pleasantly over the chips which I had made.

By the middle of April, for I made no haste in my work, but rather made the most of it, my house was framed and ready for the raising. I had already bought the shanty of James Collins, an Irishman who worked on the Fitchburg Railroad, for boards. James Collins' shanty was considered an uncommonly fine one. When I called to see it he was not at home. I walked about the outside, at first unobserved from within, the window was so deep and high. It was of small dimensions, with a peaked cottage roof, and not much else to be seen, the dirt being raised five feet all around as if it were a compost heap. The roof was the soundest part, though a good deal warped and made brittle by the sun. Door-sill there was none, but a perennial passage for the hens under the door board. Mrs. C. came to the door and asked me to view it from the inside. The hens were driven in by my approach. It was dark, and had a dirt floor for the most part, dank, clammy, and aguish, only here a board and there a board which would not bear removal. She lighted a lamp to show me the inside of the roof and the walls, and also that the board floor extended under the bed, warning me not to step into the cellar, a sort of dust hole two feet deep. In her own words, they were "good boards overhead, good boards all around, and a good window," — of two whole squares originally, only the cat had passed out that way lately. There was a stove, a bed, and a place to sit, an infant in the house where it was born, a silk parasol, gilt-framed looking-glass, and a patent new coffee-mill nailed to an oak sapling, all told. The bargain was soon concluded, for James had in the mean while returned. I to pay four dollars and twenty-five cents to-night, he to vacate at five to-morrow morning, selling to nobody else meanwhile: I to take possession at six. It were well, he said, to be there early, and anticipate certain indistinct but wholly unjust claims on the score of ground rent and fuel. This he assured me was the only encumbrance. At six I passed him and his family on the road. One large bundle held their all, — bed, coffee-mill, looking-glass, hens, — all but the cat; she took to the woods and became a wild cat, and, as I learned afterward, trod in a trap set for woodchucks, and so became a dead cat at last.

I took down this dwelling the same morning, drawing the nails, and removed it to the pond side by small car-loads, spreading the boards on the grass there to bleach and warp back again in the sun. One early thrush gave me a note or two as I drove along the woodland path. I was informed treacherously by a young Patrick that neighbor Seeley, an Irishman, in the intervals of the carting, transferred the still tolerable, straight, and drivable nails, staples, and spikes to his pocket, and then stood when I came back to pass the time of day, and look freshly up, unconcerned, with spring thoughts, at the devastation; there being a dearth of work, as he said. He was there to represent spectatordom, and help make this seemingly insignificant event one with the removal of the gods of Troy.

I dug my cellar in the side of a hill sloping to the south, where a woodchuck had formerly dug his burrow, down through sumach and blackberry roots, and the lowest stain of vegetation, six feet square by seven deep, to a fine sand where potatoes would not freeze in any winter. The sides were left shelving, and not stoned; but the sun having never shone on them, the sand still keeps its place. It was but two hours' work. I took particular pleasure in this breaking of ground, for in almost all latitudes men dig into the earth for an equable temperature. Under the most splendid house in the city is still to be found the cellar where they store their roots as of old, and long after the superstructure has disappeared posterity remark its dent in the earth. The house is still but a sort of porch at the entrance of a burrow.

At length, in the beginning of May, with the help of some of my acquaintances, rather to improve so good an occasion for neighborliness than from any necessity, I set up the frame of my house. No man was ever more honored in the character of his raisers than I.[1] They are destined, I trust, to assist at the raising of loftier structures one day. I began to occupy my house on the 4th of July, as soon as it was boarded and roofed, for the boards were carefully feather-edged and lapped, so that it was perfectly impervious to rain, but before boarding I laid the foundation of a chimney at one end, bringing two cartloads of stones up the hill from the pond in my arms. I built the

---

[1] His raisers were Emerson, Alcott, William Ellery Channing, the younger, and George William Curtis. In the case of Emerson, and perhaps Alcott, "raisers" was undoubtedly a pun.

chimney after my hoeing in the fall, before a fire became necessary for warmth, doing my cooking in the mean while out of doors on the ground, early in the morning: which mode I still think is in some respects more convenient and agreeable than the usual one. When it stormed before my bread was baked, I fixed a few boards over the fire, and sat under them to watch my loaf, and passed some pleasant hours in that way. In those days, when my hands were much employed, I read but little, but the least scraps of paper which lay on the ground, my holder, or tablecloth, afforded me as much entertainment, in fact answered the same purpose as the Iliad.

It would be worth the while to build still more deliberately than I did, considering, for instance, what foundation a door, a window, a cellar, a garret, have in the nature of man, and perchance never raising any superstructure until we found a better reason for it than our temporal necessities even. There is some of the same fitness in a man's building his own house that there is in a bird's building his own nest. Who knows but if men constructed their dwellings with their own hands, and provided food for themselves and families simply and honestly enough, the poetic faculty would be universally developed, as birds universally sing when they are so engaged? But alas! we do like cowbirds and cuckoos, which lay their eggs in nests which other birds have built, and cheer no traveller with their chattering and unmusical notes. Shall we forever resign the pleasure of construction to the carpenter? What does architecture amount to in the experience of the mass of men? I never in all my walks came across a man engaged in so simple and natural an occupation as building his house. We belong to the community. It is not the tailor alone who is the ninth part of a man; it is as much the preacher, and the merchant, and the farmer. Where is this division of labor to end? and what object does it finally serve? No doubt another *may* also think for me; but it is not therefore desirable that he should do so to the exclusion of my thinking for myself.

True, there are architects so called in this country, and I have heard of one at least possessed with the idea of making architectural ornaments have a core of truth, a necessity, and hence a beauty, as if it were a revelation to him.[1] All very well perhaps from his point of view, but

[1] Thoreau was referring to Horatio Greenough whose theories of functionalism he had learned of from Greenough's letter to Emerson. He was rather hard on Greenough because he misunderstood him — and perhaps because Emerson approved of his theory. No one, however, better exemplified Greenough's theory of form and function and the beauty of utility than Thoreau.

only a little better than the common dilettantism. A sentimental reformer in architecture, he began at the cornice, not at the foundation.
It was only now to put a core of truth within the ornaments, that every
sugar plum in fact might have an almond or caraway seed in it, —
though I hold that almonds are most wholesome without the sugar, —
and not how the inhabitant, the indweller, might build truly within and
without, and let the ornaments take care of themselves. What reasonable man ever supposed that ornaments were something outward and
in the skin merely, — that the tortoise got his spotted shell, or the
shellfish its mother-o'-pearl tints, by such a contract as the inhabitants
of Broadway their Trinity Church? But a man has no more to do with
the style of architecture of his house than a tortoise with that of its
shell: nor need the soldier be so idle as to try to paint the precise *color*
of his virtue on his standard. The enemy will find it out. He may
turn pale when the trial comes. This man seemed to me to lean over
the cornice, and timidly whisper his half truth to the rude occupants
who really knew it better than he. What of architectural beauty I
now see, I know has gradually grown from within outward, out of the
necessities and character of the indweller, who is the only builder, —
out of some unconscious truthfulness, and nobleness, without ever a
thought for the appearance; and whatever additional beauty of this
kind is destined to be produced will be preceded by a like unconscious
beauty of life. The most interesting dwellings in this country, as the
painter knows, are the most unpretending, humble log huts and cot-
tages of the poor commonly; it is the life of the inhabitants whose shells
they are, and not any peculiarity in their surfaces merely, which makes
them *picturesque;* and equally interesting will be the citizen's suburban
box, when his life shall be as simple and as agreeable to the imagination, and there is as little straining after effect in the style of his
dwelling. A great proportion of architectural ornaments are literally
hollow, and a September gale would strip them off, like borrowed
plumes, without injury to the substantials. They can do without *architecture* who have no olives nor wines in the cellar. What if an equal
ado were made about the ornaments of style in literature, and the
architects of our bibles spent as much time about their cornices as the
architects of our churches do? So are made the *belles-lettres* and the
beaux-arts and their professors. Much it concerns a man, forsooth,
how a few sticks are slanted over him or under him, and what colors
are daubed upon his box. It would signify somewhat, if, in any earnest sense, *he* slanted them and daubed it; but the spirit having departed

out of the tenant, it is of a piece with constructing his own coffin, — the architecture of the grave, and "carpenter," is but another name for "coffin-maker." One man says, in his despair or indifference to life, take up a handful of the earth at your feet, and paint your house that color. Is he thinking of his last and narrow house? Toss up a copper for it as well. What an abundance of leisure he must have! Why do you take up a handful of dirt? Better paint your house your own complexion; let it turn pale or blush for you. An enterprise to improve the style of cottage architecture! When you have got my ornaments ready I will wear them.

Before winter I built a chimney, and shingled the sides of my house, which were already impervious to rain, with imperfect and sappy shingles made of the first slice of the log, whose edges I was obliged to straighten with a plane.

I have thus a tight shingled and plastered house, ten feet wide by fifteen long, and eight-feet posts, with a garret and a closet, a large window on each side, two trap doors, one door at the end, and a brick fireplace opposite. The exact cost of my house, paying the usual price for such materials as I used, but not counting the work, all of which was done by myself, was as follows; and I give the details because very few are able to tell exactly what their houses cost, and fewer still, if any, the separate cost of the various materials which compose them: —

Boards	$8 03½,	mostly shanty boards.
Refuse shingles for roof and sides . .	4 00	
Laths	1 25	
Two second-hand windows with glass	2 43	
One thousand old brick	4 00	
Two casks of lime	2 40	That was high.
Hair	0 31	More than I needed.
Mantle-tree iron	0 15	
Nails	3 90	
Hinges and screws	0 14	
Latch	0 10	
Chalk	0 01	
Transportation	1 40	} I carried a good part on my back.
In all	$28 12½	

These are all the materials excepting the timber, stones, and sand, which I claimed by squatter's right. I have also a small woodshed adjoining, made chiefly of the stuff which was left after building the house.

I intend to build me a house which will surpass any on the main street in Concord in grandeur and luxury, as soon as it pleases me as much and will cost me no more than my present one.

I thus found that the student who wishes for a shelter can obtain one for a lifetime at an expense not greater than the rent which he now pays annually. If I seem to boast more than is becoming, my excuse is that I brag for humanity rather than for myself; and my shortcomings and inconsistencies do not affect the truth of my statement. Notwithstanding much cant and hypocrisy, — chaff which I find it difficult to separate from my wheat, but for which I am as sorry as any man, — I will breathe freely and stretch myself in this respect, it is such a relief to both the moral and physical system; and I am resolved that I will not through humility become the devil's attorney. I will endeavor to speak a good word for the truth. At Cambridge College the mere rent of a student's room, which is only a little larger than my own, is thirty dollars each year, though the corporation had the advantage of building thirty-two side by side and under one roof, and the occupant suffers the inconvenience of many and noisy neighbors, and perhaps a residence in the fourth story. I cannot but think that if we had more true wisdom in these respects, not only less education would be needed, because, forsooth, more would already have been acquired, but the pecuniary expense of getting an education would in a great measure vanish. Those conveniences which the student requires at Cambridge or elsewhere cost him or somebody else ten times as great a sacrifice of life as they would with proper management on both sides. Those things for which the most money is demanded are never the things which the student most wants. Tuition, for instance, is an important item in the term bill, while for the far more valuable education which he gets by associating with the most cultivated of his contemporaries no charge is made. The mode of founding a college is, commonly, to get up a subscription of dollars and cents, and then following blindly the principles of a division of labor to its extreme, a principle which should never be followed but with circumspection, — to call in a contractor who makes this a subject of speculation, and he employs Irishmen or other operatives actually to lay the foundations, while the students that are to be are said to be fitting themselves for it; and for these oversights successive generations have to pay. I think that it would be *better than this*, for the students, or those who desire to be benefited by it, even to lay the foundation themselves. The student who secures his coveted leisure and retirement by systematically shirking any labor necessary to man obtains but an ignoble and unprofitable leisure, defrauding himself of the experience which alone can make leisure fruitful. "But," says one, "you do not mean that the students should go to work with their hands instead of their heads?" I do not mean that exactly, but I mean something which he might think a good deal like that; I mean that they should not *play* life, or *study* it merely, while the community supports them at this expensive game, but earnestly *live* it from beginning to end. How could youths better learn to live than by at once trying the experiment of living? Methinks this would exercise their minds as much as mathematics. If I wished a boy to know something about the arts and sciences, for instance, I would not pursue the common course, which is merely to send him into the neighborhood of some professor, where anything is professed and practised but the art of life; — to survey the world through a telescope or a microscope, and never with his natural eye; to study chemistry, and not learn how his bread is made, or mechanics, and not learn how it is earned; to discover new satellites to Neptune, and not detect the motes in his eyes, or to what vagabond he is a satellite himself; or to be devoured by the monsters that swarm all around him, while contemplating the monsters in a drop of vinegar. Which would have advanced the most at the end of a month, — the boy who had made his own jackknife from the ore which he had dug and smelted, reading as much as would be necessary for this — or the boy who had attended the lectures on metallurgy at the Institute in the meanwhile, and had received a Rogers' penknife from his father? Which would be most likely to cut his fingers? ... To my astonishment I was informed on leaving college that I had studied navigation! — why, if I had taken one turn down the harbor I should have known more about it. Even the *poor* student studies and is taught only *political* economy, while that economy of living which is synonymous with philosophy is not even sincerely professed in our colleges. The consequence is, that while he is reading Adam Smith, Ricardo, and Say, he runs his father in debt irretrievably.[1]

As with our colleges, so with a hundred "modern improvements;"

[1] Though consonant with the organic life, Thoreau's theory of education as experience did not do justice to his own education at Harvard College. For Harvard taught him by experience to be the scholar — the omnivorous reader, and the writer of books.

there is an illusion about them; there is not always a positive advance. The devil goes on exacting compound interest to the last for his early share and numerous succeeding investments in them. Our inventions are wont to be pretty toys, which distract our attention from serious things. They are but improved means to an unimproved end, an end which it was already but too easy to arrive at; as railroads lead to Boston or New York. We are in great haste to construct a magnetic telegraph from Maine to Texas; but Maine and Texas, it may be, have nothing important to communicate. Either is in such a predicament as the man who was earnest to be introduced to a distinguished deaf woman, but when he was presented, and one end of her ear trumpet was put into his hand, had nothing to say. As if the main object were to talk fast and not to talk sensibly. We are eager to tunnel under the Atlantic and bring the old world some weeks nearer to the new; but perchance the first news that will leak through into the broad, flapping American ear will be that the Princess Adelaide has the whooping cough. After all, the man whose horse trots a mile in a minute does not carry the most important messages; he is not an evangelist, nor does he come round eating locusts and wild honey. I doubt if Flying Childers ever carried a peck of corn to mill.

One says to me, "I wonder that you do not lay up money; you love to travel; you might take the cars and go to Fitchburg to-day and see the country." But I am wiser than that. I have learned that the swiftest traveller is he that goes afoot. I say to my friend, Suppose we try who will get there first. The distance is thirty miles; the fare ninety cents. That is almost a day's wages. I remember when wages were sixty cents a day for laborers on this very road. Well, I start now on foot, and get there before night; I have travelled at that rate by the week together. You will in the mean while have earned your fare, and arrive there some time to-morrow, or possibly this evening, if you are lucky enough to get a job in season. Instead of going to Fitchburg, you will be working here the greater part of the day. And so, if the railroad reached round the world, I think that I should keep ahead of you; and as for seeing the country and getting experience of that kind, I should have to cut your acquaintance altogether.

Such is the universal law, which no man can ever outwit, and with regard to the railroad even we may say it is as broad as it is long. To make a railroad round the world available to all mankind is equivalent to grading the whole surface of the planet. Men have an indistinct notion that if they keep up this activity of joint stocks and spades long enough all will at length ride somewhere, in next to no time, and for nothing; but though a crowd rushes to the depot, and the conductor shouts "All aboard!" when the smoke is blown away and the vapor condensed, it will be perceived that a few are riding, but the rest are run over, — and it will be called, and will be, "A melancholy accident." No doubt they can ride at last who shall have earned their fare, that is, if they survive so long, but they will probably have lost their elasticity and desire to travel by that time. This spending of the best part of one's life earning money in order to enjoy a questionable liberty during the least valuable part of it, reminds me of the Englishman who went to India to make a fortune first, in order that he might return to England and live the life of a poet. He should have gone up garret at once. "What!" exclaim a million Irishmen starting up from all the shanties in the land, "is not this railroad which we have built a good thing?" Yes, I answer, *comparatively* good, that is, you might have done worse; but I wish, as you are brothers of mine, that you could have spent your time better than digging in this dirt.

Before I finished my house, wishing to earn ten or twelve dollars by some honest and agreeable method, in order to meet my unusual expenses, I planted about two acres and a half of light and sandy soil near it chiefly with beans, but also a small part with potatoes, corn, peas, and turnips. The whole lot contains eleven acres, mostly growing up to pines and hickories, and was sold the preceding season for eight dollars and eight cents an acre. One farmer said that it was "good for nothing but to raise cheeping squirrels on." I put no manure whatever on this land, not being the owner, but merely a squatter, and not expecting to cultivate so much again, and I did not quite hoe it all once. I got out several cords of stumps in ploughing, which supplied me with fuel for a long time, and left small circles of virgin mould, easily distinguishable through the summer by the greater luxuriance of the beans there. The dead and for the most part unmerchantable wood behind my house, and the driftwood from the pond, have supplied the remainder of my fuel. I was obliged to hire a team and a man for the ploughing, though I held the plough myself. My farm outgoes for the first season were, for implements, seed, work, etc., \$14.72½. The seed corn was given me. This never costs anything to speak of, unless you plant more than enough. I got twelve bushels of beans, and eighteen bushels of potatoes, beside some peas and sweet corn. The yellow corn and turnips were too late to come to anything. My whole income from the farm was

$23 44

Deducting the outgoes . . . 14 72½
_____

There are left . . . . . . $ 8 71½,

beside produce consumed and on hand at the time this estimate was made of the value of $4.50, — the amount on hand much more than balancing a little grass which I did not raise. All things considered, that is, considering the importance of a man's soul and of to-day, notwithstanding the short time occupied by my experiment, nay, partly even because of its transient character, I believe that that was doing better than any farmer in Concord did that year.

The next year I did better still, for I spaded up all the land which I required, about a third of an acre, and I learned from the experience of both years, not being in the least awed by many celebrated works on husbandry, Arthur Young among the rest, that if one would live simply and eat only the crop which he raised, and raise no more than he ate, and not exchange it for an insufficient quantity of more luxurious and expensive things, he would need to cultivate only a few rods of ground, and that it would be cheaper to spade up that than to use oxen to plough it, and to select a fresh spot from time to time than to manure the old, and he could do all his necessary farm work as it were with his left hand at odd hours in the summer; and thus he would not be tied to an ox, or horse, or cow, or pig, as at present. I desire to speak impartially on this point, and as one not interested in the success or failure of the present economical and social arrangements. I was more independent than any farmer in Concord, for I was not anchored to a house or farm, but could follow the bent of my genius, which is a very crooked one, every moment. Beside being better off than they already, if my house had been burned or my crops had failed, I should have been nearly as well off as before.

I am wont to think that men are not so much the keepers of herds as herds are the keepers of men, the former are so much the freer. Men and oxen exchange work; but if we consider necessary work only, the oxen will be seen to have greatly the advantage, their farm is so much the larger. Man does some of his part of the exchange work in his six weeks of haying, and it is no boy's play. Certainly no nation that lived simply in all respects, that is, no nation of philosophers, would commit so great a blunder as to use the labor of animals. True, there never was and is not likely soon to be a nation of philosophers, nor am I certain it is desirable that there should be. However, *I* should never have broken a horse or bull and taken him to board for any work he might do for me, for fear I should become a horse-man or a herds-man merely; and if society seems to be the gainer by so doing, are we certain that what is one man's gain is not another's loss, and that the stable-boy has equal cause with his master to be satisfied? Granted that some public works would not have been constructed without this aid, and let man share the glory of such with the ox and horse; does it follow that he could not have accomplished works yet more worthy of himself in that case? When men begin to do, not merely unnecessary or artistic, but luxurious and idle work, with their assistance, it is inevitable that a few do all the exchange work with the oxen, or, in other words, become the slaves of the strongest. Man thus not only works for the animal within him, but, for a symbol of this, he works for the animal without him. Though we have many substantial houses of brick or stone, the prosperity of the farmer is still measured by the degree to which the barn overshadows the house. This town is said to have the largest houses for oxen, cows, and horses here-abouts, and it is not behindhand in its public buildings; but there are very few halls for free worship or free speech in this county. It should not be by their architecture, but why not even by their power of ab-stract thought, that nations should seek to commemorate themselves? How much more admirable the Bhagvat-Geeta than all the ruins of the East! [1] Towers and temples are the luxury of princes. A simple and independent mind does not toil at the bidding of any prince. Genius is not a retainer to any emperor, nor is its material silver, or gold, or marble, except to a trifling extent. To what end, pray, is so much stone hammered? In Arcadia, when I was there, I did not see any hammering stone. Nations are possessed with an insane ambition to perpetuate the memory of themselves by the amount of hammered stone they leave. What if equal pains were taken to smooth and polish their manners? One piece of good sense would be more memorable than a monument as high as the moon. I love better to see stones in place. The grandeur of Thebes was a vulgar grandeur. More sensible is a rod of stone wall that bounds an honest man's field than a hundred-gated Thebes that has wandered farther from the true end of life. The religion and civilization which are barbaric and heathenish build splendid temples; but what you might call Christianity does not. Most of the stone a nation hammers goes toward its tomb only. It buries itself alive. As for the Pyramids, there is nothing to wonder at in them so much as the fact that so many men could be found degraded

[1] Thoreau wrote his sister Helen in 1840: "An honest book's the noblest work of man."

enough to spend their lives constructing a tomb for some ambitious booby, whom it would have been wiser and manlier to have drowned in the Nile, and then given his body to the dogs. I might possibly invent some excuse for them and him, but I have no time for it. As for the religion and love of art of the builders, it is much the same all the world over, whether the building be an Egyptian temple or the United States Bank. It costs more than it comes to. The mainspring is vanity, assisted by the love of garlic and bread and butter. Mr. Balcom, a promising young architect, designs it on the back of his Vitruvius, with hard pencil and ruler, and the job is let out to Dobson & Sons, stonecutters. When the thirty centuries begin to look down on it, mankind begin to look up at it. As for your high towers and monuments, there was a crazy fellow once in this town who undertook to dig through to China, and he got so far that, as he said, he heard the Chinese pots and kettles rattle; but I think that I shall not go out of my way to admire the hole which he made. Many are concerned about the monuments of the West and the East, — to know who built them. For my part, I should like to know who in those days did not build them, — who were above such trifling. But to proceed with my statistics.

By surveying, carpentry, and day-labor of various other kinds in the village in the mean while, for I have as many trades as fingers, I had earned $13.34. The expense of food for eight months, namely, from July 4th to March 1st, the time when these estimates were made, though I lived there more than two years, — not counting potatoes, a little green corn, and some peas, which I had raised, nor considering the value of what was on hand at the last date, was

Rice	$1 73½	
Molasses	1 73	Cheapest form of the saccharine.
Rye meal	1 04¾	
Indian meal . . .	0 99¾	Cheaper than rye.
Pork	0 22	
Flour	0 88	Costs more than Indian meal, both money and trouble.
Sugar	0 80	
Lard	0 65	
Apples	0 25	
Dried apple . . .	0 22	
Sweet potatoes . .	0 10	
One pumpkin . .	0 6	
One watermelon . .	0 2	
Salt	0 3	

All experiments which failed.

Yes, I did eat $8.74, all told; but I should not thus unblushingly publish my guilt, if I did not know that most of my readers were equally guilty with myself, and that their deeds would look no better in print. The next year I sometimes caught a mess of fish for my dinner, and once I went so far as to slaughter a woodchuck which ravaged my bean-field, — effect his transmigration, as a Tartar would say, — and devour him, partly for experiment's sake; but though it afforded me a momentary enjoyment, notwithstanding a musky flavor, I saw that the longest use would not make that a good practice, however it might seem to have your woodchucks ready dressed by the village butcher.

Clothing and some incidental expenses within the same dates, though little can be inferred from this item, amounted to

$8 40¾
Oil and some household utensils . . 2 00

So that all the pecuniary outgoes, excepting for washing and mending, which for the most part were done out of the house, and their bills have not yet been received, — and these are all and more than all the ways by which money necessarily goes out in this part of the world, — were

House	$28 12½
Farm one year	14 72½
Food eight months	8 74
Clothing, etc., eight months . .	8 40¾
Oil, etc., eight months	2 00
In all	$61 99¾

I address myself now to those of my readers who have a living to get. And to meet this I have for farm produce sold

	$23 44
Earned by day-labor	13 34
In all	$36 78,

which subtracted from the sum of the outgoes leaves a balance of $25.21¾ on the one side, — this being very nearly the means with which I started, and the measure of expenses to be incurred, — and on the other, beside the leisure and independence and health thus secured, a comfortable house for me as long as I choose to occupy it.

These statistics, however accidental and therefore uninstructive they may appear, as they have a certain completeness, have a certain value also. Nothing was given me of which I have not rendered some account. It appears from the above estimate, that my food alone cost me in money about twenty-seven cents a week. It was, for nearly two years after this, rye and Indian meal without yeast, potatoes, rice, a very little salt pork, molasses, and salt; and my drink, water. It was fit that I should live on rice, mainly, who loved so well the philosophy of India. To meet the objections of some inveterate cavillers, I may as well state, that if I dined out occasionally, as I always had done, and I trust shall have opportunities to do again, it was frequently to the detriment of my domestic arrangements. But the dining out, being, as I have stated, a constant element, does not in the least affect a comparative statement like this.

I learned from my two years' experience that it would cost incredibly little trouble to obtain one's necessary food, even in this latitude; that a man may use as simple a diet as the animals, and yet retain health and strength. I have made a satisfactory dinner, satisfactory on several accounts, simply off a dish of purslane (*Portulaca oleracea*) which I gathered in my cornfield, boiled and salted. I give the Latin on account of the savoriness of the trivial name. And pray what more can a reasonable man desire, in peaceful times, in ordinary noons, than a sufficient number of ears of green sweet-corn boiled, with the addition of salt? Even the little variety which I used was a yielding to the demands of appetite, and not of health. Yet men have come to such a pass that they frequently starve, not for want of necessaries, but for want of luxuries; and I know a good woman who thinks that her son lost his life because he took to drinking water only.

The reader will perceive that I am treating the subject rather from an economic than a dietetic point of view, and he will not venture to put my abstemiousness to the test unless he has a well-stocked larder.

Bread I at first made of pure Indian meal and salt, genuine hoe-cakes, which I baked before my fire out of doors on a shingle or the end of a stick of timber sawed off in building my house; but it was wont to get smoked and to have a piny flavor. I tried flour also; but have at last found a mixture of rye and Indian meal most convenient and agreeable. In cold weather it was no little amusement to bake several small loaves of this in succession, tending and turning them as carefully as an Egyptian his hatching eggs. They were a real cereal fruit which I ripened, and they had to my senses a fragrance like that of other noble fruits, which I kept in as long as possible by wrapping them in cloths. I made a study of the ancient and indispensable art of bread-making,

consulting such authorities as offered, going back to the primitive days
and first invention of the unleavened kind, when from the wildness of
nuts and meats men first reached the mildness and refinement of this
diet, and travelling gradually down in my studies through that accidental souring of the dough which, it is supposed, taught the leavening
process, and through the various fermentations thereafter, till I came
to "good, sweet, wholesome bread," the staff of life. Leaven, which
some deem the soul of bread, the *spiritus* which fills its cellular tissue,
which is religiously preserved like the vestal fire, — some precious
bottle-full, I suppose, first brought over in the Mayflower, did the
business for America, and its influence is still rising, swelling, spreading, in cerealian billows over the land, — this seed I regularly and
faithfully procured from the village, till at length one morning I forgot
the rules, and scalded my yeast; by which accident I discovered that
even this was not indispensable, — for my discoveries were not by the
synthetic but analytic process, — and I have gladly omitted it since,
though most housewives earnestly assured me that safe and wholesome
bread without yeast might not be, and elderly people prophesied a
speedy decay of the vital forces. Yet I find it not to be an essential
ingredient, and after going without it for a year am still in the land of
the living; and I am glad to escape the trivialness of carrying a bottle-
full in my pocket, which would sometimes pop and discharge its
contents to my discomfiture. It is simpler and more respectable to
omit it. Man is an animal who more than any other can adapt himself
to all climates and circumstances. Neither did I put any sal-soda, or
other acid or alkali, into my bread. It would seem that I made it according to the recipe which Marcus Porcius Cato gave about two centuries before Christ. "Panem depsticium sic facito. Manus mortari-
umque bene lavato. Farinam in mortarium indito, aquæ paulatim
addito, subigitoque pulchre. Ubi bene subegeris, defingito, coquitoque
sub testu." Which I take to mean, "Make kneaded bread thus. Wash
your hands and trough well. Put the meal into the trough, add water
gradually, and knead it thoroughly. When you have kneaded it well,
mould it, and bake it under a cover," that is, in a baking-kettle. Not a
word about leaven. But I did not always use this staff of life. At one
time, owing to the emptiness of my purse, I saw none of it for more
than a month.

Every New Englander might easily raise all his own breadstuffs in
this land of rye and Indian corn, and not depend on distant and fluctuating markets for them. Yet so far are we from simplicity and inde-

pendence that, in Concord, fresh and sweet meal is rarely sold in the shops, and hominy and corn in a still coarser form are hardly used by any. For the most part the farmer gives to his cattle and hogs the grain of his own producing, and buys flour, which is at least no more wholesome, at a greater cost, at the store. I saw that I could easily raise my bushel or two of rye and Indian corn, for the former will grow on the poorest land, and the latter does not require the best, and grind them in a hand-mill, and so do without rice and pork; and if I must have some concentrated sweet, I found by experiment that I could make a very good molasses either of pumpkins or beets, and I knew that I needed only to set out a few maples to obtain it more easily still, and while these were growing I could use various substitutes beside those which I have named. "For," as the Forefathers sang, —

> "we can make liquor to sweeten our lips
> Of pumpkins and parsnips and walnut-tree chips."

Finally, as for salt, that grossest of groceries, to obtain this might be a fit occasion for a visit to the seashore, or, if I did without it altogether, I should probably drink the less water. I do not learn that the Indians ever troubled themselves to go after it.

Thus I could avoid all trade and barter, so far as my food was concerned, and having a shelter already, it would only remain to get clothing and fuel. The pantaloons which I now wear were woven in a farmer's family, — thank Heaven there is so much virtue still in man; for I think the fall from the farmer to the operative as great and memorable as that from the man to the farmer; — and in a new country, fuel is an encumbrance. As for a habitat, if I were not permitted still to squat, I might purchase one acre at the same price for which the land I cultivated was sold — namely, eight dollars and eight cents. But as it was, I considered that I enhanced the value of the land by squatting on it.

There is a certain class of unbelievers who sometimes ask me such questions as, if I think that I can live on vegetable food alone; and to strike at the root of the matter at once, — for the root is faith, — I am accustomed to answer such, that I can live on board nails. If they cannot understand that, they cannot understand much that I have to say. For my part, I am glad to hear of experiments of this kind being tried; as that a young man tried for a fortnight to live on hard, raw corn on the ear, using his teeth for all mortar. The squirrel tribe tried the same and succeeded. The human race is interested in these experiments, though a few old women who are incapacitated for them, or who own their thirds in mills, may be alarmed.

My furniture, part of which I made myself, and the rest cost me nothing of which I have not rendered an account, consisted of a bed, a table, a desk, three chairs, a looking-glass three inches in diameter, a pair of tongs and andirons, a kettle, a skillet, and a frying-pan, a dipper, a wash-bowl, two knives and forks, three plates, one cup, one spoon, a jug for oil, a jug for molasses, and a japanned lamp. None is so poor that he need sit on a pumpkin. That is shiftlessness. There is a plenty of such chairs as I like best in the village garrets to be had for taking them away. Furniture! Thank God, I can sit and I can stand without the aid of a furniture warehouse. What man but a philosopher would not be ashamed to see his furniture packed in a cart and going up country exposed to the light of heaven and the eyes of men, a beggarly account of empty boxes? That is Spaulding's furniture. I could never tell from inspecting such a load whether it belonged to a so-called rich man or a poor one; the owner always seemed poverty-stricken. Indeed, the more you have of such things the poorer you are. Each load looks as if it contained the contents of a dozen shanties; and if one shanty is poor, this is a dozen times as poor. Pray, for what do we *move* ever but to get rid of our furniture, our *exuviæ*; at last to go from this world to another newly furnished, and leave this to be burned? It is the same as if all these traps were buckled to a man's belt, and he could not move over the rough country where our lines are cast without dragging them, — dragging his trap. He was a lucky fox that left his tail in the trap. The muskrat will gnaw his third leg off to be free. No wonder man has lost his elasticity. How often he is at a dead set! "Sir, if I may be so bold, what do you mean by a dead set?" If you are a seer, whenever you meet a man you will see all that he owns, ay, and much that he pretends to disown, behind him, even to his kitchen furniture and all the trumpery which he saves and will not burn, and he will appear to be harnessed to it and making what headway he can. I think that the man is at a dead set who has got through a knot hole or gateway where his sledge load of furniture cannot follow him. I cannot but feel compassion when I hear some trig, compact-looking man, seemingly free, all girded and ready, speak of his "furniture," as whether it is insured or not. "But what shall I do with my furniture?" My gay butterfly is entangled in a spider's web then. Even those who seem for a long while not to have any, if you inquire

more narrowly you will find have some stored in somebody's barn.
I look upon England to-day as an old gentleman who is travelling with
a great deal of baggage, trumpery which has accumulated from long
housekeeping, which he has not the courage to burn; great trunk, little
trunk, bandbox and bundle. Throw away the first three at least. It
would surpass the powers of a well man nowadays to take up his bed
and walk, and I should certainly advise a sick one to lay down his bed
and run. When I have met an immigrant tottering under a bundle
which contained his all — looking like an enormous wen which had
grown out of the nape of his neck — I have pitied him, not because that
was his all, but because he had all *that* to carry. If I have got to drag
my trap, I will take care that it be a light one and do not nip me in a
vital part. But perchance it would be wisest never to put one's paw
into it.

I would observe, by the way, that it costs me nothing for curtains,
for I have no gazers to shut out but the sun and moon, and I am willing
that they should look in. The moon will not sour milk nor taint meat
of mine, nor will the sun injure my furniture or fade my carpet; and if
he is sometimes too warm a friend, I find it still better economy to
retreat behind some curtain which nature has provided, than to add a
single item to the details of housekeeping. A lady once offered me a
mat, but as I had no room to spare within the house, nor time to spare
within or without to shake it, I declined it, preferring to wipe my feet
on the sod before my door. It is best to avoid the beginnings of evil.

Not long since I was present at the auction of a deacon's effects, for
his life had not been ineffectual: —

"The evil that men do lives after them."

As usual, a great proportion was trumpery which had begun to accumulate in his father's day. Among the rest was a dried tapeworm.
And now, after lying half a century in his garret and other dust holes,
these things were not burned; instead of a *bonfire*, or purifying destruction of them, there was an *auction*, or increasing of them. The neighbors eagerly collected to view them, bought them all, and carefully
transported them to their garrets and dust holes, to lie there till their
estates were settled, when they will start again. When a man dies he
kicks the dust.

The customs of some savage nations might, perchance, be profitably
imitated by us, for they at least go through the semblance of casting
their slough annually; they have the idea of the thing, whether they

have the reality or not. Would it not be well if we were to celebrate such a "busk," or "feast of first fruits," as Bartram describes to have been the custom of the Mucclasse Indians? "When a town celebrates the busk," says he, "having previously provided themselves with new clothes, new pots, pans, and other household utensils and furniture, they collect all their worn out clothes and other despicable things, sweep and cleanse their houses, squares, and the whole town, of their filth, which with all the remaining grain and other old provisions they cast together into one common heap, and consume it with fire. After having taken medicine, and fasted for three days, all the fire in the town is extinguished. During this fast they abstain from the gratification of every appetite and passion whatever. A general amnesty is proclaimed; all malefactors may return to their town."

"On the fourth morning, the high priest, by rubbing dry wood together, produces new fire in the public square, from whence every habitation in the town is supplied with the new and pure flame."

They then feast on the new corn and fruits, and dance and sing for three days, "and the four following days they receive visits and rejoice with their friends from neighboring towns who have in like manner purified and prepared themselves."

The Mexicans also practised a similar purification at the end of every fifty-two years, in the belief that it was time for the world to come to an end.

I have scarcely heard of a truer sacrament, that is, as the dictionary defines it, "outward and visible sign of an inward and spiritual grace," than this, and I have no doubt that they were originally inspired directly from Heaven to do thus, though they have no biblical record of the revelation.[1]

For more than five years I maintained myself thus solely by the labor of my hands, and I found, that by working about six weeks in a year, I could meet all the expenses of living. The whole of my winters, as well as most of my summers, I had free and clear for study. I have thoroughly tried school-keeping, and found that my expenses were in proportion, or rather out of proportion, to my income, for I

---

[1] Much has been made of the "busk" as the total rejection and destruction of tradition. The organic metaphors of *Walden*, however, make it clear that Thoreau was the partisan of transformations. The busk, in fact, was a purificatory rite, a sacrament or sign of the inner purification which "purifying destruction" in itself could not bring about. For the busk was only one part of a vegetation ritual that also required fasting, abstinence, and other disciplines of inner change.

was obliged to dress and train, not to say think and believe, accordingly, and I lost my time into the bargain. As I did not teach for the good of my fellow-men, but simply for a livelihood, this was a failure. I have tried trade; but I found that it would take ten years to get under way in that, and that then I should probably be on my way to the devil. I was actually afraid that I might by that time be doing what is called a good business. When formerly I was looking about to see what I could do for a living, some sad experience in conforming to the wishes of friends being fresh in my mind to tax my ingenuity, I thought often and seriously of picking huckleberries; that surely I could do, and its small profits might suffice, — for my greatest skill has been to want but little, — so little capital is required, so little distraction from my wonted moods, I foolishly thought. While my acquaintances went unhesitatingly into trade or the professions, I contemplated this occupation as most like theirs; ranging the hills all summer to pick the berries which came in my way, and thereafter carelessly dispose of them; so, to keep the flocks of Admetus. I also dreamed that I might gather the wild herbs, or carry evergreens to such villagers as loved to be reminded of the woods, even to the city, by hay-cart loads. But I have since learned that trade curses everything it handles; and though you trade in messages from heaven, the whole curse of trade attaches to the business.

As I preferred some things to others, and especially valued my freedom, as I could fare hard and yet succeed well, I did not wish to spend my time in earning rich carpets or other fine furniture, or delicate cookery, or a house in the Grecian or the Gothic style just yet. If there are any to whom it is no interruption to acquire these things, and who know how to use them when acquired, I relinquish to them the pursuit. Some are "industrious," and appear to love labor for its own sake, or perhaps because it keeps them out of worse mischief; to such I have at present nothing to say. Those who would not know what to do with more leisure than they now enjoy, I might advise to work twice as hard as they do, — work till they pay for themselves, and get their free papers. For myself I found that the occupation of a day-laborer was the most independent of any, especially as it required only thirty or forty days in a year to support one. The laborer's day ends with the going down of the sun, and he is then free to devote himself to his chosen pursuit, independent of his labor; but his employer, who speculates from month to month, has no respite from one end of the year to the other.

In short, I am convinced, both by faith and experience, that to maintain one's self on this earth is not a hardship but a pastime, if we will live simply and wisely; as the pursuits of the simpler nations are still the sports of the more artificial. It is not necessary that a man should earn his living by the sweat of his brow, unless he sweats easier than I do.

One young man of my acquaintance, who has inherited some acres, told me that he thought he should live as I did, *if he had the means.* I would not have any one adopt *my* mode of living on any account; for, beside that before he has fairly learned it I may have found out another for myself, I desire that there may be as many different persons in the world as possible; but I would have each one be very careful to find out and pursue *his own* way, and not his father's or his mother's or his neighbor's instead. The youth may build or plant or sail, only let him not be hindered from doing that which he tells me he would like to do. It is by a mathematical point only that we are wise, as the sailor or the fugitive slave keeps the polestar in his eye; but that is sufficient guidance for all our life. We may not arrive at our port within a calculable period, but we would preserve the true course.

Undoubtedly, in this case, what is true for one is truer still for a thousand, as a large house is not proportionally more expensive than a small one, since one roof may cover, one cellar underlie, and one wall separate several apartments. But for my part, I preferred the solitary dwelling. Moreover, it will commonly be cheaper to build the whole yourself than to convince another of the advantage of the common wall; and when you have done this, the common partition, to be much cheaper, must be a thin one, and that other may prove a bad neighbor, and also not keep his side in repair. The only coöperation which is commonly possible is exceedingly partial and superficial; and what little true coöperation there is, is as if it were not, being a harmony inaudible to men. If a man has faith, he will coöperate with equal faith everywhere; if he has not faith, he will continue to live like the rest of the world, whatever company he is joined to. To coöperate in the highest as well as the lowest sense, means *to get our living together.* I heard it proposed lately that two young men should travel together over the world, the one without money, earning his means as he went, before the mast and behind the plough, the other carrying a bill of exchange in his pocket. It was easy to see that they could not long be companions or coöperate, since one would not *operate* at all. They would part at the first interesting crisis in their adventures. Above all, as I have implied, the man who goes alone can start today; but he who travels with another must wait till that other is ready, and it may be a long time before they get off.

But all this is very selfish, I have heard some of my townsmen say. I confess that I have hitherto indulged very little in philanthropic enterprises. I have made some sacrifices to a sense of duty, and among others have sacrificed this pleasure also. There are those who have used all their arts to persuade me to undertake the support of some poor family in the town; and if I had nothing to do — for the devil finds employment for the idle — I might try my hand at some such pastime as that. However, when I have thought to indulge myself in this respect, and lay their Heaven under an obligation by maintaining certain poor persons in all respects as comfortably as I maintain myself, and have even ventured so far as to make them the offer, they have one and all unhesitatingly preferred to remain poor. While my townsmen and women are devoted in so many ways to the good of their fellows, I trust that one at least may be spared to other and less humane pursuits. You must have a genius for charity as well as for anything else. As for Doing-good, that is one of the professions which are full. Moreover, I have tried fairly, and, strange as it may seem, am satisfied that it does not agree with my constitution. Probably I should not consciously and deliberately forsake my particular calling to do the good which society demands of me, to save the universe from annihilation; and I believe that a like but infinitely greater steadfastness elsewhere is all that now preserves it. But I would not stand between any man and his genius; and to him who does this work, which I decline, with his whole heart and soul and life, I would say, Persevere, even if the world call it doing evil, as it is most likely they will.

I am far from supposing that my case is a peculiar one; no doubt many of my readers would make a similar defence. At doing something, — I will not engage that my neighbors shall pronounce it good, — I do not hesitate to say that I should be a capital fellow to hire; but what that is, it is for my employer to find out. What *good* I do, in the common sense of that word, must be aside from my main path, and for the most part wholly unintended. Men say, practically, Begin where you are and such as you are, without aiming mainly to become of more worth, and with kindness aforethought go about doing good. If I were to preach at all in this strain, I should say rather, Set about being good. As if the sun should stop when he had kindled his fires up to the splendor of a moon or a star of the sixth magnitude, and go about like a Robin Goodfellow, peeping in at every cottage window, inspiring lunatics, and tainting meats, and making darkness visible, instead of steadily increasing his genial heat and beneficence till he is of such brightness that no mortal can look him in the face, and then, and in the mean while too, going about the world in his own orbit, doing it good, or rather, as a truer philosophy has discovered, the world going about him getting good. When Phaeton, wishing to prove his heavenly birth by his beneficence, had the sun's chariot but one day, and drove out of the beaten track, he burned several blocks of houses in the lower streets of heaven, and scorched the surface of the earth, and dried up every spring, and made the great desert of Sahara, till at length Jupiter hurled him headlong to the earth with a thunderbolt, and the sun, through grief at his death, did not shine for a year.

There is no odor so bad as that which arises from goodness tainted. It is human, it is divine, carrion. If I knew for a certainty that a man was coming to my house with the conscious design of doing me good, I should run for my life, as from that dry and parching wind of the African deserts called the simoom, which fills the mouth and nose and ears and eyes with dust till you are suffocated, for fear that I should get some of his good done to me, — some of its virus mingled with my blood. No, — in this case I would rather suffer evil the natural way. A man is not a good *man* to me because he will feed me if I should be starving, or warm me if I should be freezing, or pull me out of a ditch if I should ever fall into one. I can find you a Newfoundland dog that will do as much. Philanthropy is not love for one's fellow-man in the broadest sense. Howard was no doubt an exceedingly kind and worthy man in his way, and has his reward; but, comparatively speaking, what are a hundred Howards to *us*, if their philanthropy do not help *us* in our best estate, when we are most worthy to be helped? I never heard of a philanthropic meeting in which it was sincerely proposed to do any good to me, or the like of me.

The Jesuits were quite balked by those Indians who, being burned at the stake, suggested new modes of torture to their tormentors. Being superior to physical suffering, it sometimes chanced that they were superior to any consolation which the missionaries could offer; and the law to do as you would be done by fell with less persuasiveness on the ears of those who, for their part, did not care how they were done by, who loved their enemies after a new fashion, and came very near freely forgiving them all they did.

Be sure that you give the poor the aid they most need, though it be your example which leaves them far behind. If you give money, spend yourself with it, and do not merely abandon it to them. We make curious mistakes sometimes. Often the poor man is not so cold and hungry as he is dirty and ragged and gross. It is partly his taste, and not merely his misfortune. If you give him money, he will perhaps buy more rags with it. I was wont to pity the clumsy Irish laborers who cut ice on the pond, in such mean and ragged clothes, while I shivered in my more tidy and somewhat more fashionable garments, till, one bitter cold day, one who had slipped into the water came to my house to warm him, and I saw him strip off three pairs of pants and two pairs of stockings ere he got down to the skin, though they were dirty and ragged enough, it is true, and that he could afford to refuse the *extra* garments which I offered him, he had so many *intra* ones. This ducking was the very thing he needed. Then I began to pity myself, and I saw that it would be a greater charity to bestow on me a flannel shirt than a whole slop-shop on him. There are a thousand hacking at the branches of evil to one who is striking at the root, and it may be that he who bestows the largest amount of time and money on the needy is doing the most by his mode of life to produce that misery which he strives in vain to relieve. It is the pious slave-breeder devoting the proceeds of every tenth slave to buy a Sunday's liberty for the rest. Some show their kindness to the poor by employing them in their kitchens. Would they not be kinder if they employed themselves there? You boast of spending a tenth part of your income in charity; may be you should spend the nine tenths so, and done with it. Society recovers only a tenth part of the property then. Is this owing to the generosity of him in whose possession it is found, or to the remissness of the officers of justice?

Philanthropy is almost the only virtue which is sufficiently appreciated by mankind. Nay, it is greatly overrated; and it is our selfishness which overrates it. A robust poor man, one sunny day here in Concord, praised a fellow-townsman to me, because, as he said, he was kind to the poor; meaning himself. The kind uncles and aunts of the race are more esteemed than its true spiritual fathers and mothers. I once heard a reverend lecturer on England, a man of learning and intelligence, after enumerating her scientific, literary, and political worthies, Shakespeare, Bacon, Cromwell, Milton, Newton, and others, speak next of her Christian heroes, whom, as if his profession required it of him, he elevated to a place far above all the rest, as the greatest of the great. They were Penn, Howard, and Mrs. Fry. Every one must feel the falsehood and cant of this. The last were not England's best men and women; only, perhaps, her best philanthropists.

I would not subtract anything from the praise that is due to philanthropy, but merely demand justice for all who by their lives and works are a blessing to mankind. I do not value chiefly a man's uprightness and benevolence, which are, as it were, his stem and leaves. Those plants of whose greenness withered we make herb tea for the sick serve but a humble use, and are most employed by quacks. I want the flower and fruit of a man; that some fragrance be wafted over from him to me, and some ripeness flavor our intercourse. His goodness must not be a partial and transitory act, but a constant superfluity, which costs him nothing and of which he is unconscious. This is a charity that hides a multitude of sins. The philanthropist too often surrounds mankind with the remembrance of his own cast-off griefs as an atmosphere, and calls it sympathy. We should impart our courage, and not our despair, our health and ease, and not our disease, and take care that this does not spread by contagion. From what southern plains comes up the voice of wailing? Under what latitudes reside the heathen to whom we would send light? Who is that intemperate and brutal man whom we would redeem? If anything ail a man, so that he does not perform his functions, if he have a pain in his bowels even, — for that is the seat of sympathy, — he forthwith sets about reforming — the world. Being a microcosm himself, he discovers — and it is true discovery, and he is the man to make it — that the world has been eating green apples; to his eyes, in fact, the globe itself is a great green apple, which there is danger awful to think of that the children of men will nibble before it is ripe; and straightway his drastic philanthropy seeks out the Esquimaux and the Patagonian, and embraces the populous Indian and Chinese villages; and thus, by a few years of philanthropic activity, the powers in the mean while using him for their own ends, no doubt, he cures himself of his dyspepsia, the globe acquires a faint blush on one or both of its cheeks, as if it were beginning to be ripe, and life loses its crudity and is once more sweet and wholesome to live. I never dreamed of any enormity greater than I have committed. I never knew, and never shall know, a worse man than myself.

I believe that what so saddens the reformer is not his sympathy with his fellows in distress, but, though he be the holiest son of God, is his private ail. Let this be righted, let the spring come to him, the morning rise over his couch, and he will forsake his generous companions without apology. My excuse for not lecturing against the use of tobacco is, that I never chewed it, that is a penalty which reformed tobacco-chewers have to pay; though there are things enough I have chewed which I could lecture against. If you should ever be betrayed into any of these philanthropies, do not let your left hand know what your right hand does, for it is not worth knowing. Rescue the drowning and tie your shoestrings. Take your time, and set about some free labor.

Our manners have been corrupted by communication with the saints. Our hymn-books resound with a melodious cursing of God and enduring him forever. One would say that even the prophets and redeemers had rather consoled the fears than confirmed the hopes of man. There is nowhere recorded a simple and irrepressible satisfaction with the gift of life, any memorable praise of God. All health and success does me good, however far off and withdrawn it may appear; all disease and failure helps to make me sad and does me evil, however much sympathy it may have with me or I with it. If, then, we would indeed restore mankind by truly Indian, botanic, magnetic, or natural means, let us first be as simple and well as Nature ourselves, dispel the clouds which hang over our own brows, and take up a little life into our pores. Do not stay to be an overseer of the poor, but endeavor to become one of the worthies of the world.

I read in the Gulistan, or Flower Garden, of Sheik Sadi of Shiraz, that "They asked a wise man, saying: Of the many celebrated trees which the Most High God has created lofty and umbrageous, they call none azad, or free, excepting the cypress, which bears no fruit; what mystery is there in this? He replied: Each has its appropriate produce, and appointed season, during the continuance of which it is fresh and blooming, and during their absence dry and withered; to neither of which states is the cypress exposed, being always flourishing; and of this nature are the azads, or religious independents. — Fix not thy heart on that which is transitory; for the Dijlah, or Tigris, will continue to flow through Bagdad after the race of caliphs is extinct: if thy hand has plenty, be liberal as the date tree; but if it affords nothing to give away, be an azad, or free man, like the cypress."

COMPLEMENTAL VERSES.

THE PRETENSIONS OF POVERTY.

Thou dost presume too much, poor needy wretch.
To claim a station in the firmament
Because thy humble cottage, or thy tub,
Nurses some lazy or pedantic virtue
In the cheap sunshine or by shady springs,
With roots and pot-herbs; where thy right hand,
Tearing those humane passions from the mind,
Upon whose stocks fair blooming virtues flourish,
Degradeth nature, and benumbeth sense,
And, Gorgon-like, turns active men to stone.
We not require the dull society
Of your necessitated temperance,
Or that unnatural stupidity
That knows nor joy nor sorrow; nor your forc'd
Falsely exalted passive fortitude
Above the active. This low abject brood,
That fix their seats in mediocrity,
Become your servile minds; but we advance
Such virtues only as admit excess,
Brave, bounteous acts, regal magnificence,
All-seeing prudence, magnanimity
That knows no bound, and that heroic virtue
For which antiquity hath left no name,
But patterns only, such as Hercules,
Achilles, Theseus. Back to thy loath'd cell;
And when thou seest the new enlightened sphere,
Study to know but what those worthies were.

T. CAREW.

II. WHERE I LIVED,
AND WHAT I LIVED FOR ˙

AT a certain season of our life we are accustomed to consider every spot as the possible site of a house. I have thus surveyed the country on every side within a dozen miles of where I live. In imagination I have bought all the farms in succession, for all were to be bought, and I knew their price. I walked over each farmer's premises, tasted his wild apples, discoursed on husbandry with him, took his farm at his price, at any price, mortgaging it to him in my mind; even put a higher price on it, — took everything but a deed of it, — took his word for his deed, for I dearly love to talk, — cultivated it, and him too to some extent, I trust, and withdrew when I had enjoyed it long enough, leaving him to carry it on. This experience entitled me to be regarded as a sort of real-estate broker by my friends. Wherever I sat, there I might live, and the landscape radiated from me accordingly. What is a house but a *sedes*, a seat? — better if a country seat. I discovered many a site for a house not likely to be soon improved, which some might have thought too far from the village, but to my eyes the village was too far from it. Well, there I might live, I said; and there I did live, for an hour, a summer and a winter life; saw how I could let the years run off, buffet the winter through, and see the spring come in. The future inhabitants of this region, wherever they may place their houses, may be sure that they have been anticipated. An afternoon sufficed to lay out the land into orchard, woodlot, and pasture, and to decide what fine oaks or pines should be left to stand before the door, and whence each blasted tree could be seen to the best advantage; and then I let it lie, fallow perchance, for a man is rich in proportion to the number of things which he can afford to let alone.

My imagination carried me so far that I even had the refusal of several farms, — the refusal was all I wanted, — but I never got my fingers burned by actual possession. The nearest that I came to actual possession was when I bought the Hollowell place, and had begun to sort my seeds, and collected materials with which to make a wheelbarrow to carry it on or off with; but before the owner gave me a deed of it, his wife — every man has such a wife — changed her mind and wished to keep it, and he offered me ten dollars to release him. Now, to speak the truth, I had but ten cents in the world, and it surpassed my arithmetic to tell, if I was the man who had ten cents, or who had a farm, or ten dollars, or all together. However, I let him keep the ten dollars and the farm too, for I had carried it far enough; or rather, to be generous, I sold him the farm for just what I gave for it, and, as he was not a rich man, made him a present of ten dollars, and still had my ten cents, and seeds, and materials for a wheelbarrow left. I found thus that I had been a rich man without any damage to my poverty. But I retained the landscape, and I have since annually carried off what it yielded without a wheelbarrow. With respect to landscapes, —

> "I am monarch of all I *survey*,
> My right there is none to dispute."

I have frequently seen a poet withdraw, having enjoyed the most valuable part of a farm, while the crusty farmer supposed that he had got a few wild apples only. Why, the owner does not know it for many years when a poet has put his farm in rhyme, the most admirable kind of invisible fence, has fairly impounded it, milked it, skimmed it, and got all the cream, and left the farmer only the skimmed milk.

The real attractions of the Hollowell farm, to me, were: its complete retirement, being about two miles from the village, half a mile from the nearest neighbor, and separated from the highway by a broad field; its bounding on the river, which the owner said protected it by its fogs from frosts in the spring, though that was nothing to me; the gray color and ruinous state of the house and barn, and the dilapidated fences, which put such an interval between me and the last occupant; the hollow and lichen-covered apple trees, gnawed by rabbits, showing what kind of neighbors I should have; but above all, the recollection I had of it from my earliest voyages up the river, when the house was concealed behind a dense grove of red maples, through which I heard the house-dog bark. I was in haste to buy it, before the proprietor finished getting out some rocks, cutting down the hollow apple trees, and grubbing up some young birches which had sprung up in the pasture, or, in short, had made any more of his improvements. To enjoy these advantages I was ready to carry it on; like Atlas, to take the world on my shoulders, — I never heard what compensation he received for that, — and do all those things which had no other motive or excuse but that I might pay for it and be unmolested in my possession of it; for I knew all the while that it would yield the most abundant crop of the kind I wanted if I could only afford to let it alone. But it turned out as I have said.

All that I could say, then, with respect to farming on a large scale, (I have always cultivated a garden,) was, that I had had my seeds ready. Many think that seeds improve with age. I have no doubt that time discriminates between the good and the bad; and when at last I shall plant, I shall be less likely to be disappointed. But I would say to my fellows, once for all, As long as possible live free and un-committed. It makes but little difference whether you are committed to a farm or the county jail.

Old Cato, whose "De Re Rusticâ" is my "Cultivator," says, and the only translation I have seen makes sheer nonsense of the passage, "When you think of getting a farm turn it thus in your mind, not to buy greedily; nor spare your pains to look at it, and do not think it enough to go round it once. The oftener you go there the more it will please you, if it is good." I think I shall not buy greedily, but go round and round it as long as I live, and be buried in it first, that it may please me the more at last.

The present was my next experiment of this kind, which I purpose to describe more at length, for convenience, putting the experience of two years into one. As I have said, I do not propose to write an ode to dejection, but to brag as lustily as chanticleer in the morning, stand-ing on his roost, if only to wake my neighbors up.

When first I took up my abode in the woods, that is, began to spend my nights as well as days there, which, by accident, was on Inde-pendence day, or the fourth of July, 1845, my house was not finished for winter, but was merely a defence against the rain, without plaster-ing or chimney, the walls being of rough weather-stained boards, with wide chinks, which made it cool at night. The upright white hewn studs and freshly planed door and window casings gave it a clean and airy look, especially in the morning, when its timbers were saturated with dew, so that I fancied that by noon some sweet gum would exude from them. To my imagination it retained throughout the day more or less of this auroral character, reminding me of a certain house on a mountain which I had visited a year before. This was an airy and unplastered cabin, fit to entertain a travelling god, and where a goddess might trail her garments. The winds which passed over my dwelling were such as sweep over the ridges of mountains, bearing the broken strains, or celestial parts only, of terrestrial music. The morning wind forever blows, the poem of creation is uninterrupted; but few are the ears that hear it. Olympus is but the outside of the earth everywhere.

The only house I had been the owner of before, if I except a boat, was a tent, which I used occasionally when making excursions in the summer, and this is still rolled up in my garret; but the boat, after passing from hand to hand, has gone down the stream of time. With this more substantial shelter about me, I had made some progress toward settling in the world. This frame, so slightly clad, was a sort of crystallization around me, and reacted on the builder. It was suggestive somewhat as a picture in outlines. I did not need to go out doors to take the air, for the atmosphere within had lost none of its freshness. It was not so much within doors as behind a door where I sat, even in the rainiest weather. The Harivansa says, "An abode without birds is like a meat without seasoning." Such was not my abode, for I found myself suddenly neighbor to the birds; not by having imprisoned one, but having caged myself near them. I was not only nearer to some of those which commonly frequent the garden and the orchard, but to those wilder and more thrilling songsters of the forest which never, or rarely, serenade a villager, — the wood-thrush, the veery, the scarlet tanager, the field-sparrow, the whippoorwill, and many others.

I was seated by the shore of a small pond, about a mile and a half south of the village of Concord and somewhat higher than it, in the midst of an extensive wood between that town and Lincoln, and about two miles south of that our only field known to fame, Concord Battle Ground; but I was so low in the woods that the opposite shore, half a mile off, like the rest, covered with wood, was my most distant horizon. For the first week, whenever I looked out on the pond it impressed me like a tarn high up on the side of a mountain, its bottom far above the surface of other lakes, and, as the sun arose, I saw it throwing off its nightly clothing of mist, and here and there, by degrees, its soft ripples or its smooth reflecting surface was revealed, while the mists, like ghosts, were stealthily withdrawing in every direction into the woods, as at the breaking up of some nocturnal conventicle. The very dew seemed to hang upon the trees later into the day than usual, as on the sides of mountains.

This small lake was of most value as a neighbor in the intervals of a gentle rain storm in August, when, both air and water being perfectly still, but the sky overcast, mid-afternoon had all the serenity of evening, and the wood-thrush sang around, and was heard from shore to shore. A lake like this is never smoother than at such a time; and the clear portion of the air above it being shallow and darkened by clouds, the water, full of light and reflections, becomes a lower heaven itself so much the more important. From a hill top near by, where the wood had been recently cut off, there was a pleasing vista southward across the pond, through a wide indentation in the hills which form the shore there, where their opposite sides sloping toward each other suggested a stream flowing out in that direction through a wooded valley, but stream there was none. That way I looked between and over the near green hills to some distant and higher ones in the horizon, tinged with blue. Indeed, by standing on tiptoe I could catch a glimpse of some of the peaks of the still bluer and more distant mountain ranges in the north-west, those true-blue coins from heaven's own mint, and also of some portion of the village. But in other directions, even from this point, I could not see over or beyond the woods which surrounded me. It is well to have some water in your neighborhood, to give buoyancy to and float the earth. One value even of the smallest well is, that when you look into it you see that earth is not continent but insular. This is as important as that it keeps butter cool. When I looked across the pond from this peak toward the Sudbury meadows, which in time of flood I distinguished elevated perhaps by a mirage in their seething valley, like a coin in a basin, all the earth beyond the pond appeared like a thin crust insulated and floated even by this small sheet of intervening water, and I was reminded that this on which I dwelt was but *dry land*.

Though the view from my door was still more contracted, I did not feel crowded or confined in the least. There was pasture enough for my imagination. The low shrub-oak plateau to which the opposite shore arose, stretched away toward the prairies of the West and the steppes of Tartary, affording ample room for all the roving families of men. "There are none happy in the world but beings who enjoy freely a vast horizon," — said Damodara, when his herds required new and larger pastures.

Both place and time were changed, and I dwelt nearer to those parts of the universe and to those eras in history which had most attracted me. Where I lived was as far off as many a region viewed nightly by astronomers. We are wont to imagine rare and delectable places in some remote and more celestial corner of the system, behind the constellation of Cassiopeia's Chair, far from noise and disturbance. I discovered that my house actually had its site in such a withdrawn, but forever new and unprofaned, part of the universe. If it were worth the while to settle in those parts near to the Pleiades or the Hyades, to

Aldebaran or Altair, then I was really there, or at an equal remoteness
from the life which I had left behind, dwindled and twinkling with as
fine a ray to my nearest neighbor, and to be seen only in moonless
nights by him. Such was that part of creation where I had squatted; —

> "There was a shepherd that did live,
>   And held his thoughts as high
> As were the mounts whereon his flocks
>   Did hourly feed him by."

What should we think of the shepherd's life if his flocks always wandered to higher pastures than his thoughts?

Every morning was a cheerful invitation to make my life of equal
simplicity, and I may say innocence, with Nature herself. I have been
as sincere a worshipper of Aurora as the Greeks. I got up early and
bathed in the pond; that was a religious exercise, and one of the best
things which I did. They say that characters were engraven on the
bathing tub of king Tching-thang to this effect: "Renew thyself completely each day; do it again, and again, and forever again." I can
understand that. Morning brings back the heroic ages. I was as
much affected by the faint hum of a mosquito making its invisible and
unimaginable tour through my apartment at earliest dawn, when I was
sitting with door and windows open, as I could be by any trumpet that
ever sang of fame. It was Homer's requiem; itself an Iliad and Odys-
sey in the air, singing its own wrath and wanderings. There was
something cosmical about it; a standing advertisement, till forbidden,
of the everlasting vigor and fertility of the world. The morning,
which is the most memorable season of the day, is the awakening hour.
Then there is least somnolence in us; and for an hour, at least, some
part of us awakes which slumbers all the rest of the day and night.
Little is to be expected of that day, if it can be called a day, to which
we are not awakened by our Genius, but by the mechanical nudgings
of some servitor, are not awakened by our own newly-acquired force
and aspirations from within, accompanied by the undulations of celestial music, instead of factory bells, and a fragrance filling the air — to
a higher life than we fell asleep from; and thus the darkness bear its
fruit, and prove itself to be good, no less than the light. That man
who does not believe that each day contains an earlier, more sacred,
and auroral hour than he has yet profaned, has despaired of life, and is
pursuing a descending and darkening way. After a partial cessation
of his sensuous life, the soul of man, or its organs rather, are reinvigor-

ated each day, and his Genius tries again what noble life it can make. All memorable events, I should say, transpire in morning time and in a morning atmosphere. The Vedas say, "All intelligences awake with the morning." Poetry and art, and the fairest and most memorable of the actions of men, date from such an hour. All poets and heroes, like Memnon, are the children of Aurora, and emit their music at sunrise. To him whose elastic and vigorous thought keeps pace with the sun, the day is a perpetual morning. It matters not what the clocks say or the attitudes and labors of men. Morning is when I am awake and there is a dawn in me. Moral reform is the effort to throw off sleep. Why is it that men give so poor an account of their day if they have not been slumbering? They are not such poor calculators. If they had not been overcome with drowsiness they would have performed something. The millions are awake enough for physical labor; but only one in a million is awake enough for effective intellectual exertion, only one in a hundred millions to a poetic or divine life. To be awake is to be alive. I have never yet met a man who was quite awake. How could I have looked him in the face?

We must learn to reawaken and keep ourselves awake, not by mechanical aids, but by an infinite expectation of the dawn, which does not forsake us in our soundest sleep. I know of no more encouraging fact than the unquestionable ability of man to elevate his life by a conscious endeavor. It is something to be able to paint a particular picture, or to carve a statue, and so to make a few objects beautiful; but it is far more glorious to carve and paint the very atmosphere and medium through which we look, which morally we can do. To affect the quality of the day, that is the highest of arts. Every man is tasked to make his life, even in its details, worthy of the contemplation of his most elevated and critical hour. If we refused, or rather used up, such paltry information as we get, the oracles would distinctly inform us how this might be done.

I went to the woods because I wished to live deliberately, to front only the essential facts of life, and see if I could not learn what it had to teach, and not, when I came to die, discover that I had not lived. I did not wish to live what was not life, living is so dear; nor did I wish to practise resignation, unless it was quite necessary. I wanted to live deep and suck out all the marrow of life, to live so sturdily and Spartan-like as to put to rout all that was not life, to cut a broad swath and shave close, to drive life into a corner, and reduce it to its lowest terms, and, if it proved to be mean, why then to get the whole and genuine meanness of it, and publish its meanness to the world; or if it were sublime, to know it by experience, and be able to give a true account of it in my next excursion. For most men, it appears to me, are in a strange uncertainty about it, whether it is of the devil or of God, and have *somewhat hastily* concluded that it is the chief end of man here to "glorify God and enjoy him forever."

Still we live meanly, like ants; though the fable tells us that we were long ago changed into men; like pygmies we fight with cranes; it is error upon error, and clout upon clout, and our best virtue has for its occasion a superfluous and evitable wretchedness. Our life is frittered away by detail. An honest man has hardly need to count more than his ten fingers, or in extreme cases he may add his ten toes, and lump the rest. Simplicity, simplicity, simplicity! I say, let your affairs be as two or three, and not a hundred or a thousand; instead of a million count half a dozen, and keep your accounts on your thumb nail. In the midst of this chopping sea of civilized life, such are the clouds and storms and quicksands and thousand-and-one items to be allowed for, that a man has to live, if he would not founder and go to the bottom and not make his port at all, by dead reckoning, and he must be a great calculator indeed who succeeds. Simplify, simplify. Instead of three meals a day, if it be necessary eat but one; instead of a hundred dishes, five; and reduce other things in proportion. Our life is like a German Confederacy, made up of petty states, with its boundary forever fluctuating, so that even a German cannot tell you how it is bounded at any moment. The nation itself, with all its so-called internal improvements, which, by the way are all external and superficial, is just such an unwieldy and overgrown establishment, cluttered with furniture and tripped up by its own traps, ruined by luxury and heedless expense, by want of calculation and a worthy aim, as the million households in the land; and the only cure for it as for them is in a rigid economy, a stern and more than Spartan simplicity of life and elevation of purpose. It lives too fast. Men think that it is essential that the *Nation* have commerce, and export ice, and talk through a telegraph, and ride thirty miles an hour, without a doubt, whether *they* do or not; but whether we should live like baboons or like men, is a little uncertain. If we do not get out sleepers, and forge rails, and devote days and nights to the work, but go to tinkering upon our *lives* to improve *them*, who will build railroads? And if railroads are not built, how shall we get to heaven in season? But if we stay at home and mind our business, who will want railroads? We do not ride on the railroad; it rides upon us.

Did you ever think what those sleepers are that underlie the railroad? Each one is a man, an Irishman, or a Yankee man. The rails are laid on them, and they are covered with sand, and the cars run smoothly over them. They are sound sleepers, I assure you. And every few years a new lot is laid down and run over; so that, if some have the pleasure of riding on a rail, others have the misfortune to be ridden upon. And when they run over a man that is walking in his sleep, a supernumerary sleeper in the wrong position, and wake him up, they suddenly stop the cars, and make a hue and cry about it, as if this were an exception. I am glad to know that it takes a gang of men for every five miles to keep the sleepers down and level in their beds as it is, for this is a sign that they may sometime get up again.[1]

Why should we live with such hurry and waste of life? We are determined to be starved before we are hungry. Men say that a stitch in time saves nine, and so they take a thousand stitches to-day to save nine to-morrow. As for *work*, we have n't any of any consequence. We have the Saint Vitus' dance, and cannot possibly keep our heads still. If I should only give a few pulls at the parish bell-rope, as for a fire, that is, without setting the bell, there is hardly a man on his farm in the outskirts of Concord, notwithstanding that press of engagements which was his excuse so many times this morning, nor a boy, nor a woman, I might almost say, but would forsake all and follow that sound, not mainly to save property from the flames, but, if we will confess the truth, much more to see it burn, since burn it must, and we, be it known, did not set it on fire, — or to see it put out, and have a hand in it, if that is done as handsomely; yes, even if it were the parish church itself. Hardly a man takes a half hour's nap after dinner, but when he wakes he holds up his head and asks, "What's the news?" as if the rest of mankind had stood his sentinels. Some give directions to be waked every half hour, doubtless for no other purpose; and then, to pay for it, they tell what they have dreamed. After a night's sleep the news is as indispensable as the breakfast. "Pray tell me anything new that has happened to a man anywhere on this globe," — and he reads it over his coffee and rolls, that a man has had his eyes gouged out this morning on the Wachito River; never dreaming the while that he lives in the dark unfathomed mammoth cave of this world, and has but the rudiment of an eye himself.

[1] Thoreau's attitude toward reform did not mean that he was indifferent to social ills. See also his remarks on the factory system at the close of the passage on clothing in "Economy."

For my part, I could easily do without the post-office. I think that there are very few important communications made through it. To speak critically, I never received more than one or two letters in my life — I wrote this some years ago — that were worth the postage. The penny-post is, commonly, an institution through which you seriously offer a man that penny for his thoughts which is so often safely offered in jest. And I am sure that I never read any memorable news in a newspaper. If we read of one man robbed, or murdered, or killed by accident, or one house burned, or one vessel wrecked, or one steamboat blown up, or one cow run over on the Western Railroad, or one mad dog killed, or one lot of grasshoppers in the winter, — we never need read of another. One is enough. If you are acquainted with the principle, what do you care for a myriad instances and applications? To a philosopher all *news*, as it is called, is gossip, and they who edit and read it are old women over their tea. Yet not a few are greedy after this gossip. There was such a rush, as I hear, the other day at one of the offices to learn the foreign news by the last arrival, that several large squares of plate glass belonging to the establishment were broken by the pressure, — news which I seriously think a ready wit might write a twelvemonth or twelve years beforehand with sufficient accuracy. As for Spain, for instance, if you know how to throw in Don Carlos and the Infanta, and Don Pedro and Seville and Granada, from time to time in the right proportions, — they may have changed the names a little since I saw the papers, — and serve up a bull-fight when other entertainments fail, it will be true to the letter, and give us as good an idea of the exact state or ruin of things in Spain as the most succinct and lucid reports under this head in the newspapers: and as for England, almost the last significant scrap of news from that quarter was the revolution of 1649; and if you have learned the history of her crops for an average year, you never need attend to that thing again, unless your speculations are of a merely pecuniary character. If one may judge who rarely looks into the newspapers, nothing new does ever happen in foreign parts, a French revolution not excepted.

What news! how much more important to know what that is which was never old! "Kieou-he-yu (great dignitary of the state of Wei) sent a man to Khoung-tseu to know his news. Khoung-tseu caused the messenger to be seated near him, and questioned him in these terms: What is your master doing? The messenger answered with respect: My master desires to diminish the number of his faults, but he cannot come to the end of them. The messenger being gone, the philosopher

remarked: What a worthy messenger! What a worthy messenger!"
The preacher, instead of vexing the ears of drowsy farmers on their
day of rest at the end of the week, — for Sunday is the fit conclusion
of an ill-spent week, and not the fresh and brave beginning of a new
one, — with this one other draggle-tail of a sermon, should shout with
thundering voice, — "Pause! Avast! Why so seeming fast, but
deadly slow?"

Shams and delusions are esteemed for soundest truths, while reality
is fabulous. If men would steadily observe realities only, and not
allow themselves to be deluded, life, to compare it with such things as
we know, would be like a fairy tale and the Arabian Nights' Entertainments. If we respected only what is inevitable and has a right to
be, music and poetry would resound along the streets. When we are
unhurried and wise, we perceive that only great and worthy things
have any permanent and absolute existence, — that petty fears and
petty pleasures are but the shadow of the reality. This is always
exhilarating and sublime. By closing the eyes and slumbering, and
consenting to be deceived by shows, men establish and confirm their
daily life of routine and habit everywhere, which still is built on purely
illusory foundations. Children, who play life, discern its true law and
relations more clearly than men, who fail to live it worthily, but who
think that they are wiser by experience, that is, by failure. I have
read in a Hindoo book, that "there was a king's son, who, being expelled in infancy from his native city, was brought up by a forester,
and, growing up to maturity in that state, imagined himself to belong to
the barbarous race with which he lived. One of his father's ministers
having discovered him, revealed to him what he was, and the miscon-
ception of his character was removed, and he knew himself to be a
prince. So soul," continues the Hindoo philosopher, "from the circumstances in which it is placed, mistakes its own character, until the
truth is revealed to it by some holy teacher, and then it knows itself to
be *Brahme*." I perceive that we inhabitants of New England live this
mean life that we do because our vision does not penetrate the surface
of things. We think that that *is* which *appears* to be. If a man should
walk through this town and see only the reality, where, think you,
would the "Mill-dam" go to? If he should give us an account of the
realities he beheld there, we should not recognize the place in his
description. Look at a meeting-house, or a courthouse, or a jail, or a
shop, or a dwelling-house, and say what that thing really is before a
true gaze, and they would all go to pieces in your account of them.

Men esteem truth remote, in the outskirts of the system, behind the farthest star, before Adam and after the last man. In eternity there is indeed something true and sublime. But all these times and places and occasions are now and here. God himself culminates in the present moment, and will never be more divine in the lapse of all the ages. And we are enabled to apprehend at all what is sublime and noble only by the perpetual instilling and drenching of the reality that surrounds us. The universe constantly and obediently answers to our conceptions; whether we travel fast or slow, the track is laid for us. Let us spend our lives in conceiving then. The poet or the artist never yet had so fair and noble a design but some of his posterity at least could accomplish it.

Let us spend one day as deliberately as Nature, and not be thrown off the track by every nutshell and mosquito's wing that falls on the rails. Let us rise early and fast, or break fast, gently and without perturbation; let company come and let company go, let the bells ring and the children cry, — determined to make a day of it. Why should we knock under and go with the stream? Let us not be upset and overwhelmed in that terrible rapid and whirlpool called a dinner, situated in the meridian shallows. Weather this danger and you are safe, for the rest of the way is down hill. With unrelaxed nerves, with morning vigor, sail by it, looking another way, tied to the mast like Ulysses. If the engine whistles, let it whistle till it is hoarse for its pains. If the bell rings, why should we run? We will consider what kind of music they are like. Let us settle ourselves, and work and wedge our feet downward through the mud and slush of opinion, and prejudice, and tradition, and delusion, and appearance, that alluvion which covers the globe, through Paris and London, through New York and Boston and Concord, through church and state, through poetry and philosophy and religion, till we come to a hard bottom and rocks in place, which we can call *reality*, and say, This is, and no mistake; and then begin, having a *point d'appui*, below freshet and frost and fire, a place where you might found a wall or a state, or set a lamppost safely, or perhaps a gauge, not a Nilometer, but a Realometer, that future ages might know how deep a freshet of shams and appearances had gathered from time to time. If you stand right fronting and face to face to a fact, you will see the sun glimmer on both its surfaces, as if it were a cimeter, and feel its sweet edge dividing you through the heart and marrow, and so you will happily conclude your mortal career. Be it life or death, we crave only reality. If we are really dying, let us hear the rattle in our throats and feel cold in the extremities; if we are alive, let us go about our business.

Time is but the stream I go a-fishing in. I drink at it; but while I drink I see the sandy bottom and detect how shallow it is. Its thin current slides away, but eternity remains. I would drink deeper; fish in the sky, whose bottom is pebbly with stars. I cannot count one. I know not the first letter of the alphabet. I have always been regretting that I was not as wise as the day I was born. The intellect is a cleaver; it discerns and rifts its way into the secret of things. I do not wish to be any more busy with my hands than is necessary. My head is hands and feet. I feel all my best faculties concentrated in it. My instinct tells me that my head is an organ for burrowing, as some creatures use their snout and fore-paws, and with it I would mine and burrow my way through these hills. I think that the richest vein is somewhere hereabouts; so by the divining rod and thin rising vapors I judge; and here I will begin to mine.

III. READING[1]

WITH a little more deliberation in the choice of their pursuits, all men would perhaps become essentially students and observers, for certainly their nature and destiny are interesting to all alike. In accumulating property for ourselves or our posterity, in founding a family or a state, or acquiring fame even, we are mortal; but in dealing with truth we are immortal, and need fear no change nor accident. The

[1] This chapter is an extension of the discussion of literature and "scripture" in the *Week*. As in building his house and his life, Thoreau again shows his indebtedness to the past, his desire, in Emerson's words, to "digest and correct past experience; and blend it with the new and divine life." Literature was one of his borrowings, and like the book he wanted to write, its ultimate test was to stir one to action. Having been inspired by the scriptures of the past (that is why the chapter is appropriately placed as the prelude of his experiment), he went in search of the living revelation: "Reading" was followed by "Sounds." The whole book, in fact, related his search for the conditions of new life or revelation, for the miracle of experience; by his own definition it was scripture, to be placed among the "Vedas and Zendavestas and Bibles, with Homers and Dantes and Shakespeares. . . ."

oldest Egyptian or Hindoo philosopher raised a corner of the veil from the statue of the divinity; and still the trembling robe remains raised, and I gaze upon as fresh a glory as he did, since it was I in him that was then so bold, and it is he in me that now reviews the vision. No dust has settled on that robe; no time has elapsed since that divinity was revealed. That time which we really improve, or which is improvable, is neither past, present, nor future.

My residence was more favorable, not only to thought, but to serious reading, than a university; and though I was beyond the range of the ordinary circulating library, I had more than ever come within the influence of those books which circulate round the world, whose sentences were first written on bark, and are now merely copied from time to time on to linen paper. Says the poet Mîr Camar Uddîn Mast, "Being seated to run through the region of the spiritual world; I have had this advantage in books. To be intoxicated by a single glass of wine; I have experienced this pleasure when I have drunk the liquor of the esoteric doctrines." I kept Homer's Iliad on my table through the summer, though I looked at his page only now and then. Incessant labor with my hands, at first, for I had my house to finish and my beans to hoe at the same time, made more study impossible. Yet I sustained myself by the prospect of such reading in future. I read one or two shallow books of travel in the intervals of my work, till that employment made me ashamed of myself, and I asked where it was then that *I* lived.

The student may read Homer or Æschylus in the Greek without danger of dissipation or luxuriousness, for it implies that he in some measure emulate their heroes, and consecrate morning hours to their pages. The heroic books, even if printed in the character of our mother tongue, will always be in a language dead to degenerate times; and we must laboriously seek the meaning of each word and line, conjecturing a larger sense than common use permits out of what wisdom and valor and generosity we have. The modern cheap and fertile press, with all its translations, has done little to bring us nearer to the heroic writers of antiquity. They seem as solitary, and the letter in which they are printed as rare and curious, as ever. It is worth the expense of youthful days and costly hours, if you learn only some words of an ancient language, which are raised out of the trivialness of the street, to be perpetual suggestions and provocations. It is not in vain that the farmer remembers and repeats the few Latin words which he has heard. Men sometimes speak as if the study of the classics would at length make way for more modern and practical studies; but the adventurous student will always study classics, in whatever language they may be written and however ancient they may be. For what are the classics but the noblest recorded thoughts of man? They are the only oracles which are not decayed, and there are such answers to the most modern inquiry in them as Delphi and Dodona never gave. We might as well omit to study Nature because she is old. To read well, that is, to read true books in a true spirit, is a noble exercise, and one that will task the reader more than any exercise which the customs of the day esteem. It requires a training such as the athletes underwent, the steady intention almost of the whole life to this object. Books must be read as deliberately and reservedly as they were written. It is not enough even to be able to speak the language of that nation by which they are written, for there is a memorable interval between the spoken and the written language, the language heard and the language read. The one is commonly transitory, a sound, a tongue, a dialect merely, almost brutish, and we learn it unconsciously, like the brutes, of our mothers. The other is the maturity and experience of that; if that is our mother tongue, this is our father tongue, a reserved and select expression, too significant to be heard by the ear, which we must be born again in order to speak. The crowds of men who merely *spoke* the Greek and Latin tongues in the middle ages were not entitled by the accident of birth to *read* the works of genius written in those languages; for these were not written in that Greek or Latin which they knew, but in the select language of literature. They had not learned the nobler dialects of Greece and Rome, but the very materials on which they were written were waste paper to them, and they prized instead a cheap contemporary literature. But when the several nations of Europe had acquired distinct though rude written languages of their own, sufficient for the purposes of their rising literatures, then first learning revived, and scholars were enabled to discern from that remoteness the treasures of antiquity. What the Roman and Grecian multitude could not *hear*, after the lapse of ages a few scholars *read*, and a few scholars only are still reading it.

However much we may admire the orator's occasional bursts of eloquence, the noblest written words are commonly as far behind or above the fleeting spoken language as the firmament with its stars is behind the clouds. *There* are the stars, and they who can may read them. The astronomers forever comment on and observe them. They are not exhalations like our daily colloquies and vaporous breath.

What is called eloquence in the forum is commonly found to be rhetoric in the study. The orator yields to the inspiration of a transient occasion, and speaks to the mob before him, to those who can *hear* him; but the writer, whose more equable life is his occasion, and who would be distracted by the event and the crowd which inspire the orator, speaks to the intellect and heart of mankind, to all in any age who can *understand* him.

No wonder that Alexander carried the Iliad with him on his expeditions in a precious casket. A written word is the choicest of relics. It is something at once more intimate with us and more universal than any other work of art. It is the work of art nearest to life itself. It may be translated into every language, and not only be read but actually breathed from all human lips; — not be represented on canvas or in marble only, but be carved out of the breath of life itself. The symbol of an ancient man's thought becomes a modern man's speech. Two thousand summers have imparted to the monuments of Grecian literature, as to her marbles, only a maturer golden and autumnal tint, for they have carried their own serene and celestial atmosphere into all lands to protect them against the corrosion of time. Books are the treasured wealth of the world and the fit inheritance of generations and nations. Books, the oldest and the best, stand naturally and rightfully on the shelves of every cottage. They have no cause of their own to plead, but while they enlighten and sustain the reader his common sense will not refuse them. Their authors are a natural and irresistible aristocracy in every society, and, more than kings or emperors, exert an influence on mankind. When the illiterate and perhaps scornful trader has earned by enterprise and industry his coveted leisure and independence, and is admitted to the circles of wealth and fashion, he turns inevitably at last to those still higher but yet inaccessible circles of intellect and genius, and is sensible only of the imperfection of his culture and the vanity and insufficiency of all his riches, and further proves his good sense by the pains which he takes to secure for his children that intellectual culture whose want he so keenly feels; and thus it is that he becomes the founder of a family.

Those who have not learned to read the ancient classics in the language in which they were written must have a very imperfect knowledge of the history of the human race; for it is remarkable that no transcript of them has ever been made into any modern tongue, unless our civilization itself may be regarded as such a transcript. Homer has never yet been printed in English, nor Æschylus, nor Virgil even, —

works as refined, as solidly done, and as beautiful almost as the morning itself; for later writers, say what we will of their genius, have
rarely, if ever, equalled the elaborate beauty and finish and the lifelong
and heroic literary labors of the ancients. They only talk of forgetting
them who never knew them. It will be soon enough to forget them
when we have the learning and the genius which will enable us to
attend to and appreciate them. That age will be rich indeed when
those relics which we call Classics, and the still older and more than
classic but even less known Scriptures of the nations, shall have still
further accumulated, when the Vaticans shall be filled with Vedas and
Zendavestas and Bibles, with Homers and Dantes and Shakespeares,
and all the centuries to come shall have successively deposited their
trophies in the forum of the world. By such a pile we may hope to
scale heaven at last.

The works of the great poets have never yet been read by mankind,
for only great poets can read them. They have only been read as the
multitude read the stars, at most astrologically, not astronomically.
Most men have learned to read to serve a paltry convenience, as they
have learned to cipher in order to keep accounts and not be cheated in
trade; but of reading as a noble intellectual exercise they know little
or nothing; yet this only is reading, in a high sense, not that which
lulls us as a luxury and suffers the nobler faculties to sleep the while,
but what we have to stand on tip-toe to read and devote our most alert
and wakeful hours to.

I think that having learned our letters we should read the best that
is in literature, and not be forever repeating our a b abs, and words of
one syllable, in the fourth or fifth classes, sitting on the lowest and
foremost form all our lives. Most men are satisfied if they read or
hear read, and perchance have been convicted by the wisdom of one
good book, the Bible, and for the rest of their lives vegetate and dissi-
pate their faculties in what is called easy reading. There is a work in
several volumes in our Circulating Library entitled Little Reading,
which I thought referred to a town of that name which I had not been
to. There are those who, like cormorants and ostriches, can digest all
sorts of this, even after the fullest dinner of meats and vegetables, for
they suffer nothing to be wasted. If others are the machines to provide this provender, they are the machines to read it. They read the
nine thousandth tale about Zebulon and Sephronia, and how they loved
as none had ever loved before, and neither did the course of their true
love run smooth, — at any rate, how it did run and stumble, and get up

again and go on! how some poor unfortunate got up on to a steeple, who had better never have gone up as far as the belfry; and then, having needlessly got him up there, the happy novelist rings the bell for all the world to come together and hear, O dear! how he did get down again! For my part, I think that they had better metamorphose all such aspiring heroes of universal noveldom into man weather-cocks, as they used to put heroes among the constellations, and let them swing round there till they are rusty, and not come down at all to bother honest men with their pranks. The next time the novelist rings the bell I will not stir though the meeting-house burn down. "The Skip of the Tip-Toe-Hop, a Romance of the Middle Ages, by the celebrated author of 'Tittle-Tol-Tan,' to appear in monthly parts; a great rush; don't all come together." All this they read with saucer eyes, and erect and primitive curiosity, and with unwearied gizzard, whose corrugations even yet need no sharpening, just as some little four-year-old bencher his two-cent gilt-covered edition of Cinderella, — without any improvement, that I can see, in the pronunciation, or accent, or emphasis, or any more skill in extracting or inserting the moral. The result is dulness of sight, a stagnation of the vital circulations, and a general deliquium and sloughing off of all the intellectual faculties. This sort of gingerbread is baked daily and more sedulously than pure wheat or rye-and-Indian in almost every oven, and finds a surer market.

The best books are not read even by those who are called good readers. What does our Concord culture amount to? There is in this town, with a very few exceptions, no taste for the best or for very good books even in English literature, whose words all can read and spell. Even the college-bred and so-called liberally educated men here and elsewhere have really little or no acquaintance with the English classics; and as for the recorded wisdom of mankind, the ancient classics and Bibles, which are accessible to all who will know of them, there are the feeblest efforts anywhere made to become acquainted with them. I know a woodchopper, of middle age, who takes a French paper, not for news as he says, for he is above that, but to "keep himself in practice," he being a Canadian by birth; and when I ask him what he considers the best thing he can do in this world, he says, beside this, to keep up and add to his English. This is about as much as the college-bred generally do or aspire to do, and they take an English paper for the purpose. One who has just come from reading perhaps one of the best English books will find how many with whom he can converse about it? Or suppose he comes from reading a Greek or Latin classic in the original, whose praises are familiar even to the so-called illiterate; he will find nobody at all to speak to, but must keep silence about it. Indeed, there is hardly the professor in our colleges, who, if he has mastered the difficulties of the language, has proportionally mastered the difficulties of the wit and poetry of a Greek poet, and has any sympathy to impart to the alert and heroic reader; and as for the sacred Scriptures, or Bibles of mankind, who in this town can tell me even their titles? Most men do not know that any nation but the Hebrews have had a scripture. A man, any man, will go considerably out of his way to pick up a silver dollar; but here are golden words, which the wisest men of antiquity have uttered, and whose worth the wise of every succeeding age have assured us of; — and yet we learn to read only as far as Easy Reading, the primers and class-books, and when we leave school, the "Little Reading," and story books, which are for boys and beginners; and our reading, our conversation and thinking, are all on a very low level, worthy only of pygmies and manikins.

I aspire to be acquainted with wiser men than this our Concord soil has produced, whose names are hardly known here. Or shall I hear the name of Plato and never read his book? As if Plato were my townsman and I never saw him, — my next neighbor and I never heard him speak or attended to the wisdom of his words. But how actually is it? His Dialogues, which contain what was immortal in him, lie on the next shelf, and yet I never read them. We are under-bred and low-lived and illiterate; and in this respect I confess I do not make any very broad distinction between the illiterateness of my townsman who cannot read at all and the illiterateness of him who has learned to read only what is for children and feeble intellects. We should be as good as the worthies of antiquity, but partly by first knowing how good they were. We are a race of tit-men, and soar but little higher in our intellectual flights than the columns of the daily paper.

It is not all books that are as dull as their readers. There are probably words addressed to our condition exactly, which, if we could really hear and understand, would be more salutary than the morning or the spring to our lives, and possibly put a new aspect on the face of things for us. How many a man has dated a new era in his life from the reading of a book. The book exists for us perchance which will explain our miracles and reveal new ones. The at present unutterable things we may find somewhere uttered. These same questions that disturb and puzzle and confound us have in their turn occurred to all the wise men; not one has been omitted; and each has answered them, according to his ability, by his words and his life. Moreover, with wisdom we shall learn liberality. The solitary hired man on a farm in the outskirts of Concord, who has had his second birth and peculiar religious experience, and is driven as he believes into silent gravity and exclusiveness by his faith, may think it is not true; but Zoroaster, thousands of years ago, travelled the same road and had the same experience; but he, being wise, knew it to be universal, and treated his neighbors accordingly, and is even said to have invented and established worship among men. Let him humbly commune with Zoroaster then, and through the liberalizing influence of all the worthies, with Jesus Christ himself, and let "our church" go by the board.

We boast that we belong to the nineteenth century and are making the most rapid strides of any nation. But consider how little this village does for its own culture. I do not wish to flatter my townsmen, nor to be flattered by them, for that will not advance either of us. We need to be provoked, — goaded like oxen, as we are, into a trot. We have a comparatively decent system of common schools, schools for infants only; but excepting the half-starved Lyceum in the winter, and latterly the puny beginning of a library suggested by the state, no school for ourselves. We spend more on almost any article of bodily aliment or ailment than on our mental aliment. It is time that we had uncommon schools, that we did not leave off our education when we begin to be men and women. It is time that villages were universities, and their elder inhabitants the fellows of universities, with leisure — if they are indeed so well off — to pursue liberal studies the rest of their lives. Shall the world be confined to one Paris or one Oxford forever? Cannot students be boarded here and get a liberal education under the skies of Concord? Can we not hire some Abelard to lecture to us? Alas! what with foddering the cattle and tending the store, we are kept from school too long, and our education is sadly neglected. In this country, the village should in some respects take the place of the nobleman of Europe. It should be the patron of the fine arts. It is rich enough. It wants only the magnanimity and refinement. It can spend money enough on such things as farmers and traders value, but it is thought Utopian to propose spending money for things which more intelligent men know to be of far more worth. This town has spent seventeen thousand dollars on a town-house, thank fortune or politics, but probably it will not spend so much on living wit, the true meat to put into that shell, in a hundred years. The one hundred and twenty-five dollars annually subscribed for a Lyceum in the winter is better spent than any other equal sum raised in the town. If we live in the nineteenth century, why should we not enjoy the advantages which the nineteenth century offers? Why should our life be in any respect provincial? If we will read newspapers, why not skip the gossip of Boston and take the best newspaper in the world at once? — not be sucking the pap of "neutral family" papers, or browsing "Olive-Branches" here in New England. Let the reports of all the learned societies come to us, and we will see if they know anything. Why should we leave it to Harper & Brothers and Redding & Co. to select our reading? As the nobleman of cultivated taste surrounds himself with whatever conduces to his culture, — genius — learning — wit — books — paintings — statuary — music — philosophical instruments, and the like; so let the village do, — not stop short at a pedagogue, a parson, a sexton, a parish library, and three selectmen, because our pilgrim forefathers got through a cold winter once on a bleak rock with these. To act collectively is according to the spirit of our institutions; and I am confident that, as our circumstances are more flourishing, our means are greater than the nobleman's. New England can hire all the wise men in the world to come and teach her, and board them round the while, and not be provincial at all. That is the *uncommon* school we want. Instead of noblemen, let us have noble villages of men. If it is necessary, omit one bridge over the river, go round a little there, and throw one arch at least over the darker gulf of ignorance which surrounds us.[1]

[1] As early as his college essays, Thoreau proposed that the state provide compulsory public education. Though an individualist, he always subscribed to legislation for the general welfare. He himself acted "collectively" in behalf of the higher education of the community, not only by lecturing some twenty times for the Concord Lyceum, but by taking a guiding role in its proceedings. From 1838 to 1840, and in 1842, 1843, and 1845, as curator, he organized the lecture series.

IV. SOUNDS [1]

BUT while we are confined to books, though the most select and classic, and read only particular written languages, which are themselves but dialects and provincial, we are in danger of forgetting the language which all things and events speak without metaphor, which alone is copious and standard. Much is published, but little printed. The rays which stream through the shutter will be no longer remembered when the shutter is wholly removed. No method nor discipline can supersede the necessity of being forever on the alert. What is a course of history or philosophy, or poetry, no matter how well selected, or the best society, or the most admirable routine of life, compared with the discipline of looking always at what is to be seen? Will you be a reader, a student merely, or a seer? Read your fate, see what is before you, and walk on into futurity.

I did not read books the first summer; I hoed beans. Nay, I often did better than this. There were times when I could not afford to sacrifice the bloom of the present moment to any work, whether of the head or hands. I love a broad margin to my life. Sometimes, in a summer morning, having taken my accustomed bath, I sat in my sunny doorway from sunrise till noon, rapt in a revery, amidst the pines and hickories and sumachs, in undisturbed solitude and stillness, while the birds sang around or flitted noiseless through the house, until by the sun falling in at my west window, or the noise of some traveller's wagon on the distant highway, I was reminded of the lapse of time. I grew in those seasons like corn in the night, and they were far better than any work of the hands would have been. They were not time subtracted from my life, but so much over and above my usual allowance. I realized what the Orientals mean by contemplation and the forsaking of works. For the most part, I minded not how the hours

[1] If "Reading" instructed the reader in the discipline of using the past, "Sounds" showed him how to read the universal, living language of Nature. As this chapter shows, Thoreau's sense of hearing was especially acute. In fact, hearing was his primary sense and passport into Nature; sounds told him of Nature's healthy or "sound" state, and his responsiveness to her sounds was a measure of his health or communion. The chapter also shows the more fanciful and literary correspondences that in time — and later in the book — yielded to more exact expressions of the meaning of Nature.

went. The day advanced as if to light some work of mine; it was morning, and lo, now it is evening, and nothing memorable is accomplished. Instead of singing like the birds, I silently smiled at my incessant good fortune. As the sparrow had its trill, sitting on the hickory before my door, so had I my chuckle or suppressed warble which he might hear out of my nest. My days were not days of the week, bearing the stamp of any heathen deity, nor were they minced into hours and fretted by the ticking of a clock; for I lived like the Puri Indians, of whom it is said that "for yesterday, to-day, and to-morrow they have only one word, and they express the variety of meaning by pointing backward for yesterday, forward for to-morrow, and overhead for the passing day." This was sheer idleness to my fellow-townsmen, no doubt; but if the birds and flowers had tried me by their standard, I should not have been found wanting. A man must find his occasions in himself, it is true. The natural day is very calm, and will hardly reprove his indolence.

I had this advantage, at least, in my mode of life, over those who were obliged to look abroad for amusement, to society and the theatre, that my life itself was become my amusement and never ceased to be novel. It was a drama of many scenes and without an end. If we were always indeed getting our living, and regulating our lives according to the last and best mode we had learned, we should never be troubled with ennui. Follow your genius closely enough, and it will not fail to show you a fresh prospect every hour. Housework was a pleasant pastime. When my floor was dirty, I rose early, and, setting all my furniture out of doors on the grass, bed and bedstead making but one budget, dashed water on the floor, and sprinkled white sand from the pond on it, and then with a broom scrubbed it clean and white; and by the time the villagers had broken their fast the morning sun had dried my house sufficiently to allow me to move in again, and my meditations were almost uninterrupted. It was pleasant to see my whole household effects out on the grass, making a little pile like a gypsy's pack, and my three-legged table, from which I did not remove the books and pen and ink, standing amid the pines and hickories. They seemed glad to get out themselves, and as if unwilling to be brought in. I was sometimes tempted to stretch an awning over them and take my seat there. It was worth the while to see the sun shine on these things, and hear the free wind blow on them; so much more interesting most familiar objects look out of doors than in the house. A bird sits on the next bough, life-everlasting grows under the table, and blackberry vines run round its legs; pine cones, chestnut burs, and strawberry leaves are strewn about. It looked as if this was the way these forms came to be transferred to our furniture, to tables, chairs, and bedsteads, — because they once stood in their midst.

My house was on the side of a hill, immediately on the edge of the larger wood, in the midst of a young forest of pitch pines and hickories, and half a dozen rods from the pond, to which a narrow footpath led down the hill. In my front yard grew the strawberry, blackberry, and life-everlasting, johnswort and golden-rod, shrub-oaks and sand-cherry, blueberry and ground-nut. Near the end of May, the sand-cherry (*cerasus pumila*) adorned the sides of the path with its delicate flowers arranged in umbels cylindrically about its short stems, which last, in the fall, weighed down with good sized and handsome cherries, fell over in wreaths like rays on every side. I tasted them out of compliment to Nature, though they were scarcely palatable. The sumach (*rhus glabra*) grew luxuriantly about the house, pushing up through the embankment which I had made, and growing five or six feet the first season. Its broad pinnate tropical leaf was pleasant though strange to look on. The large buds, suddenly pushing out late in the spring from dry sticks which had seemed to be dead, developed themselves as by magic into graceful green and tender boughs, an inch in diameter; and sometimes, as I sat at my window, so heedlessly did they grow and tax their weak joints, I heard a fresh and tender bough suddenly fall like a fan to the ground, when there was not a breath of air stirring, broken off by its own weight. In August, the large masses of berries, which, when in flower, had attracted many wild bees, gradually assumed their bright velvety crimson hue, and by their weight again bent down and broke the tender limbs.

As I sit at my window this summer afternoon, hawks are circling about my clearing; the tantivy of wild pigeons, flying by twos and threes athwart my view, or perching restless on the white-pine boughs behind my house, gives a voice to the air; a fishhawk dimples the glassy surface of the pond and brings up a fish; a mink steals out of the marsh before my door and seizes a frog by the shore; the sedge is bending under the weight of the red-birds flitting hither and thither; and for the last half hour I have heard the rattle of railroad cars, now dying away and then reviving like the beat of a partridge, conveying travellers from Boston to the country. For I did not live so out of the world as that boy, who, as I hear, was put out to a farmer in the east part of

the town, but ere long ran away and came home again, quite down at
the heel and homesick. He had never seen such a dull and out-of-the-
way place; the folks were all gone off; why, you could n't even hear
the whistle! I doubt if there is such a place in Massachusetts now: —

> "In truth, our village has become a butt
> For one of those fleet railroad shafts, and o'er
> Our peaceful plain its soothing sound is — Concord."

The Fitchburg Railroad touches the pond about a hundred rods south
of where I dwell. I usually go to the village along its causeway, and
am, as it were, related to society by this link. The men on the freight
trains, who go over the whole length of the road, bow to me as to an
old acquaintance, they pass me so often, and apparently they take me
for an employee; and so I am. I too would fain be a track-repairer
somewhere in the orbit of the earth.

The whistle of the locomotive penetrates my woods summer and
winter, sounding like the scream of a hawk sailing over some farmer's
yard, informing me that many restless city merchants are arriving
within the circle of the town, or adventurous country traders from the
other side. As they come under one horizon, they shout their warning
to get off the track to the other, heard sometimes through the circles of
two towns. Here come your groceries, country; your rations, coun-
trymen! Nor is there any man so independent on his farm that he can
say them nay. And here's your pay for them! screams the country-
man's whistle; timber like long battering rams going twenty miles an
hour against the city's walls, and chairs enough to seat all the weary and
heavy laden that dwell within them. With such huge and lumbering
civility the country hands a chair to the city. All the Indian huckleberry hills are stripped, all the cranberry meadows are raked into the
city. Up comes the cotton, down goes the woven cloth; up comes the
silk, down goes the woollen; up come the books, but down goes the
wit that writes them.

When I meet the engine with its train of cars moving off with
planetary motion, — or, rather, like a comet, for the beholder knows
not if with that velocity and with that direction it will ever revisit this
system, since its orbit does not look like a returning curve, — with
its steam cloud like a banner streaming behind in golden and silver
wreaths, like many a downy cloud which I have seen, high in the
heavens, unfolding its masses to the light, — as if this travelling demi-
god, this cloud-compeller, would ere long take the sunset sky for the

livery of his train; when I hear the iron horse make the hills echo with his snort like thunder, shaking the earth with his feet, and breathing fire and smoke from his nostrils, (what kind of winged horse or fiery dragon they will put into the new Mythology I don't know,) it seems as if the earth had got a race now worthy to inhabit it. If all were as it seems, and men made the elements their servants for noble ends! If the cloud that hangs over the engine were the perspiration of heroic deeds, or as beneficent as that which floats over the farmer's fields, then the elements and Nature herself would cheerfully accompany men on their errands and be their escort.

I watch the passage of the morning cars with the same feeling that I do the rising of the sun, which is hardly more regular. Their train of clouds stretching far behind and rising higher and higher, going to heaven while the cars are going to Boston, conceals the sun for a minute and casts my distant field into the shade, a celestial train beside which the petty train of cars which hugs the earth is but the barb of the spear. The stabler of the iron horse was up early this winter morning by the light of the stars amid the mountains, to fodder and harness his steed. Fire, too, was awakened thus early to put the vital heat in him and get him off. If the enterprise were as innocent as it is early! If the snow lies deep, they strap on his snow-shoes, and with the giant plough plough a furrow from the mountains to the seaboard, in which the cars, like a following drill-barrow, sprinkle all the restless men and floating merchandise in the country for seed. All day the fire-steed flies over the country, stopping only that his master may rest, and I am awakened by his tramp and defiant snort at midnight, when in some remote glen in the woods he fronts the elements incased in ice and snow; and he will reach his stall only with the morning star, to start once more on his travels without rest or slumber. Or perchance, at evening, I hear him in his stable blowing off the superfluous energy of the day, that he may calm his nerves and cool his liver and brain for a few hours of iron slumber. If the enterprise were as heroic and commanding as it is protracted and unwearied!

Far through unfrequented woods on the confines of towns, where once only the hunter penetrated by day, in the darkest night dart these bright saloons without the knowledge of their inhabitants; this moment stopping at some brilliant station-house in town or city, where a social crowd is gathered, the next in the Dismal Swamp, scaring the owl and fox. The startings and arrivals of the cars are now the epochs in the village day. They go and come with such regularity and precision, and their whistle can be heard so far, that the farmers set their clocks by them, and thus one well conducted institution regulates a whole country. Have not men improved somewhat in punctuality since the railroad was invented? Do they not talk and think faster in the depot than they did in the stage-office? There is something electrifying in the atmosphere of the former place. I have been astonished at the miracles it has wrought; that some of my neighbors, who, I should have prophesied, once for all, would never get to Boston by so prompt a conveyance, are on hand when the bell rings. To do things "railroad fashion" is now the byword; and it is worth the while to be warned so often and so sincerely by any power to get off its track. There is no stopping to read the riot act, no firing over the heads of the mob, in this case. We have constructed a fate, an *Atropos*, that never turns aside. (Let that be the name of your engine.) Men are advertised that at a certain hour and minute these bolts will be shot toward particular points of the compass; yet it interferes with no man's business, and the children go to school on the other track. We live the steadier for it. We are all educated thus to be sons of Tell. The air is full of invisible bolts. Every path but your own is the path of fate. Keep on your own track, then.

What recommends commerce to me is its enterprise and bravery. It does not clasp its hands and pray to Jupiter. I see these men every day go about their business with more or less courage and content, doing more even than they suspect, and perchance better employed than they could have consciously devised. I am less affected by their heroism who stood up for half an hour in the front line at Buena Vista, than by the steady and cheerful valor of the men who inhabit the snow-plough for their winter quarters; who have not merely the three-o'-clock in the morning courage, which Bonaparte thought was the rarest, but whose courage does not go to rest so early, who go to sleep only when the storm sleeps or the sinews of their iron steed are frozen. On this morning of the Great Snow, perchance, which is still raging and chilling men's blood, I hear the muffled tone of their engine bell from out the fog bank of their chilled breath, which announces that the cars *are coming*, without long delay, notwithstanding the veto of a New England north-east snow-storm, and I behold the ploughmen covered with snow and rime, their heads peering above the mould-board which is turning down other than daisies and the nests of field-mice, like bowlders of the Sierra Nevada, that occupy an outside place in the universe.

Commerce is unexpectedly confident and serene, alert, adventurous, and unwearied. It is very natural in its methods withal, far more so than many fantastic enterprises and sentimental experiments, and hence its singular success. I am refreshed and expanded when the freight train rattles past me, and I smell the stores which go dispensing their odors all the way from Long Wharf to Lake Champlain, reminding me of foreign parts, of coral reefs, and Indian oceans, and tropical climes, and the extent of the globe. I feel more like a citizen of the world at the sight of the palm-leaf which will cover so many flaxen New England heads the next summer, the Manilla hemp and cocoa-nut husks, the old junk, gunny bags, scrap iron, and rusty nails. This car-load of torn sails is more legible and interesting now than if they should be wrought into paper and printed books. Who can write so graphically the history of the storms they have weathered as these rents have done? They are proof-sheets which need no correction. Here goes lumber from the Maine woods, which did not go out to sea in the last freshet, risen four dollars on the thousand because of what did go out or was split up; pine, spruce, cedar, — first, second, third and fourth qualities, so lately all of one quality, to wave over the bear, and moose, and caribou. Next rolls Thomaston lime, a prime lot, which will get far among the hills before it gets slacked. These rags in bales, of all hues and qualities, the lowest condition to which cotton and linen descend, the final result of dress, — of patterns which are now no longer cried up, unless it be in Milwaukee, as those splendid articles, English, French, or American prints, ginghams, muslins, etc., gathered from all quarters both of fashion and poverty, going to become paper of one color or a few shades only, on which forsooth will be written tales of real life, high and low, and founded on fact! This closed car smells of salt fish, the strong New England and commercial scent, reminding me of the Grand Banks and the fisheries. Who has not seen a salt fish, thoroughly cured for this world, so that nothing can spoil it, and putting the perseverance of the saints to the blush? with which you may sweep or pave the streets, and split your kindlings, and the teamster shelter himself and his lading against sun, wind, and rain behind it, — and the trader, as a Concord trader once did, hang it up by his door for a sign when he commences business, until at last his oldest customer cannot tell surely whether it be animal, vegetable, or mineral, and yet it shall be as pure as a snowflake, and if it be put into a pot and boiled, will come out an excellent dun fish for a Saturday's dinner. Next Spanish hides, with the tails still preserving their twist and the angle of elevation they had when the oxen that wore them were careering over the pampas of the Spanish main, — a type of all obstinacy, and evincing how almost hopeless and incurable are all constitutional vices. I confess, that practically speaking, when I have learned a man's real disposition, I have no hopes of changing it for the better or worse in this state of existence. As the Orientals say, "A cur's tail may be warmed, and pressed, and bound round with ligatures, and after a twelve years' labor bestowed upon it, still it will retain its natural form." The only effectual cure for such inveteracies as these tails exhibit is to make glue of them, which I believe is what is usually done with them, and then they will stay put and stick. Here is a hogshead of molasses or of brandy directed to John Smith, Cuttingsville, Vermont, some trader among the Green Mountains, who imports for the farmers near his clearing, and now perchance stands over his bulk-head and thinks of the last arrivals on the coast, how they may affect the price for him, telling his customers this moment, as he has told them twenty times before this morning, that he expects some by the next train of prime quality. It is advertised in the Cuttingsville Times.

While these things go up other things come down. Warned by the whizzing sound, I look up from my book and see some tall pine, hewn on far northern hills, which has winged its way over the Green Mountains and the Connecticut, shot like an arrow through the township within ten minutes, and scarce another eye beholds it; going

> "to be the mast
> Of some great ammiral."

And hark! here comes the cattle-train bearing the cattle of a thousand hills, sheepcots, stables, and cow-yards in the air, drovers with their sticks, and shepherd boys in the midst of their flocks, all but the mountain pastures, whirled along like leaves blown from the mountains by the September gales. The air is filled with the bleating of calves and sheep, and the hustling of oxen, as if a pastoral valley were going by. When the old bell-weather at the head rattles his bell, the mountains do indeed skip like rams and the little hills like lambs. A car-load of drovers, too, in the midst, on a level with their droves now, their vocation gone, but still clinging to their useless sticks as their badge of office. But their dogs, where are they? It is a stampede to them; they are quite thrown out; they have lost the scent. Methinks I hear them barking behind the Peterboro' Hills, or panting up the western slope of

the Green Mountains. They will not be in at the death. Their vocation, too, is gone. Their fidelity and sagacity are below par now
They will slink back to their kennels in disgrace, or perchance run
wild and strike a league with the wolf and the fox. So is your pastoral
life whirled past and away. But the bell rings, and I must get off the
track and let the cars go by; —

> What's the railroad to me?
> I never go to see
> Where it ends.
> It fills a few hollows,
> And makes banks for the swallows,
> It sets the sand a-blowing,
> And the blackberries a-growing,

but I cross it like a cart-path in the woods. I will not have my eyes
put out and my ears spoiled by its smoke and steam and hissing.

Now that the cars are gone by and all the restless world with them,
and the fishes in the pond no longer feel their rumbling, I am more
alone than ever. For the rest of the long afternoon, perhaps, my meditations are interrupted only by the faint rattle of a carriage or team
along the distant highway.

Sometimes, on Sundays, I heard the bells, the Lincoln, Acton, Bed-
ford, or Concord bell, when the wind was favorable, a faint, sweet,
and, as it were, natural melody, worth importing into the wilderness.
At a sufficient distance over the woods this sound acquires a certain
vibratory hum, as if the pine needles in the horizon were the strings
of a harp which it swept. All sound heard at the greatest possible distance produces one and the same effect, a vibration of the universal
lyre, just as the intervening atmosphere makes a distant ridge of earth
interesting to our eyes by the azure tint it imparts to it. There came
to me in this case a melody which the air had strained, and which had
conversed with every leaf and needle of the wood, that portion of the
sound which the elements had taken up and modulated and echoed
from vale to vale. The echo is, to some extent, an original sound, and
therein is the magic and charm of it. It is not merely a repetition of
what was worth repeating in the bell, but partly the voice of the wood,
the same trivial words and notes sung by a wood-nymph.

At evening, the distant lowing of some cow in the horizon beyond
the woods sounded sweet and melodious, and at first I would mistake
it for the voices of certain minstrels by whom I was sometimes ser-

enaded, who might be straying over hill and dale; but soon I was not unpleasantly disappointed when it was prolonged into the cheap and natural music of the cow. I do not mean to be satirical, but to express my appreciation of those youths' singing, when I state that I perceived clearly that it was akin to the music of the cow, and they were at length one articulation of Nature.

Regularly at half past seven, in one part of the summer, after the evening train had gone by, the whippoorwills chanted their vespers for half an hour, sitting on a stump by my door, or upon the ridge-pole of the house. They would begin to sing almost with as much precision as a clock, within five minutes of a particular time, referred to the setting of the sun, every evening. I had a rare opportunity to become acquainted with their habits. Sometimes I heard four or five at once in different parts of the wood, by accident one a bar behind another, and so near me that I distinguished not only the cluck after each note, but often that singular buzzing sound like a fly in a spider's web, only proportionally louder. Sometimes one would circle round and round me in the woods a few feet distant as if tethered by a string, when probably I was near its eggs. They sang at intervals throughout the night, and were again as musical as ever just before and about dawn.

When other birds are still the screech owls take up the strain, like mourning women their ancient u-lu-lu. Their dismal scream is truly Ben Jonsonian. Wise midnight hags! It is no honest and blunt tu-whit tu-who of the poets, but, without jesting, a most solemn grave-yard ditty, the mutual consolations of suicide lovers remembering the pangs and the delights of supernal love in the infernal groves. Yet I love to hear their wailing, their doleful responses, trilled along the woodside; reminding me sometimes of music and singing birds; as if it were the dark and tearful side of music, the regrets and sighs that would fain be sung. They are the spirits, the low spirits and melancholy forebodings, of fallen souls that once in human shape night-walked the earth and did the deeds of darkness, now expiating their sins with their wailing hymns or threnodies in the scenery of their transgressions. They give me a new sense of the variety and capacity of that nature which is our common dwelling. *Oh-o-o-o-o that I never had been bor-r-r-r-n!* sighs one on this side of the pond, and circles with the restlessness of despair to some new perch on the gray oaks. Then — *that I never had been bor-r-r-n!* echoes another on the farther side with tremulous sincerity, and — *bor-r-r-n!* comes faintly from far in the Lincoln woods.

I was also serenaded by a hooting owl. Near at hand you could fancy it the most melancholy sound in Nature, as if she meant by this to stereotype and make permanent in her choir the dying moans of a human being, — some poor weak relic of mortality who has left hope behind, and howls like an animal, yet with human sobs, on entering the dark valley, made more awful by a certain gurgling melodiousness, — I find myself beginning with the letters gl when I try to imitate it, — expressive of a mind which has reached the gelatinous mildewy stage in the mortification of all healthy and courageous thought. It reminded me of ghouls and idiots and insane howlings. But now one answers from far woods in a strain made really melodious by distance, — *Hoo hoo hoo, hoorer hoo;* and indeed for the most part it suggested only pleasing associations, whether heard by day or night, summer or winter.

I rejoice that there are owls. Let them do the idiotic and maniacal hooting for men. It is a sound admirably suited to swamps and twilight woods which no day illustrates, suggesting a vast and undeveloped nature which men have not recognized. They represent the stark twilight and unsatisfied thoughts which all have. All day the sun has shone on the surface of some savage swamp, where the single spruce stands hung with usnea lichens, and small hawks circulate above, and the chickadee lisps amid the evergreens, and the partridge and rabbit skulk beneath; but now a more dismal and fitting day dawns, and a different race of creatures awakes to express the meaning of Nature there.

Late in the evening I heard the distant rumbling of wagons over bridges, — a sound heard farther than almost any other at night, — the baying of dogs, and sometimes again the lowing of some disconsolate cow in a distant barn-yard. In the mean while all the shore rang with the trump of bullfrogs, the sturdy spirits of ancient wine-bibbers and wassailers, still unrepentant, trying to sing a catch in their Stygian lake, — if the Walden nymphs will pardon the comparison, for though there are almost no weeds, there are frogs there, — who would fain keep up the hilarious rules of their old festal tables, though their voices have waxed hoarse and solemnly grave, mocking at mirth, and the wine has lost its flavor, and become only liquor to distend their paunches, and sweet intoxication never comes to drown the memory of the past, but mere saturation and waterloggedness and distention. The most aldermanic, with his chin upon a heart-leaf, which serves for a napkin to his drooling chaps, under this northern shore quaffs a deep draught of the once scorned water, and passes round the cup with the ejaculation *tr-r-r-oonk, tr-r-r-oonk, tr-r-r-oonk!* and straightway comes over the water from some distant cove the same password repeated, where the next in seniority and girth has gulped down to his mark; and when this observance has made the circuit of the shores, then ejaculates the master of ceremonies, with satisfaction, *tr-r-r-oonk!* and each in his turn repeats the same down to the least distended, leakiest, and flabbiest paunched, that there be no mistake; and then the bowl goes round again and again, until the sun disperses the morning mist, and only the patriarch is not under the pond, but vainly bellowing *troonk* from time to time, and pausing for a reply.

I am not sure that I ever heard the sound of cock-crowing from my clearing, and I thought that it might be worth the while to keep a cockerel for his music merely, as a singing bird. The note of this once wild Indian pheasant is certainly the most remarkable of any bird's, and if they could be naturalized without being domesticated, it would soon become the most famous sound in our woods, surpassing the clangor of the goose and the hooting of the owl; and then imagine the cackling of the hens to fill the pauses when their lords' clarions rested! No wonder that man added this bird to his tame stock, — to say nothing of the eggs and drumsticks. To walk in a winter morning in a wood where these birds abounded, their native woods, and hear the wild cockerels crow on the trees, clear and shrill for miles over the resounding earth, drowning the feebler notes of other birds, — think of it! It would put nations on the alert. Who would not be early to rise, and rise earlier and earlier every successive day of his life, till he became unspeakably healthy, wealthy, and wise? This foreign bird's note is celebrated by the poets of all countries along with the notes of their native songsters. All climates agree with brave Chanticleer. He is more indigenous even than the natives. His health is ever good, his lungs are sound, his spirits never flag. Even the sailor on the Atlantic and Pacific is awakened by his voice; but its shrill sound never roused me from my slumbers. I kept neither dog, cat, cow, pig, nor hens, so that you would have said there was a deficiency of domestic sounds; neither the churn, nor the spinning-wheel, nor even the singing of the kettle, nor the hissing of the urn, nor children crying, to comfort one. An old-fashioned man would have lost his senses or died of ennui before this. Not even rats in the wall, for they were starved out, or rather were never baited in, — only squirrels on the roof and under the floor, a whippoorwill on the ridge-pole, a blue-jay screaming beneath the window, a hare or woodchuck under the house, a screech-owl or a cat-owl behind it, a flock of wild geese or a laughing loon on the pond, and a fox to bark in the night.   Not even a lark or an oriole, those mild plantation birds, ever visited my clearing.   No cockerels to crow nor hens to cackle in the yard.   No yard! but unfenced Nature reaching up to your very sills.   A young forest growing up under your windows, and wild sumachs and blackberry vines breaking through into your cellar; sturdy pitch-pines rubbing and creaking against the shingles for want of room, their roots reaching quite under the house.   Instead of a scuttle or a blind blown off in the gale, — a pine tree snapped off or torn up by the roots behind your house for fuel.   Instead of no path to the front-yard gate in the Great Snow, — no gate — no front-yard, — and no path to the civilized world.

V. SOLITUDE

THIS is a delicious evening, when the whole body is one sense, and imbibes delight through every pore.   I go and come with a strange liberty in Nature, a part of herself.   As I walk along the stony shore of the pond in my shirt sleeves, though it is cool as well as cloudy and windy, and I see nothing special to attract me, all the elements are unusually congenial to me.   The bullfrogs trump to usher in the night, and the note of the whippoorwill is borne on the rippling wind from over the water.   Sympathy with the fluttering alder and poplar leaves almost takes away my breath; yet, like the lake, my serenity is rippled but not ruffled.   These small waves raised by the evening wind are as remote from storm as the smooth reflecting surface.   Though it is now dark, the wind still blows and roars in the wood, the waves still dash, and some creatures lull the rest with their notes.   The repose is never complete.   The wildest animals do not repose, but seek their prey now; the fox, and skunk, and rabbit, now roam the fields and woods without fear.   They are Nature's watchmen, — links which connect the days of animated life.

When I return to my house I find that visitors have been there and left their cards, either a bunch of flowers, or a wreath of evergreen, or a name in pencil on a yellow walnut leaf or a chip. They who come rarely to the woods take some little piece of the forest into their hands to play with by the way, which they leave, either intentionally or accidentally. One has peeled a willow wand, woven it into a ring, and dropped it on my table. I could always tell if visitors had called in my absence, either by the bended twigs or grass, or the print of their shoes, and generally of what sex or age or quality they were by some slight trace left, as a flower dropped, or a bunch of grass plucked and thrown away, even as far off as the railroad, half a mile distant, or by the lingering odor of a cigar or pipe. Nay, I was frequently notified of the passage of a traveller along the highway sixty rods off by the scent of his pipe.

There is commonly sufficient space about us. Our horizon is never quite at our elbows. The thick wood is not just at our door, nor the pond, but somewhat is always clearing, familiar and worn by us, appropriated and fenced in some way, and reclaimed from Nature. For what reason have I this vast range and circuit, some square miles of unfrequented forest, for my privacy, abandoned to me by men? My nearest neighbor is a mile distant, and no house is visible from any place but the hill-tops within half a mile of my own. I have my horizon bounded by woods all to myself; a distant view of the railroad where it touches the pond on the one hand, and of the fence which skirts the woodland road on the other. But for the most part it is as solitary where I live as on the prairies. It is as much Asia or Africa as New England. I have, as it were, my own sun and moon and stars, and a little world all to myself. At night there was never a traveller passed my house, or knocked at my door, more than if I were the first or last man; unless it were in the spring, when at long intervals some came from the village to fish for pouts, — they plainly fished much more in the Walden Pond of their own natures, and baited their hooks with darkness, — but they soon retreated, usually with light baskets, and left "the world to darkness and to me," and the black kernel of the night was never profaned by any human neighborhood. I believe that men are generally still a little afraid of the dark, though the witches are all hung, and Christianity and candles have been introduced.

Yet I experienced sometimes that the most sweet and tender, the most innocent and encouraging society may be found in any natural object, even for the poor misanthrope and most melancholy man. There can be no very black melancholy to him who lives in the midst of Nature and has his senses still. There was never yet such a storm but it was Æolian music to a healthy and innocent ear. Nothing can rightly compel a simple and brave man to a vulgar sadness. While I enjoy the friendship of the seasons I trust that nothing can make life a burden to me. The gentle rain which waters my beans and keeps me in the house to-day is not drear and melancholy, but good for me too. Though it prevents my hoeing them, it is of far more worth than my hoeing. If it should continue so long as to cause the seeds to rot in the ground and destroy the potatoes in the low lands, it would still be good for the grass on the uplands, and, being good for the grass, it would be good for me. Sometimes, when I compare myself with other men, it seems as if I were more favored by the gods than they, beyond any deserts that I am conscious of; as if I had a warrant and surety at their hands which my fellows have not, and were especially guided and guarded. I do not flatter myself, but if it be possible they flatter me. I have never felt lonesome, or in the least oppressed by a sense of solitude, but once, and that was a few weeks after I came to the woods, when, for an hour, I doubted if the near neighborhood of man was not essential to a serene and healthy life. To be alone was something unpleasant. But I was at the same time conscious of a slight insanity in my mood, and seemed to foresee my recovery. In the midst of a gentle rain while these thoughts prevailed, I was suddenly sensible of such sweet and beneficent society in Nature, in the very pattering of the drops, and in every sound and sight around my house, an infinite and unaccountable friendliness all at once like an atmosphere sustaining me, as made the fancied advantages of human neighborhood insignificant, and I have never thought of them since. Every little pine needle expanded and swelled with sympathy and befriended me. I was so distinctly made aware of the presence of something kindred to me, even in scenes which we are accustomed to call wild and dreary, and also that the nearest of blood to me and humanest was not a person nor a villager, that I thought no place could ever be strange to me again. —

> "Mourning untimely consumes the sad;
> Few are their days in the land of the living,
> Beautiful daughter of Toscar."

Some of my pleasantest hours were during the long rain storms in the spring or fall, which confined me to the house for the afternoon as well as the forenoon, soothed by their ceaseless roar and pelting; when an early twilight ushered in a long evening in which many thoughts

had time to take root and unfold themselves. In those driving north-
east rains which tried the village houses so, when the maids stood
ready with mop and pail in front entries to keep the deluge out, I sat
behind my door in my little house, which was all entry, and thoroughly
enjoyed its protection. In one heavy thunder shower the lightning
struck a large pitch-pine across the pond, making a very conspicuous
and perfectly regular spiral groove from top to bottom, an inch or
more deep, and four or five inches wide, as you would groove a walk-
ing-stick. I passed it again the other day, and was struck with awe
on looking up and beholding that mark, now more distinct than ever,
where a terrific and resistless bolt came down out of the harmless sky
eight years ago. Men frequently say to me, "I should think you would
feel lonesome down there, and want to be nearer to folks, rainy and
snowy days and nights especially." I am tempted to reply to such, —
This whole earth which we inhabit is but a point in space. How far
apart, think you, dwell the two most distant inhabitants of yonder
star, the breadth of whose disk cannot be appreciated by our instruments? Why should I feel lonely? is not our planet in the Milky
Way? This which you put seems to me not to be the most important
question. What sort of space is that which separates a man from his
fellows and makes him solitary? I have found that no exertion of the
legs can bring two minds much nearer to one another. What do we
want most to dwell near to? Not to many men surely, the depot, the
post-office, the bar-room, the meeting-house, the school-house, the
grocery, Beacon Hill, or the Five Points, where men most congregate,
but to the perennial source of our life, whence in all our experience we
have found that to issue, as the willow stands near the water and sends
out its roots in that direction. This will vary with different natures,
but this is the place where a wise man will dig his cellar. . . . I one
evening overtook one of my townsmen, who has accumulated what is
called "a handsome property," — though I never got a *fair* view of it,
— on the Walden road, driving a pair of cattle to market, who inquired to me how I could bring my mind to give up so many of the
comforts of life. I answered that I was very sure I liked it passably
well; I was not joking. And so I went home to my bed, and left him
to pick his way through the darkness and the mud to Brighton, — or
Bright-town, — which place he would reach some time in the
morning.

Any prospect of awakening or coming to life to a dead man makes
indifferent all times and places. The place where that may occur is

always the same, and indescribably pleasant to all our senses. For the most part we allow only outlying and transient circumstances to make our occasions. They are, in fact, the cause of our distraction. Nearest to all things is that power which fashions their being. *Next* to us the grandest laws are continually being executed. *Next* to us is not the workman whom we have hired, with whom we love so well to talk, but the workman whose work we are.

"How vast and profound is the influence of the subtle powers of Heaven and of Earth!"

"We seek to perceive them, and we do not see them; we seek to hear them, and we do not hear them; identified with the substance of things, they cannot be separated from them."

"They cause that in all the universe men purify and sanctify their hearts, and clothe themselves in their holiday garments to offer sacrifices and oblations to their ancestors. It is an ocean of subtle intelligences. They are everywhere, above us, on our left, on our right; they environ us on all sides."

We are the subjects of an experiment which is not a little interesting to me. Can we not do without the society of our gossips a little while under these circumstances, — have our own thoughts to cheer us? Confucius says truly, "Virtue does not remain as an abandoned orphan; it must of necessity have neighbors."

With thinking we may be beside ourselves in a sane sense. By a conscious effort of the mind we can stand aloof from actions and their consequences; and all things, good and bad, go by us like a torrent. We are not wholly involved in Nature. I may be either the drift-wood in the stream, or Indra in the sky looking down on it. I *may* be affected by a theatrical exhibition; on the other hand, I *may not* be affected by an actual event which appears to concern me much more. I only know myself as a human entity; the scene, so to speak, of thoughts and affections; and am sensible of a certain doubleness by which I can stand as remote from myself as from another. However intense my experience, I am conscious of the presence and criticism of a part of me, which, as it were, is not a part of me, but spectator, sharing no experience, but taking note of it; and that is no more I than it is you. When the play, it may be the tragedy, of life is over, the spectator goes his way. It was a kind of fiction, a work of the imagination only, so far as he was concerned. This doubleness may easily make us poor neighbors and friends sometimes.

I find it wholesome to be alone the greater part of the time. To be in company, even with the best, is soon wearisome and dissipating. I love to be alone. I never found the companion that was so companionable as solitude. We are for the most part more lonely when we go abroad among men than when we stay in our chambers. A man thinking or working is always alone, let him be where he will. Solitude is not measured by the miles of space that intervene between a man and his fellows. The really diligent student in one of the crowded hives of Cambridge College is as solitary as a dervis in the desert. The farmer can work alone in the field or the woods all day, hoeing or chopping, and not feel lonesome, because he is employed; but when he comes home at night he cannot sit down in a room alone, at the mercy of his thoughts, but must be where he can "see the folks," and recreate, and as he thinks remunerate, himself for his day's solitude; and hence he wonders how the student can sit alone in the house all night and most of the day without ennui and "the blues;" but he does not realize that the student, though in the house, is still at work in *his* field, and chopping in *his* woods, as the farmer in his, and in turn seeks the same recreation and society that the latter does, though it may be a more condensed form of it.

Society is commonly too cheap. We meet at very short intervals, not having had time to acquire any new value for each other. We meet at meals three times a day, and give each other a new taste of that old musty cheese that we are. We have had to agree on a certain set of rules, called etiquette and politeness, to make this frequent meeting tolerable and that we need not come to open war. We meet at the post-office, and at the sociable, and about the fireside every night; we live thick and are in each other's way, and stumble over one another, and I think that we thus lose some respect for one another. Certainly less frequency would suffice for all important and hearty communications. Consider the girls in a factory, — never alone, hardly in their dreams. It would be better if there were but one inhabitant to a square mile, as where I live. The value of a man is not in his skin, that we should touch him.

I have heard of a man lost in the woods and dying of famine and exhaustion at the foot of a tree, whose loneliness was relieved by the grotesque visions with which, owing to bodily weakness, his diseased imagination surrounded him, and which he believed to be real. So also, owing to bodily and mental health and strength, we may be continually cheered by a like but more normal and natural society, and come to know that we are never alone.

I have a great deal of company in my house; especially in the morning, when nobody calls. Let me suggest a few comparisons, that some one may convey an idea of my situation. I am no more lonely than the loon in the pond that laughs so loud, or than Walden Pond itself. What company has that lonely lake, I pray? And yet it has not the blue devils, but the blue angels in it, in the azure tint of its waters. The sun is alone, except in thick weather, when there sometimes appear to be two, but one is a mock sun. God is alone, — but the devil, he is far from being alone; he sees a great deal of company; he is legion. I am no more lonely than a single mullein or dandelion in a pasture, or a bean leaf, or sorrel, or a horse-fly, or a humble-bee. I am no more lonely than the Mill Brook, or a weathercock, or the north star, or the south wind, or an April shower, or a January thaw, or the first spider in a new house.

I have occasional visits in the long winter evenings, when the snow falls fast and the wind howls in the wood, from an old settler and original proprietor, who is reported to have dug Walden Pond, and stoned it, and fringed it with pine woods; who tells me stories of old time and of new eternity; and between us we manage to pass a cheerful evening with social mirth and pleasant views of things, even without apples or cider, — a most wise and humorous friend, whom I love much, who keeps himself more secret than ever did Goffe or Whalley; and though he is thought to be dead, none can show where he is buried. An elderly dame, too, dwells in my neighborhood, invisible to most persons, in whose odorous herb garden I love to stroll sometimes, gathering simples and listening to her fables; for she has a genius of unequalled fertility, and her memory runs back farther than mythology, and she can tell me the original of every fable, and on what fact every one is founded, for the incidents occurred when she was young. A ruddy and lusty old dame, who delights in all weathers and seasons, and is likely to outlive all her children yet.

The indescribable innocence and beneficence of Nature, — of sun and wind and rain, of summer and winter, — such health, such cheer, they afford forever! and such sympathy have they ever with our race, that all Nature would be affected, and the sun's brightness fade, and the winds would sigh humanely, and the clouds rain tears, and the woods shed their leaves and put on mourning in midsummer, if any man should ever for a just cause grieve. Shall I not have intelligence with the earth? Am I not partly leaves and vegetable mould myself?

What is the pill which will keep us well, serene, contented? Not my or thy great-grandfather's, but our great-grandmother Nature's universal, vegetable, botanic medicines, by which she has kept herself young always, outlived so many old Parrs in her day, and fed her health with their decaying fatness. For my panacea, instead of one of those quack vials of a mixture dipped from Acheron and the Dead Sea, which come out of those long shallow black-schooner looking wagons which we sometimes see made to carry bottles, let me have a draught of undiluted morning air. Morning air! If men will not drink of this at the fountain-head of the day, why, then, we must even bottle up some and sell it in the shops, for the benefit of those who have lost their subscription ticket to morning time in this world. But remember, it will not keep quite till noonday even in the coolest cellar, but drive out the stopples long ere that and follow westward the steps of Aurora. I am no worshipper of Hygeia, who was the daughter of that old herb-doctor Æsculapius, and who is represented on monuments holding a serpent in one hand, and in the other a cup out of which the serpent sometimes drinks; but rather of Hebe, cupbearer to Jupiter, who was the daughter of Juno and wild lettuce, and who had the power of restoring gods and men to the vigor of youth. She was probably the only thoroughly sound-conditioned, healthy, and robust young lady that ever walked the globe, and wherever she came it was spring.

VI. VISITORS

I THINK that I love society as much as most, and am ready enough to fasten myself like a bloodsucker for the time to any full-blooded man that comes in my way. I am naturally no hermit, but might possibly sit out the sturdiest frequenter of the bar-room, if my business called me thither.

I had three chairs in my house; one for solitude, two for friendship, three for society. When visitors came in larger and unexpected numbers there was but the third chair for them all, but they generally economized the room by standing up. It is surprising how many great men and women a small house will contain. I have had twenty-five or thirty souls, with their bodies, at once under my roof, and yet we often

parted without being aware that we had come very near to one another. Many of our houses, both public and private, with their almost
innumerable apartments, their huge halls and their cellars for the stor-
age of wines and other munitions of peace, appear to me extravagantly
large for their inhabitants. They are so vast and magnificent that the
latter seem to be only vermin which infest them. I am surprised when
the herald blows his summons before some Tremont or Astor or Middlesex House, to see come creeping out over the piazza for all inhabitants a ridiculous mouse, which soon again slinks into some hole in the
pavement.

One inconvenience I sometimes experienced in so small a house, the
difficulty of getting to a sufficient distance from my guest when we
began to utter the big thoughts in big words. You want room for your
thoughts to get into sailing trim and run a course or two before they
make their port. The bullet of your thought must have overcome its
lateral and ricochet motion and fallen into its last and steady course
before it reaches the ear of the hearer, else it may plough out again
through the side of his head. Also, our sentences wanted room to
unfold and form their columns in the interval. Individuals, like nations, must have suitable broad and natural boundaries, even a considerable neutral ground, between them. I have found it a singular luxury
to talk across the pond to a companion on the opposite side. In my
house we were so near that we could not begin to hear, — we could
not speak low enough to be heard; as when you throw two stones into
calm water so near that they break each other's undulations. If we are
merely loquacious and loud talkers, then we can afford to stand very
near together, cheek by jowl, and feel each other's breath; but if we
speak reservedly and thoughtfully, we want to be farther apart, that
all animal heat and moisture may have a chance to evaporate. If we
would enjoy the most intimate society with that in each of us which is
without, or above, being spoken to, we must not only be silent, but
commonly so far apart bodily that we cannot possibly hear each other's
voice in any case. Referred to this standard, speech is for the convenience of those who are hard of hearing; but there are many fine
things which we cannot say if we have to shout. As the conversation
began to assume a loftier and grander tone, we gradually shoved our
chairs farther apart till they touched the wall in opposite corners, and
then commonly there was not room enough.

My "best" room, however, my withdrawing room, always ready
for company, on whose carpet the sun rarely fell, was the pine wood

behind my house. Thither in summer days, when distinguished guests came, I took them, and a priceless domestic swept the floor and dusted the furniture and kept the things in order.

If one guest came he sometimes partook of my frugal meal, and it was no interruption to conversation to be stirring a hasty-pudding, or watching the rising and maturing of a loaf of bread in the ashes, in the mean while. But if twenty came and sat in my house there was nothing said about dinner, though there might be bread enough for two, more than if eating were a forsaken habit; but we naturally practised abstinence; and this was never felt to be an offence against hospitality, but the most proper and considerate course. The waste and decay of physical life, which so often needs repair, seemed miraculously retarded in such a case, and the vital vigor stood its ground. I could entertain thus a thousand as well as twenty; and if any ever went away disappointed or hungry from my house when they found me at home, they may depend upon it that I sympathized with them at least. So easy is it, though many housekeepers doubt it, to establish new and better customs in the place of the old. You need not rest your reputation on the dinners you give. For my own part, I was never so effectually deterred from frequenting a man's house, by any kind of Cerberus whatever, as by the parade one made about dining me, which I took to be a very polite and roundabout hint never to trouble him so again. I think I shall never revisit those scenes. I should be proud to have for the motto of my cabin those lines of Spenser which one of my visitors inscribed on a yellow walnut leaf for a card: —

> "Arrivéd there, the little house they fill,
> Ne looke for entertainment where none was;
> Rest is their feast, and all things at their will:
> The noblest mind the best contentment has."

When Winslow, afterward governor of the Plymouth Colony, went with a companion on a visit of ceremony to Massasoit on foot through the woods, and arrived tired and hungry at his lodge, they were well received by the king, but nothing was said about eating that day. When the night arrived, to quote their own words, — "He laid us on the bed with himself and his wife, they at the one end and we at the other, it being only plank, laid a foot from the ground, and a thin mat upon them. Two more of his chief men, for want of room, pressed by and upon us; so that we were worse weary of our lodging than of our journey." At one o'clock the next day Massasoit "brought two fishes that he had shot," about thrice as big as a bream; "these being boiled, there were at least forty looked for a share in them. The most ate of them. This meal only we had in two nights and a day; and had not one of us bought a partridge, we had taken our journey fasting." Fearing that they would be light-headed for want of food and also sleep, owing to "the savages' barbarous singing, (for they used to sing themselves asleep,)" and that they might get home while they had strength to travel, they departed. As for lodging, it is true they were but poorly entertained, though what they found an inconvenience was no doubt intended for an honor; but as far as eating was concerned, I do not see how the Indians could have done better. They had nothing to eat themselves, and they were wiser than to think that apologies could supply the place of food to their guests; so they drew their belts tighter and said nothing about it. Another time when Winslow visited them, it being a season of plenty with them, there was no deficiency in this respect.

As for men, they will hardly fail one anywhere. I had more visitors while I lived in the woods at than any other period of my life; I mean that I had some. I met several there under more favorable circumstances than I could anywhere else. But fewer came to see me on trivial business. In this respect, my company was winnowed by my mere distance from town. I had withdrawn so far within the great ocean of solitude, into which the rivers of society empty, that for the most part, so far as my needs were concerned, only the finest sediment was deposited around me. Beside, there were wafted to me evidences of unexplored and uncultivated continents on the other side.

Who should come to my lodge this morning but a true Homeric or Paphlagonian man, — he had so suitable and poetic a name that I am sorry I cannot print it here,[1] — a Canadian, a wood-chopper and post-maker, who can hole fifty posts in a day, who made his last supper on a woodchuck which his dog caught. He, too, has heard of Homer, and, "if it were not for books," would "not know what to do rainy days," though perhaps he has not read one wholly through for many rainy seasons. Some priest who could pronounce the Greek itself taught him to read his verse in the testament in his native parish far away; and now I must translate to him, while he holds the book, Achilles' reproof

[1] Alek Therien. The wood-chopper, of course, was such a summerman as Thoreau might have been in his youth — at home in Nature, with a "slumbering" mind, whose seeds had not yet been awakened and ripened by discipline (as in "The Bean-Field") into expression. The requirements of art, Thoreau found as early as his stay with Emerson, destroyed this unconscious communion.

to Patroclus for his sad countenance. — "Why are you in tears, Patroclus, like a young girl?" —

> "Or have you alone heard some news from Phthia?
> They say that Menœtius lives yet, son of Actor,
> And Peleus lives, son of Æacus, among the Myrmidons,
> Either of whom having died, we should greatly grieve."

He says, "That's good." He has a great bundle of white-oak bark under his arm for a sick man, gathered this Sunday morning. "I suppose there's no harm in going after such a thing to-day," says he. To him Homer was a great writer, though what his writing was about he did not know. A more simple and natural man it would be hard to find. Vice and disease, which cast such a sombre moral hue over the world, seemed to have hardly any existence for him. He was about twenty-eight years old, and had left Canada and his father's house a dozen years before to work in the States, and earn money to buy a farm with at last, perhaps in his native country. He was cast in the coarsest mould; a stout but sluggish body, yet gracefully carried, with a thick sunburnt neck, dark bushy hair, and dull sleepy blue eyes, which were occasionally lit up with expression. He wore a flat gray cloth cap, a dingy wool-colored great-coat, and cowhide boots. He was a great consumer of meat, usually carrying his dinner to his work a couple of miles past my house, — for he chopped all summer, — in a tin pail; cold meats, often cold woodchucks, and coffee in a stone bottle which dangled by a string from his belt; and sometimes he offered me a drink. He came along early, crossing my bean-field, though without anxiety or haste to get to his work, such as Yankees exhibit. He wasn't a-going to hurt himself. He didn't care if he only earned his board. Frequently he would leave his dinner in the bushes, when his dog had caught a woodchuck by the way, and go back a mile and a half to dress it and leave it in the cellar of the house where he boarded, after deliberating first for half an hour whether he could not sink it in the pond safely till nightfall, — loving to dwell long upon these themes. He would say, as he went by in the morning, "How thick the pigeons are! If working every day were not my trade, I could get all the meat I should want by hunting, — pigeons, woodchucks, rabbits, partridges, — by gosh! I could get all I should want for a week in one day."

He was a skilful chopper, and indulged in some flourishes and ornaments in his art. He cut his trees level and close to the ground, that the sprouts which came up afterward might be more vigorous and a sled might slide over the stumps; and instead of leaving a whole tree to support his corded wood, he would pare it away to a slender stake or splinter which you could break off with your hand at last.

He interested me because he was so quiet and solitary and so happy withal; a well of good humor and contentment which overflowed at his eyes. His mirth was without alloy. Sometimes I saw him at his work in the woods, felling trees, and he would greet me with a laugh of inexpressible satisfaction, and a salutation in Canadian French, though he spoke English as well. When I approached him he would suspend his work, and with half-suppressed mirth lie along the trunk of a pine which he had felled, and, peeling off the inner bark, roll it up into a ball and chew it while he laughed and talked. Such an exuberance of animal spirits had he that he sometimes tumbled down and rolled on the ground with laughter at anything which made him think and tickled him. Looking round upon the trees he would exclaim, — "By George! I can enjoy myself well enough here chopping; I want no better sport." Sometimes, when at leisure, he amused himself all day in the woods with a pocket pistol, firing salutes to himself at regular intervals as he walked. In the winter he had a fire by which at noon he warmed his coffee in a kettle; and as he sat on a log to eat his dinner the chickadees would sometimes come round and alight on his arm and peck at the potato in his fingers; and he said that he "liked to have the little *fellers* about him."

In him the animal man chiefly was developed. In physical endurance and contentment he was cousin to the pine and the rock. I asked him once if he was not sometimes tired at night, after working all day; and he answered, with a sincere and serious look, "Gorrappit, I never was tired in my life." But the intellectual and what is called spiritual man in him were slumbering as in an infant. He had been instructed only in that innocent and ineffectual way in which the Catholic priests teach the aborigines, by which the pupil is never educated to the degree of consciousness, but only to the degree of trust and reverence, and a child is not made a man, but kept a child. When Nature made him, she gave him a strong body and contentment for his portion, and propped him on every side with reverence and reliance, that he might live out his threescore years and ten a child. He was so genuine and unsophisticated that no introduction would serve to introduce him, more than if you introduced a woodchuck to your neighbor. He had got to find him out as you did. He would not play any part. Men paid him wages for work, and so helped to feed and clothe him; but he never exchanged opinions with them. He was so simply and naturally humble — if he can be called humble who never aspires — that humility was no distinct quality in him, nor could he conceive of it. Wiser men were demigods to him. If you told him that such a one was coming, he did as if he thought that anything so grand would expect nothing of himself, but take all the responsibility on itself, and let him be forgotten still. He never heard the sound of praise. He particularly reverenced the writer and the preacher. Their performances were miracles. When I told him that I wrote considerably, he thought for a long time that it was merely the handwriting which I meant, for he could write a remarkably good hand himself. I sometimes found the name of his native parish handsomely written in the snow by the highway, with the proper French accent, and knew that he had passed. I asked him if he ever wished to write his thoughts. He said that he had read and written letters for those who could not, but he never tried to write thoughts, — no, he could not, he could not tell what to put first, it would kill him, and then there was spelling to be attended to at the same time!

I heard that a distinguished wise man and reformer asked him if he did not want the world to be changed; but he answered with a chuckle of surprise in his Canadian accent, not knowing that the question had ever been entertained before, "No, I like it well enough." It would have suggested many things to a philosopher to have dealings with him. To a stranger he appeared to know nothing of things in general; yet I sometimes saw in him a man whom I had not seen before, and I did not know whether he was as wise as Shakespeare or as simply ignorant as a child, whether to suspect him of a fine poetic consciousness or of stupidity. A townsman told me that when he met him sauntering through the village in his small close-fitting cap, and whistling to himself, he reminded him of a prince in disguise.

His only books were an almanac and an arithmetic, in which last he was considerably expert. The former was a sort of cyclopædia to him, which he supposed to contain an abstract of human knowledge, as indeed it does to a considerable extent. I loved to sound him on the various reforms of the day, and he never failed to look at them in the most simple and practical light. He had never heard of such things before. Could he do without factories? I asked. He had worn the home-made Vermont gray, he said, and that was good. Could he dispense with tea and coffee? Did this country afford any beverage beside water? He had soaked hemlock leaves in water and drank it, and thought that was better than water in warm weather. When I asked him if he could do without money, he showed the convenience of money in such a way as to suggest and coincide with the most philosophical accounts of the origin of this institution, and the very derivation of the word *pecunia*. If an ox were his property, and he wished to get needles and thread at the store, he thought it would be inconvenient and impossible soon to go on mortgaging some portion of the creature each time to that amount. He could defend many institutions better than any philosopher, because, in describing them as they concerned him, he gave the true reason for their prevalence, and speculation had not suggested to him any other. At another time, hearing Plato's definition of a man, — a biped without feathers, — and that one exhibited a cock plucked and called it Plato's man, he thought it an important difference that the *knees* bent the wrong way. He would sometimes exclaim, "How I love to talk! By George, I could talk all day!" I asked him once, when I had not seen him for many months, if he had got a new idea this summer. "Good Lord," said he, "a man that has to work as I do, if he does not forget the ideas he has had, he will do well. May be the man you hoe with is inclined to race; then, by gorry, your mind must be there; you think of weeds." He would sometimes ask me first on such occasions, if I had made any improvement. One winter day I asked him if he was always satisfied with himself, wishing to suggest a substitute within him for the priest without, and some higher motive for living. "Satisfied!" said he; "some men are satisfied with one thing, and some with another. One man, perhaps, if he has got enough, will be satisfied to sit all day with his back to the fire and his belly to the table, by George!" Yet I never, by any manœuvring, could get him to take the spiritual view of things; the highest that he appeared to conceive of was a simple expediency, such as you might expect an animal to appreciate; and this, practically, is true of most men. If I suggested any improvement in his mode of life, he merely answered, without expressing any regret, that it was too late. Yet he thoroughly believed in honesty and the like virtues.

There was a certain positive originality, however slight, to be detected in him, and I occasionally observed that he was thinking for himself and expressing his own opinion, a phenomenon so rare that I would any day walk ten miles to observe it, and it amounted to the re-origination of many of the institutions of society. Though he hesitated, and perhaps failed to express himself distinctly, he always had a presentable thought behind. Yet his thinking was so primitive and immersed in his animal life that, though more promising than a merely learned man's, it rarely ripened to anything which can be reported. He suggested that there might be men of genius in the lowest grades of life, however permanently humble and illiterate, who take their own view always, or do not pretend to see at all; who are as bottomless even as Walden Pond was thought to be, though they may be dark and muddy.

Many a traveller came out of his way to see me and the inside of my house, and, as an excuse for calling, asked for a glass of water. I told them that I drank at the pond, and pointed thither, offering to lend them a dipper. Far off as I lived, I was not exempted from that annual visitation which occurs, methinks, about the first of April, when everybody is on the move; and I had my share of good luck, though there were some curious specimens among my visitors. Half-witted men from the almshouse and elsewhere came to see me; but I endeavored to make them exercise all the wit they had, and make their confessions to me; in such cases making wit the theme of our conversation; and so was compensated. Indeed, I found some of them to be wiser than the so-called *overseers* of the poor and selectmen of the town, and thought it was time that the tables were turned. With respect to wit, I learned that there was not much difference between the half and the whole. One day, in particular, an inoffensive, simple-minded pauper, whom with others I had often seen used as fencing stuff, standing or sitting on a bushel in the fields to keep cattle and himself from straying, visited me, and expressed a wish to live as I did. He told me, with the utmost simplicity and truth, quite superior, or rather *inferior*, to anything that is called humility, that he was "deficient in intellect." These were his words. The Lord had made him so, yet he supposed the Lord cared as much for him as for another. "I have always been so," said he, "from my childhood; I never had much mind; I was not like other children; I am weak in the head. It was the Lord's will, I suppose." And there he was to prove the truth of his words. He was a metaphysical puzzle to me. I have rarely met a fellowman on such promising ground, — it was so simple and sincere and so true all that he said. And, true enough, in proportion as he appeared to humble himself was he exalted. I did not know at first but it was the result of a wise policy. It seemed that from such a basis of truth and frankness as the poor weak-headed pauper had laid, our intercourse might go forward to something better than the intercourse of sages.

I had some guests from those not reckoned commonly among the town's poor, but who should be; who are among the world's poor, at any rate; guests who appeal, not to your hospitality, but to your *hospitalality;* who earnestly wish to be helped, and preface their appeal with the information that they are resolved, for one thing, never to help themselves. I require of a visitor that he be not actually starving, though he may have the very best appetite in the world, however he got it. Objects of charity are not guests. Men who did not know when their visit had terminated, though I went about my business again, answering them from greater and greater remoteness. Men of almost every degree of wit called on me in the migrating season. Some who had more wits than they knew what to do with; runaway slaves with plantation manners, who listened from time to time, like the fox in the fable, as if they heard the hounds a-baying on their track, and looked at me beseechingly, as much as to say, —

"O Christian, will you send me back?"

One real runaway slave, among the rest, whom I helped to forward toward the north-star. Men of one idea, like a hen with one chicken, and that a duckling; men of a thousand ideas, and unkempt heads, like those hens which are made to take charge of a hundred chickens, all in pursuit of one bug, a score of them lost in every morning's dew, — and become frizzled and mangy in consequence; men of ideas instead of legs, a sort of intellectual centipede that made you crawl all over. One man proposed a book in which visitors should write their names, as at the White Mountains; but, alas! I have too good a memory to make that necessary.

I could not but notice some of the peculiarities of my visitors. Girls and boys and young women generally seemed glad to be in the woods. They looked in the pond and at the flowers, and improved their time. Men of business, even farmers, thought only of solitude and employment, and of the great distance at which I dwelt from something or other; and though they said that they loved a ramble in the woods occasionally, it was obvious that they did not. Restless committed men, whose time was all taken up in getting a living or keeping it; ministers who spoke of God as if they enjoyed a monopoly of the subject, who could not bear all kinds of opinions; doctors, lawyers, uneasy housekeepers who pried into my cupboard and bed when I was out, —

how came Mrs. —— to know that my sheets were not as clean as hers? — young men who had ceased to be young, and had concluded that it was safest to follow the beaten track of the professions, — all these generally said that it was not possible to do so much good in my position. Ay! there was the rub. The old and infirm and the timid, of whatever age or sex, thought most of sickness, and sudden accident and death; to them life seemed full of danger, — what danger is there if you don't think of any? — and they thought that a prudent man would carefully select the safest position, where Dr. B. might be on hand at a moment's warning. To them the village was literally a *com-munity*, a league for mutual defence, and you would suppose that they would not go a-huckleberrying without a medicine chest. The amount of it is, if a man is alive, there is always *danger* that he may die, though the danger must be allowed to be less in proportion as he is dead-and-alive to begin with. A man sits as many risks as he runs. Finally, there were the self-styled reformers, the greatest bores of all, who thought that I was forever singing, —

> This is the house that I built;
> This is the man that lives in the house that I built;

but they did not know that the third line was, —

> These are the folks that worry the man
> That lives in the house that I built.

I did not fear the hen-harriers, for I kept no chickens; but I feared the men-harriers rather.

I had more cheering visitors than the last. Children come a-berrying, railroad men taking a Sunday morning walk in clean shirts, fishermen and hunters, poets and philosophers; in short, all honest pilgrims, who came out to the woods for freedom's sake, and really left the village behind, I was ready to greet with, — "Welcome, Englishmen! welcome, Englishmen!" for I had had communication with that race.

VII. THE BEAN-FIELD

MEANWHILE my beans, the length of whose rows, added together, was seven miles already planted, were impatient to be hoed, for the earliest had grown considerably before the latest were in the ground; indeed they were not easily to be put off. What was the meaning of this so steady and self-respecting, this small Herculean labor, I knew not. I came to love my rows, my beans, though so many more than I wanted. They attached me to the earth, and so I got strength like Antæus. But why should I raise them? Only Heaven knows. This was my curious labor all summer, — to make this portion of the earth's surface, which had yielded only cinquefoil, blackberries, johnswort, and the like, before, sweet wild fruits and pleasant flowers, produce instead this pulse. What shall I learn of beans or beans of me? I cherish them, I hoe them, early and late I have an eye to them; and this is my day's work. It is a fine broad leaf to look on. My auxiliaries are the dews and rains which water this dry soil, and what fertility is in the soil itself, which for the most part is lean and effete. My enemies are worms, cool days, and most of all woodchucks. The last have nibbled for me a quarter of an acre clean. But what right had I to oust johnswort and the rest, and break up their ancient herb garden? Soon, however, the remaining beans will be too tough for them, and go forward to meet new foes.

When I was four years old, as I well remember, I was brought from Boston to this my native town, through these very woods and this field, to the pond. It is one of the oldest scenes stamped on my memory. And now to-night my flute has waked the echoes over that very water. The pines still stand here older than I; or, if some have fallen, I have cooked my supper with their stumps, and a new growth is rising all around, preparing another aspect for new infant eyes. Almost the same johnswort springs from the same perennial root in this pasture, and even I have at length helped to clothe that fabulous landscape of my infant dreams, and one of the results of my presence and influence is seen in these bean leaves, corn blades, and potato vines.

I planted about two acres and a half of upland; and as it was only about fifteen years since the land was cleared, and I myself had got out two or three cords of stumps, I did not give it any manure; but in the

course of the summer it appeared by the arrow-heads which I turned
up in hoeing, that an extinct nation had anciently dwelt here and
planted corn and beans ere white men came to clear the land, and so,
to some extent, had exhausted the soil for this very crop.

Before yet any woodchuck or squirrel had run across the road, or
the sun had got above the shrub-oaks, while all the dew was on, though
the farmers warned me against it, — I would advise you to do all your
work if possible while the dew is on, — I began to level the ranks of
haughty weeds in my bean-field and throw dust upon their heads.
Early in the morning I worked barefooted, dabbling like a plastic artist
in the dewy and crumbling sand, but later in the day the sun blistered
my feet. There the sun lighted me to hoe beans, pacing slowly backward and forward over that yellow gravelly upland, between the long
green rows, fifteen rods, the one end terminating in a shrub oak copse
where I could rest in the shade, the other in a blackberry field where
the green berries deepened their tints by the time I had made another
bout. Removing the weeds, putting fresh soil about the bean stems,
and encouraging this weed which I had sown, making the yellow soil
express its summer thought in bean leaves and blossoms rather than
in wormwood and piper and millet grass, making the earth say beans
instead of grass, — this was my daily work. As I had little aid from
horses or cattle, or hired men or boys, or improved implements of husbandry, I was much slower, and became much more intimate with my
beans than usual. But labor of the hands, even when pursued to the
verge of drudgery, is perhaps never the worst form of idleness. It has
a constant and imperishable moral, and to the scholar it yields a classic
result. A very *agricola laboriosus* was I to travellers bound westward
through Lincoln and Wayland to nobody knows where; they sitting
at their ease in gigs, with elbows on knees, and reins loosely hanging in
festoons; I the home-staying, laborious native of the soil. But soon my
homestead was out of their sight and thought. It was the only open
and cultivated field for a great distance on either side of the road, so
they made the most of it; and sometimes the man in the field heard
more of travellers' gossip and comment than was meant for his ear:
"Beans so late! peas so late!" — for I continued to plant when others
had begun to hoe, — the ministerial husbandman had not suspected it.
"Corn, my boy, for fodder; corn for fodder." "Does he *live* there?"
asks the black bonnet of the gray coat; and the hard-featured farmer
reins up his grateful dobbin to inquire what you are doing where he
sees no manure in the furrow, and recommends a little chip dirt, or any

little waste stuff, or it may be ashes or plaster. But here were two acres and a half of furrows, and only a hoe for cart and two hands to draw it, — there being an aversion to other carts and horses, — and chip dirt far away. Fellow-travellers as they rattled by compared it aloud with the fields which they had passed, so that I came to know how I stood in the agricultural world. This was one field not in Mr. Coleman's report. And, by the way, who estimates the value of the crop which Nature yields in the still wilder fields unimproved by man? The crop of *English* hay is carefully weighed, the moisture calculated, the silicates and the potash; but in all dells and pond holes in the woods and pastures and swamps grows a rich and various crop only unreaped by man. Mine was, as it were, the connecting link between wild and cultivated fields; as some states are civilized, and others half-civilized, and others savage or barbarous, so my field was, though not in a bad sense, a half-cultivated field. They were beans cheerfully returning to their wild and primitive state that I cultivated, and my hoe played the *Ranz des Vaches* for them.

Near at hand, upon the topmost spray of a birch, sings the brown-thrasher — or red mavis, as some love to call him — all the morning, glad of your society, that would find out another farmer's field if yours were not here. While you are planting the seed, he cries, — "Drop it, drop it, — cover it up, cover it up, — pull it up, pull it up, pull it up." But this was not corn, and so it was safe from such enemies as he. You may wonder what his rigmarole, his amateur Paganini performances on one string or on twenty, have to do with your planting, and yet prefer it to leached ashes or plaster. It was a cheap sort of top dressing in which I had entire faith.

As I drew a still fresher soil about the rows with my hoe, I disturbed the ashes of unchronicled nations who in primeval years lived under these heavens, and their small implements of war and hunting were brought to the light of this modern day. They lay mingled with other natural stones, some of which bore the marks of having been burned by Indian fires, and some by the sun, and also bits of pottery and glass brought hither by the recent cultivators of the soil. When my hoe tinkled against the stones, that music echoed to the woods and the sky, and was an accompaniment to my labor which yielded an instant and immeasurable crop. It was no longer beans that I hoed, nor I that hoed beans; and I remembered with as much pity as pride, if I remembered at all, my acquaintances who had gone to the city to attend the oratorios. The night-hawk circled overhead in the sunny afternoons — for I sometimes made a day of it — like a mote in the eye, or in heaven's eye, falling from time to time with a swoop and a sound as if the heavens were rent, torn at last to very rags and tatters, and yet a seamless cope remained; small imps that fill the air and lay their eggs on the ground on bare sand or rocks on the tops of hills, where few have found them; graceful and slender like ripples caught up from the pond, as leaves are raised by the wind to float in the heavens; such kindredship is in Nature. The hawk is aerial brother of the wave which he sails over and surveys, those his perfect air-inflated wings answering to the elemental unfledged pinions of the sea. Or sometimes I watched a pair of hen-hawks circling high in the sky, alternately soaring and descending, approaching and leaving one another, as if they were the embodiment of my own thoughts. Or I was attracted by the passage of wild pigeons from this wood to that, with a slight quivering winnowing sound and carrier haste; or from under a rotten stump my hoe turned up a sluggish portentous and outlandish spotted salamander, a trace of Egypt and the Nile, yet our contemporary. When I paused to lean on my hoe, these sounds and sights I heard and saw anywhere in the row, a part of the inexhaustible entertainment which the country offers.

On gala days the town fires its great guns, which echo like popguns to these woods, and some waifs of martial music occasionally penetrate thus far. To me, away there in my bean-field at the other end of the town, the big guns sounded as if a puff ball had burst; and when there was a military turnout of which I was ignorant, I have sometimes had a vague sense all the day of some sort of itching and disease in the horizon, as if some eruption would break out there soon, either scarlatina or canker-rash, until at length some more favorable puff of wind, making haste over the fields and up the Wayland road, brought me information of the "trainers." It seemed by the distant hum as if somebody's bees had swarmed, and that the neighbors, according to Virgil's advice, by a faint *tintinnabulum* upon the most sonorous of their domestic utensils, were endeavoring to call them down into the hive again. And when the sound died quite away, and the hum had ceased, and the most favorable breezes told no tale, I knew that they had got the last drone of them all safely into the Middlesex hive, and that now their minds were bent on the honey with which it was smeared.

I felt proud to know that the liberties of Massachusetts and of our fatherland were in such safe keeping; and as I turned to my hoeing again I was filled with an inexpressible confidence, and pursued my labor cheerfully with a calm trust in the future.

When there were several bands of musicians, it sounded as if all the village was a vast bellows, and all the buildings expanded and collapsed alternately with a din. But sometimes it was a really noble and inspiring strain that reached these woods, and the trumpet that sings of fame, and I felt as if I could spit a Mexican with a good relish, — for why should we always stand for trifles? — and looked round for a woodchuck or a skunk to exercise my chivalry upon. These martial strains seemed as far away as Palestine, and reminded me of a march of crusaders in the horizon, with a slight tantivy and tremulous motion of the elm-tree tops which overhang the village. This was one of the *great* days; though the sky had from my clearing only the same everlastingly great look that it wears daily, and I saw no difference in it.

It was a singular experience that long acquaintance which I cultivated with beans, what with planting, and hoeing, and harvesting, and threshing, and picking over and selling them, — the last was the hardest of all, — I might add eating, for I did taste. I was determined to know beans. When they were growing, I used to hoe from five o'clock in the morning till noon, and commonly spent the rest of the day about other affairs. Consider the intimate and curious acquaintance one makes with various kinds of weeds, — it will bear some iteration in the account, for there was no little iteration in the labor, — disturbing their delicate organizations so ruthlessly, and making such invidious distinctions with his hoe, levelling whole ranks of one species, and sedulously cultivating another. That's Roman wormwood, — that's pigweed, — that's sorrel, — that's piper-grass, — have at him, chop him up, turn his roots upward to the sun, don't let him have a fibre in the shade, if you do he'll turn himself t'other side up and be as green as a leek in two days. A long war, not with cranes, but with weeds, those Trojans who had sun and rain and dews on their side. Daily the beans saw me come to their rescue armed with a hoe, and thin the ranks of their enemies, filling up the trenches with weedy dead. Many a lusty crest-waving Hector, that towered a whole foot above his crowding comrades, fell before my weapon and rolled in the dust.

Those summer days which some of my contemporaries devoted to the fine arts in Boston or Rome, and others to contemplation in India, and others to trade in London or New York, I thus, with the other farmers of New England, devoted to husbandry. Not that I wanted beans to eat, for I am by nature a Pythagorean, so far as beans are con-

cerned, whether they mean porridge or voting, and exchanged them
for rice; but, perchance, as some must work in fields if only for the
sake of tropes and expression, to serve a parable-maker one day. It
was on the whole a rare amusement, which, continued too long, might
have become a dissipation. Though I gave them no manure, and did
not hoe them all once, I hoed them unusually well as far as I went, and
was paid for it in the end, "there being in truth," as Evelyn says, "no
compost or lætation whatsoever comparable to this continual motion,
repastination, and turning of the mould with the spade." "The earth,"
he adds elsewhere, "especially if fresh, has a certain magnetism in it,
by which it attracts the salt, power, or virtue (call it either) which
gives it life, and is the logic of all the labor and stir we keep about it,
to sustain us; all dungings and other sordid temperings being but the
vicars succedaneous to this improvement." Moreover, this being one
of those "worn-out and exhausted lay fields which enjoy their sabbath," had perchance, as Sir Kenelm Digby thinks likely, attracted
"vital spirits" from the air. I harvested twelve bushels of beans.

But to be more particular, for it is complained that Mr. Coleman
has reported chiefly the expensive experiments of gentlemen farmers,
my outgoes were, —

For a hoe, ...	$0 54	
Ploughing, harrowing, and furrowing,	7 50	Too much.
Beans for seed, ...	3 12½	
Potatoes "	1 33	
Peas "	0 40	
Turnip seed, ...	0 06	
White line for crow fence, . . .	0 02	
Horse cultivator and boy three hours,	1 00	
Horse and cart to get crop, . . .	0 75	
In all, ...	$14 72½	

My income was, (patremfamilias vendacem, non emacem esse
oportet,) from

Nine bushels and twelve quarts of beans sold, . .	$16 94
Five " large potatoes, ...	2 50
Nine " small, ...	2 25
Grass, ...	1 00
Stalks, ...	0 75
In all, ...	$23 44

Leaving a pecuniary profit, as I have elsewhere said, of $8 71½.

This is the result of my experience in raising beans. Plant the common small white bush bean about the first of June, in rows three feet by eighteen inches apart, being careful to select fresh round and unmixed seed. First look out for worms, and supply vacancies by planting anew. Then look out for woodchucks, if it is an exposed place, for they will nibble off the earliest tender leaves almost clean as they go; and again, when the young tendrils make their appearance, they have notice of it, and will shear them off with both buds and young pods, sitting erect like a squirrel. But above all harvest as early as possible, if you would escape frosts and have a fair and salable crop; you may save much loss by this means.

This further experience also I gained. I said to myself, I will not plant beans and corn with so much industry another summer, but such seeds, if the seed is not lost, as sincerity, truth, simplicity, faith, innocence, and the like, and see if they will not grow in this soil, even with less toil and manurance, and sustain me, for surely it has not been exhausted for these crops.[1] Alas! I said this to myself; but now another summer is gone, and another, and another, and I am obliged to say to you, Reader, that the seeds which I planted, if indeed they *were* the seeds of those virtues, were wormeaten or had lost their vitality, and so did not come up. Commonly men will only be brave as their fathers were brave, or timid. This generation is very sure to plant corn and beans each new year precisely as the Indians did centuries ago and taught the first settlers to do, as if there were a fate in it. I saw an old man the other day, to my astonishment, making the holes with a hoe for the seventieth time at least, and not for himself to lie down in! But why should not the New Englander try new adventures, and not lay so much stress on his grain, his potato and grass crop, and his orchards, — raise other crops than these? Why concern ourselves so much about our beans for seed, and not be concerned at all about a new generation of men? We should really be fed and cheered if when we met a man we were sure to see that some of the qualities which I have named, which we all prize more than those other productions, but which are for the most part broadcast and floating in the air, had taken root and grown in him. Here comes such a subtile and ineffable quality, for instance, as truth or justice, though the slightest amount or new

[1] Thoreau wrote in the *Week:* "He who eats the fruit, should at least plant the seed; aye, if possible, a better seed than that whose fruit he has enjoyed. . . . Defray thy debt to the world; eat not the seeds of institutions, as the luxurious do, but plant it rather. . . ."

variety of it, along the road. Our ambassadors should be instructed to
send home such seeds as these, and Congress help to distribute them
over all the land. We should never stand upon ceremony with sincerity. We should never cheat and insult and banish one another by
our meanness, if there were present the kernel of worth and friendliness. We should not meet thus in haste. Most men I do not meet at
all, for they seem not to have time; they are busy about their beans.
We would not deal with a man thus plodding ever, leaning on a hoe or
a spade as a staff between his work, not as a mushroom, but partially
risen out of the earth, something more than erect, like swallows
alighted and walking on the ground: —

> "And as he spake, his wings would now and then
> Spread, as he meant to fly, then close again, —"

so that we should suspect that we might be conversing with an angel.
Bread may not always nourish us; but it always does us good, it even
takes stiffness out of our joints, and makes us supple and buoyant,
when we knew not what ailed us, to recognize any generosity in man
or Nature, to share any unmixed and heroic joy.

Ancient poetry and mythology suggest, at least, that husbandry was
once a sacred art; but it is pursued with irreverent haste and heedless-
ness by us, our object being to have large farms and large crops merely.
We have no festival, nor procession, nor ceremony, not excepting our
Cattle-shows and so called Thanksgivings, by which the farmer expresses a sense of the sacredness of his calling, or is reminded of its
sacred origin. It is the premium and the feast which tempt him. He
sacrifices not to Ceres and the Terrestrial Jove, but to the infernal
Plutus rather. By avarice and selfishness, and a grovelling habit, from
which none of us is free, of regarding the soil as property, or the means
of acquiring property chiefly, the landscape is deformed, husbandry is
degraded with us, and the farmer leads the meanest of lives. He knows
Nature but as a robber. Cato says that the profits of agriculture are
particularly pious or just, (*maximeque pius quæstus,*) and according to
Varro the old Romans "called the same earth Mother and Ceres, and
thought that they who cultivated it led a pious and useful life, and that
they alone were left of the race of King Saturn."

We are wont to forget that the sun looks on our cultivated fields and
on the prairies and forests without distinction. They all reflect and
absorb his rays alike, and the former make but a small part of the
glorious picture which he beholds in his daily course. In his view the

earth is all equally cultivated like a garden. Therefore we should receive the benefit of his light and heat with a corresponding trust and magnanimity. What though I value the seed of these beans, and harvest that in the fall of the year? This broad field which I have looked at so long looks not to me as the principal cultivator, but away from me to influences more genial to it, which water and make it green. These beans have results which are not harvested by me. Do they not grow for woodchucks partly? The ear of wheat, (in Latin *spica*, obsoletely *speca*, from *spe*, hope,) should not be the only hope of the husbandman; its kernel or grain (*granum*, from *gerendo*, bearing,) is not all that it bears. How, then, can our harvest fail? Shall I not rejoice also at the abundance of the weeds whose seeds are the granary of the birds? It matters little comparatively whether the fields fill the farmer's barns. The true husbandman will cease from anxiety, as the squirrels manifest no concern whether the woods will bear chestnuts this year or not, and finish his labor with every day, relinquishing all claim to the produce of his fields, and sacrificing in his mind not only his first but his last fruits also.

VIII. THE VILLAGE

AFTER hoeing, or perhaps reading and writing, in the forenoon, I usually bathed again in the pond, swimming across one of its coves for a stint, and washed the dust of labor from my person, or smoothed out the last wrinkle which study had made, and for the afternoon was absolutely free. Every day or two I strolled to the village to hear some of the gossip which is incessantly going on there, circulating either from mouth to mouth, or from newspaper to newspaper, and which, taken in homœopathic doses, was really as refreshing in its way as the rustle of leaves and the peeping of frogs. As I walked in the woods to see the birds and squirrels, so I walked in the village to see the men and boys; instead of the wind among the pines I heard the carts rattle. In one direction from my house there was a colony of musk-rats in the river meadows; under the grove of elms and buttonwoods in the other horizon was a village of busy men, as curious to me as if they had been prairie dogs, each sitting at the mouth of its burrow, or running out to a neighbor's to gossip. I went there frequently to observe their habits. The village appeared to me a great news room; and on one side, to support it, as once at Redding & Company's on State Street, they kept nuts and raisins, or salt and meal and other groceries. Some have such a vast appetite for the former commodity, that is, the news, and such sound digestive organs, that they can sit forever in public avenues without stirring, and let it simmer and whisper through them like the Etesian winds, or as if inhaling ether, it only producing numbness and insensibility to pain, — otherwise it would often be painful to hear, — without affecting the consciousness. I hardly ever failed, when I rambled through the village, to see a row of such worthies, either sitting on a ladder sunning themselves, with their bodies inclined forward and their eyes glancing along the line this way and that, from time to time, with a voluptuous expression, or else leaning against a barn with their hands in their pockets, like caryatides, as if to prop it up. They, being commonly out of doors, heard whatever was in the wind. These are the coarsest mills, in which all gossip is first rudely digested or cracked up before it is emptied into finer and more delicate hoppers within doors. I observed that the vitals of the village were the grocery, the bar-room, the post-office, and the bank; and, as a necessary part of the machinery, they kept a bell, a big gun, and a fire-engine, at convenient places; and the houses were so arranged as to make the most of mankind, in lanes and fronting one another, so that every traveller had to run the gauntlet, and every man, woman, and child might get a lick at him. Of course, those who were stationed nearest to the head of the line, where they could most see and be seen, and have the first blow at him, paid the highest prices for their places; and the few straggling inhabitants in the outskirts, where long gaps in the line began to occur, and the traveller could get over walls or turn aside into cow-paths, and so escape, paid a very slight ground or window tax. Signs were hung out on all sides to allure him; some to catch him by the appetite, as the tavern and victualling cellar; some by the fancy, as the dry goods store and the jeweller's; and others by the hair or the feet or the skirts, as the barber, the shoemaker, or the tailor. Besides, there was a still more terrible standing invitation to call at every one of these houses, and company expected about these times. For the most part I escaped wonderfully from these dangers, either by proceeding at once boldly and without deliberation to the goal, as is recommended to those who run the gauntlet, or by keeping my thoughts on high things, like Orpheus, who, "loudly singing the praises of the gods to his lyre, drowned the voices of the Sirens, and kept out of danger." Sometimes I bolted suddenly, and nobody could tell my whereabouts, for I did not stand much about gracefulness, and never hesitated at a gap in a fence. I was even accustomed to make an irruption into some houses, where I was well entertained, and after learning the kernels and very last sieve-ful of news, what had subsided, the prospects of war and peace, and whether the world was likely to hold together much longer, I was let out through the rear avenues, and so escaped to the woods again.

It was very pleasant, when I stayed late in town, to launch myself into the night, especially if it was dark and tempestuous, and set sail from some bright village parlor or lecture room, with a bag of rye or Indian meal upon my shoulder, for my snug harbor in the woods, having made all tight without and withdrawn under hatches with a merry crew of thoughts, leaving only my outer man at the helm, or even tying up the helm when it was plain sailing. I had many a genial thought by the cabin fire "as I sailed." I was never cast away nor distressed in any weather, though I encountered some severe storms. It is darker in the woods, even in common nights, than most suppose. I frequently had to look up at the opening between the trees above the path in order to learn my route, and, where there was no cart-path, to feel with my feet the faint track which I had worn, or steer by the known relation of particular trees which I felt with my hands, passing between two pines for instance, not more than eighteen inches apart, in the midst of the woods, invariably in the darkest night. Sometimes, after coming home thus late in a dark and muggy night, when my feet felt the path which my eyes could not see, dreaming and absent-minded all the way, until I was aroused by having to raise my hand to lift the latch, I have not been able to recall a single step of my walk, and I have thought that perhaps my body would find its way home if its master should forsake it, as the hand finds its way to the mouth without assistance. Several times, when a visitor chanced to stay into evening, and it proved a dark night, I was obliged to conduct him to the cart-path in the rear of the house, and then point out to him the direction he was to pursue, and in keeping which he was to be guided rather by his feet than his eyes. One very dark night I directed thus on their way two young men who had been fishing in the pond. They lived about a mile off through the woods, and were quite used to the route. A day or two after one of them told me that they wandered about the greater part of the night, close by their own premises, and did not get home till toward morning, by which time, as there had been several heavy showers in the mean while, and the leaves were very wet, they were drenched to their skins. I have heard of many going astray even in the village streets, when the darkness was so thick that you could cut it with a knife, as the saying is. Some who live in the outskirts, having come to town a-shopping in their wagons, have been obliged to put up for the night; and gentlemen and ladies making a call have gone half a mile out of their way, feeling the sidewalk only with their feet, and not knowing when they turned. It is a surprising and memorable, as well as valuable experience, to be lost in the woods any time. Often in a snow storm, even by day, one will come out upon a well-known road and yet find it impossible to tell which way leads to the village. Though he knows that he has travelled it a thousand times, he cannot recognize a feature in it, but it is as strange to him as if it were a road in Siberia. By night, of course, the perplexity is infinitely greater. In our most trivial walks, we are constantly, though unconsciously, steering like pilots by certain well-known beacons and headlands, and if we go beyond our usual course we still carry in our minds the bearing of some neighboring cape; and not till we are completely lost, or turned round, — for a man needs only to be turned round once with his eyes shut in this world to be lost, — do we appreciate the vastness and strangeness of Nature. Every man has to learn the points of compass again as often as he awakes, whether from sleep or any abstraction. Not till we are lost, in other words, not till we have lost the world, do we begin to find ourselves, and realize where we are and the infinite extent of our relations.

One afternoon, near the end of the first summer, when I went to the village to get a shoe from the cobbler's, I was seized and put into jail, because, as I have elsewhere related,[1] I did not pay a tax to, or recognize the authority of, the state which buys and sells men, women, and children, like cattle at the door of its senate-house. I had gone down to the woods for other purposes. But, wherever a man goes, men will pursue and paw him with their dirty institutions, and, if they can, constrain him to belong to their desperate odd-fellow society. It is true, I might have resisted forcibly with more or less effect, might have run "amok" against society; but I preferred that society should run "amok" against me, it being the desperate party. However, I was re-

[1] "Civil Disobedience." In the *Week*, he also discussed the issue by relating the significant passages of the *Antigone*.

leased the next day, obtained my mended shoe, and returned to the woods in season to get my dinner of huckleberries on Fair Haven Hill. I was never molested by any person but those who represented the state. I had no lock nor bolt but for the desk which held my papers, not even a nail to put over my latch or windows. I never fastened my door night or day, though I was to be absent several days; not even when the next fall I spent a fortnight in the woods of Maine. And yet my house was more respected than if it had been surrounded by a file of soldiers. The tired rambler could rest and warm himself by my fire, the literary amuse himself with the few books on my table, or the curious, by opening my closet door, see what was left of my dinner, and what prospect I had of a supper. Yet, though many people of every class came this way to the pond, I suffered no serious inconvenience from these sources, and I never missed anything but one small book, a volume of Homer, which perhaps was improperly gilded, and this I trust a soldier of our camp has found by this time. I am convinced, that if all men were to live as simply as I then did, thieving and robbery would be unknown. These take place only in communities where some have got more than is sufficient while others have not enough. The Pope's Homers would soon get properly distributed —

> "Nec bella fuerunt,
> Faginus astabat dum scyphus ante dapes."
> "Nor wars did men molest,
> When only beechen bowls were in request."

"You who govern public affairs, what need have you to employ punishments? Love virtue, and the people will be virtuous. The virtues of a superior man are like the wind; the virtues of a common man are like the grass; the grass, when the wind passes over it, bends."

IX. THE PONDS

Sometimes, having had a surfeit of human society and gossip, and worn out all my village friends, I rambled still farther westward than I habitually dwell, into yet more unfrequented parts of the town, "to fresh woods and pastures new," or, while the sun was setting, made my supper of huckleberries and blueberries on Fair Haven Hill, and laid up a store for several days. The fruits do not yield their true flavor to the purchaser of them, nor to him who raises them for the market. There is but one way to obtain it, yet few take that way. If you would know the flavor of huckleberries, ask the cow-boy or the partridge. It is a vulgar error to suppose that you have tasted huckleberries who never plucked them. A huckleberry never reaches Boston; they have not been known there since they grew on her three hills. The ambrosial and essential part of the fruit is lost with the bloom which is rubbed off in the market cart, and they become mere provender. As long as Eternal Justice reigns, not one innocent huckleberry can be transported thither from the country's hills.

Occasionally, after my hoeing was done for the day, I joined some impatient companion who had been fishing on the pond since morning, as silent and motionless as a duck or a floating leaf, and, after practising various kinds of philosophy, had concluded commonly, by the time I arrived, that he belonged to the ancient sect of Cœnobites. There was one older man, an excellent fisher and skilled in all kinds of woodcraft, who was pleased to look upon my house as a building erected for the convenience of fishermen; and I was equally pleased when he sat in my doorway to arrange his lines. Once in a while we sat together on the pond, he at one end of the boat, and I at the other; but not many words passed between us, for he had grown deaf in his later years, but he occasionally hummed a psalm, which harmonized well enough with my philosophy. Our intercourse was thus altogether one of unbroken harmony, far more pleasing to remember than if it had been carried on by speech. When, as was commonly the case, I had none to commune with, I used to raise the echoes by striking with a paddle on the side of my boat, filling the surrounding woods with circling and dilating sound, stirring them up as the keeper of a menagerie his wild beasts, until I elicited a growl from every wooded vale and hill-side.

In warm evenings I frequently sat in the boat playing the flute, and saw the perch, which I seem to have charmed, hovering around me, and the moon travelling over the ribbed bottom, which was strewed with the wrecks of the forest. Formerly I had come to this pond adventurously, from time to time, in dark summer nights, with a companion, and making a fire close to the water's edge, which we thought attracted the fishes, we caught pouts with a bunch of worms strung on a thread, and when we had done, far in the night, threw the burning brands high into the air like skyrockets, which, coming down into the pond, were quenched with a loud hissing, and we were suddenly groping in total darkness. Through this, whistling a tune, we took our way to the haunts of men again. But now I had made my home by the shore.

Sometimes, after staying in a village parlor till the family had all retired, I have returned to the woods, and, partly with a view to the next day's dinner, spent the hours of midnight fishing from a boat by moonlight, serenaded by owls and foxes, and hearing, from time to time, the creaking note of some unknown bird close at hand. These experiences were very memorable and valuable to me, — anchored in forty feet of water, and twenty or thirty rods from the shore, surrounded sometimes by thousands of small perch and shiners, dimpling the surface with their tails in the moonlight, and communicating by a long flaxen line with mysterious nocturnal fishes which had their dwelling forty feet below, or sometimes dragging sixty feet of line about the pond as I drifted in the gentle night breeze, now and then feeling a slight vibration along it, indicative of some life prowling about its extremity, of dull uncertain blundering purpose there, and slow to make up its mind. At length you slowly raise, pulling hand over hand, some horned pout squeaking and squirming to the upper air. It was very queer, especially in dark nights, when your thoughts had wandered to vast and cosmogonal themes in other spheres, to feel this faint jerk, which came to interrupt your dreams and link you to Nature again. It seemed as if I might next cast my line upward into the air, as well as downward into this element, which was scarcely more dense. Thus I caught two fishes as it were with one hook.

The scenery of Walden is on a humble scale, and, though very beautiful, does not approach to grandeur, nor can it much concern one who has not long frequented it or lived by its shore; yet this pond is so remarkable for its depth and purity as to merit a particular description. It is a clear and deep green well, half a mile long and a mile and three quarters in circumference, and contains about sixty-one and a half acres; a perennial spring in the midst of pine and oak woods, without any visible inlet or outlet except by the clouds and evaporation. The surrounding hills rise abruptly from the water to the height of forty to eighty feet, though on the south-east and east they attain to about one hundred and one hundred and fifty feet respectively, within a quarter and a third of a mile. They are exclusively woodland. All our Concord waters have two colors at least; one when viewed at a distance, and another, more proper, close at hand. The first depends more on the light, and follows the sky. In clear weather, in summer, they appear blue at a little distance, especially if agitated, and at a great distance all appear alike. In stormy weather they are sometimes of a dark slate color. The sea, however, is said to be blue one day and green another without any perceptible change in the atmosphere. I have seen our river, when, the landscape being covered with snow, both water and ice were almost as green as grass. Some consider blue "to be the color of pure water, whether liquid or solid." But, looking directly down into our waters from a boat, they are seen to be of very different colors. Walden is blue at one time and green at another, even from the same point of view. Lying between the earth and the heavens, it partakes of the color of both. Viewed from a hill-top it reflects the color of the sky; but near at hand it is of a yellowish tint next the shore where you can see the sand, then a light green, which gradually deepens to a uniform dark green in the body of the pond. In some lights, viewed even from a hill-top, it is of a vivid green next the shore. Some have referred this to the reflection of the verdure; but it is equally green there against the railroad sand-bank, and in the spring, before the leaves are expanded, and it may be simply the result of the prevailing blue mixed with the yellow of the sand. Such is the color of its iris. This is that portion, also, where in the spring, the ice being warmed by the heat of the sun reflected from the bottom, and also transmitted through the earth, melts first and forms a narrow canal about the still frozen middle. Like the rest of our waters, when much agitated, in clear weather, so that the surface of the waves may reflect the sky at the right angle, or because there is more light mixed with it, it appears at a little distance of a darker blue than the sky itself; and at such a time, being on its surface, and looking with divided vision, so as to see the reflection, I have discerned a matchless and indescribable light blue, such as watered or changeable silks and sword blades suggest, more cerulean than the sky itself, alternating with the original dark green on the opposite sides of the waves, which last appeared but muddy in comparison. It is a vitreous greenish blue, as I remember it, like those patches of the winter sky seen through cloud vistas in the west before sundown. Yet a single glass of its water held up to the light is as colorless as an equal quantity of air. It is well known that a large plate of glass will have a green tint, owing, as the makers say, to its "body," but a small piece of the same will be colorless. How large

a body of Walden water would be required to reflect a green tint I
have never proved. The water of our river is black or a very dark
brown to one looking directly down on it, and, like that of most ponds,
imparts to the body of one bathing in it a yellowish tinge; but this
water is of such crystalline purity that the body of the bather appears
of an alabaster whiteness, still more unnatural, which, as the limbs are
magnified and distorted withal, produces a monstrous effect, making
fit studies for a Michael Angelo.

The water is so transparent that the bottom can easily be discerned
at the depth of twenty-five or thirty feet. Paddling over it, you may
see many feet beneath the surface the schools of perch and shiners,
perhaps only an inch long, yet the former easily distinguished by their
transverse bars, and you think that they must be ascetic fish that find a
subsistence there. Once, in the winter, many years ago, when I had
been cutting holes through the ice in order to catch pickerel, as I
stepped ashore I tossed my axe back on to the ice, but, as if some evil
genius had directed it, it slid four or five rods directly into one of the
holes, where the water was twenty-five feet deep. Out of curiosity,
I lay down on the ice and looked through the hole, until I saw the axe
a little on one side, standing on its head, with its helve erect and gently
swaying to and fro with the pulse of the pond; and there it might have
stood erect and swaying till in the course of time the handle rotted off,
if I had not disturbed it. Making another hole directly over it with
an ice chisel which I had, and cutting down the longest birch which I
could find in the neighborhood with my knife, I made a slip-noose,
which I attached to its end, and, letting it down carefully, passed it
over the knob of the handle, and drew it by a line along the birch, and
so pulled the axe out again.

The shore is composed of a belt of smooth rounded white stones
like paving-stones, excepting one or two short sand beaches, and is so
steep that in many places a single leap will carry you into water over
your head; and were it not for its remarkable transparency, that would
be the last to be seen of its bottom till it rose on the opposite side.
Some think it is bottomless. It is nowhere muddy, and a casual observer would say that there were no weeds at all in it; and of noticeable plants, except in the little meadows recently overflowed, which
do not properly belong to it, a closer scrutiny does not detect a flag nor
a bulrush, nor even a lily, yellow or white, but only a few small heart-
leaves and potamogetons, and perhaps a water-target or two; all which
however a bather might not perceive; and these plants are clean and

bright like the element they grow in.   The stones extend a rod or two
into the water, and then the bottom is pure sand, except in the deepest
parts, where there is usually a little sediment, probably from the decay
of the leaves which have been wafted on to it so many successive falls,
and a bright green weed is brought up on anchors even in midwinter.

We have one other pond just like this, White Pond, in Nine Acre
Corner, about two and a half miles westerly; but, though I am acquainted with most of the ponds within a dozen miles of this centre, I
do not know a third of this pure and well-like character.   Successive
nations perchance have drank at, admired, and fathomed it, and passed
away, and still its water is green and pellucid as ever.   Not an inter-
mitting spring!   Perhaps on that spring morning when Adam and Eve
were driven out of Eden Walden Pond was already in existence, and
even then breaking up in a gentle spring rain accompanied with mist
and a southerly wind, and covered with myriads of ducks and geese,
which had not heard of the fall, when still such pure lakes sufficed
them.   Even then it had commenced to rise and fall, and had clarified
its waters and colored them of the hue they now wear, and obtained a
patent of Heaven to be the only Walden Pond in the world and distiller
of celestial dews.   Who knows in how many unremembered nations'
literatures this has been the Castalian Fountain? or what nymphs presided over it in the Golden Age?   It is a gem of the first water which
Concord wears in her coronet.

Yet perchance the first who came to this well have left some trace of
their footsteps.   I have been surprised to detect encircling the pond,
even where a thick wood has just been cut down on the shore, a narrow
shelf-like path in the steep hill-side, alternately rising and falling,
approaching and receding from the water's edge, as old probably as
the race of man here, worn by the feet of aboriginal hunters, and still
from time to time unwittingly trodden by the present occupants of the
land.   This is particularly distinct to one standing on the middle of the
pond in winter, just after a light snow has fallen, appearing as a clear
undulating white line, unobscured by weeds and twigs, and very obvious a quarter of a mile off in many places where in summer it is hardly
distinguishable close at hand.   The snow reprints it, as it were, in
clear white type alto-relievo.   The ornamented grounds of villas which
will one day be built here may still preserve some trace of this.

The pond rises and falls, but whether regularly or not, and within
what period, nobody knows, though, as usual, many pretend to know.
It is commonly higher in the winter and lower in the summer, though

not corresponding to the general wet and dryness. I can remember when it was a foot or two lower, and also when it was at least five feet higher, than when I lived by it. There is a narrow sand-bar running into it, with very deep water on one side, on which I helped boil a kettle of chowder, some six rods from the main shore, about the year 1824, which it has not been possible to do for twenty-five years; and, on the other hand, my friends used to listen with incredulity when I told them, that a few years later I was accustomed to fish from a boat in a secluded cove in the woods, fifteen rods from the only shore they knew, which place was long since converted into a meadow. But the pond has risen steadily for two years, and now, in the summer of '52, is just five feet higher than when I lived there, or as high as it was thirty years ago, and fishing goes on again in the meadow. This makes a difference of level, at the outside, of six or seven feet; and yet the water shed by the surrounding hills is insignificant in amount, and this overflow must be referred to causes which affect the deep springs. This same summer the pond has begun to fall again. It is remarkable that this fluctuation, whether periodical or not, appears thus to require many years for its accomplishment. I have observed one rise and a part of two falls, and I expect that a dozen or fifteen years hence the water will again be as low as I have ever known it. Flints' Pond, a mile eastward, allowing for the disturbance occasioned by its inlets and outlets, and the smaller intermediate ponds also, sympathize with Walden, and recently attained their greatest height at the same time with the latter. The same is true, as far as my observation goes, of White Pond.

This rise and fall of Walden at long intervals serves this use at least; the water standing at this great height for a year or more, though it makes it difficult to walk round it, kills the shrubs and trees which have sprung up about its edge since the last rise, — pitch-pines, birches, alders, aspens, and others, — and, falling again, leaves an unobstructed shore; for, unlike many ponds and all waters which are subject to a daily tide, its shore is cleanest when the water is lowest. On the side of the pond next my house a row of pitch-pines, fifteen feet high, has been killed and tipped over as if by a lever, and thus a stop put to their encroachments; and their size indicates how many years have elapsed since the last rise to this height. By this fluctuation the pond asserts its title to a shore, and thus the *shore* is *shorn*, and the trees cannot hold it by right of possession. These are the lips of the lake on which no beard grows. It licks its chaps from time to time. When the water is at its height, the alders, willows, and maples send forth a mass of fibrous red roots several feet long from all sides of their stems in the water, and to the height of three or four feet from the ground, in the effort to maintain themselves; and I have known the high-blueberry bushes about the shore, which commonly produce no fruit, bear an abundant crop under these circumstances.

Some have been puzzled to tell how the shore became so regularly paved. My townsmen have all heard the tradition, the oldest people tell me that they heard it in their youth, that anciently the Indians were holding a pow-wow upon a hill here, which rose as high into the heavens as the pond now sinks deep into the earth, and they used much profanity, as the story goes, though this vice is one of which the Indians were never guilty, and while they were thus engaged the hill shook and suddenly sank, and only one old squaw, named Walden, escaped, and from her the pond was named. It has been conjectured that when the hill shook these stones rolled down its side and became the present shore. It is very certain, at any rate, that once there was no pond here, and now there is one; and this Indian fable does not in any respect conflict with the account of that ancient settler whom I have mentioned, who remembers so well when he first came here with his divining rod, saw a thin vapor rising from the sward, and the hazel pointed steadily downward, and he concluded to dig a well here. As for the stones, many still think that they are hardly to be accounted for by the action of the waves on these hills; but I observe that the surrounding hills are remarkably full of the same kind of stones, so that they have been obliged to pile them up in walls on both sides of the railroad cut nearest the pond; and, moreover, there are most stones where the shore is most abrupt; so that, unfortunately, it is no longer a mystery to me. I detect the paver. If the name was not derived from that of some English locality, — Saffron Walden, for instance, — one might suppose that it was called originally *Walled-in* Pond.

The pond was my well ready dug. For four months in the year its water is as cold as it is pure at all times; and I think that it is then as good as any, if not the best, in the town. In the winter, all water which is exposed to the air is colder than springs and wells which are protected from it. The temperature of the pond water which had stood in the room where I sat from five o'clock in the afternoon till noon the next day, the sixth of March, 1846, the thermometer having been up to 65° or 70° some of the time, owing partly to the sun on the roof, was 42°, or one degree colder than the water of one of the coldest wells in the village just drawn. The temperature of the Boiling Spring the same day was 45°, or the warmest of any water tried, though it is the coldest that I know of in summer, when, beside, shallow and stagnant surface water is not mingled with it. Moreover, in summer, Walden never becomes so warm as most water which is exposed to the sun, on account of its depth. In the warmest weather I usually placed a pailful in my cellar, where it became cool in the night, and remained so during the day; though I also resorted to a spring in the neighborhood. It was as good when a week old as the day it was dipped, and had no taste of the pump. Whoever camps for a week in summer by the shore of a pond, needs only bury a pail of water a few feet deep in the shade of his camp to be independent of the luxury of ice.

There have been caught in Walden pickerel, one weighing seven pounds, — to say nothing of another which carried off a reel with great velocity, which the fisherman safely set down at eight pounds because he did not see him, — perch and pouts, some of each weighing over two pounds, shiners, chivins or roach, (*Leuciscus pulchellus*,) a very few breams, and a couple of eels, one weighing four pounds, — I am thus particular because the weight of a fish is commonly its only title to fame, and these are the only eels I have heard of here; — also, I have a faint recollection of a little fish some five inches long, with silvery sides and a greenish back, somewhat dace-like in its character, which I mention here chiefly to link my facts to fable. Nevertheless, this pond is not very fertile in fish. Its pickerel, though not abundant, are its chief boast. I have seen at one time lying on the ice pickerel of at least three different kinds: a long and shallow one, steel-colored, most like those caught in the river; a bright golden kind, with greenish reflections and remarkably deep, which is the most common here; and another, golden-colored, and shaped like the last, but peppered on the sides with small dark brown or black spots, intermixed with a few faint blood-red ones, very much like a trout. The specific name *reticulatus* would not apply to this; it should be *guttatus* rather. These are all very firm fish, and weigh more than their size promises. The shiners, pouts, and perch also, and indeed all the fishes which inhabit this pond, are much cleaner, handsomer, and firmer fleshed than those in the river and most other ponds, as the water is purer, and they can easily be distinguished from them. Probably many ichthyologists would make new varieties of some of them. There are also a clean race of frogs and tortoises, and a few muscles in it; muskrats and minks leave their traces about it, and occasionally a travelling mud-turtle visits it. Sometimes, when I pushed off my boat in the morning, I disturbed a great mud-turtle which had secreted himself under the boat in the night. Ducks and geese frequent it in the spring and fall, the white-bellied swallows (*Hirundo bicolor*) skim over it, and the peet-weets (*Totanus macularius*) "teter" along its stony shores all summer. I have sometimes disturbed a fish-hawk sitting on a white-pine over the water; but I doubt if it is ever profaned by the wing of a gull, like Fair Haven. At most, it tolerates one annual loon. These are all the animals of consequence which frequent it now.

You may see from a boat, in calm weather, near the sandy eastern shore, where the water is eight or ten feet deep, and also in some other parts of the pond, some circular heaps half a dozen feet in diameter by a foot in height, consisting of small stones less than a hen's egg in size, where all around is bare sand. At first you wonder if the Indians could have formed them on the ice for any purpose, and so, when the ice melted, they sank to the bottom; but they are too regular and some of them plainly too fresh for that. They are similar to those found in rivers; but as there are no suckers nor lampreys here, I know not by what fish they could be made. Perhaps they are the nests of the chivin. These lend a pleasing mystery to the bottom.

The shore is irregular enough not to be monotonous. I have in my mind's eye the western indented with deep bays, the bolder northern, and the beautifully scolloped southern shore, where successive capes overlap each other and suggest unexplored coves between. The forest has never so good a setting, nor is so distinctly beautiful, as when seen from the middle of a small lake amid hills which rise from the water's edge; for the water in which it is reflected not only makes the best foreground in such a case, but, with its winding shore, the most natural and agreeable boundary to it. There is no rawness nor imperfection in its edge there, as where the axe has cleared a part, or a cultivated field abuts on it. The trees have ample room to expand on the water side, and each sends forth its most vigorous branch in that direction. There Nature has woven a natural selvage, and the eye rises by just gradations from the low shrubs of the shore to the highest trees. There are few traces of man's hand to be seen. The water laves the shore as it did a thousand years ago.

A lake is the landscape's most beautiful and expressive feature. It is earth's eye; looking into which the beholder measures the depth of his own nature. The fluviatile trees next the shore are the slender eyelashes which fringe it, and the wooded hills and cliffs around are its overhanging brows.

Standing on the smooth sandy beach at the east end of the pond, in a calm September afternoon, when a slight haze makes the opposite shore line indistinct, I have seen whence came the expression, "the glassy surface of a lake." When you invert your head, it looks like a thread of finest gossamer stretched across the valley, and gleaming against the distant pine woods, separating one stratum of the atmosphere from another. You would think that you could walk dry under it to the opposite hills, and that the swallows which skim over might perch on it. Indeed, they sometimes dive below the line, as it were by mistake, and are undeceived. As you look over the pond westward you are obliged to employ both your hands to defend your eyes against the reflected as well as the true sun, for they are equally bright; and if, between the two, you survey its surface critically, it is literally as smooth as glass, except where the skater insects, at equal intervals scattered over its whole extent, by their motions in the sun produce the finest imaginable sparkle on it, or, perchance, a duck plumes itself, or, as I have said, a swallow skims so low as to touch it. It may be that in the distance a fish describes an arc of three or four feet in the air, and there is one bright flash where it emerges, and another where it strikes the water; sometimes the whole silvery arc is revealed; or here and there, perhaps, is a thistle-down floating on its surface, which the fishes dart at and so dimple it again. It is like molten glass cooled but not congealed, and the few motes in it are pure and beautiful like the imperfections in glass. You may often detect a yet smoother and darker water, separated from the rest as if by an invisible cobweb, boom of the water nymphs, resting on it. From a hill-top you can see a fish leap in almost any part; for not a pickerel or shiner picks an insect from this smooth surface but it manifestly disturbs the equilibrium of the whole lake. It is wonderful with what elaborateness this simple fact is advertised, — this piscine murder will out, — and from my distant perch I distinguish the circling undulations when they are half a dozen rods in diameter. You can even detect a water-bug (*Gyrinus*) ceaselessly progressing over the smooth surface a quarter of a mile off; for they furrow the water slightly, making a conspicuous ripple bounded by two diverging lines, but the skaters glide over it without rippling it perceptibly. When the surface is considerably agitated there are no skaters nor water-bugs on it, but apparently, in calm days, they leave their havens and adventurously glide forth from the shore by short impulses till they completely cover it. It is a soothing employment, on one of those fine days in the fall when all the warmth of the sun is fully appreciated, to sit on a stump on such a height as this, overlooking the pond, and study the dimpling circles which are incessantly inscribed on its otherwise invisible surface amid the reflected skies and trees. Over this great expanse there is no disturbance but it is thus at once gently smoothed away and assuaged, as, when a vase of water is jarred, the trembling circles seek the shore and all is smooth again. Not a fish can leap or an insect fall on the pond but it is thus reported in circling dimples, in lines of beauty, as it were the constant welling up of its fountain, the gentle pulsing of its life, the heaving of its breast. The thrills of joy and thrills of pain are undistinguishable. How peaceful the phenomena of the lake! Again the works of man shine as in the spring. Ay, every leaf and twig and stone and cobweb sparkles now at mid-afternoon as when covered with dew in a spring morning. Every motion of an oar or an insect produces a flash of light; and if an oar falls, how sweet the echo!

In such a day, in September or October, Walden is a perfect forest mirror, set round with stones as precious to my eye as if fewer or rarer. Nothing so fair, so pure, and at the same time so large, as a lake, perchance, lies on the surface of the earth. Sky water. It needs no fence. Nations come and go without defiling it. It is a mirror which no stone can crack, whose quicksilver will never wear off, whose gilding Nature continually repairs; no storms, no dust, can dim its surface ever fresh; — a mirror in which all impurity presented to it sinks, swept and dusted by the sun's hazy brush, — this the light dust-cloth, — which retains no breath that is breathed on it, but sends its own to float as clouds high above its surface, and be reflected in its bosom still.

A field of water betrays the spirit that is in the air. It is continually receiving new life and motion from above. It is intermediate in its nature between land and sky. On land only the grass and trees wave, but the water itself is rippled by the wind. I see where the breeze dashes across it by the streaks or flakes of light. It is remarkable that we can look down on its surface. We shall, perhaps, look down thus on the surface of air at length, and mark where a still subtler spirit sweeps over it.

The skaters and water-bugs finally disappear in the latter part of October, when the severe frosts have come; and then and in November, usually, in a calm day, there is absolutely nothing to ripple the surface. One November afternoon, in the calm at the end of a rain storm of several days' duration, when the sky was still completely

overcast and the air was full of mist, I observed that the pond was remarkably smooth, so that it was difficult to distinguish its surface;
though it no longer reflected the bright tints of October, but the sombre November colors of the surrounding hills. Though I passed over
it as gently as possible, the slight undulations produced by my boat
extended almost as far as I could see, and gave a ribbed appearance to
the reflections. But, as I was looking over the surface, I saw here and
there at a distance a faint glimmer, as if some skater insects which had
escaped the frosts might be collected there, or, perchance, the surface,
being so smooth, betrayed where a spring welled up from the bottom.
Paddling gently to one of these places, I was surprised to find myself
surrounded by myriads of small perch, about five inches long, of a rich
bronze color in the green water, sporting there, and constantly rising
to the surface and dimpling it, sometimes leaving bubbles on it. In
such transparent and seemingly bottomless water, reflecting the
clouds, I seemed to be floating through the air as in a balloon, and their
swimming impressed me as a kind of flight or hovering, as if they were
a compact flock of birds passing just beneath my level on the right or
left, their fins, like sails, set all around them. There were many such
schools in the pond, apparently improving the short season before
winter would draw an icy shutter over their broad skylight, sometimes
giving to the surface an appearance as if a slight breeze struck it, or a
few rain-drops fell there. When I approached carelessly and alarmed
them, they made a sudden plash and rippling with their tails, as if one
had struck the water with a brushy bough, and instantly took refuge in
the depths. At length the wind rose, the mist increased, and the waves
began to run, and the perch leaped much higher than before, half out of
water, a hundred black points, three inches long, at once above the
surface. Even as late as the fifth of December, one year, I saw some
dimples on the surface, and thinking it was going to rain hard immediately, the air being full of mist, I made haste to take my place at the
oars and row homeward; already the rain seemed rapidly increasing,
though I felt none on my cheek, and I anticipated a thorough soaking.
But suddenly the dimples ceased, for they were produced by the perch,
which the noise of my oars had scared into the depths, and I saw their
schools dimly disappearing; so I spent a dry afternoon after all.

An old man who used to frequent this pond nearly sixty years ago,
when it was dark with surrounding forests, tells me that in those days
he sometimes saw it all alive with ducks and other water fowl, and that
there were many eagles about it. He came here a-fishing, and used an
old log canoe which he found on the shore. It was made of two white-

pine logs dug out and pinned together, and was cut off square at the ends. It was very clumsy, but lasted a great many years before it became water-logged and perhaps sank to the bottom. He did not know whose it was; it belonged to the pond. He used to make a cable for his anchor of strips of hickory bark tied together. An old man, a potter, who lived by the pond before the Revolution, told him once that there was an iron chest at the bottom, and that he had seen it. Sometimes it would come floating up to the shore; but when you went toward it, it would go back into deep water and disappear. I was pleased to hear of the old log canoe, which took the place of an Indian one of the same material but more graceful construction, which perchance had first been a tree on the bank, and then, as it were, fell into the water, to float there for a generation, the most proper vessel for the lake. I remember that when I first looked into these depths there were many large trunks to be seen indistinctly lying on the bottom, which had either been blown over formerly, or left on the ice at the last cutting, when wood was cheaper; but now they have mostly disappeared.

When I first paddled a boat on Walden, it was completely surrounded by thick and lofty pine and oak woods, and in some of its coves grape-vines had run over the trees next the water and formed bowers under which a boat could pass. The hills which form its shores are so steep, and the woods on them were then so high, that, as you looked down from the west end, it had the appearance of an amphitheatre for some kind of sylvan spectacle. I have spent many an hour, when I was younger, floating over its surface as the zephyr willed, having paddled my boat to the middle, and lying on my back across the seats, in a summer forenoon, dreaming awake, until I was aroused by the boat touching the sand, and I arose to see what shore my fates had impelled me to; days when idleness was the most attractive and productive industry. Many a forenoon have I stolen away, preferring to spend thus the most valued part of the day; for I was rich, if not in money, in sunny hours and summer days, and spent them lavishly; not do I regret that I did not waste more of them in the workshop or the teacher's desk. But since I left those shores the woodchoppers have still further laid them waste, and now for many a year there will be no more rambling through the aisles of the wood, with occasional vistas through which you see the water. My Muse may be excused if she is silent henceforth. How can you expect the birds to sing when their groves are cut down?

Now the trunks of trees on the bottom, and the old log canoe, and the dark surrounding woods, are gone, and the villagers, who scarcely know where it lies, instead of going to the pond to bathe or drink, are thinking to bring its water, which should be as sacred as the Ganges at least, to the village in a pipe, to wash their dishes with! — to earn their Walden by the turning of a cock or drawing of a plug! That devilish Iron Horse, whose ear-rending neigh is heard throughout the town, has muddied the Boiling Spring with his foot, and he it is that has browsed off all the woods on Walden shore, that Trojan horse, with a thousand men in his belly, introduced by mercenary Greeks! Where is the country's champion, the Moore of Moore Hall, to meet him at the Deep Cut and thrust an avenging lance between the ribs of the bloated pest?

Nevertheless, of all the characters I have known, perhaps Walden wears best, and best preserves its purity. Many men have been likened to it, but few deserve that honor. Though the woodchoppers have laid bare first this shore and then that, and the Irish have built their sties by it, and the railroad has infringed on its border, and the ice-men have skimmed it once, it is itself unchanged, the same water which my youthful eyes fell on; all the change is in me. It has not acquired one permanent wrinkle after all its ripples. It is perennially young, and I may stand and see a swallow dip apparently to pick an insect from its surface as of yore. It struck me again to-night, as if I had not seen it almost daily for more than twenty years, — Why, here is Walden, the same woodland lake that I discovered so many years ago; where a forest was cut down last winter another is springing up by its shore as lustily as ever; the same thought is welling up to its surface that was then; it is the same liquid joy and happiness to itself and its Maker, ay, and it *may* be to me. It is the work of a brave man surely, in whom there was no guile! He rounded this water with his hand, deepened and clarified it in his thought, and in his will bequeathed it to Concord. I see by its face that it is visited by the same reflection; and I can almost say, Walden, is it you?

> It is no dream of mine,
> To ornament a line;
> I cannot come nearer to God and Heaven
> Than I live to Walden even.
> I am its stony shore,
> And the breeze that passes o'er;
> In the hollow of my hand
> Are its water and its sand,
> And its deepest resort
> Lies high in my thought.

The cars never pause to look at it; yet I fancy that the engineers and firemen and brakemen, and those passengers who have a season ticket and see it often, are better men for the sight. The engineer does not forget at night, or his nature does not, that he has beheld this vision of serenity and purity once at least during the day. Though seen but once, it helps to wash out State-street and the engine's soot. One proposes that it be called "God's Drop."

I have said that Walden has no visible inlet nor outlet, but it is on the one hand distantly and indirectly related to Flints' Pond, which is more elevated, by a chain of small ponds coming from that quarter, and on the other directly and manifestly to Concord River, which is lower, by a similar chain of ponds through which in some other geological period it may have flowed, and by a little digging, which God forbid, it can be made to flow thither again. If by living thus reserved and austere, like a hermit in the woods, so long, it has acquired such wonderful purity, who would not regret that the comparatively impure waters of Flints' Pond should be mingled with it, or itself should ever go to waste its sweetness in the ocean wave?

Flints', or Sandy Pond, in Lincoln, our greatest lake and inland sea, lies about a mile east of Walden. It is much larger, being said to contain one hundred and ninety-seven acres, and is more fertile in fish; but it is comparatively shallow, and not remarkably pure. A walk through the woods thither was often my recreation. It was worth the while, if only to feel the wind blow on your cheek freely, and see the waves run, and remember the life of mariners. I went a-chestnutting there in the fall, on windy days, when the nuts were dropping into the water and were washed to my feet; and one day, as I crept along its sedgy shore, the fresh spray blowing in my face, I came upon the mouldering wreck of a boat, the sides gone, and hardly more than the impression of its flat bottom left amid the rushes; yet its model was sharply defined, as if it were a large decayed pad, with its veins. It was as impressive a wreck as one could imagine on the sea-shore, and had as good a moral. It is by this time mere vegetable mould and undistinguishable pond shore, through which rushes and flags have pushed up. I used to admire the ripple marks on the sandy bottom, at the north end of this pond, made firm and hard to the feet of the wader by the pressure of the water, and the rushes which grew in Indian file, in waving lines, corresponding to these marks, rank behind rank, as if the waves had planted them. There also I have found, in considerable quantities, curious balls, composed apparently of fine grass or roots, of pipewort perhaps, from half an inch to four inches in diameter, and perfectly spherical. These wash back and forth in shallow water on a sandy bottom, and are sometimes cast on the shore. They are either solid grass, or have a little sand in the middle. At first you would say that they were formed by the action of the waves, like a pebble; yet the smallest are made of equally coarse materials, half an inch long, and they are produced only at one season of the year. Moreover, the waves, I suspect, do not so much construct as wear down a material which has already acquired consistency. They preserve their form when dry for an indefinite period.

Flints' Pond! Such is the poverty of our nomenclature. What right had the unclean and stupid farmer, whose farm abutted on this sky water, whose shores he has ruthlessly laid bare, to give his name to it? Some skin-flint, who loved better the reflecting surface of a dollar, or a bright cent, in which he could see his own brazen face; who regarded even the wild ducks which settled in it as trespassers; his fingers grown into crooked and horny talons from the long habit of grasping harpy-like; — so it is not named for me. I go not there to see him nor to hear of him; who never *saw* it, who never bathed in it, who never *loved* it, who never protected it, who never spoke a good word for it, nor thanked God that he had made it. Rather let it be named from the fishes that swim in it, the wild fowl or quadrupeds which frequent it, the wild flowers which grow by its shores, or some wild man or child the thread of whose history is interwoven with its own; not from him who could show no title to it but the deed which a like-minded neighbor or legislature gave him, — him who thought only of its money value; whose presence perchance cursed all the shore; who exhausted the land around it, and would fain have exhausted the waters within it; who regretted only that it was not English hay or cranberry meadow, — there was nothing to redeem it, forsooth, in his eyes, — and would have drained and sold it for the mud at its bottom. It did not turn his mill, and it was no *privilege* to him to behold it. I respect not his labors, his farm where everything has its price, who would carry the landscape, who would carry his God, to market, if he could get anything for him; who goes to market *for* his god as it is; on whose farm nothing grows free, whose fields bear no crops, whose meadows no flowers, whose trees no fruits, but dollars; who loves not the beauty of his fruits, whose fruits are not ripe for him till they are turned to dollars. Give me the poverty that enjoys true wealth. Farmers are respectable and interesting to me in proportion as they are poor, — poor farmers. A model farm! where the house stands like a fungus in a muck-heap, chambers for men, horses, oxen, and swine, cleansed and uncleansed, all contiguous to one another! Stocked with men! A great grease-spot, redolent of manures and buttermilk! Under a high state of cultivation, being manured with the hearts and brains of men! As if you were to raise your potatoes in the churchyard! Such is a model farm.

No, no; if the fairest features of the landscape are to be named after men, let them be the noblest and worthiest men alone. Let our lakes receive as true names at least as the Icarian Sea, where "still the shore" a "brave attempt resounds."

Goose Pond, of small extent, is on my way to Flints'; Fair Haven, an expansion of Concord River, said to contain some seventy acres, is a mile south-west; and White Pond, of about forty acres, is a mile and a half beyond Fair Haven. This is my lake country. These, with Concord River, are my water privileges; and night and day, year in year out, they grind such grist as I carry to them.

Since the wood-cutters, and the railroad, and I myself have profaned Walden, perhaps the most attractive, if not the most beautiful, of all our lakes, the gem of the woods, is White Pond; — a poor name from its commonness, whether derived from the remarkable purity of its waters or the color of its sands. In these as in other respects, however, it is a lesser twin of Walden. They are so much alike that you would say they must be connected under ground. It has the same stony shore, and its waters are of the same hue. As at Walden, in sultry dog-day weather, looking down through the woods on some of its bays which are not so deep but that the reflection from the bottom tinges them, its waters are of a misty bluish-green or glaucous color. Many years since I used to go there to collect the sand by cart-loads, to make sand-paper with, and I have continued to visit it ever since. One who frequents it proposes to call it Virid Lake. Perhaps it might be called Yellow-Pine Lake, from the following circumstance. About fifteen years ago you could see the top of a pitch-pine, of the kind called yellow-pine hereabouts, though it is not a distinct species, projecting above the surface in deep water, many rods from the shore. It was even supposed by some that the pond had sunk, and this was one of the primitive forest that formerly stood there. I find that even so long ago as 1792, in a "Topographical Description of the Town of

Concord," by one of its citizens, in the Collections of the Massachu-setts Historical Society, the author, after speaking of Walden and White Ponds, adds: "In the middle of the latter may be seen, when the water is very low, a tree which appears as if it grew in the place where it now stands, although the roots are fifty feet below the surface of the water; the top of this tree is broken off, and at that place measures fourteen inches in diameter." In the spring of '49 I talked with the man who lives nearest the pond in Sudbury, who told me that it was he who got out this tree ten or fifteen years before. As near as he could remember, it stood twelve or fifteen rods from the shore, where the water was thirty or forty feet deep. It was in the winter, and he had been getting out ice in the forenoon, and had resolved that in the afternoon, with the aid of his neighbors, he would take out the old yellow-pine. He sawed a channel in the ice toward the shore, and hauled it over and along and out on to the ice with oxen; but, before he had gone far in his work, he was surprised to find that it was wrong end upward, with the stumps of the branches pointing down, and the small end firmly fastened in the sandy bottom. It was about a foot in diameter at the big end, and he had expected to get a good saw-log, but it was so rotten as to be fit only for fuel, if for that. He had some of it in his shed then. There were marks of an axe and of woodpeckers on the butt. He thought that it might have been a dead tree on the shore, but was finally blown over into the pond, and after the top had become water-logged, while the butt-end was still dry and light, had drifted out and sunk wrong end up. His father, eighty years old, could not remember when it was not there. Several pretty large logs may still be seen lying on the bottom, where, owing to the undulation of the surface, they look like huge water snakes in motion.

This pond has rarely been profaned by a boat, for there is little in it to tempt a fisherman. Instead of the white lily, which requires mud, or the common sweet flag, the blue flag (*Iris versicolor*) grows thinly in the pure water, rising from the stony bottom all around the shore, where it is visited by humming birds in June; and the color both of its bluish blades and its flowers and especially their reflections, are in singular harmony with the glaucous water.

White Pond and Walden are great crystals on the surface of the earth, Lakes of Light. If they were permanently congealed, and small enough to be clutched, they would, perchance, be carried off by slaves, like precious stones, to adorn the heads of emperors; but being liquid, and ample, and secured to us and our successors forever, we disregard them, and run after the diamond of Kohinoor. They are too pure to have a market value; they contain no muck. How much more beautiful than our lives, how much more transparent than our characters, are they! We never learned meanness of them. How much fairer than the pool before the farmer's door, in which his ducks swim! Hither the clean wild ducks come. Nature has no human inhabitant who appreciates her. The birds with their plumage and their notes are in harmony with the flowers, but what youth or maiden conspires with the wild luxuriant beauty of Nature? She flourishes most alone, far from the towns where they reside. Talk of Heaven! ye disgrace earth.

X. BAKER FARM

SOMETIMES I rambled to pine groves, standing like temples, or like fleets at sea, full-rigged, with wavy boughs, and rippling with light, so soft and green and shady that the Druids would have forsaken their oaks to worship in them; or to the cedar wood beyond Flints' Pond, where the trees, covered with hoary blue berries, spiring higher and higher, are fit to stand before Valhalla, and the creeping juniper covers the ground with wreaths full of fruit; or to swamps where the usnea lichen hangs in festoons from the white-spruce trees, and toadstools, round tables of the swamp gods, cover the ground, and more beautiful fungi adorn the stumps, like butterflies or shells, vegetable winkles; where the swamp-pink and dogwood grow, the red alderberry glows like eyes of imps, the waxwork grooves and crushes the hardest woods in its folds, and the wild-holly berries make the beholder forget his home with their beauty, and he is dazzled and tempted by nameless other wild forbidden fruits, too fair for mortal taste. Instead of calling on some scholar, I paid many a visit to particular trees, of kinds which are rare in this neighborhood, standing far away in the middle of some pasture, or in the depths of a wood or swamp, or on a hill-top; such as the black-birch, of which we have some handsome specimens two feet in diameter; its cousin, the yellow-birch, with its loose golden vest, perfumed like the first; the beech, which has so neat a bole and beautifully lichen-painted, perfect in all its details, of which, excepting scattered specimens, I know but one small grove of sizable trees left in the township, supposed by some to have been planted by the pigeons that were once baited with beech nuts near by; it is worth the while to see the silver grain sparkle when you split this wood; the bass; the hornbeam; the *celtis occidentalis*, or false elm, of which we have but one well-grown; some taller mast of a pine, a shingle tree, or a more perfect hemlock than usual, standing like a pagoda in the midst of the woods; and many others I could mention. These were the shrines I visited both summer and winter.

Once it chanced that I stood in the very abutment of a rainbow's arch, which filled the lower stratum of the atmosphere, tinging the grass and leaves around, and dazzling me as if I looked through colored crystal. It was a lake of rainbow light, in which, for a short while, I lived like a dolphin. If it had lasted longer it might have tinged my employments and life. As I walked on the railroad causeway, I used to wonder at the halo of light around my shadow, and would fain fancy myself one of the elect. One who visited me declared that the shadows of some Irishmen before him had no halo about them, that it was only natives that were so distinguished. Benvenuto Cellini tells us in his memoirs, that, after a certain terrible dream or vision which he had during his confinement in the castle of St. Angelo a resplendent light appeared over the shadow of his head at morning and evening, whether he was in Italy or France, and it was particularly conspicuous when the grass was moist with dew. This was probably the same phenomenon to which I have referred, which is especially observed in the morning, but also at other times, and even by moonlight. Though a constant one, it is not commonly noticed, and, in the case of an excitable imagination like Cellini's, it would be basis enough for superstition. Beside, he tells us that he showed it to very few. But are they not indeed distinguished who are conscious that they are regarded at all?

I set out one afternoon to go a-fishing to Fair Haven, through the woods, to eke out my scanty fare of vegetables. My way led through Pleasant Meadow, an adjunct of the Baker Farm, that retreat of which a poet has since sung, beginning, —

> "Thy entry is a pleasant field,
> Which some mossy fruit trees yield
> Partly to a ruddy brook,
> By gliding musquash undertook,
> And mercurial trout,
> Darting about."

I thought of living there before I went to Walden. I "hooked" the apples, leaped the brook, and scared the musquash and the trout. It was one of those afternoons which seem indefinitely long before one, in which many events may happen, a large portion of our natural life, though it was already half spent when I started. By the way there came up a shower, which compelled me to stand half an hour under a pine, piling boughs over my head, and wearing my handkerchief for a shed; and when at length I had made one cast over the pickerel-weed, standing up to my middle in water, I found myself suddenly in the shadow of a cloud, and the thunger began to rumble with such emphasis that I could do no more than listen to it. The gods must be proud, thought I, with such forked flashes to rout a poor unarmed fisherman. So I made haste for shelter to the nearest hut, which stood half a mile from any road, but so much the nearer to the pond, and had long been uninhabited: —

> "And here a poet builded,
>   In the completed years,
> For behold a trivial cabin
>   That to destruction steers."

So the Muse fables. But therein, as I found, dwelt now John Field, an Irishman, and his wife, and several children, from the broad-faced boy who assisted his father at his work, and now came running by his side from the bog to escape the rain, to the wrinkled, sibyl-like, cone-headed infant that sat upon its father's knee as in the palaces of nobles, and looked out from its home in the midst of wet and hunger inquisitively upon the stranger, with the privilege of infancy, not knowing but it was the last of a noble line, and the hope and cynosure of the world, instead of John Field's poor starveling brat. There we sat together under that part of the roof which leaked the least, while it showered and thundered without. I had sat there many times of old before the ship was built that floated this family to America. An honest, hard-working, but shiftless man plainly was John Field; and his wife, she too was brave to cook so many successive dinners in the recesses of that lofty stove; with round greasy face and bare breast, still thinking to improve her condition one day; with the never absent mop in one hand, and yet no effects of it visible anywhere. The chickens, which had also taken shelter here from the rain, stalked about the room like members of the family, too humanized methought to roast well. They stood and looked in my eye or pecked at my shoe significantly.   Meanwhile my host told me his story, how hard he worked "bogging" for a neighboring farmer, turning up a meadow with a spade or bog hoe at the rate of ten dollars an acre and the use of the land with manure for one year, and his little broad-faced son worked cheerfully at his father's side the while, not knowing how poor a bargain the latter had made.   I tried to help him with my experience, telling him that he was one of my nearest neighbors, and that I too, who came a-fishing here, and looked like a loafer, was getting my living like himself; that I lived in a tight, light, and clean house, which hardly cost more than the annual rent of such a ruin as his commonly amounts to; and how, if he chose, he might in a month or two build himself a palace of his own; that I did not use tea, nor coffee, nor butter, nor milk, nor fresh meat, and so did not have to work to get them; again, as I did not work hard, I did not have to eat hard, and it cost me but a trifle for my food; but as he began with tea, and coffee, and butter, and milk, and beef, he had to work hard to pay for them, and when he had worked hard he had to eat hard again to repair the waste of his system, — and so it was as broad as it was long, indeed it was broader than it was long, for he was discontented and wasted his life into the bargain; and yet he had rated it as a gain in coming to America, that here you could get tea, and coffee, and meat every day.   But the only true America is that country where you are at liberty to pursue such a mode of life as may enable you to do without these, and where the state does not endeavor to compel you to sustain the slavery and war and other superfluous expenses which directly or indirectly result from the use of such things.   For I purposely talked to him as if he were a philosopher, or desired to be one. I should be glad if all the meadows on the earth were left in a wild state, if that were the consequence of men's beginning to redeem themselves.   A man will not need to study history to find out what is best for his own culture.   But alas! the culture of an Irishman is an enterprise to be undertaken with a sort of moral bog hoe.   I told him, that as he worked so hard at bogging, he required thick boots and stout clothing, which yet were soon soiled and worn out, but I wore light shoes and thin clothing, which cost not half so much, though he might think that I was dressed like a gentleman, (which, however, was not the case,) and in an hour or two, without labor, but as a recreation, I could, if I wished, catch as many fish as I should want for two days, or earn enough money to support me a week.   If he and his family would live simply, they might all go a-huckleberrying in the summer for their amusement. John heaved a sigh at this, and his wife stared with arms a-kimbo, and both appeared to be wondering if they had capital enough to begin such a course with, or arithmetic enough to carry it through. It was sailing by dead reckoning to them, and they saw not clearly how to make their port so; therefore I suppose they still take life bravely, after their fashion, face to face, giving it tooth and nail, not having skill to split its massive columns with any fine entering wedge, and rout it in detail; — thinking to deal with it roughly, as one should handle a thistle. But they fight at an overwhelming disadvantage, — living, John Field, alas! without arithmetic, and failing so.

"Do you ever fish?" I asked. "O yes, I catch a mess now and then when I am lying by; good perch I catch." "What's your bait?" "I catch shiners with fishworms, and bait the perch with them." "You'd better go now, John," said his wife, with glistening and hopeful face; but John demurred.

The shower was now over, and a rainbow above the eastern woods promised a fair evening; so I took my departure. When I had got without I asked for a dish, hoping to get a sight of the well bottom, to complete my survey of the premises; but there, alas! are shallows and quicksands, and rope broken withal, and bucket irrecoverable. Meanwhile the right culinary vessel was selected, water was seemingly distilled, and after consultation and long delay passed out to the thirsty one, — not yet suffered to cool, not yet to settle. Such gruel sustains life here, I thought; so, shutting my eyes, and excluding the motes by a skilfully directed undercurrent, I drank to genuine hospitality the heartiest draught I could. I am not squeamish in such cases when manners are concerned.

As I was leaving the Irishman's roof after the rain, bending my steps again to the pond, my haste to catch pickerel, wading in retired meadows, in sloughs and bog-holes, in forlorn and savage places, appeared for an instant trivial to me who had been sent to school and college; but as I ran down the hill toward the reddening west, with the rainbow over my shoulder, and some faint tinkling sounds borne to my ear through the cleansed air, from I know not what quarter, my Good Genius seemed to say, — Go fish and hunt far and wide day by day, — farther and wider, — and rest thee by many brooks and hearth-sides without misgiving. Remember thy Creator in the days of thy youth. Rise free from care before the dawn, and seek adventures. Let the noon find thee by other lakes, and the night overtake thee everywhere at home. There are no larger fields than these, no worthier games than may here be played. Grow wild according to thy nature, like these sedges and brakes, which will never become English hay. Let the thunder rumble; what if it threaten ruin to farmers' crops? that is not its errand to thee. Take shelter under the cloud, while they flee to carts and sheds. Let not to get a living be thy trade, but thy sport. Enjoy the land, but own it not. Through want of enterprise and faith men are where they are, buying and selling, and spending their lives like serfs.

O Baker Farm!

> "Landscape where the richest element
> Is a little sunshine innocent." . . .

> "No one runs to revel
> On thy rail-fenced lea." . . .

> "Debate with no man hast thou,
>   With questions art never perplexed,
> As tame at the first sight as now,
>   In thy plain russet gabardine dressed." . . .

> "Come ye who love,
>   And ye who hate,
> Children of the Holy Dove,
>   And Guy Faux of the state,
> And hang conspiracies
> From the tough rafters of the trees!"

Men come tamely home at night only from the next field or street, where their household echoes haunt, and their life pines because it breathes its own breath over again; their shadows morning and evening reach farther than their daily steps. We should come home from far, from adventures, and perils, and discoveries every day, with new experience and character.

Before I had reached the pond some fresh impulse had brought out John Field, with altered mind, letting go "bogging" ere this sunset. But he, poor man, disturbed only a couple of fins while I was catching a fair string, and he said it was his luck; but when we changed seats in the boat luck changed seats too. Poor John Field! — I trust he does not read this, unless he will improve by it, — thinking to live by some derivative old country mode in this primitive new country, — to catch perch with shiners. It is good bait sometimes, I allow. With his horizon all his own, yet he a poor man, born to be poor, with his inherited Irish poverty or poor life, his Adam's grandmother and boggy ways, not to rise in this world, he nor his posterity, till their wading webbed bog-trotting feet get *talaria* to their heels.

XI. HIGHER LAWS

As I came home through the woods with my string of fish, trailing my pole, it being now quite dark, I caught a glimpse of a woodchuck stealing across my path, and felt a strange thrill of savage delight, and was strongly tempted to seize and devour him raw; not that I was hungry then, except for that wildness which he represented. Once or twice, however, while I lived at the pond, I found myself ranging the woods, like a half-starved hound, with a strange abandonment, seeking some kind of venison which I might devour, and no morsel could have been too savage for me. The wildest scenes had become unaccountably familiar. I found in myself, and still find, an instinct toward a higher, or, as it is named, spiritual life, as do most men, and another toward a primitive rank and savage one, and I reverence them both. I love the wild not less than the good. The wildness and adventure that are in fishing still recommended it to me. I like sometimes to take rank hold on life and spend my day more as the animals do. Perhaps I have owed to this employment and to hunting, when quite young, my closest acquaintance with Nature. They early introduce us to and detain us in scenery with which otherwise, at that age, we should have little acquaintance. Fishermen, hunters, woodchoppers, and others, spending their lives in the fields and woods, in a peculiar sense a part of Nature themselves, are often in a more favorable mood for observing her, in the intervals of their pursuits, than philosophers or poets even, who approach her with expectation. She is not afraid to exhibit herself to them. The traveller on the prairie is naturally a hunter, on the head waters of the Missouri and Columbia a trapper, and at the Falls of St. Mary a fisherman. He who is only a traveller learns things at second-hand and by the halves, and is poor authority. We are most interested when science reports what those men already know practically or instinctively, for that alone is a true *humanity*, or account of human experience.

They mistake who assert that the Yankee has few amusements, because he has not so many public holidays, and men and boys do not play so many games as they do in England, for here the more primitive but solitary amusements of hunting, fishing, and the like have not yet given place to the former. Almost every New England boy among my contemporaries shouldered a fowling piece between the ages of ten and fourteen; and his hunting and fishing grounds were not limited, like the preserves of an English nobleman, but were more boundless even than those of a savage. No wonder, then, that he did not oftener stay to play on the common. But already a change is taking place, owing, not to an increased humanity, but to an increased scarcity of game, for perhaps the hunter is the greatest friend of the animals hunted, not excepting the Humane Society.

Moreover, when at the pond, I wished sometimes to add fish to my fare for variety. I have actually fished from the same kind of necessity that the first fishers did. Whatever humanity I might conjure up against it was all factitious, and concerned my philosophy more than my feelings. I speak of fishing only now, for I had long felt differently about fowling, and sold my gun before I went to the woods. Not that I am less humane than others, but I did not perceive that my feelings were much affected. I did not pity the fishes nor the worms. This was habit. As for fowling, during the last years that I carried a gun my excuse was that I was studying ornithology, and sought only new or rare birds. But I confess that I am now inclined to think that there is a finer way of studying ornithology than this. It requires so much closer attention to the habits of the birds, that, if for that reason only, I have been willing to omit the gun. Yet notwithstanding the objection on the score of humanity, I am compelled to doubt if equally valuable sports are ever substituted for these; and when some of my friends have asked me anxiously about their boys, whether they should let them hunt, I have answered, yes, — remembering that it was one of the best parts of my education, — *make* them hunters, though sportsmen only at first, if possible, mighty hunters at last, so that they shall not find game large enough for them in this or any vegetable wilderness, — hunters as well as fishers of men. Thus far I am of the opinion of Chaucer's nun, who

> "yave not of the text a pulled hen
> That saith that hunters ben not holy men."

There is a period in the history of the individual, as of the race, when the hunters are the "best men," as the Algonquins called them. We cannot but pity the boy who has never fired a gun; he is no more humane, while his education has been sadly neglected. This was my answer with respect to those youths who were bent on this pursuit, trusting that they would soon outgrow it. No humane being, past the thoughtless age of boyhood, will wantonly murder any creature, which holds its life by the same tenure that he does. The hare in its extremity cries like a child. I warn you, mothers, that my sympathies do not always make the usual phil-*anthropic* distinctions.

Such is oftenest the young man's introduction to the forest, and the most original part of himself. He goes thither at first as a hunter and fisher, until at last, if he has the seeds of a better life in him, he distinguishes his proper objects, as a poet or naturalist it may be, and leaves the gun and fish-pole behind. The mass of men are still and always young in this respect. In some countries a hunting parson is no uncommon sight. Such a one might make a good shepherd's dog, but is far from being the Good Shepherd. I have been surprised to consider that the only obvious employment, except wood-chopping, ice-cutting, or the like business, which ever to my knowledge detained at Walden Pond for a whole half day any of my fellow-citizens, whether fathers or children of the town, with just one exception, was fishing. Commonly they did not think that they were lucky, or well paid for their time, unless they got a long string of fish, though they had the opportunity of seeing the pond all the while. They might go there a thousand times before the sediment of fishing would sink to the bottom and leave their purpose pure; but no doubt such a clarifying process would be going on all the while. The governor and his council faintly remember the pond, for they went a-fishing there when they were boys; but now they are too old and dignified to go a-fishing, and so they know it no more forever. Yet even they expect to go to heaven at last. If the legislature regards it, it is chiefly to regulate the number of hooks to be used there; but they know nothing about the hook of hooks with which to angle for the pond itself, impaling the legislature for a bait. Thus, even in civilized communities, the embryo man passes through the hunter stage of development.

I have found repeatedly, of late years, that I cannot fish without falling a little in self-respect. I have tried it again and again. I have skill at it, and, like many of my fellows, a certain instinct for it, which revives from time to time, but always when I have done I feel that it would have been better if I had not fished. I think that I do not mistake. It is a faint intimation, yet so are the first streaks of morning. There is unquestionably this instinct in me which belongs to the lower orders of creation; yet with every year I am less a fisherman, though without more humanity or even wisdom; at present I am no fisherman at all. But I see that if I were to live in a wilderness I should again be tempted to become a fisher and hunter in earnest. Beside, there is something essentially unclean about this diet and all flesh, and I began to see where housework commences, and whence the endeavor, which costs so much, to wear a tidy and respectable appearance each day, to keep the house sweet and free from all ill odors and sights. Having been my own butcher and scullion and cook, as well as the gentleman for whom the dishes were served up, I can speak from an unusually complete experience. The practical objection to animal food in my case was its uncleanness; and besides, when I had caught and cleaned and cooked and eaten my fish, they seemed not to have fed me essentially. It was insignificant and unnecessary, and cost more than it came to. A little bread or a few potatoes would have done as well, with less trouble and filth. Like many of my contemporaries, I had rarely for many years used animal food, or tea, or coffee, etc.; not so much because of any ill effects which I had traced to them, as because they were not agreeable to my imagination. The repugnance to animal food is not the effect of experience, but is an instinct. It appeared more beautiful to live low and fare hard in many respects; and though I never did so, I went far enough to please my imagination. I believe that every man who has ever been earnest to preserve his higher or poetic faculties in the best condition has been particularly inclined to abstain from animal food, and from much food of any kind. It is a significant fact, stated by entomologists, I find it in Kirby and Spence, that "some insects in their perfect state, though furnished with organs of feeding, make no use of them;" and they lay it down as "a general rule, that almost all insects in this state eat much less than in that of larvæ. The voracious caterpillar when transformed into a butterfly," ... "and the gluttonous maggot when become a fly," content themselves with a drop or two of honey or some other sweet liquid. The abdomen under the wings of the butterfly still represents the larva. This is the tidbit which tempts his insectivorous fate. The gross feeder is a man in the larva state; and there are whole nations in that condition, nations without fancy or imagination, whose vast abdomens betray them.

It is hard to provide and cook so simple and clean a diet as will not offend the imagination; but this, I think, is to be fed when we feed the body; they should both sit down at the same table. Yet perhaps this may be done. The fruits eaten temperately need not make us ashamed of our appetites, nor interrupt the worthiest pursuits. But put an extra condiment into your dish, and it will poison you. It is not worth the while to live by rich cookery. Most men would feel shame if caught preparing with their own hands precisely such a dinner, whether of animal or vegetable food, as is every day prepared for them by others. Yet till this is otherwise we are not civilized, and, if gentlemen and ladies, are not true men and women. This certainly suggests what change is to be made. It may be vain to ask why the imagination will not be reconciled to flesh and fat. I am satisfied that it is not. Is it not a reproach that man is a carnivorous animal? True, he can and does live, in a great measure, by preying on other animals; but this is a miserable way, — as any one who will go to snaring rabbits, or slaughtering lambs, may learn, — and he will be regarded as a benefactor of his race who shall teach man to confine himself to a more innocent and wholesome diet. Whatever my own practice may be, I have no doubt that it is a part of the destiny of the human race, in its gradual improvement, to leave off eating animals, as surely as the savage tribes have left off eating each other when they came in contact with the more civilized.

If one listens to the faintest but constant suggestions of his genius, which are certainly true, he sees not to what extremes, or even insanity, it may lead him; and yet that way, as he grows more resolute and faithful, his road lies. The faintest assured objection which one healthy man feels will at length prevail over the arguments and customs of mankind. No man ever followed his genius till it misled him. Though the result were bodily weakness, yet perhaps no one can say that the consequences were to be regretted, for these were a life in conformity to higher principles. If the day and the night are such that you greet them with joy, and life emits a fragrance like flowers and sweet-scented herbs, is more elastic, more starry, more immortal, — that is your success. All nature is your congratulation, and you have cause momentarily to bless yourself. The greatest gains and values are farthest from being appreciated. We easily come to doubt if they exist. We soon forget them. They are the highest reality. Perhaps the facts most astounding and most real are never communicated by man to man. The true harvest of my daily life is somewhat as intangible and indescribable as the tints of morning or evening. It is a little star-dust caught, a segment of the rainbow which I have clutched.

Yet, for my part, I was never unusually squeamish; I could sometimes eat a fried rat with a good relish, if it were necessary. I am glad to have drunk water so long, for the same reason that I prefer the natural sky to an opium-eater's heaven. I would fain keep sober always; and there are infinite degrees of drunkenness. I believe that water is the only drink for a wise man; wine is not so noble a liquor; and think of dashing the hopes of a morning with a cup of warm coffee, or of an evening with a dish of tea! Ah, how low I fall when I am tempted by them! Even music may be intoxicating. Such apparently slight causes destroyed Greece and Rome, and will destroy England and America. Of all ebriosity, who does not prefer to be intoxicated by the air he breathes? I have found it to be the most serious objection to coarse labors long continued, that they compelled me to eat and drink coarsely also. But to tell the truth, I find myself at present somewhat less particular in these respects. I carry less religion to the table, ask no blessing; not because I am wiser than I was, but, I am obliged to confess, because, however much it is to be regretted, with years I have grown more coarse and indifferent. Perhaps these questions are entertained only in youth, as most believe of poetry. My practice is "nowhere," my opinion is here. Nevertheless I am far from regarding myself as one of those privileged ones to whom the Ved refers when it says, that "he who has true faith in the Omnipresent Supreme Being may eat all that exists," that is, is not bound to inquire what is his food, or who prepares it; and even in their case it is to be observed, as a Hindoo commentator has remarked, that the Vedant limits this privilege to "the time of distress."

Who has not sometimes derived an inexpressible satisfaction from his food in which appetite had no share? I have been thrilled to think that I owed a mental perception to the commonly gross sense of taste, that I have been inspired through the palate, that some berries which I had eaten on a hill-side had fed my genius. "The soul not being mistress of herself," says Thseng-tseu, "one looks, and one does not see; one listens, and one does not hear; one eats, and one does not know the savor of food." He who distinguishes the true savor of his food can never be a glutton; he who does not cannot be otherwise. A puritan may go to his brown-bread crust with as gross an appetite as ever an alderman to his turtle. Not that food which entereth into

the mouth defileth a man, but the appetite with which it is eaten. It
is neither the quality nor the quantity, but the devotion to sensual
savors; when that which is eaten is not a viand to sustain our animal,
or inspire our spiritual life, but food for the worms that possess us.
If the hunter has a taste for mud-turtles, muskrats, and other such
savage tid-bits, the fine lady indulges a taste for jelly made of a calf's
foot, or for sardines from over the sea, and they are even. He goes to
the millpond, she to her preserve-pot. The wonder is how they, how
you and I, can live this slimy beastly life, eating and drinking.

Our whole life is startlingly moral. There is never an instant's
truce between virtue and vice. Goodness is the only investment that
never fails. In the music of the harp which trembles round the
world it is the insisting on this which thrills us. The harp is the
travelling patterer for the Universe's Insurance Company, recom-
mending its laws, and our little goodness is all the assessment that
we pay. Though the youth at last grows indifferent, the laws of the
universe are not indifferent, but are forever on the side of the most
sensitive. Listen to every zephyr for some reproof, for it is surely
there, and he is unfortunate who does not hear it. We cannot touch
a string or move a stop but the charming moral transfixes us. Many
an irksome noise, go a long way off, is heard as music, a proud sweet
satire on the meanness of our lives.

We are conscious of an animal in us, which awakens in proportion
as our higher nature slumbers. It is reptile and sensual, and perhaps
cannot be wholly expelled; like the worms which, even in life and
health, occupy our bodies. Possibly we may withdraw from it, but
never change its nature. I fear that it may enjoy a certain health of
its own; that we may be well, yet not pure. The other day I picked
up the lower jaw of a hog, with white and sound teeth and tusks,
which suggested that there was an animal health and vigor distinct
from the spiritual. This creature succeeded by other means than
temperance and purity. "That in which men differ from brute beasts,"
says Mencius, "is a thing very inconsiderable; the common herd lose
it very soon; superior men preserve it carefully." Who knows what
sort of life would result if we had attained to purity? If I knew so
wise a man as could teach me purity I would go to seek him forthwith. "A command over our passions, and over the external senses of
the body, and good acts, are declared by the Ved to be indispensable
in the mind's approximation to God." Yet the spirit can for the time
pervade and control every member and function of the body, and

transmute what in form is the grossest sensuality into purity and devotion. The generative energy, which, when we are loose, dissipates and makes us unclean, when we are continent invigorates and inspires us. Chastity is the flowering of man; and what are called Genius, Heroism, Holiness, and the like, are but various fruits which succeed it. Man flows at once to God when the channel of purity is open. By turns our purity inspires and our impurity casts us down. He is blessed who is assured that the animal is dying out in him day by day, and the divine being established. Perhaps there is none but has cause for shame on account of the inferior and brutish nature to which he is allied. I fear that we are such gods or demigods only as fauns and satyrs, the divine allied to beasts, the creatures of appetite, and that, to some extent, our very life is our disgrace. —

> "How happy 's he who hath due place assigned
> To his beasts and disafforested his mind!
> . . . .
> Can use his horse, goat, wolf, and ev'ry beast,
> And is not ass himself to all the rest!
> Else man not only is the herd of swine,
> But he's those devils too which did incline
> Them to a headlong rage, and made them worse."

All sensuality is one, though it takes many forms; all purity is one. It is the same whether a man eat, or drink, or cohabit, or sleep sensually. They are but one appetite, and we only need to see a person do any one of these things to know how great a sensualist he is. The impure can neither stand nor sit with purity. When the reptile is attacked at one mouth of his burrow, he shows himself at another. If you would be chaste, you must be temperate. What is chastity? How shall a man know if he is chaste? He shall not know it. We have heard of this virtue, but we know not what it is. We speak conformably to the rumor which we have heard. From exertion come wisdom and purity; from sloth ignorance and sensuality. In the student sensuality is a sluggish habit of mind. An unclean person is universally a slothful one, one who sits by a stove, whom the sun shines on prostrate, who reposes without being fatigued. If you would avoid uncleanness, and all the sins, work earnestly, though it be at cleaning a stable. Nature is hard to be overcome, but she must be overcome. What avails it that you are Christian, if you are not purer than the heathen, if you deny yourself no more, if you are not

more religious? I know of many systems of religion esteemed heathenish whose precepts fill the reader with shame, and provoke him
to new endeavors, though it be to the performance of rites merely.

I hesitate to say these things, but it is not because of the subject, —
I care not how obscene my *words* are, — but because I cannot speak of
them without betraying my impurity. We discourse freely without
shame of one form of sensuality, and are silent about another. We
are so degraded that we cannot speak simply of the necessary functions of human nature. In earlier ages, in some countries, every function was reverently spoken of and regulated by law. Nothing was
too trivial for the Hindoo lawgiver, however offensive it may be to
modern taste. He teaches how to eat, drink, cohabit, void excrement
and urine, and the like, elevating what is mean, and does not falsely
excuse himself by calling these things trifles.

Every man is the builder of a temple, called his body, to the god he
worships, after a style purely his own, nor can he get off by hammering marble instead. We are all sculptors and painters, and our material is our own flesh and blood and bones. Any nobleness begins at
once to refine a man's features, any meanness or sensuality to imbrute
them.

John Farmer sat at his door one September evening, after a hard
day's work, his mind still running on his labor more or less. Having
bathed he sat down to recreate his intellectual man. It was a rather
cool evening, and some of his neighbors were apprehending a frost.
He had not attended to the train of his thoughts long when he heard
some one playing on a flute, and that sound harmonized with his mood.
Still he thought of his work; but the burden of his thought was, that
though this kept running in his head, and he found himself planning
and contriving it against his will, yet it concerned him very little.
It was no more than the scurf of his skin, which was constantly shuf-
fled off. But the notes of the flute came home to his ears out of a
different sphere from that he worked in, and suggested work for certain faculties which slumbered in him. They gently did away with
the street, and the village, and the state in which he lived. A voice
said to him, — Why do you stay here and live this mean moiling life,
when a glorious existence is possible for you? Those same stars
twinkle over other fields than these. — But how to come out of this
condition and actually migrate thither? All that he could think of
was to practise some new austerity, to let his mind descend into his
body and redeem it, and treat himself with ever increasing respect.

XII. BRUTE NEIGHBORS

SOMETIMES I had a companion in my fishing, who came through the village to my house from the other side of the town, and the catching of the dinner was as much a social exercise as the eating of it.

Hermit. I wonder what the world is doing now. I have not heard so much as a locust over the sweet-fern these three hours. The pigeons are all asleep upon their roosts, — no flutter from them. Was that a farmer's noon horn which sounded from beyond the woods just now? The hands are coming in to boiled salt beef and cider and Indian bread. Why will men worry themselves so? He that does not eat need not work. I wonder how much they have reaped. Who would live there where a body can never think for the barking of Bose? And O, the housekeeping! to keep bright the devil's doorknobs, and scour his tubs this bright day! Better not keep a house. Say, some hollow tree; and then for morning calls and dinner-parties! Only a woodpecker tapping. O, they swarm; the sun is too warm there; they are born too far into life for me. I have water from the spring, and a loaf of brown bread on the shelf. — Hark! I hear a rustling of the leaves. Is it some ill-fed village hound yielding to the instinct of the chase? or the lost pig which is said to be in these woods, whose tracks I saw after the rain? It comes on apace; my sumachs and sweetbriers tremble. — Eh, Mr. Poet, is it you? How do you like the world to-day?

Poet. See those clouds; how they hang! That's the greatest thing I have seen to-day. There's nothing like it in old paintings, nothing like it in foreign lands, — unless when we were off the coast of Spain. That's a true Mediterranean sky. I thought, as I have my living to get, and have not eaten to-day, that I might go a-fishing. That's the true industry for poets. It is the only trade I have learned. Come, let's along.[1]

Hermit. I cannot resist. My brown bread will soon be gone. I will go with you gladly soon, but I am just concluding a serious medi-

[1] The "Poet" was Thoreau's most frequent companion and first biographer, William Ellery Channing, the younger. While Thoreau was at the pond, Emerson solicited money from his friends to advance Channing's education in Europe. The allusions to Europe in the above passage, even more than Channing's *Conversations in Rome*, were the longest-lived memorial of that excursion.

tation.   I think that I am near the end of it.   Leave me alone, then, for
a while.   But that we may not be delayed, you shall be digging the
bait meanwhile.   Angle-worms are rarely to be met with in these
parts, where the soil was never fattened with manure; the race is
nearly extinct.   The sport of digging the bait is nearly equal to that
of catching the fish, when one's appetite is not too keen; and this
you may have all to yourself to-day.   I would advise you to set in the
spade down yonder among the ground-nuts, where you see the johnswort waving.   I think that I may warrant you one worm to every
three sods you turn up, if you look well in among the roots of the
grass, as if you were weeding.   Or, if you choose to go farther, it will
not be unwise, for I have found the increase of fair bait to be very
nearly as the squares of the distances.

Hermit alone.   Let me see; where was I?   Methinks I was nearly
in this frame of mind; the world lay about at this angle.   Shall I go
to heaven or a-fishing?   If I should soon bring this meditation to an
end, would another so sweet occasion be likely to offer?   I was as
near being resolved into the essence of things as ever I was in my life.
I fear my thoughts will not come back to me.   If it would do any good,
I would whistle for them.   When they make us an offer, is it wise to
say, We will think of it?   My thoughts have left no track, and I cannot find the path again.   What was it that I was thinking of?   It was
a very hazy day.   I will just try these three sentences of Confut-see;
they may fetch that state about again.   I know not whether it was
the dumps or a budding ecstasy.   Mem.   There never is but one opportunity of a kind.

Poet.   How now, Hermit, is it too soon?   I have got just thirteen
whole ones, beside several which are imperfect or undersized; but
they will do for the smaller fry; they do not cover up the hook so
much.   Those village worms are quite too large; a shiner may make
a meal off one without finding the skewer.

Hermit.   Well, then, let's be off.   Shall we to the Concord?
There's good sport there if the water be not too high.

Why do precisely these objects which we behold make a world?
Why has man just these species of animals for his neighbors; as if
nothing but a mouse could have filled this crevice?   I suspect that
Pilpay & Co. have put animals to their best use, for they are all beasts
of burden, in a sense, made to carry some portion of our thoughts.

The mice which haunted my house were not the common ones,

which are said to have been introduced into the country, but a wild
native kind not found in the village. I sent one to a distinguished
naturalist, and it interested him much. When I was building, one of
these had its nest underneath the house, and before I had laid the
second floor, and swept out the shavings, would come out regularly
at lunch time and pick up the crumbs at my feet. It probably had
never seen a man before; and it soon became quite familiar, and would
run over my shoes and up my clothes. It could readily ascend the
sides of the room by short impulses, like a squirrel, which it resembled
in its motions. At length, as I leaned with my elbow on the bench
one day, it ran up my clothes, and along my sleeve, and round and
round the paper which held my dinner, while I kept the latter close,
and dodged and played at bo-peep with it; and when at last I held still
a piece of cheese between my thumb and finger, it came and nibbled
it, sitting in my hand, and afterward cleaned its face and paws, like a
fly, and walked away.

A phœbe soon built in my shed, and a robin for protection in a pine
which grew against the house. In June the partridge, (*Tetrao um-
bellus*,) which is so shy a bird, led her brood past my windows, from
the woods in the rear to the front of my house, clucking and calling
to them like a hen, and in all her behavior proving herself the hen of
the woods. The young suddenly disperse on your approach, at a
signal from the mother, as if a whirlwind had swept them away, and
they so exactly resemble the dried leaves and twigs that many a traveller has placed his foot in the midst of a brood, and heard the whir of
the old bird as she flew off, and her anxious calls and mewing, or seen
her trail her wings to attract his attention, without suspecting their
neighborhood. The parent will sometimes roll and spin round before
you in such a dishabille, that you cannot, for a few moments, detect
what kind of creature it is. The young squat still and flat, often running their heads under a leaf, and mind only their mother's directions
given from a distance, nor will your approach make them run again
and betray themselves. You may even tread on them, or have your
eyes on them for a minute, without discovering them. I have held
them in my open hand at such a time, and still their only care, obedient
to their mother and their instinct, was to squat there without fear or
trembling. So perfect is this instinct, that once, when I had laid them
on the leaves again, and one accidentally fell on its side, it was found
with the rest in exactly the same position ten minutes afterward.
They are not callow like the young of most birds, but more perfectly

developed and precocious even than chickens. The remarkably adult yet innocent expression of their open and serene eyes is very memorable. All intelligence seems reflected in them. They suggest not merely the purity of infancy, but a wisdom clarified by experience. Such an eye was not born when the bird was, but is coeval with the sky it reflects. The woods do not yield another such a gem. The traveller does not often look into such a limpid well. The ignorant or reckless sportsman often shoots the parent at such a time, and leaves these innocents to fall a prey to some prowling beast or bird, or gradually mingle with the decaying leaves which they so much resemble. It is said that when hatched by a hen they will directly disperse on some alarm, and so are lost, for they never hear the mother's call which gathers them again. These were my hens and chickens.

It is remarkable how many creatures live wild and free though secret in the woods, and still sustain themselves in the neighborhood of towns, suspected by hunters only. How retired the otter manages to live here! He grows to be four feet long, as big as a small boy, perhaps without any human being getting a glimpse of him. I formerly saw the raccoon in the woods behind where my house is built, and probably still heard their whinnering at night. Commonly I rested an hour or two in the shade at noon, after planting, and ate my lunch, and read a little by a spring which was the source of a swamp and of a brook, oozing from under Brister's Hill, half a mile from my field. The approach to this was through a succession of descending grassy hollows, full of young pitch-pines, into a larger wood about the swamp. There, in a very secluded and shaded spot, under a spreading white-pine, there was yet a clean firm sward to sit on. I had dug out the spring and made a well of clear gray water, where I could dip up a pailful without roiling it, and thither I went for this purpose almost every day in mid-summer, when the pond was warmest. Thither too the wood-cock led her brood, to probe the mud for worms, flying but a foot above them down the bank, while they ran in a troop beneath; but at last, spying me, she would leave her young and circle round and round me, nearer and nearer till within four or five feet, pretending broken wings and legs, to attract my attention, and get off her young, who would already have taken up their march, with faint wiry peep, single file through the swamp, as she directed. Or I heard the peep of the young when I could not see the parent bird. There too the turtle-doves sat over the spring, or fluttered from bough to bough of the soft white-pines over my head; or the red squirrel, coursing down the nearest bough, was particularly familiar and inquisitive. You only need sit still long enough in some attractive spot in the woods that all its inhabitants may exhibit themselves to you by turns.

I was witness to events of a less peaceful character. One day when I went out to my wood-pile, or rather my pile of stumps, I observed two large ants, the one red, the other much larger, nearly half an inch long, and black, fiercely contending with one another. Having once got hold they never let go, but struggled and wrestled and rolled on the chips incessantly. Looking farther, I was surprised to find that the chips were covered with such combatants, that it was not a *duellum*, but a *bellum*, a war between two races of ants, the red always pitted against the black, and frequently two red ones to one black. The legions of these Myrmidons covered all the hills and vales in my wood-yard, and the ground was already strewn with the dead and dying, both red and black. It was the only battle which I have ever witnessed, the only battle-field I ever trod while the battle was raging; internecine war; the red republicans on the one hand, and the black imperialists on the other.[1] On every side they were engaged in deadly combat, yet without any noise that I could hear, and human soldiers never fought so resolutely. I watched a couple that were fast locked in each other's embraces, in a little sunny valley amid the chips, now at noon-day prepared to fight till the sun went down, or life went out. The smaller red champion had fastened himself like a vice to his adversary's front, and through all the tumblings on that field never for an instant ceased to gnaw at one of his feelers near the root, having already caused the other to go by the board; while the stronger black one dashed him from side to side, and, as I saw on looking nearer, had already divested him of several of his members. They fought with more pertinacity than bull-dogs. Neither manifested the least disposition to retreat. It was evident that their battle-cry was Conquer or die. In the mean while there came along a single red ant on the hillside of this valley, evidently full of excitement, who either had despatched his foe, or had not yet taken part in the battle; probably the latter, for he had lost none of his limbs; whose mother had charged him to return with his shield or upon it. Or perchance he was some Achilles, who had nourished his wrath apart, and had now come to avenge or rescue his Patroclus. He saw this unequal combat from afar, — for the blacks were nearly twice the size of the

[1] Perhaps Thoreau was alluding to the Mexican War. He also described the ant-war in "My Books I'd Fain Cast Off, I Cannot Read" (1842).

red, — he drew near with rapid pace till he stood on his guard within half an inch of the combatants; then, watching his opportunity, he sprang upon the black warrior, and commenced his operations near the root of his right fore-leg, leaving the foe to select among his own members; and so there were three united for life, as if a new kind of attraction had been invented which put all other locks and cements to shame. I should not have wondered by this time to find that they had their respective musical bands stationed on some eminent chip, and playing their national airs the while, to excite the slow and cheer the dying combatants. I was myself excited somewhat even as if they had been men. The more you think of it, the less the difference. And certainly there is not the fight recorded in Concord history, at least, if in the history of America, that will bear a moment's comparison with this, whether for the numbers engaged in it, or for the patriotism and heroism displayed. For numbers and for carnage it was an Austerlitz or Dresden. Concord Fight! Two killed on the patriots' side, and Luther Blanchard wounded! Why here every ant was a Buttrick, — "Fire! for God's sake fire!" — and thousands shared the fate of Davis and Hosmer. There was not one hireling there. I have no doubt that it was a principle they fought for, as much as our ancestors, and not to avoid a three-penny tax on their tea; and the results of this battle will be as important and memorable to those whom it concerns as those of the battle of Bunker Hill, at least.

I took up the chip on which the three I have particularly described were struggling, carried it into my house, and placed it under a tumbler on my window-sill, in order to see the issue. Holding a microscope to the first-mentioned red ant, I saw that, though he was assiduously gnawing at the near foreleg of his enemy, having severed his remaining feeler, his own breast was all torn away, exposing what vitals he had there to the jaws of the black warrior, whose breastplate was apparently too thick for him to pierce; and the dark carbuncles of the sufferer's eyes shone with ferocity such as war only could excite. They struggled half an hour longer under the tumbler, and when I looked again the black soldier had severed the heads of his foes from their bodies, and the still living heads were hanging on either side of him like ghastly trophies at his saddle-bow, still apparently as firmly fastened as ever, and he was endeavoring with feeble struggles, being without feelers and with only the remnant of a leg, and I know not how many other wounds, to divest himself of them; which at length, after half an hour more, he accomplished. I raised the glass, and he went off over the window-sill in that crippled state. Whether he finally survived that combat, and spent the remainder of his days in some Hotel des Invalides, I do not know; but I thought that his in- dustry would not be worth much thereafter. I never learned which party was victorious, nor the cause of the war; but I felt for the rest of that day as if I had had my feelings excited and harrowed by wit- nessing the struggle, the ferocity and carnage, of a human battle before my door.

Kirby and Spence tell us that the battles of ants have long been celebrated and the date of them recorded, though they say that Huber is the only modern author who appears to have witnessed them. "Æneas Sylvius," say they, "after giving a very circumstantial ac- count of one contested with great obstinacy by a great and small species on the trunk of a pear tree," adds that " 'This action was fought in the pontificate of Eugenius the Fourth, in the presence of Nicholas Pistoriensis, an eminent lawyer, who related the whole history of the battle with the greatest fidelity.' A similar engage- ment between great and small ants is recorded by Olaus Magnus, in which the small ones, being victorious, are said to have buried the bodies of their own soldiers, but left those of their giant enemies a prey to the birds. This event happened previous to the expulsion of the tyrant Christiern the Second from Sweden." The battle which I witnessed took place in the Presidency of Polk, five years before the passage of Webster's Fugitive-Slave Bill.

Many a village Bose, fit only to course a mud-turtle in a victualling cellar, sported his heavy quarters in the woods, without the knowledge of his master, and ineffectually smelled at old fox burrows and wood- chucks' holes; led perchance by some slight cur which nimbly threaded the wood, and might still inspire a natural terror in its denizens; now far behind his guide, barking like a canine bull toward some small squirrel which had treed itself for scrutiny, then, cantering off, bend- ing the bushes with his weight, imagining that he is on the track of some stray member of the jerbilla family. Once I was surprised to see a cat walking along the stony shore of the pond, for they rarely wander so far from home. The surprise was mutual. Nevertheless the most domestic cat, which has lain on a rug all her days, appears quite at home in the woods, and, by her sly and stealthy behavior, proves herself more native there than the regular inhabitants. Once, when berrying, I met with a cat with young kittens in the woods, quite wild, and they all, like their mother, had their backs up and were fiercely spitting at me. A few years before I lived in the woods there was what was called a "winged cat" in one of the farm-houses in Lincoln nearest the pond, Mr. Gilian Baker's. When I called to see her in June, 1842, she was gone a-hunting in the woods, as was her wont, (I am not sure whether it was a male or female, and so use the more common pronoun,) but her mistress told me that she came into the neighborhood a little more than a year before, in April, and was finally taken into their house; that she was of a dark brownish-gray color, with a white spot on her throat, and white feet, and had a large bushy tail like a fox; that in the winter the fur grew thick and flatted out along her sides, forming strips ten or twelve inches long by two and a half wide, and under her chin like a muff, the upper side loose, the under matted like felt, and in the spring these appendages dropped off. They gave me a pair of her "wings," which I keep still. There is no appearance of a membrane about them. Some thought it was part flying-squirrel or some other wild animal, which is not impossible, for, according to naturalists, prolific hybrids have been produced by the union of the marten and domestic cat. This would have been the right kind of cat for me to keep, if I had kept any; for why should not a poet's cat be winged as well as his horse?

In the fall the loon (*Colymbus glacialis*) came, as usual, to moult and bathe in the pond, making the woods ring with his wild laughter before I had risen. At rumor of his arrival all the Mill-dam sportsmen are on the alert, in gigs and on foot, two by two and three by three, with patent rifles and conical balls and spy-glasses. They come rustling through the woods like autumn leaves, at least ten men to one loon. Some station themselves on this side of the pond, some on that, for the poor bird cannot be omnipresent; if he dive here he must come up there. But now the kind October wind rises, rustling the leaves and rippling the surface of the water, so that no loon can be heard or seen, though his foes sweep the pond with spy-glasses, and make the woods resound with their discharges. The waves generously rise and dash angrily, taking sides with all waterfowl, and our sportsmen must beat a retreat to town and shop and unfinished jobs. But they were too often successful. When I went to get a pail of water early in the morning I frequently saw this stately bird sailing out of my cove within a few rods. If I endeavored to overtake him in a boat, in order to see how he would manœuvre, he would dive and be completely lost, so that I did not discover him again, sometimes, till the latter part of the day. But I was more than a match for him on the surface. He commonly went off in a rain.

As I was paddling along the north shore one very calm October afternoon, for such days especially they settle on to the lakes, like the milkweed down, having looked in vain over the pond for a loon, suddenly one, sailing out from the shore toward the middle a few rods in front of me, set up his wild laugh and betrayed himself. I pursued with a paddle and he dived, but when he came up I was nearer than before. He dived again, but I miscalculated the direction he would take, and we were fifty rods apart when he came to the surface this time, for I had helped to widen the interval; and again he laughed long and loud, and with more reason than before. He manœuvred so cunningly that I could not get within half a dozen rods of him. Each time, when he came to the surface, turning his head this way and that, he coolly surveyed the water and the land, and apparently chose his course so that he might come up where there was the widest expanse of water and at the greatest distance from the boat. It was surprising how quickly he made up his mind and put his resolve into execution. He led me at once to the widest part of the pond, and could not be driven from it. While he was thinking one thing in his brain, I was endeavoring to divine his thought in mine. It was a pretty game, played on the smooth surface of the pond, a man against a loon. Suddenly your adversary's checker disappears beneath the board, and the problem is to place yours nearest to where his will appear again. Sometimes he would come up unexpectedly on the opposite side of me, having apparently passed directly under the boat. So long-winded was he and so unweariable, that when he had swum farthest he would immediately plunge again, nevertheless; and then no wit could divine where in the deep pond, beneath the smooth surface, he might be speeding his way like a fish, for he had time and ability to visit the bottom of the pond in its deepest part. It is said that loons have been caught in the New York lakes eighty feet beneath the surface, with hooks set for trout, — though Walden is deeper than that. How surprised must the fishes be to see this ungainly visitor from another sphere speeding his way amid their schools! Yet he appeared to know his course as surely under water as on the surface, and swam much faster there. Once or twice I saw a ripple where he approached the surface, just put his head out to reconnoitre, and instantly dived again. I found that it was as well for me to rest on my oars and wait his reappearing as to endeavor to

calculate where he would rise; for again and again, when I was straining my eyes over the surface one way, I would suddenly be startled by
his unearthly laugh behind me. But why, after displaying so much
cunning, did he invariably betray himself the moment he came up by
that loud laugh? Did not his white breast enough betray him? He
was indeed a silly loon, I thought. I could commonly hear the plash
of the water when he came up, and so also detected him. But after
an hour he seemed as fresh as ever, dived as willingly, and swam yet
farther than at first. It was surprising to see how serenely he sailed
off with unruffled breast when he came to the surface, doing all the
work with his webbed feet beneath. His usual note was this demoniac laughter, yet somewhat like that of a water-fowl; but occasionally, when he had balked me most successfully and come up a
long way off, he uttered a long-drawn unearthly howl, probably more
like that of a wolf than any bird; as when a beast puts his muzzle to the
ground and deliberately howls. This was his looning, — perhaps
the wildest sound that is ever heard here, making the woods ring far
and wide. I concluded that he laughed in derision of my efforts, confident of his own resources. Though the sky was by this time overcast, the pond was so smooth that I could see where he broke the
surface when I did not hear him. His white breast, the stillness of
the air, and the smoothness of the water were all against him. At
length, having come up fifty rods off, he uttered one of those prolonged
howls, as if calling on the god of loons to aid him, and immediately
there came a wind from the east and rippled the surface, and filled the
whole air with misty rain, and I was impressed as if it were the prayer
of the loon answered, and his god was angry with me; and so I left
him disappearing far away on the tumultuous surface.

For hours, in fall days, I watched the ducks cunningly tack and
veer and hold the middle of the pond, far from the sportsman; tricks
which they will have less need to practise in Louisiana bayous.
When compelled to rise they would sometimes circle round and
round and over the pond at a considerable height, from which they
could easily see to other ponds and the river, like black motes in the
sky; and, when I thought they had gone off thither long since, they
would settle down by a slanting flight of a quarter of a mile on to a
distant part which was left free; but what beside safety they got by
sailing in the middle of Walden I do not know, unless they love its
water for the same reason that I do.

XIII. HOUSE-WARMING

IN October I went a-graping to the river meadows, and loaded myself with clusters more precious for their beauty and fragrance than for food. There too I admired, though I did not gather, the cranberries, small waxen gems, pendants of the meadow grass, pearly and red, which the farmer plucks with an ugly rake, leaving the smooth meadow in a snarl, heedlessly measuring them by the bushel and the dollar only, and sells the spoils of the meads to Boston and New York; destined to be *jammed*, to satisfy the tastes of lovers of Nature there. So butchers rake the tongues of bison out of the prairie grass, regardless of the torn and drooping plant. The barberry's brilliant fruit was likewise food for my eyes merely; but I collected a small store of wild apples for coddling, which the proprietor and travellers had overlooked. When chestnuts were ripe I laid up half a bushel for winter. It was very exciting at that season to roam the then boundless chestnut woods of Lincoln, — they now sleep their long sleep under the railroad, — with a bag on my shoulder, and a stick to open burrs with in my hand, for I did not always wait for the frost, amid the rustling of leaves and the loud reproofs of the red-squirrels and the jays, whose half-consumed nuts I sometimes stole, for the burrs which they had selected were sure to contain sound ones. Occasionally I climbed and shook the trees. They grew also behind my house, and one large tree, which almost overshadowed it, was, when in flower, a bouquet which scented the whole neighborhood, but the squirrels and the jays got most of its fruit; the last coming in flocks early in the morning and picking the nuts out of the burrs before they fell. I relinquished these trees to them and visited the more distant woods composed wholly of chestnut. These nuts, as far as they went, were a good substitute for bread. Many other substitutes might, perhaps, be found. Digging one day for fish-worms I discovered the ground-nut (*Apios tuberosa*) on its string, the potato of the aborigines, a sort of fabulous fruit, which I had begun to doubt if I had ever dug and eaten in childhood, as I had told, and had not dreamed it. I had often since seen its crimpled red velvety blossom supported by the stems of other plants without knowing it to be the same. Cultivation has well-nigh exterminated it. It has a sweetish taste, much like that of a frost-bitten potato, and I found it better boiled than roasted. This tuber seemed like a faint promise of Nature to rear her own children and feed them simply here at some future period. In these days of fatted cattle and waving grain-fields this humble root, which was once the *totem* of an Indian tribe, is quite forgotten, or known only by its flowering vine; but let wild Nature reign here once more, and the tender and luxurious English grains will probably disappear before a myriad of foes, and without the care of man the crow may carry back even the last seed of corn to the great corn-field of the Indian's God in the south-west, whence he is said to have brought it; but the now almost exterminated ground-nut will perhaps revive and flourish in spite of frosts and wilderness, prove itself indigenous, and resume its ancient importance and dignity as the diet of the hunter tribe. Some Indian Ceres or Minerva must have been the inventor and bestower of it; and when the reign of poetry commences here, its leaves and string of nuts may be represented on our works of art.

Already, by the first of September, I had seen two or three small maples turned scarlet across the pond, beneath where the white stems of three aspens diverged, at the point of a promontory, next the water. Ah, many a tale their color told! And gradually from week to week the character of each tree came out, and it admired itself reflected in the smooth mirror of the lake. Each morning the manager of this gallery substituted some new picture, distinguished by more brilliant or harmonious coloring, for the old upon the walls.

The wasps came by thousands to my lodge in October, as to winter quarters, and settled on my windows within and on the walls overhead, sometimes deterring visitors from entering. Each morning, when they were numbed with cold, I swept some of them out, but I did not trouble myself much to get rid of them; I even felt complimented by their regarding my house as a desirable shelter. They never molested me seriously, though they bedded with me; and they gradually disappeared, into what crevices I do not know, avoiding winter and unspeakable cold.

Like the wasps, before I finally went into winter quarters in November, I used to resort to the north-east side of Walden, which the sun, reflected from the pitch-pine woods and the stony shore, made the fireside of the pond; it is so much pleasanter and wholesomer to be warmed by the sun while you can be, than by an artificial fire. I thus warmed myself by the still glowing embers which the summer, like a departed hunter, had left.

When I came to build my chimney I studied masonry. My bricks being second-hand ones required to be cleaned with a trowel, so that I learned more than usual of the qualities of bricks and trowels. The mortar on them was fifty years old, and was said to be still growing harder; but this is one of those sayings which men love to repeat whether they are true or not. Such sayings themselves grow harder and adhere more firmly with age, and it would take many blows with a trowel to clean an old wiseacre of them. Many of the villages of Mesopotamia are built of second-hand bricks of a very good quality, obtained from the ruins of Babylon, and the cement on them is older and probably harder still. However that may be, I was struck by the peculiar toughness of the steel which bore so many violent blows without being worn out. As my bricks had been in a chimney before, though I did not read the name of Nebuchadnezzar on them, I picked out as many fireplace bricks as I could find, to save work and waste, and I filled the spaces between the bricks about the fireplace with stones from the pond shore, and also made my mortar with the white sand from the same place. I lingered most about the fireplace, as the most vital part of the house. Indeed, I worked so deliberately, that though I commenced at the ground in the morning, a course of bricks raised a few inches above the floor served for my pillow at night; yet I did not get a stiff neck for it that I remember; my stiff neck is of older date. I took a poet to board for a fortnight about those times, which caused me to be put to it for room. He brought his own knife, though I had two, and we used to scour them by thrusting them into the earth. He shared with me the labors of cooking. I was pleased to see my work rising so square and solid by degrees, and reflected, that, if it proceeded slowly, it was calculated to endure a long time. The chimney is to some extent an independent structure, standing on the ground, and rising through the house to the heavens; even after the house is burned it still stands sometimes, and its importance and independence are apparent. This was toward the end of summer. It was now November.

The north wind had already begun to cool the pond, though it took many weeks of steady blowing to accomplish it, it is so deep. When I began to have a fire at evening, before I plastered my house, the chimney carried smoke particularly well, because of the numerous chinks between the boards. Yet I passed some cheerful evenings in that cool and airy apartment, surrounded by the rough brown boards full of knots, and rafters with the bark on high overhead. My house

never pleased my eye so much after it was plastered, though I was
obliged to confess that it was more comfortable. Should not every
apartment in which man dwells be lofty enough to create some obscurity overhead, where flickering shadows may play at evening
about the rafters? These forms are more agreeable to the fancy and
imagination than fresco paintings or other the most expensive furniture. I now first began to inhabit my house, I may say, when I began
to use it for warmth as well as shelter. I had got a couple of old fire-
dogs to keep the wood from the hearth, and it did me good to see the
soot form on the back of the chimney which I had built, and I poked
the fire with more right and more satisfaction than usual. My dwelling was small, and I could hardly entertain an echo in it; but it seemed
larger for being a single apartment and remote from neighbors. All
the attractions of a house were concentrated in one room; it was
kitchen, chamber, parlor, and keeping-room; and whatever satisfaction parent or child, master or servant, derive from living in a house,
I enjoyed it all. Cato says, the master of a family (*patremfamilias*)
must have in his rustic villa "cellam oleariam, vinariam, dolia multa,
uti lubeat caritatem expectare, et rei, et virtuti, et gloriæ erit," that
is, "an oil and wine cellar, many casks, so that it may be pleasant to
expect hard times; it will be for his advantage, and virtue, and glory."
I had in my cellar a firkin of potatoes, about two quarts of peas with
the weevil in them, and on my shelf a little rice, a jug of molasses, and
of rye and Indian meal a peck each.

I sometimes dream of a larger and more populous house, standing
in a golden age, of enduring materials, and without gingerbread work,
which shall still consist of only one room a vast, rude, substantial,
primitive hall, without ceiling or plastering, with bare rafters and
purlins supporting a sort of lower heaven over one's head, — useful
to keep off rain and snow, where the king and queen posts stand out
to receive your homage, when you have done reverence to the prostrate Saturn of an older dynasty on stepping over the sill; a cavernous
house, wherein you must reach up a torch upon a pole to see the roof;
where some may live in the fireplace, some in the recess of a window,
and some on settles, some at one end of the hall, some at another, and
some aloft on rafters with the spiders, if they choose; a house which
you have got into when you have opened the outside door, and the
ceremony is over; where the weary traveller may wash, and eat, and
converse, and sleep, without further journey; such a shelter as you
would be glad to reach in a tempestuous night, containing all the es-

sentials of a house, and nothing for house-keeping; where you can see all the treasures of the house at one view, and everything hangs upon its peg that a man should use; at once kitchen, pantry, parlor, chamber, storehouse, and garret; where you can see so necessary a thing as a barrel or a ladder, so convenient a thing as a cupboard, and hear the pot boil, and pay your respects to the fire that cooks your dinner, and the oven that bakes your bread, and the necessary furniture and utensils are the chief ornaments; where the washing is not put out, nor the fire, nor the mistress, and perhaps you are sometimes requested to move from off the trap-door, when the cook would descend into the cellar, and so learn whether the ground is solid or hollow beneath you without stamping. A house whose inside is as open and manifest as a bird's nest, and you cannot go in at the front door and out at the back without seeing some of its inhabitants; where to be a guest is to be presented with the freedom of the house, and not to be carefully excluded from seven eighths of it, shut up in a particular cell, and told to make yourself at home there, — in solitary confinement. Nowadays the host does not admit you to *his* hearth, but has got the mason to build one for yourself somewhere in his alley, and hospitality is the art of *keeping* you at the greatest distance. There is as much secrecy about the cooking as if he had a design to poison you. I am aware that I have been on many a man's premises, and might have been legally ordered off, but I am not aware that I have been in many men's houses. I might visit in my old clothes a king and queen who lived simply in such a house as I have described, if I were going their way; but backing out of a modern palace will be all that I shall desire to learn, if ever I am caught in one.

It would seem as if the very language of our parlors would lose all its nerve and degenerate into *parlaver* wholly, our lives pass at such remoteness from its symbols, and its metaphors and tropes are necessarily so far fetched, through slides and dumb-waiters, as it were; in other words, the parlor is so far from the kitchen and workshop. The dinner even is only the parable of a dinner, commonly. As if only the savage dwelt near enough to Nature and Truth to borrow a trope from them. How can the scholar, who dwells away in the North West Territory of the Isle of Man, tell what is parliamentary in the kitchen?

However, only one or two of my guests were ever bold enough to stay and eat a hasty-pudding with me; but when they saw that crisis approaching they beat a hasty retreat rather, as if it would shake the house to its foundations. Nevertheless, it stood through a great many hasty-puddings.

I did not plaster till it was freezing weather. I brought over some whiter and cleaner sand for this purpose from the opposite shore of the pond in a boat, a sort of conveyance which would have tempted me to go much farther if necessary. My house had in the mean while been shingled down to the ground on every side. In lathing I was pleased to be able to send home each nail with a single blow of the hammer, and it was my ambition to transfer the plaster from the board to the wall neatly and rapidly. I remembered the story of a conceited fellow, who, in fine clothes, was wont to lounge about the village once, giving advice to workmen. Venturing one day to substitute deeds for words, he turned up his cuffs, seized a plasterer's board, and having loaded his trowel without mishap, with a complacent look toward the lathing overhead, made a bold gesture thitherward; and straightway, to his complete discomfiture, received the whole contents in his ruffled bosom. I admired anew the economy and convenience of plastering, which so effectually shuts out the cold and takes a handsome finish, and I learned the various casualties to which the plasterer is liable. I was surprised to see how thirsty the bricks were which drank up all the moisture in my plaster before I had smoothed it, and how many pailfuls of water it takes to christen a new hearth. I had the previous winter made a small quantity of lime by burning the shells of the *Unio fluviatilis*, which our river affords, for the sake of the experiment; so that I knew where my materials came from. I might have got good limestone within a mile or two and burned it myself, if I had cared to do so.

The pond had in the mean while skimmed over in the shadiest and shallowest coves, some days or even weeks before the general freezing. The first ice is especially interesting and perfect, being hard, dark, and transparent, and affords the best opportunity that ever offers for examining the bottom where it is shallow; for you can lie at your length on ice only an inch thick, like a skater insect **on** the surface of the water, and study the bottom at your leisure, only two or three inches distant, like a picture behind a glass, and the water is necessarily always smooth then. There are many furrows in the sand where some creature has travelled about and doubled on its tracks; and, for wrecks, it is strewn with the cases of caddis worms made of minute grains of white quartz. Perhaps these have creased it, for you find some of their cases in the furrows, though they are deep and broad for them to make. But the ice itself is the object of most interest, though you must improve the earliest opportunity to study it. If you examine it closely the morning after it freezes, you find that the greater part of the bubbles, which at first appeared to be within it, are against its under surface, and that more are continually rising from the bottom; while the ice is as yet comparatively solid and dark, that is, you see the water through it. These bubbles are from an eightieth to an eighth of an inch in diameter, very clear and beautiful, and you see your face reflected in them through the ice. There may be thirty or forty of them to a square inch. There are also already within the ice narrow oblong perpendicular bubbles about half an inch long, sharp cones with the apex upward; or oftener, if the ice is quite fresh, minute spherical bubbles one directly above another, like a string of beads. But these within the ice are not so numerous nor obvious as those beneath. I sometimes used to cast on stones to try the strength of the ice, and those which broke through carried in air with them, which formed very large and conspicuous white bubbles beneath. One day when I came to the same place forty-eight hours afterward, I found that those large bubbles were still perfect, though an inch more of ice had formed, as I could see distinctly by the seam in the edge of a cake. But as the last two days had been very warm, like an Indian summer, the ice was not now transparent, showing the dark green color of the water, and the bottom, but opaque and whitish or gray, and though twice as thick was hardly stronger than before, for the air bubbles had greatly expanded under this heat and run together, and lost their regularity; they were no longer one directly over another, but often like silvery coins poured from a bag, one overlapping another, or in thin flakes, as if occupying slight cleavages. The beauty of the ice was gone, and it was too late to study the bottom. Being curious to know what position my great bubbles occupied with regard to the new ice, I broke out a cake containing a middling sized one, and turned it bottom upward. The new ice had formed around and under the bubble, so that it was included between the two ices. It was wholly in the lower ice, but close against the upper, and was flattish, or perhaps slightly lenticular, with a rounded edge, a quarter of an inch deep by four inches in diameter; and I was surprised to find that directly under the bubble the ice was melted with great regularity in the form of a saucer reversed, to the height of five eighths of an inch in the middle, leaving a thin partition there between the water and the bubble, hardly an eighth of an inch thick; and in many places the small bubbles in this partition had burst out downward, and probably there was no ice at all under the largest bubbles, which were a foot in diameter. I inferred that the infinite number of minute bubbles which I had first seen against the under surface of the ice were now frozen in likewise, and that each, in its degree, had operated like a burning glass on the ice beneath to melt and rot it. These are the little air-guns which contribute to make the ice crack and whoop.

At length the winter set in in good earnest, just as I had finished plastering, and the wind began to howl around the house as if it had not had permission to do so till then. Night after night the geese came lumbering in in the dark with a clangor and a whistling of wings, even after the ground was covered with snow, some to alight in Walden, and some flying low over the woods toward Fair Haven, bound for Mexico. Several times, when returning from the village at ten or eleven o'clock at night I heard the tread of a flock of geese, or else ducks, on the dry leaves in the woods by a pond-hole behind my dwelling, where they had come up to feed, and the faint honk or quack of their leader as they hurried off. In 1845 Walden froze entirely over for the first time on the night of the 22d of December, Flints' and other shallower ponds and the river having been frozen ten days or more; in '46, the 16th; in '49, about the 31st; and in '50, about the 27th of December; in '52, the 5th of January; in '53, the 31st of December. The snow had already covered the ground since the 25th of November, and surrounded me suddenly with the scenery of winter. I withdrew yet farther into my shell, and endeavored to keep a bright fire both within my house and within my breast. My employment out of doors now was to collect the dead wood in the forest, bringing it in my hands or on my shoulders, or sometimes trailing a dead pine-tree under each arm to my shed. An old forest fence which had seen its best days was a great haul for me. I sacrificed it to Vulcan, for it was past serving the god Terminus. How much more interesting an event is that man's supper who has just been forth in the snow to hunt, nay, you might say, steal, the fuel to cook it with! His bread and meat are sweet. There are enough fagots and waste wood of all kinds in the forests of most of our towns to support many fires, but which at present warm none, and, some think, hinder the growth of the young wood. There was also the driftwood of the pond. In the course of the summer I had discovered a raft of pitch-pine logs with the bark on, pinned together by the Irish when the railroad was built. This I hauled up partly on the shore. After soaking two years and then lying high six months it was perfectly sound, though waterlogged past drying. I amused myself one winter day with sliding this piece-meal across the pond, nearly half a mile, skating behind with one end of a log fifteen feet long on my shoulder, and the other on the ice; or I tied several logs together with a birch withe, and then, with a longer birch or alder which had a hook at the end, dragged them across. Though completely waterlogged and almost as heavy as lead, they not only burned long, but made a very hot fire; nay, I thought that they burned better for the soaking, as if the pitch, being confined by the water, burned longer as in a lamp.

Gilpin, in his account of the forest borderers of England, says that "the encroachments of trespassers, and the houses and fences thus raised on the borders of the forest," were "considered as great nuisances by the old forest law, and were severely punished under the name of *purprestures*, as tending *ad terrorem ferarum — ad nocumentum forestæ*, etc.," to the frightening of the game and the detriment of the forest. But I was interested in the preservation of the venison and the vert more than the hunters or wood-choppers, and as much as though I had been the Lord Warden himself; and if any part was burned, though I burned it myself by accident, I grieved with a grief that lasted longer and was more inconsolable than that of the proprietors; nay, I grieved when it was cut down by the proprietors themselves. I would that our farmers when they cut down a forest felt some of that awe which the old Romans did when they came to thin, or let in the light to, a consecrated grove, (*lucum conlucare*,) that is, would believe that it is sacred to some god. The Roman made an expiatory offering, and prayed, Whatever god or goddess thou art to whom this grove is sacred, be propitious to me, my family, and children, etc.

It is remarkable what a value is still put upon wood even in this age and in this new country, a value more permanent and universal than that of gold. After all our discoveries and inventions no man will go by a pile of wood. It is as precious to us as it was to our Saxon and Norman ancestors. If they made their bows of it, we make our gunstocks of it. Michaux, more than thirty years ago, says that the price of wood for fuel in New York and Philadelphia "nearly equals, and sometimes exceeds, that of the best wood in Paris, though this immense capital annually requires more than three hundred thousand cords, and is surrounded to the distance of three hundred miles by cultivated plains." In this town the price of wood rises almost steadily, and the only question is, how much higher it is to be this year than it was the last. Mechanics and tradesmen who come in person to the forest on no other errand, are sure to attend the wood auction, and even pay a high price for the privilege of gleaning after the woodchopper. It is now many years that men have resorted to the forest for fuel and the materials of the arts: the New Englander and the New Hollander, the Parisian and the Celt, the farmer and Robinhood, Goody Blake and Harry Gill; in most parts of the world the prince and the peasant, the scholar and the savage, equally require still a few sticks from the forest to warm them and cook their food. Neither could I do without them.

Every man looks at his wood-pile with a kind of affection. I loved to have mine before my window, and the more chips the better to re-mind me of my pleasing work. I had an old axe which nobody claimed, with which by spells in winter days, on the sunny side of the house, I played about the stumps which I had got out of my bean-field. As my driver prophesied when I was ploughing, they warmed me twice, — once while I was splitting them, and again when they were on the fire, so that no fuel could give out more heat. As for the axe, I was advised to get the village blacksmith to "jump" it; but I jumped him, and, putting a hickory helve from the woods into it, made it do. If it was dull, it was at least hung true.

A few pieces of fat pine were a great treasure. It is interesting to remember how much of this food for fire is still concealed in the bowels of the earth. In previous years I had often gone "prospecting" over some bare hill side, where a pitch-pine wood had formerly stood, and got out the fat pine roots. They are almost indestructible. Stumps thirty or forty years old, at least, will still be sound at the core, though the sapwood has all become vegetable mould, as appears by the scales of the thick bark forming a ring level with the earth four or five inches distant from the heart. With axe and shovel you ex-plore this mine, and follow the marrowy store, yellow as beef tallow, or as if you had struck on a vein of gold, deep into the earth. But commonly I kindled my fire with the dry leaves of the forest, which I had stored up in my shed before the snow came. Green hickory finely split makes the wood-chopper's kindlings, when he has a camp in the woods. Once in a while I got a little of this. When the vil-lagers were lighting their fires beyond the horizon, I too gave notice to the various wild inhabitants of Walden vale, by a smoky streamer from my chimney, that I was awake. —

> Light-winged Smoke, Icarian bird,
> Melting thy pinions in thy upward flight,
> Lark without song, and messenger of dawn,
> Circling above the hamlets as thy nest;
> Or else, departing dream, and shadowy form
> Of midnight vision, gathering up thy skirts;
> By night star-veiling, and by day
> Darkening the light and blotting out the sun;
> Go thou my incense upward from this hearth,
> And ask the gods to pardon this clear flame.

Hard green wood just cut, though I used but little of that, answered my purpose better than any other. I sometimes left a good fire when I went to take a walk in a winter afternoon; and when I returned, three or four hours afterward, it would be still alive and glowing. My house was not empty though I was gone. It was as if I had left a cheerful housekeeper behind. It was I and Fire that lived there; and commonly my housekeeper proved trustworthy. One day, however, as I was splitting wood, I thought that I would just look in at the window and see if the house was not on fire; it was the only time I remember to have been particularly anxious on this score; so I looked and saw that a spark had caught my bed, and I went in and extinguished it when it had burned a place as big as my hand. But my house occupied so sunny and sheltered a position, and its roof was so low, that I could afford to let the fire go out in the middle of almost any winter day.

The moles nested in my cellar, nibbling every third potato, and making a snug bed even there of some hair left after plastering and of brown paper; for even the wildest animals love comfort and warmth as well as man, and they survive the winter only because they are so careful to secure them. Some of my friends spoke as if I was coming to the woods on purpose to freeze myself. The animal merely makes a bed, which he warms with his body, in a sheltered place; but man, having discovered fire, boxes up some air in a spacious apartment, and warms that, instead of robbing himself, makes that his bed, in which he can move about divested of more cumbrous clothing, maintain a kind of summer in the midst of winter, and by means of windows even admit the light, and with a lamp lengthen out the day. Thus he goes a step or two beyond instinct, and saves a little time for the fine arts. Though, when I had been exposed to the rudest blasts a long time, my whole body began to grow torpid, when I reached the genial atmosphere of my house I soon recovered my faculties and prolonged my life. But the most luxuriously housed has little to boast of in this respect, nor need we trouble ourselves to speculate how the human race may be at last destroyed. It would be easy to cut their threads any time with a little sharper blast from the north. We go on dating from Cold Fridays and Great Snows; but a little colder Friday, or greater snow would put a period to man's existence on the globe.

The next winter I used a small cooking-stove for economy, since I did not own the forest; but it did not keep fire so well as the open fireplace. Cooking was then, for the most part, no longer a poetic, but merely a chemic process. It will soon be forgotten, in these days of stoves, that we used to roast potatoes in the ashes, after the Indian fashion. The stove not only took up room and scented the house, but it concealed the fire, and I felt as if I had lost a companion. You can always see a face in the fire. The laborer, looking into it at evening, purifies his thoughts of the dross and earthiness which they have accumulated during the day. But I could no longer sit and look into the fire, and the pertinent words of a poet recurred to me with new force. —

> "Never, bright flame, may be denied to me
> Thy dear, life imaging, close sympathy.
> What but my hopes shot upward e'er so bright?
> What but my fortunes sunk so low in night?
> Why art thou banished from our hearth and hall,
> Thou who art welcomed and beloved by all?
> Was thy existence then too fanciful
> For our life's common light, who are so dull?
> Did thy bright gleam mysterious converse hold
> With our congenial souls? secrets too bold?
>
> Well, we are safe and strong, for now we sit
> Beside a hearth where no dim shadows flit,
> Where nothing cheers nor saddens, but a fire
> Warms feet and hands — nor does to more aspire;
> By whose compact utilitarian heap
> The present may sit down and go to sleep,
> Nor fear the ghosts who from the dim past walked,
> And with us by the unequal light of the old wood
>   fire talked."

XIV. FORMER INHABITANTS; AND WINTER VISITORS

I WEATHERED some merry snow storms, and spent some cheerful winter evenings by my fireside, while the snow whirled wildly without, and even the hooting of the owl was hushed. For many weeks I met no one in my walks but those who came occasionally to cut wood and sled it to the village. The elements, however, abetted me in making a path through the deepest snow in the woods, for when I had once gone through the wind blew the oak leaves into my tracks, where they lodged, and by absorbing the rays of the sun melted the snow, and so not only made a dry bed for my feet, but in the night their dark line was my guide. For human society I was obliged to conjure up the former occupants of these woods. Within the memory of many of my townsmen the road near which my house stands resounded with the laugh and gossip of inhabitants, and the woods which border it were notched and dotted here and there with their little gardens and dwellings, though it was then much more shut in by the forest than now. In some places, within my own remembrance, the pines would scrape both sides of a chaise at once, and women and children who were compelled to go this way to Lincoln alone and on foot did it with fear, and often ran a good part of the distance. Though mainly but a humble route to neighboring villages, or for the woodman's team, it once amused the traveller more than now by its variety, and lingered longer in his memory. Where now firm open fields stretch from the village to the woods, it then ran through a maple swamp on a foundation of logs, the remnants of which, doubtless, still underlie the present dusty highway, from the Stratten, now the Alms House, Farm, to Brister's Hill.

East of my bean-field, across the road, lived Cato Ingraham, slave of Duncan Ingraham, Esquire, gentleman, of Concord village, who built his slave a house, and gave him permission to live in Walden Woods; — Cato, not Uticensis, but Concordiensis. Some say that he was a Guinea Negro. There are a few who remember his little patch among the walnuts, which he let grow up till he should be old and need them; but a younger and whiter speculator got them at last. He too, however, occupies an equally narrow house at present. Cato's half-obliterated cellar hole still remains, though known to few, being concealed from the traveller by a fringe of pines. It is now filled with the smooth sumach, (*Rhus glabra*,) and one of the earliest species of goldenrod (*Solidago stricta*) grows there luxuriantly.

Here, by the very corner of my field, still nearer to town, Zilpha, a colored woman, had her little house, where she spun linen for the townsfolk, making the Walden Woods ring with her shrill singing, for she had a loud and notable voice. At length, in the war of 1812, her dwelling was set on fire by English soldiers, prisoners on parole, when she was away, and her cat and dog and hens were all burned up together. She led a hard life, and somewhat inhumane. One old frequenter of these woods remembers, that as he passed her house one noon he heard her muttering to herself over her gurgling pot, — "Ye are all bones, bones!" I have seen bricks amid the oak copse there.

Down the road, on the right hand, on Brister's Hill, lived Brister Freeman, "a handy Negro," slave of Squire Cummings once, — there where grow still the apple-trees which Brister planted and tended; large old trees now, but their fruit still wild and ciderish to my taste. Not long since I read his epitaph in the old Lincoln burying-ground, a little on one side, near the unmarked graves of some British grena- diers who fell in the retreat from Concord, — where he is styled "Sippio Brister," — Scipio Africanus he had some title to be called, — "a man of color," as if he were discolored. It also told me, with staring emphasis, when he died; which was but an indirect way of in- forming me that he ever lived. With him dwelt Fenda, his hospitable wife, who told fortunes, yet pleasantly, — large, round, and black, blacker than any of the children of night, such a dusky orb as never rose on Concord before or since.

Farther down the hill, on the left, on the old road in the woods, are marks of some homestead of the Stratten family; whose orchard once covered all the slope of Brister's Hill, but was long since killed out by pitch-pines, excepting a few stumps, whose old roots furnish still the wild stocks of many a thrifty village tree.

Nearer yet to town, you come to Breed's location, on the other side of the way, just on the edge of the wood; ground famous for the pranks of a demon not distinctly named in old mythology, who has acted a prominent and astounding part in our New England life, and deserves, as much as any mythological character, to have his biog- raphy written one day; who first comes in the guise of a friend or hired man, and then robs and murders the whole family, — New-

England Rum. But history must not yet tell the tragedies enacted here; let time intervene in some measure to assuage and lend an azure tint to them. Here the most indistinct and dubious tradition says that once a tavern stood; the well the same, which tempered the traveller's beverage and refreshed his steed. Here then men saluted one another, and heard and told the news, and went their ways again.

Breed's hut was standing only a dozen years ago, though it had long been unoccupied. It was about the size of mine. It was set on fire by mischievous boys, one Election night, if I do not mistake. I lived on the edge of the village then, and had just lost myself over Davenant's Gondibert, that winter that I labored with a lethargy, — which, by the way, I never knew whether to regard as a family complaint, having an uncle who goes to sleep shaving himself, and is obliged to sprout potatoes in a cellar Sundays, in order to keep awake and keep the Sabbath, or as the consequence of my attempt to read Chalmers' collection of English poetry without skipping. It fairly overcame my Nervii. I had just sunk my head on this when the bells rung fire, and in hot haste the engines rolled that way, led by a straggling troop of men and boys, and I among the foremost, for I had leaped the brook. We thought it was far south over the woods, — we who had run to fires before, — barn, shop, or dwelling-house, or all together. "It's Baker's barn," cried one. "It is the Codman Place," affirmed another. And then fresh sparks went up above the wood, as if the roof fell in, and we all shouted "Concord to the rescue!" Wagons shot past with furious speed and crushing loads, bearing, perchance, among the rest, the agent of the Insurance Company, who was bound to go however far; and ever and anon the engine bell tinkled behind, more slow and sure; and rearmost of all, as it was afterward whispered, came they who set the fire and gave the alarm. Thus we kept on like true idealists, rejecting the evidence of our senses, until at a turn in the road we heard the crackling and actually felt the heat of the fire from over the wall, and realized, alas! that we were there. The very nearness of the fire but cooled our ardor. At first we thought to throw a frog-pond on to it; but concluded to let it burn, it was so far gone and so worthless. So we stood round our engine, jostled one another, expressed our sentiments through speaking-trumpets, or in lower tone referred to the great conflagrations which the world has witnessed, including Bascom's shop, and, between ourselves, we thought that, were we there in season with our "tub," and a full frog-pond by, we could turn that

threatened last and universal one into another flood. We finally retreated without doing any mischief, — returned to sleep and Gondibert. But as for Gondibert, I would except that passage in the preface
about wit being the soul's powder, — "but most of mankind are
strangers to wit, as Indians are to powder."

It chanced that I walked that way across the fields the following
night, about the same hour, and hearing a low moaning at this spot,
I drew near in the dark, and discovered the only survivor of the family
that I know, the heir of both its virtues and its vices, who alone was
interested in this burning, lying on his stomach and looking over the
cellar wall at the still smoldering cinders beneath, muttering to himself, as is his wont. He had been working far off in the river meadows
all day, and had improved the first moments that he could call his own
to visit the home of his fathers and his youth. He gazed into the cellar from all sides and points of view by turns, always lying down to
it, as if there was some treasure, which he remembered, concealed
between the stones, where there was absolutely nothing but a heap
of bricks and ashes. The house being gone, he looked at what there
was left. He was soothed by the sympathy which my mere presence
implied, and showed me, as well as the darkness permitted, where the
well was covered up; which, thank Heaven, could never be burned;
and he groped along about the wall to find the well-sweep which his
father had cut and mounted, feeling for the iron hook or staple by
which a burden had been fastened to the heavy end, — all that he
could now cling to, — to convince me that it was no common "rider."
I felt it, and still remark it almost daily in my walks, for by its hangs
the history of a family.

Once more, on the left, where are seen the well and lilac bushes by
the wall, in the now open field, lived Nutting and Le Grosse. But to
return toward Lincoln.

Farther in the woods than any of these, where the road approaches
nearest to the pond, Wyman the potter squatted, and furnished his
townsmen with earthen ware, and left descendants to succeed him.
Neither were they rich in worldly goods, holding the land by suffer-
ance while they lived; and there often the sheriff came in vain to
collect the taxes, and "attached a chip," for form's sake, as I have
read in his accounts, there being nothing else that he could lay his
hands on. One day in midsummer, when I was hoeing, a man who
was carrying a load of pottery to market stopped his horse against
my field and inquired concerning Wyman the younger. He had long

ago bought a potter's wheel of him, and wished to know what had become of him. I had read of the potter's clay and wheel in Scripture, but it had never occurred to me that the pots we use were not such as had come down unbroken from those days, or grown on trees like gourds somewhere, and I was pleased to hear that so fictile an art was ever practised in my neighborhood.

The last inhabitant of these woods before me was an Irishman, Hugh Quoil, (if I have spelt his name with coil enough,) who occupied Wyman's tenement, — Col. Quoil, he was called. Rumor said that he had been a soldier at Waterloo. If he had lived I should have made him fight his battles over again. His trade here was that of a ditcher. Napoleon went to St. Helena; Quoil came to Walden Woods. All I know of him is tragic. He was a man of manners, like one who had seen the world, and was capable of more civil speech than you could well attend to. He wore a great coat in midsummer, being affected with the trembling delirium, and his face was the color of carmine. He died in the road at the foot of Brister's Hill shortly after I came to the woods, so that I have not remembered him as a neighbor. Before his house was pulled down, when his comrades avoided it as "an unlucky castle," I visited it. There lay his old clothes curled up by use, as if they were himself, upon his raised plank bed. His pipe lay broken on the hearth, instead of a bowl broken at the fountain. The last could never have been the symbol of his death, for he confessed to me that, though he had heard of Brister's Spring, he had never seen it; and soiled cards, kings of diamonds spades and hearts, were scattered over the floor. One black chicken which the administrator could not catch, black as night and as silent, not even croaking, awaiting Reynard, still went to roost in the next apartment. In the rear there was the dim outline of a garden, which had been planted but had never received its first hoeing, owing to those terrible shaking fits, though it was now harvest time. It was overrun with Roman wormwood and beggar-ticks, which last stuck to my clothes for all fruit. The skin of a woodchuck was freshly stretched upon the back of the house, a trophy of his last Waterloo; but no warm cap or mittens would he want more.

Now only a dent in the earth marks the site of these dwellings, with buried cellar stones, and strawberries, raspberries, thimble-berries, hazel-bushes, and sumachs growing in the sunny sward there; some pitch-pine or gnarled oak occupies what was the chimney nook, and a sweet-scented blackbirch, perhaps, waves where the door-stone was. Sometimes the well dent is visible, where once a spring oozed; now dry and tearless grass; or it was covered deep, — not to be discovered till some late day, — with a flat stone under the sod, when the last of the race departed. What a sorrowful act must that be, — the covering up of wells! coincident with the opening of wells of tears. These cellar dents, like deserted fox burrows, old holes, are all that is left where once were the stir and bustle of human life, and "fate, free-will, foreknowledge absolute," in some form and dialect or other were by turns discussed. But all I can learn of their conclusions amounts to just this, that "Cato and Brister pulled wool;" which is about as edifying as the history of more famous schools of philosophy.

Still grows the vivacious lilac a generation after the door and lintel and the sill are gone, unfolding its sweet-scented flowers each spring, to be plucked by the musing traveller; planted and tended once by children's hands, in front-yard plots, — now standing by wall-sides in retired pastures, and giving place to new-rising forests; — the last of that stirp, sole survivor of that family. Little did the dusky children think that the puny slip with its two eyes only, which they stuck in the ground in the shadow of the house and daily watered, would root itself so, and outlive them, and house itself in the rear that shaded it, and grown man's garden and orchard, and tell their story faintly to the lone wanderer a half century after they had grown up and died, — blossoming as fair, and smelling as sweet, as in the first spring. I mark its still tender, civil, cheerful, lilac colors.

But this small village, germ of something more, why did it fail while Concord keeps its ground? Were there no natural advantages, — no water privileges, forsooth? Ay, the deep Walden Pond and cool Brister's Spring, — privilege to drink long and healthy draughts at these, all unimproved by these men but to dilute their glass. They were universally a thirsty race. Might not the basket, stable-broom, mat-making, corn-parching, linen-spinning, and pottery business have thrived here, making the wilderness to blossom like the rose, and a numerous posterity have inherited the land of their fathers? The sterile soil would at least have been proof against a low-land degeneracy. Alas! how little does the memory of these human inhabitants enhance the beauty of the landscape! Again, perhaps, Nature will try, with me for a first settler, and my house raised last spring to be the oldest in the hamlet.

I am not aware that any man has ever built on the spot which I occupy. Deliver me from a city built on the site of a more ancient city, whose materials are ruins, whose gardens cemeteries. The soil is blanched and accursed there, and before that becomes necessary the earth itself will be destroyed. With such reminiscences I repeopled the woods and lulled myself asleep.

At this season I seldom had a visitor. When the snow lay deepest no wanderer ventured near my house for a week or fortnight at a time, but there I lived as snug as a meadow mouse, or as cattle and poultry which are said to have survived for a long time buried in drifts, even without food; or like that early settler's family in the town of Sutton, in this state, whose cottage was completely covered by the great snow of 1717 when he was absent, and an Indian found it only by the hole which the chimney's breath made in the drift, and so relieved the family. But no friendly Indian concerned himself about me; nor needed he, for the master of the house was at home. The Great Snow! How cheerful it is to hear of! When the farmers could not get to the woods and swamps with their teams, and were obliged to cut down the shade trees before their houses, and when the crust was harder cut off the trees in the swamps ten feet from the ground, as it appeared the next spring.

In the deepest snows, the path which I used from the highway to my house, about half a mile long, might have been represented by a meandering dotted line, with wide intervals between the dots. For a week of even weather I took exactly the same number of steps, and of the same length, coming and going, stepping deliberately and with the precision of a pair of dividers in my own deep tracks, — to such routine the winter reduces us, — yet often they were filled with heaven's own blue. But no weather interfered fatally with my walks, or rather my going abroad, for I frequently tramped eight or ten miles through the deepest snow to keep an appointment with a beech-tree, or a yellow-birch, or an old acquaintance among the pines; when the ice and snow causing their limbs to droop, and so sharpening their tops, had changed the pines into fir-trees; wading to the tops of the highest hills when the snow was nearly two feet deep on a level, and shaking down another snow-storm on my head at every step; or some-times creeping and floundering thither on my hands and knees, when the hunters had gone into winter quarters. One afternoon I amused myself by watching a barred owl (*Strix nebulosa*) sitting on one of the lower dead limbs of a white-pine, close to the trunk, in broad daylight,

I standing within a rod of him. He could hear me when I moved and
cronched the snow with my feet, but could not plainly see me. When
I made most noise he would stretch out his neck, and erect his neck
feathers, and open his eyes wide; but their lids soon fell again, and he
began to nod. I too felt a slumberous influence after watching him
half an hour, as he sat thus with his eyes half open, like a cat, winged
brother of the cat. There was only a narrow slit left between their
lids, by which he preserved a peninsular relation to me; thus, with
half-shut eyes, looking out from the land of dreams, and endeavoring
to realize me, vague object or mote that interrupted his visions. At
length, on some louder noise or my nearer approach, he would grow
uneasy and sluggishly turn about on his perch, as if impatient at
having his dreams disturbed; and when he launched himself off and
flapped through the pines, spreading his wings to unexpected breadth,
I could not hear the slightest sound from them. Thus, guided amid
the pine boughs rather by a delicate sense of their neighborhood than
by sight, feeling his twilight way as it were with his sensitive pinions,
he found a new perch, where he might in peace await the dawning
of his day.

As I walked over the long causeway made for the railroad through
the meadows, I encountered many a blustering and nipping wind, for
nowhere has it freer play; and when the frost had smitten me on one
cheek, heathen as I was, I turned to it the other also. Nor was it
much better by the carriage road from Brister's Hill. For I came to
town still, like a friendly Indian, when the contents of the broad open
fields were all piled up between the walls of the Walden road, and
half an hour sufficed to obliterate the tracks of the last traveller. And
when I returned new drifts would have formed, through which I
floundered, where the busy north-west wind had been depositing the
powdery snow round a sharp angle in the road, and not a rabbit's
track, nor even the fine print, the small type, of a meadow mouse was
to be seen. Yet I rarely failed to find, even in midwinter, some warm
and springy swamp where the grass and the skunk-cabbage still put
forth with perennial verdure, and some hardier bird occasionally
awaited the return of spring.

Sometimes, notwithstanding the snow, when I returned from my
walk at evening I crossed the deep tracks of a wood-chopper leading
from my door, and found his pile of whittlings on the hearth, and my
house filled with the odor of his pipe. Or on a Sunday afternoon, if
I chanced to be at home, I heard the cronching of the snow made by

the step of a long-headed farmer,[1] who from far through the woods sought my house, to have a social "crack;" one of the few of his vocation who are "men on their farms;" who donned a frock instead of a professor's gown, and is as ready to extract the moral out of church or state as to haul a load of manure from his barn-yard. We talked of rude and simple times, when men sat about large fires in cold bracing weather, with clear heads; and when other dessert failed, we tried our teeth on many a nut which wise squirrels have long since abandoned, for those which have the thickest shells are commonly empty.

The one who came from farthest to my lodge, through deepest snows and most dismal tempests, was a poet.[2] A farmer, a hunter, a soldier, a reporter, even a philosopher, may be daunted; but nothing can deter a poet, for he is actuated by pure love. Who can predict his comings and goings? His business calls him out at all hours, even when doctors sleep. We made that small house ring with boisterous mirth and resound with the murmur of much sober talk, making amends then to Walden vale for the long silences. Broadway was still and deserted in comparison. At suitable intervals there were regular salutes of laughter, which might have been referred indifferently to the last uttered or the forth-coming jest. We made many a "bran new" theory of life over a thin dish of gruel, which combined the advantages of conviviality with the clear-headedness which philosophy requires.

I should not forget that during my last winter at the pond there was another welcome visitor,[3] who at one time came through the village, through snow and rain and darkness, till he saw my lamp through the trees, and shared with me some long winter evenings. One of the last of the philosophers, — Connecticut gave him to the world, — he peddled first her wares, afterwards, as he declares, his brains. These he peddles still, prompting God and disgracing man, bearing for fruit his brain only, like the nut its kernel. I think that he must be the man of the most faith of any alive. His words and attitude always suppose a better state of things than other men are acquainted with, and he will be the last man to be disappointed as the ages revolve. He has no venture in the present. But though comparatively disregarded now, when his day comes, laws unsuspected by most will take

---

[1] Probably George Minott, Thoreau's ideal farmer and Concord Herodotus.
[2] Willian Ellery Channing, the younger.
[3] Bronson Alcott.

effect, and masters of families and rulers will come to him for advice. —

"How blind that cannot see serenity!"

A true friend of man; almost the only friend of human progress.   An
Old Mortality, say rather an Immortality, with unwearied patience
and faith making plain the image engraven in men's bodies, the God
of whom they are but defaced and leaning monuments.   With his
hospitable intellect he embraces children, beggars, insane, and scholars,
and entertains the thought of all, adding to it commonly some breath
and elegance.   I think that he should keep a caravansary on the
world's highway, where philosophers of all nations might put up, and
on his sign should be printed, "Entertainment for man, but not for his
beast.   Enter ye that have leisure and a quiet mind, who earnestly
seek the right road."   He is perhaps the sanest man and has the fewest crotchets of any I chance to know; the same yesterday and to-
morrow.   Of yore we had sauntered and talked, and effectually put
the world behind us; for he was pledged to no institution in it, free-
born, *ingenuus*.   Whichever way we turned, it seemed that the heavens and the earth had met together, since he enhanced the beauty of
the landscape.   A blue-robed man, whose fittest roof is the overarch-
ing sky which reflects his serenity.   I do not see how he can ever die;
Nature cannot spare him.

   Having each some shingles of thought well dried, we sat and
whittled them, trying our knives, and admiring the clear yellowish
grain of the pumpkin pine.   We waded so gently and reverently, or
we pulled together so smoothly, that the fishes of thought were not
scared from the stream, nor feared any angler on the bank, but came
and went grandly, like the clouds which float through the western
sky, and the mother-o'-pearl flocks which sometimes form and dissolve there.   There we worked, revising mythology, rounding a
fable here and there, and building castles in the air for which earth
offered no worthy foundation.   Great Looker!   Great Expecter! to
converse with whom was a New England Night's Entertainment.
Ah! such discourse we had, hermit and philosopher, and the old settler
I have spoken of, — we three, — it expanded and racked my little
house; I should not dare to say how many pounds' weight there was
above the atmospheric pressure on every circular inch; it opened its
seams so that they had to be calked with much dulness thereafter to
stop the consequent leak; — but I had enough of that kind of oakum
already picked.

There was one other [1] with whom I had "solid seasons," long to be remembered, at his house in the village, and who looked in upon me from time to time; but I had no more for society there.

There too, as everywhere, I sometimes expected the Visitor who never comes. The Vishnu Purana says, "The house-holder is to remain at eventide in his court-yard as long as it takes to milk a cow, or longer if he pleases, to await the arrival of a guest." I often performed this duty of hospitality, waited long enough to milk a whole herd of cows, but did not see the man approaching from the town.

XV. WINTER ANIMALS

WHEN the ponds were firmly frozen, they afforded not only new and shorter routes to many points, but new views from their surfaces of the familiar landscape around them. When I crossed Flints' Pond, after it was covered with snow, though I had often paddled about and skated over it, it was so unexpectedly wide and so strange that I could think of nothing but Baffin's Bay. The Lincoln hills rose up around me at the extremity of a snowy plain, in which I did not remember to have stood before; and the fishermen, at an indeterminable distance over the ice, moving slowly about with their wolfish dogs, passed for sealers or Esquimaux, or in misty weather loomed like fabulous creatures, and I did not know whether they were giants or pygmies. I took this course when I went to lecture in Lincoln in the evening, travelling in no road and passing no house between my own hut and the lecture room. In Goose Pond, which lay in my way, a colony of muskrats dwelt, and raised their cabins high above the ice, though none could be seen abroad when I crossed it. Walden, being like the rest usually bare of snow, or with only shallow and interrupted drifts on it, was my yard where I could walk freely

[1] Ralph Waldo Emerson. By comparison with the generous tributes to Channing and Alcott, and in the ambiguous remark, "I had no more for society there" — implying either that he had no more friends in the village, which was untrue, or that the third person he required to make a society, in this case God, was not present — one catches a glimpse of the breakdown of Thoreau's friendship with Emerson.

when the snow was nearly two feet deep on a level elsewhere and the villagers were confined to their streets. There, far from the village street, and except at very long intervals, from the jingle of sleigh-bells, I slid and skated, as in a vast moose-yard well trodden, over-hung by oak woods and solemn pines bent down with snow or bristling with icicles.

For sounds in winter nights, and often in winter days, I heard the forlorn but melodious note of a hooting owl indefinitely far; such a sound as the frozen earth would yield if struck with a suitable plec-trum, the very *lingua vernacula* of Walden Wood, and quite familiar to me at last, though I never saw the bird while it was making it. I seldom opened my door in a winter evening without hearing it; *Hoo hoo, hoo, hoorer hoo,* sounded sonorously, and the first three syllables accented somewhat like *how der do;* or sometimes *hoo hoo* only. One night in the beginning of winter, before the pond froze over, about nine o'clock, I was startled by the loud honking of a goose, and, step-ping to the door, heard the sound of their wings like a tempest in the woods as they flew low over my house. They passed over the pond toward Fair Haven, seemingly deterred from settling by my light, their commodore honking all the while with a regular beat. Sud-denly an unmistakable cat-owl from very near me, with the most harsh and tremendous voice I ever heard from any inhabitant of the woods, responded at regular intervals to the goose, as if determined to expose and disgrace this intruder from Hudson's Bay by exhibiting a greater compass and volume of voice in a native, and *boo-hoo* him out of Concord horizon. What do you mean by alarming the citadel at this time of night consecrated to me? Do you think I am ever caught napping at such an hour, and that I have not got lungs and a larynx as well as yourself? *Boo-hoo, boo-hoo, boo-hoo!* It was one of the most thrilling discords I ever heard. And yet, if you had a discriminating ear, there were in it the elements of a concord such as these plains never saw nor heard.

I also heard the whooping of the ice in the pond, my great bed-fellow in that part of Concord, as if it were restless in its bed and would fain turn over, were troubled with flatulency and bad dreams; or I was waked by the cracking of the ground by the frost, as if some one had driven a team against my door, and in the morning would find a crack in the earth a quarter of a mile long and a third of an inch wide.

Sometimes I heard the foxes as they ranged over the snow crust, in moonlight nights, in search of a partridge or other game, barking raggedly and demoniacally like forest dogs, as if laboring with some anxiety, or seeking expression, struggling for light and to be dogs outright and run freely in the streets; for if we take the ages into our account, may there not be a civilization going on among brutes as well as men? They seemed to me to be rudimental, burrowing men, still standing on their defence, awaiting their transformation. Sometimes one came near to my window, attracted by my light, barked a vulpine curse at me, and then retreated.

Usually the red squirrel (*Sciurus Hudsonius*) waked me in the dawn, coursing over the roof and up and down the sides of the house, as if sent out of the woods for this purpose. In the course of the winter I threw out half a bushel of ears of sweet-corn, which had not got ripe, on to the snow crust by my door, and was amused by watching the motions of the various animals which were baited by it. In the twilight and the night the rabbits came regularly and made a hearty meal. All day long the red squirrels came and went, and afforded me much entertainment by their manœuvres. One would approach at first warily through the shrub-oaks, running over the snow crust by fits and starts like a leaf blown by the wind, now a few paces this way, with wonderful speed and waste of energy, making inconceivable haste with his "trotters," as if it were for a wager, and now as many paces that way, but never getting on more than half a rod at a time; and then suddenly pausing with a ludicrous expression and a gratuitous somerset, as if all the eyes in the universe were fixed on him, — for all the motions of a squirrel, even in the most solitary recesses of the forest, imply spectators as much as those of the dancing girl, — wasting more time in delay and circumspection than would have sufficed to walk the whole distance, — I never saw one walk, — and then suddenly, before you could say Jack Robinson, he would be in the top of a young pitch-pine, winding up his clock and chiding all imaginary spectators, soliloquizing and talking to all the universe at the same time, — for no reason that I could ever detect, or he himself was aware of, I suspect. At length he would reach the corn, and selecting a suitable ear, frisk about in the same uncertain trigonometrical way to the top-most stick of my wood-pile, before my window, where he looked me in the face, and there sit for hours, supplying himself with a new ear from time to time, nibbling at first voraciously and throwing the half-naked cobs about; till at length he grew more dainty still and played with his food, tasting only the inside of the kernel, and the ear, which was held balanced over the stick by one paw, slipped from his careless grasp and fell to the ground, when he would look over at it with a ludicrous expression of uncertainty, as if suspecting that it had life, with a mind not made up whether to get it again, or a new one, or be off; now thinking of corn, then listening to hear what was in the wind. So the little impudent fellow would waste many an ear in a forenoon; till at last, seizing some longer and plumper one, considerably bigger than himself, and skilfully balancing it, he would set out with it to the woods, like a tiger with a buffalo, by the same zigzag course and frequent pauses, scratching along with it as if it were too heavy for him and falling all the while, making its fall a diagonal between a perpendicular and horizontal, being determined to put it through at any rate; — a singularly frivolous and whimsical fellow; — and so he would get off with it to where he lived, perhaps carry it to the top of a pine-tree forty or fifty rods distant, and I would afterwards find the cobs strewn about the woods in various directions.

At length the jays arrive, whose discordant screams were heard long before, as they were warily making their approach an eighth of a mile off, and in a stealthy and sneaking manner they flit from tree to tree, nearer and nearer, and pick up the kernels which the squirrels have dropped. Then, sitting on a pitch-pine bough, they attempt to swallow in their haste a kernel which is too big for their throats and chokes them; and after great labor they disgorge it, and spend an hour in the endeavor to crack it by repeated blows with their bills. They were manifestly thieves, and I had not much respect for them; but the squirrels, though at first shy, went to work as if they were taking what was their own.

Meanwhile also came the chickadees in flocks, which, picking up the crumbs the squirrels had dropped, flew to the nearest twig, and, placing them under their claws, hammered away at them with their little bills, as if it were an insect in the bark, till they were sufficiently reduced for their slender throats. A little flock of these titmice came daily to pick a dinner out of my woodpile, or the crumbs at my door, with faint flitting lisping notes, like the tinkling of icicles in the grass, or else with sprightly *day day day*, or more rarely, in spring-like days, a wiry summery *phe-be* from the wood-side. They were so familiar that at length one alighted on an armful of wood which I was carrying in, and pecked at the sticks without fear. I once had a sparrow alight upon my shoulder for a moment while I was hoeing in a village garden, and I felt that I was more distinguished by that circumstance than I should have been by any epaulet I could have worn. The squirrels also grew at last to be quite familiar, and occasionally stepped upon my shoe, when that was the nearest way.

When the ground was not yet quite covered, and again near the end of winter, when the snow was melted on my south hill-side and about my wood-pile, the partridges came out of the woods morning and evening to feed there. Whichever side you walk in the woods the partridge bursts away on whirring wings, jarring the snow from the dry leaves and twigs on high, which comes sifting down in the sunbeams like golden dust, for this brave bird is not to be scared by winter. It is frequently covered up by drifts, and, it is said, "sometimes plunges from on wing into the soft snow, where it remains concealed for a day or two." I used to start them in the open land also, where they had come out of the woods at sunset to "bud" the wild apple-trees. They will come regularly every evening to particular trees, where the cunning sportsman lies in wait for them, and the distant orchards next the woods suffer thus not a little. I am glad that the partridge gets fed, at any rate. It is Nature's own bird which lives on buds and diet-drink.

In dark winter mornings, or in short winter afternoons, I sometimes heard a pack of hounds threading all the woods with hounding cry and yelp, unable to resist the instinct of the chase, and the note of the hunting horn at intervals, proving that man was in the rear. The woods ring again, and yet no fox bursts forth on to the open level of the pond, nor following pack pursuing their Actæon. And perhaps at evening I see the hunters returning with a single brush trailing from their sleigh for a trophy, seeking their inn. They tell me that if the fox would remain in the bosom of the frozen earth he would be safe, or if he would run in a straight line away no fox-hound could overtake him; but, having left his pursuers far behind, he stops to rest and listen till they come up, and when he runs he circles round to his old haunts, where the hunters await him. Sometimes, however, he will run upon a wall many rods, and then leap off far to one side, and he appears to know that water will not retain his scent. A hunter told me that he once saw a fox pursued by hounds burst out on to Walden when the ice was covered with shallow puddles, run part way across, and then return to the same shore. Ere long the hounds arrived, but here they lost the scent. Sometimes a pack hunting by themselves would pass my door, and circle round my house, and yelp and hound without regarding me, as if afflicted by a species of madness, so that nothing could divert them from the pursuit. Thus they circle until they fall upon the recent trail of a fox, for a wise hound will forsake everything else for this. One day a man came to my hut from Lexington to inquire after his hound that made a large track, and had been hunting for a week by himself. But I fear that he was not the wiser for all I told him, for every time I attempted to answer his questions he interrupted me by asking, "What do you do here?" He had lost a dog, but found a man.

One old hunter who has a dry tongue, who used to come to bathe in Walden once every year when the water was warmest, and at such times looked in upon me, told me that many years ago he took his gun one afternoon and went out for a cruise in Walden Wood; and as he walked the Wayland road he heard the cry of hounds approaching, and ere long a fox leaped the wall into the road, and as quick as thought leaped the other wall out of the road, and his swift bullet had not touched him. Some way behind came an old hound and her three pups in full pursuit, hunting on their own account, and disappeared again in the woods. Late in the afternoon, as he was resting in the thick woods south of Walden, he heard the voice of the hounds far over toward Fair Haven still pursuing the fox; and on they came, their hounding cry which made all the woods ring sounding nearer and nearer, now from Well-Meadow, now from the Baker Farm. For a long time he stood still and listened to their music, so sweet to a hunter's ear, when suddenly the fox appeared, threading the solemn aisles with an easy coursing pace, whose sound was concealed by a sympathetic rustle of the leaves, swift and still, keeping the ground, leaving his pursuers far behind; and, leaping upon a rock amid the woods, he sat erect and listening, with his back to the hunter. For a moment compassion restrained the latter's arm; but that was a short-lived mood, and as quick as thought can follow thought his piece was levelled, and *whang!* — the fox rolling over the rock lay dead on the ground. The hunter still kept his place and listened to the hounds. Still on they came, and now the near woods resounded through all their aisles with their demoniac cry. At length the old hound burst into view with muzzle to the ground, and snapping the air as if possessed, and ran directly to the rock; but spying the dead fox she suddenly ceased her hounding, as if struck dumb with amazement, and walked round and round him in silence; and one by one her pups arrived, and, like their mother, were sobered into silence by the mystery. Then the hunter came forward and stood in their midst, and the mystery was solved. They waited in silence while he skinned the fox, then followed the brush a while, and at length turned off into the woods again. That evening a Weston Squire came to the Concord hunter's cottage to inquire for his hounds, and told how for a week they had been hunting on their own account from Weston woods. The Concord hunter told him what he knew and offered him the skin; but the other declined it and departed. He did not find his hounds that night, but the next day learned that they had crossed the river and put up at a farmhouse for the night, whence, having been well fed, they took their departure early in the morning.

The hunter who told me this could remember one Sam Nutting, who used to hunt bears on Fair Haven Ledges, and exchange their skins for rum in Concord village; who told him, even, that he had seen a moose there. Nutting had a famous fox-hound named Burgoyne, — he pronounced it Bugine, — which my informant used to borrow. In the "Wast Book" of an old trader of this town, who was also a captain, town-clerk, and representative, I find the following entry. Jan. 18th, 1742–3, "John Melven Cr. by 1 Grey Fox 0 — 2 — 3;" they are not now found here; and in his ledger, Feb. 7th, 1743, Hezekiah Stratton has credit "by $\frac{1}{2}$ a Catt skin 0 — 1 — $4\frac{1}{2}$;" of course, a wild-cat, for Stratton was a sergeant in the old French war, and would not have got credit for hunting less noble game. Credit is given for deer skins also, and they were daily sold. One man still preserves the horns of the last deer that was killed in this vicinity, and another has told me the particulars of the hunt in which his uncle was engaged. The hunters were formerly a numerous and merry crew here. I remember well one gaunt Nimrod who would catch up a leaf by the road-side and play a strain on it wilder and more melodious, if my memory serves me, than any hunting horn.

At midnight, when there was a moon, I sometimes met with hounds in my path prowling about the woods, which would skulk out of my way, as if afraid, and stand silent amid the bushes till I had passed.

Squirrels and wild mice disputed for my store of nuts. There were scores of pitch-pines around my house, from one to four inches in diameter, which had been gnawed by mice the previous winter, — a Norwegian winter for them, for the snow lay long and deep, and they were obliged to mix a large proportion of pine bark with their other diet. These trees were alive and apparently flourishing at midsummer, and many of them had grown a foot, though completely girdled; but after another winter such were without exception dead. It is remarkable that a single mouse should thus be allowed a whole pine-tree for its dinner, gnawing round instead of up and down it; but perhaps it is necessary in order to thin these trees, which are wont to grow up densely.

The hares (*Lepus Americanus*) were very familiar. One had her form under my house all winter, separated from me only by the flooring, and she startled me each morning by her hasty departure when I began to stir, — thump, thump, thump, striking her head against the floor timbers in her hurry. They used to come round my door at dusk to nibble the potato parings which I had thrown out, and were so nearly the color of the ground that they could hardly be distinguished when still. Sometimes in the twilight I alternately lost and recovered sight of one sitting motionless under my window. When I opened my door in the evening, off they would go with a squeak and a bounce. Near at hand they only excited my pity. One evening one sat by my door two paces from me, at first trembling with fear, yet unwilling to move; a poor wee thing, lean and bony, with ragged ears and sharp nose, scant tail and slender paws. It looked as if Nature no longer contained the breed of nobler bloods, but stood on her last toes. Its large eyes appeared young and unhealthy, almost dropsical. I took a step, and lo, away it scud with an elastic spring over the snow crust, straightening its body and its limbs into graceful length, and soon put the forest between me and itself, — the wild free venison, asserting its vigor and the dignity of Nature. Not without reason was, its slenderness. Such then was its nature. (*Lepus, levipes*, light-foot some think.)

What is a country without rabbits and partridges? They are among the most simple and indigenous animal products; ancient and venerable families known to antiquity as to modern times; of the very hue and substance of Nature, nearest allied to leaves and to the ground, — and to one another; it is either winged or it is legged. It is hardly as if you had seen a wild creature when a rabbit or a partridge bursts away, only a natural one, as much to be expected as rustling leaves. The partridge and the rabbit are still sure to thrive, like true natives of the soil, whatever revolutions occur. If the forest is cut off, the sprouts and bushes which spring up afford them concealment, and they become more numerous than ever. That must be a poor country indeed that does not support a hare. Our woods teem with them both, and around every swamp may be seen the partridge or rabbit walk, beset with twiggy fences and horse-hair snares, which some cow-boy tends.

XVI. THE POND IN WINTER

AFTER a still winter night I awoke with the impression that some question had been put to me, which I had been endeavoring in vain to answer in my sleep, as what — how — when — where? But there was dawning Nature, in whom all creatures live, looking in at my broad windows with serene and satisfied face, and no question on *her* lips. I awoke to an answered question, to Nature and daylight. The snow lying deep on the earth dotted with young pines, and the very slope of the hill on which my house is placed, seemed to say, Forward! Nature puts no question and answers none which we mortals ask. She has long ago taken her resolution. "O Prince, our eyes contemplate with admiration and transmit to the soul the wonderful and varied spectacle of this universe. The night veils without doubt a part of this glorious creation; but day comes to reveal to us this great work, which extends from earth even into the plains of the ether."

Then to my morning work. First I take an axe and pail and go in search of water, if that be not a dream. After a cold and snowy night it needed a divining rod to find it. Every winter the liquid and trembling surface of the pond, which was so sensitive to every breath, and reflected every light and shadow, becomes solid to the depth of a foot or a foot and a half, so that it will support the heaviest teams, and perchance the snow covers it to an equal depth, and it is not to be distinguished from any level field. Like the marmots in the surrounding hills, it closes its eyelids and becomes dormant for three months or more. Standing on the snow-covered plain, as if in a pasture amid the hills, I cut my way first through a foot of snow, and then a foot of ice, and open a window under my feet, where, kneeling to drink, I look down into the quiet parlor of the fishes, pervaded by a softened light as through a window of ground glass, with its bright sanded floor the same as in summer; there a perennial waveless serenity reigns as in the amber twilight sky, corresponding to the cool and even temperament of the inhabitants. Heaven is under our feet as well as over our heads.

Early in the morning, while all things are crisp with frost, men come with fishing reels and slender lunch, and let down their fine lines through the snowy field to take pickerel and perch; wild men, who instinctively follow other fashions and trust other authorities than their townsmen, and by their goings and comings stitch towns together in parts where else they would be ripped. They sit and eat their luncheon in stout fear-naughts on the dry oak leaves on the shore, as wise in natural lore as the citizen is in artificial. They never consulted with books, and know and can tell much less than they have done. The things which they practise are said not yet to be known. Here is one fishing for pickerel with grown perch for bait. You look into his pail with wonder as into a summer pond, as if he kept summer locked up at home, or knew where she had retreated. How, pray, did he get these in midwinter? O, he got worms out of rotten logs since the ground froze, and so he caught them. His life itself passes deeper in Nature than the studies of the naturalist penetrate; himself a subject for the naturalist. The latter raises the moss and bark gently with his knife in search of insects; the former lays open logs to their core with his axe, and moss and bark fly far and wide. He gets his living by barking trees. Such a man has some right to fish, and I love to see Nature carried out in him. The perch swallows the grub-worm, the pickerel swallows the perch, and the fisherman swallows the pickerel; and so all the chinks in the scale of being are filled.

When I strolled around the pond in misty weather I was sometimes amused by the primitive mode which some ruder fisherman had adopted. He would perhaps have placed alder branches over the narrow holes in the ice, which were four or five rods apart and an equal distance from the shore, and having fastened the end of the line to a stick to prevent its being pulled through, have passed the slack line over a twig of the alder, a foot or more above the ice, and tied a dry oak leaf to it, which, being pulled down, would show when he had a bite. These alders loomed through the mist at regular intervals as you walked half way round the pond.

Ah, the pickerel of Walden! when I see them lying on the ice, or in the well which the fisherman cuts in the ice, making a little hole to admit the water, I am always surprised by their rare beauty, as if they were fabulous fishes, they are so foreign to the streets, even to the woods, foreign as Arabia to our Concord life. They possess a quite dazzling and transcendent beauty which separates them by a wide interval from the cadaverous cod and haddock whose fame is trumpeted in our streets. They are not green like the pines, nor gray like the stones, nor blue like the sky; but they have, to my eyes, if possible, yet rarer colors, like flowers and precious stones, as if they were the pearls, the animalized *nuclei* or crystals of the Walden water. They, of course, are Walden all over and all through; are themselves small Waldens in the animal kingdom, Waldenses. It is surprising that they are caught here, — that in this deep and capacious spring, far beneath the rattling teams and chaises and tinkling sleighs that travel the Walden road, this great gold and emerald fish swims. I never chanced to see its kind in any market; it would be the cynosure of all eyes there. Easily, with a few convulsive quirks, they give up their watery ghosts, like a mortal translated before his time to the thin air of heaven.

As I was desirous to recover the long lost bottom of Walden Pond, I surveyed it carefully, before the ice broke up, early in '46, with compass and chain and sounding line. There have been many stories told about the bottom, or rather no bottom, of this pond, which certainly had no foundation for themselves. It is remarkable how long men will believe in the bottomlessness of a pond without taking the trouble to sound it. I have visited two such Bottomless Ponds in one walk in this neighborhood. Many have believed that Walden reached quite through to the other side of the globe. Some who have lain flat on the ice for a long time, looking down through the illusive medium, perchance with watery eyes into the bargain, and driven to hasty conclusions by the fear of catching cold in their breasts, have seen vast holes "into which a load of hay might be driven," if there were anybody to drive it, the undoubted source of the Styx and entrance to the Infernal Regions from these parts. Others have gone down from the village with a "fifty-six" and a wagon load of inch rope, but yet have failed to find any bottom; for while the "fifty-six" was resting by the way, they were paying out the rope in the vain attempt to fathom their truly immeasurable capacity for marvellousness. But I can assure my readers that Walden has a reasonably tight bottom at a not unreasonable, though at an unusual, depth. I fathomed it easily with a cod-line and a stone weighing about a pound and a half, and could tell accurately when the stone left the bottom, by having to pull so much harder before the water got underneath to help me. The greatest depth was exactly one hundred and two feet; to which may be added the five feet which it has risen since, making one hundred and seven. This is a remarkable depth for so small an area; yet not an inch of it can be spared by the imagination. What if all ponds were shallow? Would it not react on the minds of men? I am thankful that this pond was made deep and pure for a symbol. While men believe in the infinite some ponds will be thought to be bottomless.

A factory owner, hearing what depth I had found, thought that it could not be true, for, judging from his acquaintance with dams, sand would not lie at so steep an angle. But the deepest ponds are not so deep in proportion to their area as most suppose, and, if drained, would not leave very remarkable valleys. They are not like cups between the hills; for this one, which is so unusually deep for its area, appears in a vertical section through its centre not deeper than a shallow plate. Most ponds, emptied, would leave a meadow no more hollow than we frequently see. William Gilpin, who is so admirable in all that relates to landscapes, and usually so correct, standing at the head of Loch Fyne, in Scotland, which he describes as "a bay of salt water, sixty or seventy fathoms deep, four miles in breadth," and about fifty miles long, surrounded by mountains, observes, "If we could have seen it immediately after the diluvian crash, or whatever convulsion of Nature occasioned it, before the waters gushed in, what a horrid chasm it must have appeared!

> "So high as heaved the tumid hills, so low
> Down sunk a hollow bottom, broad, and deep,
> Capacious bed of waters ———."

But if, using the shortest diameter of Loch Fyne, we apply these proportions to Walden, which, as we have seen, appears already in a vertical section only like a shallow plate, it will appear four times as shallow. So much for the *increased* horrors of the chasm of Loch Fyne when emptied. No doubt many a smiling valley with its stretching cornfields occupies exactly such a "horrid chasm," from which the waters have receded, though it requires the insight and the far sight of the geologist to convince the unsuspecting inhabitants of this fact. Often an inquisitive eye may detect the shores of a primitive lake in the low horizon hills, and no subsequent elevation of the plain have been necessary to conceal their history. But it is easiest, as they who work on the highways know, to find the hollows by the puddles after a shower. The amount of it is, the imagination, give it the least license, dives deeper and soars higher than Nature goes. So, probably, the depth of the ocean will be found to be very inconsiderable compared with its breadth.

As I sounded through the ice I could determine the shape of the bottom with greater accuracy than is possible in surveying harbors which do not freeze over, and I was surprised at its general regularity. In the deepest part there are several acres more level than almost any field which is exposed to the sun, wind, and plough. In one instance, on a line arbitrarily chosen, the depth did not vary more than one foot in thirty rods; and generally, near the middle, I could calculate the variation for each one hundred feet in any direction beforehand within three or four inches. Some are accustomed to speak of deep and dangerous holes even in quiet sandy ponds like this, but the effect of water under these circumstances is to level all inequalities. The regularity of the bottom and its conformity to the shores and the range of the neighboring hills were so perfect that a distant promontory betrayed itself in the soundings quite across the pond, and its direction could be determined by observing the opposite shore. Cape becomes bar, and plain shoal, and valley and gorge deep water and channel.

When I had mapped the pond by the scale of ten rods to an inch, and put down the soundings, more than a hundred in all, I observed this remarkable coincidence. Having noticed that the number indicating the greatest depth was apparently in the centre of the map, I laid a rule on the map lengthwise, and then breadthwise, and found, to my surprise, that the line of greatest length intersected the line of greatest breadth *exactly* at the point of greatest depth, notwithstanding that the middle is so nearly level, the outline of the pond far from regular, and the extreme length and breadth were got by measuring into the coves; and I said to myself, Who knows but this hint would conduct to the deepest part of the ocean as well as of a pond or puddle? Is not this the rule also for the height of mountains, regarded as the opposite of valleys? We know that a hill is not highest at its narrowest part.

Of five coves, three, or all which had been sounded, were observed to have a bar quite across their mouths and deeper water within, so that the bay tended to be an expansion of water within the land not

only horizontally but vertically, and to form a basin or independent
pond, the direction of the two capes showing the course of the bar.
Every harbor on the sea-coast, also, has its bar at its entrance. In
proportion as the mouth of the cove was wider compared with its
length, the water over the bar was deeper compared with that in the
basin. Given, then, the length and breadth of the cove, and the character of the surrounding shore, and you have almost elements enough
to make out a formula for all cases.

In order to see how nearly I could guess, with this experience, at
the deepest point in a pond, by observing the outlines of its surface
and the character of its shores alone, I made a plan of White Pond,
which contains about forty-one acres, and, like this, has no island in
it, nor any visible inlet or outlet; and as the line of greatest breadth
fell very near the line of least breadth, where two opposite capes approached each other and two opposite bays receded, I ventured to
mark a point a short distance from the latter line, but still on the line
of greatest length, as the deepest. The deepest part was found to be
within one hundred feet of this, still farther in the direction to which
I had inclined, and was only one foot deeper, namely, sixty feet. Of
course, a stream running through, or an island in the pond, would
make the problem much more complicated.

If we knew all the laws of Nature, we should need only one fact,
or the description of one actual phenomenon, to infer all the particular
results at that point. Now we know only a few laws, and our result
is vitiated, not, of course, by any confusion or irregularity in Nature,
but by our ignorance of essential elements in the calculation. Our
notions of law and harmony are commonly confined to those instances
which we detect; but the harmony which results from a far greater
number of seemingly conflicting, but really concurring, laws, which
we have not detected, is still more wonderful. The particular laws
are as our points of view, as, to the traveller, a mountain outline varies
with every step, and it has an infinite number of profiles, though absolutely but one form. Even when cleft or bored through it is not
comprehended in its entireness.

What I have observed of the pond is no less true in ethics. It is
the law of average. Such a rule of the two diameters not only guides
us toward the sun in the system and the heart in man, but draw lines
through the length and breadth of the aggregate of a man's particular
daily behaviors and waves of life into his coves and inlets, and where
they intersect will be the height or depth of his character. Perhaps we

need only to know how his shores trend and his adjacent country or circumstances, to infer his depth and concealed bottom. If he is sur-rounded by mountainous circumstances, an Achillean shore, whose peaks overshadow and are reflected in his bosom, they suggest a cor-responding depth in him. But a low and smooth shore proves him shallow on that side. In our bodies, a bold projecting brow falls off to and indicates a corresponding depth of thought. Also there is a bar across the entrance of our every cove, or particular inclination; each is our harbor for a season, in which we are detained and partially land-locked. These inclinations are not whimsical usually, but their form, size, and direction are determined by the promontories of the shore, the ancient axes of elevation. When this bar is gradually in-creased by storms, tides, or currents, or there is a subsidence of the waters, so that it reaches to the surface, that which was at first but an inclination in the shore in which a thought was harbored becomes an individual lake, cut off from the ocean, wherein the thought secures its own conditions, — changes, perhaps, from salt to fresh, becomes a sweet sea, dead sea, or a marsh. At the advent of each individual into this life, may we not suppose that such a bar has risen to the sur-face somewhere? It is true, we are such poor navigators that our thoughts, for the most part, stand off and on upon a harborless coast, are conversant only with the bights of the bays of poesy, or steer for the public ports of entry, and go into the dry docks of science, where they merely refit for this world, and no natural currents concur to individualize them.

As for the inlet or outlet of Walden, I have not discovered any but rain and snow and evaporation, though perhaps, with a thermom-eter and a line, such places may be found, for where the water flows into the pond it will probably be coldest in summer and warmest in winter. When the ice-men were at work here in '46–7, the cakes sent to the shore were one day rejected by those who were stacking them up there, not being thick enough to lie side by side with the rest; and the cutters thus discovered that the ice over a small space was two or three inches thinner than elsewhere, which made them think that there was an inlet there. They also showed me in another place what they thought was a "leach hole," through which the pond leaked out under a hill into a neighboring meadow, pushing me out on a cake of ice to see it. It was a small cavity under ten feet of water; but I think that I can warrant the pond not to need soldering till they find a worse leak than that. One has suggested, that if such a "leach hole" should be found, its connection with the meadow, if any existed, might be proved by conveying some colored powder or sawdust to the mouth of the hole, and then putting a strainer over the spring in the meadow, which would catch some of the particles carried through by the current.

While I was surveying, the ice, which was sixteen inches thick, undulated under a slight wind like water. It is well known that a level cannot be used on ice. At one rod from the shore its greatest fluctuation, when observed by means of a level on land directed toward a graduated staff on the ice, was three quarters of an inch, though the ice appeared firmly attached to the shore. It was probably greater in the middle. Who knows but if our instruments were delicate enough we might detect an undulation in the crust of the earth? When two legs of my level were on the shore and the third on the ice, and the sights were directed over the latter, a rise or fall of the ice of an almost infinitesimal amount made a difference of several feet on a tree across the pond. When I began to cut holes for sounding there were three or four inches of water on the ice under a deep snow which had sunk it thus far; but the water began immediately to run into these holes, and continued to run for two days in deep streams, which wore away the ice on every side, and contributed essentially, if not mainly, to dry the surface of the pond; for, as the water ran in, it raised and floated the ice. This was somewhat like cutting a hole in the bottom of a ship to let the water out. When such holes freeze, and a rain succeeds, and finally a new freezing forms a fresh smooth ice over all, it is beautifully mottled internally by dark figures, shaped somewhat like a spider's web, what you may call ice rosettes, produced by the channels worn by the water flowing from all sides to a centre. Sometimes, also, when the ice was covered with shallow puddles, I saw a double shadow of myself, one standing on the head of the other, one on the ice, the other on the trees or hill-side.

While yet it is cold January, and snow and ice are thick and solid, the prudent landlord comes from the village to get ice to cool his summer drink; impressively, even pathetically, wise, to foresee the heat and thirst of July now in January, — wearing a thick coat and mittens! when so many things are not provided for. It may be that he lays up no treasures in this world which will cool his summer drink in the next. He cuts and saws the solid pond, unroofs the house of fishes, and carts off their very element and air, held fast by chains and stakes like corded wood, through the favoring winter air, to wintry cellars, to underlie the summer there. It looks like solidified azure, as, far off, it is drawn through the streets. These ice-cutters are a merry race, full of jest and sport, and when I went among them they were wont to invite me to saw pit-fashion with them, I standing underneath.

In the winter of '46–7 there came a hundred men of Hyperborean extraction swoop down on to our pond one morning, with many carloads of ungainly-looking farming tools, — sleds, ploughs, drill-barrows, turf-knives, spades, saws, rakes, and each man was armed with a double-pointed pike-staff, such as is not described in the New-England Farmer or the Cultivator. I did not know whether they had come to sow a crop of winter rye, or some other kind of grain recently introduced from Iceland. As I saw no manure, I judged that they meant to skim the land, as I had done, thinking the soil was deep and had lain fallow long enough. They said that a gentleman farmer, who was behind the scenes, wanted to double his money, which, as I understood, amounted to half a million already; but in order to cover each one of his dollars with another, he took off the only coat, ay, the skin itself, of Walden Pond in the midst of a hard winter. They went to work at once, ploughing, harrowing, rolling, furrowing, in admirable order, as if they were bent on making this a model farm; but when I was looking sharp to see what kind of seed they dropped into the furrow, a gang of fellows by my side suddenly began to hook up the virgin mould itself, with a peculiar jerk, clean down to the sand, or rather the water, — for it was a very springy soil, — indeed all the *terra firma* there was, — and haul it away on sleds, and then I guessed that they must be cutting peat in a bog. So they came and went every day, with a peculiar shriek from the locomotive, from and to some point of the polar regions, as it seemed to me, like a flock of arctic snow-birds. But sometimes Squaw Walden had her revenge, and a hired man, walking behind his team, slipped through a crack in the ground down toward Tartarus, and he who was so brave before suddenly became but the ninth part of a man, almost gave up his animal heat, and was glad to take refuge in my house, and acknowledged that there was some virtue in a stove; or sometimes the frozen soil took a piece of steel out of a ploughshare, or a plough got set in the furrow and had to be cut out.

To speak literally, a hundred Irishmen, with Yankee overseers, came from Cambridge every day to get out the ice. They divided it into cakes by methods too well known to require description, and these, being sledded to the shore, were rapidly hauled off on to an ice platform, and raised by grappling irons and block and tackle, worked by horses, on to a stack, as surely as so many barrels of flour, and there placed evenly side by side, and row upon row, as if they formed the solid base of an obelisk designed to pierce the clouds. They told me that in a good day they could get out a thousand tons, which was the yield of about one acre. Deep ruts and "cradle holes" were worn in the ice, as on *terra firma*, by the passage of the sleds over the same track, and the horses invariably ate their oats out of cakes of ice hollowed out like buckets. They stacked up the cakes thus in the open air in a pile thirty-five feet high on one side and six or seven rods square, putting hay between the outside layers to exclude the air; for when the wind, though never so cold, finds a passage through, it will wear large cavities, leaving slight supports or studs only here and there, and finally topple it down. At first it looked like a vast blue fort or Valhalla; but when they began to tuck the coarse meadow hay into the crevices, and this became covered with rime and icicles, it looked like a venerable moss-grown and hoary ruin, built of azure-tinted marble, the abode of Winter, that old man we see in the almanac, — his shanty, as if he had a design to estivate with us. They calculated that not twenty-five per cent. of this would reach its destination, and that two or three per cent. would be wasted in the cars. However, a still greater part of this heap had a different destiny from what was intended; for, either because the ice was found not to keep so well as was expected, containing more air than usual, or for some other reason, it never got to market. This heap, made in the winter of '46-7 and estimated to contain ten thousand tons, was finally covered with hay and boards; and though it was unroofed the following July, and a part of it carried off, the rest remaining exposed to the sun, it stood over that summer and the next winter, and was not quite melted till September, 1848. Thus the pond recovered the greater part.

Like the water, the Walden ice, seen near at hand, has a green tint, but at a distance is beautifully blue, and you can easily tell it from the white ice of the river, or the merely greenish ice of some ponds, a quarter of a mile off. Sometimes one of those great cakes slips from the ice-man's sled into the village street, and lies there for a week like a great emerald, an object of interest to all passers. I have noticed that a portion of Walden which in the state of water was green will often, when frozen, appear from the same point of view blue. So the hollows about this pond will, sometimes, in the winter, be filled with a greenish water somewhat like its own, but the next day will have frozen blue. Perhaps the blue color of water and ice is due to the light and air they contain, and the most transparent is the bluest. Ice is an interesting subject for contemplation. They told me that they had some in the ice-houses at Fresh Pond five years old which was as good as ever. Why is it that a bucket of water soon becomes putrid, but frozen remains sweet forever? It is commonly said that this is the difference between the affections and the intellect.

Thus for sixteen days I saw from my window a hundred men at work like busy husbandmen, with teams and horses and apparently all the implements of farming, such a picture as we see on the first page of the almanac; and as often as I looked out I was reminded of the fable of the lark and the reapers, or the parable of the sower, and the like; and now they are all gone, and in thirty days more, probably, I shall look from the same window on the pure sea-green Walden water there, reflecting the clouds and the trees, and sending up its evaporations in solitude, and no traces will appear that a man has ever stood there. Perhaps I shall hear a solitary loon laugh as he dives and plumes himself, or shall see a lonely fisher in his boat, like a floating leaf, beholding his form reflected in the waves, where lately a hundred men securely labored.

Thus it appears that the sweltering inhabitants of Charleston and New Orleans, of Madras and Bombay and Calcutta, drink at my well. In the morning I bathe my intellect in the stupendous and cosmogonal philosophy of the Bhagvat Geeta, since whose composition years of the gods have elapsed, and in comparison with which our modern world and its literature seem puny and trivial; and I doubt if that philosophy is not to be referred to a previous state of existence, so remote is its sublimity from our conceptions. I lay down the book and go to my well for water, and lo! there I meet the servant of the Bramin, priest of Brahma and Vishnu and Indra, who still sits in his temple on the Ganges reading the Vedas, or dwells at the root of a tree with his crust and water jug. I meet his servant come to draw water for his master, and our buckets as it were grate together in the same well. The pure Walden water is mingled with the sacred water of the Ganges. With favoring winds it is wafted past the site of the fabulous islands of Atlantis and the Hesperides, makes the periplus of Hanno, and, floating by Ternate and Tidore and the mouth of the

Persian Gulf, melts in the tropic gales of the Indian seas, and is landed in ports of which Alexander only heard the names.

XVII. SPRING

THE opening of large tracts by the ice-cutters commonly causes a pond to break up earlier; for the water, agitated by the wind, even in cold weather, wears away the surrounding ice. But such was not the effect on Walden that year, for she had soon got a thick new garment to take the place of the old. This pond never breaks up so soon as the others in this neighborhood, on account both of its greater depth and its having no stream passing through it to melt or wear away the ice. I never knew it to open in the course of a winter, not excepting that of '52–3, which gave the ponds so severe a trial. It commonly opens about the first of April, a week or ten days later than Flints' Pond and Fair Haven, beginning to melt on the north side and in the shallower parts where it began to freeze. It indicates better than any water hereabouts the absolute progress of the season, being least affected by transient changes of temperature. A severe cold of a few days' duration in March may very much retard the opening of the former ponds, while the temperature of Walden increases almost uninterruptedly. A thermometer thrust into the middle of Walden on the 6th of March, 1847, stood at 32°, or freezing point; near the shore at 33°; in the middle of Flints' Pond, the same day, at $32\frac{1}{2}°$; at a dozen rods from the shore, in shallow water, under ice a foot thick, at 36°. This difference of three and a half degrees between the temperature of the deep water and the shallow in the latter pond, and the fact that a great proportion of it is comparatively shallow, show why it should break up so much sooner than Walden. The ice in the shallowest part was at this time several inches thinner than in the middle. In midwinter the middle had been the warmest and the ice thinnest there. So, also, every one who has waded about the shores of a pond in summer must have perceived how much warmer the water is close to the shore, where only three or four inches deep, than a little distance out, and on the surface where it is deep, than near the bottom. In spring the sun not only exerts an influence through the increased temperature of the air and earth, but its heat passes through ice a foot or more thick, and is reflected from the bottom in shallow water, and so also warms the water and melts the under side of the ice, at the same time that it is melting it more directly above, making it uneven, and causing the air bubbles which it contains to extend themselves upward and downward until it is completely honey-combed, and at last disappears suddenly in a single spring rain. Ice has its grain as well as wood, and when a cake begins to rot or "comb," that is, assume the appearance of honey-comb, whatever may be its position, the air cells are at right angles with what was the water surface. Where there is a rock or a log rising near to the surface the ice over it is much thinner, and is frequently quite dissolved by this reflected heat; and I have been told that in the experiment at Cambridge to freeze water in a shallow wooden pond, though the cold air circulated underneath, and so had access to both sides, the reflection of the sun from the bottom more than counterbalanced this advantage. When a warm rain in the middle of the winter melts off the snow-ice from Walden, and leaves a hard dark or transparent ice on the middle, there will be a strip of rotten though thicker white ice, a rod or more wide, about the shores, created by this reflected heat. Also, as I have said, the bubbles themselves within the ice operate as burning glasses to melt the ice beneath.

The phenomena of the year take place every day in a pond on a small scale. Every morning, generally speaking, the shallow water is being warmed more rapidly than the deep, though it may not be made so warm after all, and every evening it is being cooled more rapidly until the morning. The day is an epitome of the year. The night is the winter, the morning and evening are the spring and fall, and the noon is the summer. The cracking and booming of the ice indicate a change of temperature. One pleasant morning after a cold night, February 24th, 1850, having gone to Flints' Pond to spend the day, I noticed with surprise, that when I struck the ice with the head of my axe, it resounded like a gong for many rods around, or as if I had struck on a tight drum-head. The pond began to boom about an hour after sunrise, when it felt the influence of the sun's rays slanted upon it from over the hills; it stretched itself and yawned like a waking man with a gradually increasing tumult, which was kept up three or four hours. It took a short siesta at noon, and boomed once more toward night, as the sun was withdrawing his influence. In the right stage of the weather a pond fires its evening gun with great regularity. But in the middle of the day, being full of cracks, and the air also being less elastic, it had completely lost its resonance, and probably fishes and muskrats could not then have been stunned by a blow on it. The fishermen say that the "thundering of the pond" scares the fishes and prevents their biting. The pond does not thunder every evening, and I cannot tell surely when to expect its thundering; but though I may perceive no difference in the weather, it does. Who would have suspected so large and cold and thick-skinned a thing to be so sensitive? Yet it has its law to which it thunders obedience when it should as surely as the buds expand in the spring. The earth is all alive and covered with papillæ. The largest pond is as sensitive to atmospheric changes as the globule of mercury in its tube.

One attraction in coming to the woods to live was that I should have leisure and opportunity to see the Spring come in. The ice in the pond at length begins to be honey-combed, and I can set my heel in it as I walk. Fogs and rains and warmer suns are gradually melting the snow; the days have grown sensibly longer; and I see how I shall get through the winter without adding to my wood-pile, for large fires are no longer necessary. I am on the alert for the first signs of spring, to hear the chance note of some arriving bird, or the striped squirrel's chirp, for his stores must be now nearly exhausted, or see the woodchuck venture out of his winter quarters. On the 13th of March, after I had heard the bluebird, song-sparrow, and red-wing, the ice was still nearly a foot thick. As the weather grew warmer it was not sensibly worn away by the water, nor broken up and floated off as in rivers, but, though it was completely melted for half a rod in width about the shore, the middle was merely honey-combed and saturated with water, so that you could put your foot through it when six inches thick; but by the next day evening, perhaps, after a warm rain followed by fog, it would have wholly disappeared, all gone off with the fog, spirited away. One year I went across the middle only five days before it disappeared entirely. In 1845 Walden was first completely open on the 1st of April; in '46, the 25th of March; in '47, the 8th of April; in '51, the 28th of March; in '52, the 18th of April; in '53, the 23d of March; in '54, about the 7th of April.

Every incident connected with the breaking up of the rivers and ponds and the settling of the weather is particularly interesting to us who live in a climate of so great extremes. When the warmer days come, they who dwell near the river hear the ice crack at night with a startling whoop as loud as artillery, as if its icy fetters were rent from end to end, and within a few days see it rapidly going out. So the alligator comes out of the mud with quakings of the earth. One old man, who has been a close observer of Nature, and seems as thoroughly wise in regard to all her operations as if she had been put upon the stocks when he was a boy, and he had helped to lay her keel, — who has come to his growth, and can hardly acquire more of natural lore if he should live to the age of Methuselah, — told me, and I was surprised to hear him express wonder at any of Nature's operations, for I thought that there were no secrets between them, that one spring day he took his gun and boat, and thought that he would have a little sport with the ducks. There was ice still on the meadows, but it was all gone out of the river, and he dropped down without obstruction from Sudbury, where he lived, to Fair Haven Pond, which he found, unexpectedly, covered for the most part with a firm field of ice. It was a warm day, and he was surprised to see so great a body of ice remaining. Not seeing any ducks, he hid his boat on the north or back side of an island in the pond, and then concealed himself in the bushes on the south side, to await them. The ice was melted for three or four rods from the shore, and there was a smooth and warm sheet of water, with a muddy bottom, such as the ducks love, within, and he thought it likely that some would be along pretty soon. After he had lain still there about an hour he heard a low and seemingly very distant sound, but singularly grand and impressive, unlike anything he had ever heard, gradually swelling and increasing as if it would have a universal and memorable ending, a sullen rush and roar, which seemed to him all at once like the sound of a vast body of fowl coming in to settle there, and, seizing his gun, he started up in haste and excited; but he found, to his surprise, that the whole body of the ice had started while he lay there, and drifted in to the shore, and the sound he had heard was made by its edge grating on the shore, — at first gently nibbled and crumbled off, but at length heaving up and scattering its wrecks along the island to a considerable height before it came to a stand still.

At length the sun's rays have attained the right angle, and warm winds blow up mist and rain and melt the snow banks, and the sun dispersing the mist smiles on a checkered landscape of russet and white smoking with incense, through which the traveller picks his way from islet to islet, cheered by the music of a thousand tinkling rills and rivulets whose veins are filled with the blood of winter which they are bearing off.

Few phenomena gave me more delight than to observe the forms which thawing sand and clay assume in flowing down the sides of a deep cut on the railroad through which I passed on my way to the village, a phenomenon not very common on so large a scale, though the number of freshly exposed banks of the right material must have been greatly multiplied since railroads were invented. The material was sand of every degree of fineness and of various rich colors, commonly mixed with a little clay. When the frost comes out in the spring, and even in a thawing day in the winter, the sand begins to flow down the slopes like lava, sometimes bursting out through the snow and overflowing it where no sand was to be seen before. Innumerable little streams overlap and interlace one with another, exhibiting a sort of hybrid product, which obeys half way the law of currents, and half way that of vegetation. As it flows it takes the forms of sappy leaves or vines, making heaps of pulpy sprays a foot or more in depth, and resembling, as you look down on them, the laciniated, lobed, and imbricated thalluses of some lichens; or you are reminded of coral, of leopards' paws or birds' feet, of brains or lungs or bowels, and excrements of all kinds. It is a truly *grotesque* vegetation, whose forms and color we see imitated in bronze, a sort of architectural foliage more ancient and typical than acanthus, chiccory, ivy, vine, or any vegetable leaves; destined perhaps, under some circumstances, to become a puzzle to future geologists. The whole cut impressed me as if it were a cave with its stalactites laid open to the light. The various shades of the sand are singularly rich and agreeable, embracing the different iron colors, brown, gray, yellowish, and reddish. When the flowing mass reaches the drain at the foot of the bank it spreads out flatter into *strands*, the separate streams losing their semi-cylindrical form and gradually becoming more flat and broad, running together as they are more moist, till they form an almost flat *sand*, still variously and beautifully shaded, but in which you can trace the original forms of vegetation; till at length, in the water itself, they are converted into *banks*, like those formed off the mouths of rivers, and the forms of vegetation are lost in the ripple marks on the bottom.

The whole bank, which is from twenty to forty feet high, is sometimes overlaid with a mass of this kind of foliage, or sandy rupture, for a quarter of a mile on one or both sides, the produce of one spring day. What makes this sand foliage remarkable is its springing into existence thus suddenly. When I see on the one side the inert bank, — for the sun acts on one side first, — and on the other this luxuriant foliage, the creation of an hour, I am affected as if in a peculiar sense I stood in the laboratory of the Artist who made the world and me, — had come to where he was still at work, sporting on this bank, and with excess of energy strewing his fresh designs about. I feel as if I were nearer to the vitals of the globe, for this sandy overflow is something such a foliaceous mass as the vitals of the animal body. You find thus in the very sands an anticipation of the vegetable leaf. No wonder that the earth expresses itself outwardly in leaves, it so labors with the idea inwardly. The atoms have already learned this law, and are pregnant by it. The overhanging leaf sees here its prototype. *Internally*, whether in the globe or animal body, it is a moist thick *lobe*, a word especially applicable to the liver and lungs and the *leaves* of fat, (λείβω, *labor*, *lapsus*, to flow or slip downward, a lapsing; λοβός, *globus*, lobe, globe; also lap, flap, and many other words,) *externally*, a dry thin *leaf*, even as the *f* and *v* are a pressed and dried *b*. The radicals of lobe are *lb*, the soft mass of the *b* (single lobed, or B, doubled lobed,) with the liquid *l* behind it pressing it forward. In globe, *glb*, the guttural *g* adds to the meaning the capacity of the throat. The feathers and wings of birds are still drier and thinner leaves. Thus, also, you pass from the lumpish grub in the earth to the airy and fluttering butterfly. The very globe continually transcends and translates itself, and becomes winged in its orbit. Even ice begins with delicate crystal leaves, as if it had flowed into moulds which the fronds of water plants have impressed on the watery mirror. The whole tree itself is but one leaf, and rivers are still vaster leaves whose pulp is intervening earth, and towns and cities are the ova of insects in their axils.

When the sun withdraws the sand ceases to flow, but in the morning the streams will start once more and branch and branch again into a myriad of others. You here see perchance how blood-vessels are formed. If you look closely you observe that first there pushes forward from the thawing mass a stream of softened sand with a drop-like point, like the ball of the finger, feeling its way slowly and blindly downward, until at last with more heat and moisture, as the sun gets higher, the most fluid portion, in its effort to obey the law to which the most inert also yields, separates from the latter and forms for itself a meandering channel or artery within that, in which is seen a little silvery stream glancing like lightning from one stage of pulpy leaves or branches to another, and ever and anon swallowed up in the sand.

It is wonderful how rapidly yet perfectly the sand organizes itself as it flows, using the best material its mass affords to form the sharp edges of its channel. Such are the sources of rivers. In the silicious matter which the water deposits is perhaps the bony system, and in the still finer soil and organic matter the fleshy fibre or cellular tissue. What is man but a mass of thawing clay? The ball of the human finger is but a drop congealed. The fingers and toes flow to their extent from the thawing mass of the body. Who knows what the human body would expand and flow out to under a more genial heaven? Is not the hand a spreading *palm* leaf with its lobes and veins? The ear may be regarded, fancifully, as a lichen, *umbilicaria*, on the side of the head, with its lobe or drop. The lip — *labium*, from *labor* (?) — laps or lapses from the sides of the cavernous mouth. The nose is a manifest congealed drop or stalactite. The chin is a still larger drop, the confluent dripping of the face. The cheeks are a slide from the brows into the valley of the face, opposed and diffused by the cheek bones. Each rounded lobe of the vegetable leaf, too, is a thick and now loitering drop, larger or smaller; the lobes are the fingers of the leaf; and as many lobes as it has, in so many directions it tends to flow, and more heat or other genial influences would have caused it to flow yet farther.

Thus it seemed that this one hillside illustrated the principle of all the operations of Nature. The Maker of this earth but patented a leaf. What Champollion will decipher this hieroglyphic for us, that we may turn over a new leaf at last? This phenomenon is more exhilarating to me than the luxuriance and fertility of vineyards. True, it is somewhat excrementitious in its character, and there is no end to the heaps of liver, lights, and bowels, as if the globe were turned wrong side outward; but this suggests at least that Nature has some bowels, and there again is mother of humanity. This is the frost coming out of the ground; this is Spring. It precedes the green and flowery spring, as mythology precedes regular poetry. I know of nothing more purgative of winter fumes and indigestions. It convinces me that Earth is still in her swaddling clothes, and stretches forth baby fingers on every side. Fresh curls spring from the baldest brow. There is nothing inorganic. These foliaceous heaps lie along the bank like the slag of a furnace, showing that Nature is "in full blast" within. The earth is not a mere fragment of dead history, stratum upon stratum like the leaves of a book, to be studied by geologists and antiquaries chiefly, but living poetry like the leaves of a tree, which precede flowers and fruit, — not a fossil earth, but a living earth; compared with whose great central life all animal and vegetable life is merely parasitic. Its throes will heave our exuviæ from their graves. You may melt your metals and cast them into the most beautiful moulds you can; they will never excite me like the forms which this molten earth flows out into. And not only it, but the institutions upon it are plastic like clay in the hands of the potter.

Ere long, not only on these banks, but on every hill and plain and in every hollow, the frost comes out of the ground like a dormant quadruped from its burrow, and seeks the sea with music, or migrates to other climes in clouds. Thaw with his gentle persuasion is more powerful than Thor with his hammer. The one melts, the other but breaks in pieces.

When the ground was partially bare of snow, and a few warm days had dried its surface somewhat, it was pleasant to compare the first tender signs of the infant year just peeping forth with the stately beauty of the withered vegetation which had withstood the winter, — life-everlasting, golden-rods, pinweeds, and graceful wild grasses, more obvious and interesting frequently than in summer even, as if their beauty was not ripe till then; even cotton-grass, cat-tails, mulleins, johnswort, hard-hack, meadow-sweet, and other strong-stemmed plants, those unexhausted granaries which entertain the earliest birds, — decent weeds, at least, which widowed Nature wears. I am particularly attracted by the arching and sheaf-like top of the wool-grass; it brings back the summer to our winter memories, and is among the forms which art loves to copy, and which, in the vegetable kingdom, have the same relation to types already in the mind of man that astronomy has. It is an antique style, older than Greek or Egyptian. Many of the phenomena of Winter are suggestive of an inexpressible tenderness and fragile delicacy. We are accustomed to hear this king described as a rude and boisterous tyrant; but with the gentleness of a lover he adorns the tresses of Summer.

At the approach of spring the red-squirrels got under my house, two at a time, directly under my feet as I sat reading or writing, and kept up the queerest chuckling and chirruping and vocal pirouetting and gurgling sounds that ever were heard; and when I stamped they only chirruped the louder, as if past all fear and respect in their mad pranks, defying humanity to stop them. No you don't — chickaree — chickaree. They were wholly deaf to my arguments, or failed to perceive their force, and fell into a strain of invective that was irresistible.

The first sparrow of spring! The year beginning with younger

hope than ever! The faint silvery warblings heard over the partially
bare and moist fields from the blue-bird, the song-sparrow, and the
red-wing, as if the last flakes of winter tinkled as they fell! What at
such a time are histories, chronologies, traditions, and all written revelations? The brooks sing carols and glees to the spring. The marsh-
hawk sailing low over the meadow is already seeking the first slimy
life that awakes. The sinking sound of melting snow is heard in all
dells, and the ice dissolves apace in the ponds. The grass flames up on
the hillsides like a spring fire, — "et primitus oritur herba imbribus
primoribus evocata," — as if the earth sent forth an inward heat to
greet the returning sun; not yellow but green is the color of its flame;
— the symbol of perpetual youth, the grass-blade, like a long green
ribbon, streams from the sod into the summer, checked indeed by the
frost, but anon pushing on again, lifting its spear of last year's hay
with the fresh life below. It grows as steadily as the rill oozes out of
the ground. It is almost identical with that, for in the growing days
of June, when the rills are dry, the grass blades are their channels, and
from year to year the herds drink at this perennial green stream, and
the mower draws from it betimes their winter supply. So our human
life but dies down to its root, and still puts forth its green blade to
eternity.

Walden is melting apace. There is a canal two rods wide along the
northerly and westerly sides, and wider still at the east end. A great
field of ice has cracked off from the main body. I hear a song-sparrow
singing from the bushes on the shore, — *olit, olit, olit,* — *chip, chip,
chip, che char,* — *che wiss, wiss, wiss.* He too is helping to crack it.
How handsome the great sweeping curves in the edge of the ice, answering somewhat to those of the shore, but more regular! It is
unusually hard, owing to the recent severe but transient cold, and all
watered or waved like a palace floor. But the wind slides eastward
over its opaque surface in vain, till it reaches the living surface beyond.
It is glorious to behold this ribbon of water sparkling in the sun, the
bare face of the pond full of glee and youth, as if it spoke the joy of
the fishes within it, and of the sands on its shore, — a silvery sheen as
from the scales of a *leuciscus,* as it were all one active fish. Such is the
contrast between winter and spring. Walden was dead and is alive
again. But this spring it broke up more steadily, as I have said.

The change from storm and winter to serene and mild weather, from
dark and sluggish hours to bright and elastic ones, is a memorable
crisis which all things proclaim. It is seemingly instantaneous at last.

Suddenly an influx of light filled my house, though the evening was at hand, and the clouds of winter still overhung it, and the eaves were dripping with sleety rain. I looked out the window, and lo! where yesterday was cold gray ice there lay the transparent pond already calm and full of hope as in a summer evening, reflecting a summer evening sky in its bosom, though none was visible overhead, as if it had intelligence with some remote horizon. I heard a robin in the distance, the first I had heard for many a thousand years, methought, whose note I shall not forget for many a thousand more, — the same sweet and powerful song as of yore. O the evening robin, at the end of a New England summer day! If I could ever find the twig he sits upon! I mean *he;* I mean *the twig*. This at least is not the *Turdus migratorius*. The pitch-pines and shrub-oaks about my house, which had so long drooped, suddenly resumed their several characters, looked brighter, greener, and more erect and alive, as if effectually cleansed and restored by the rain. I knew that it would not rain any more. You may tell by looking at any twig of the forest, ay, at your very wood-pile, whether its winter is past or not. As it grew darker, I was startled by the *honking* of geese flying low over the woods, like weary travellers getting in late from southern lakes, and indulging at last in unrestrained complaint and mutual consolation. Standing at my door, I could hear the rush of their wings; when, driving toward my house, they suddenly spied my light, and with hushed clamor wheeled and settled in the pond. So I came in, and shut the door, and passed my first spring night in the woods.

In the morning I watched the geese from the door through the mist, sailing in the middle of the pond, fifty rods off, so large and tumultuous that Walden appeared like an artificial pond for their amusement. But when I stood on the shore they at once rose up with a great flapping of wings at the signal of their commander, and when they had got into rank circled about over my head, twenty-nine of them, and then steered straight to Canada, with a regular *honk* from the leader at intervals, trusting to break their fast in muddier pools. A "plump" of ducks rose at the same time and took the route to the north in the wake of their noisier cousins.

For a week I heard the circling groping clangor of some solitary goose in the foggy mornings, seeking its companion, and still peopling the woods with the sound of a larger life than they could sustain. In April the pigeons were seen again flying express in small flocks, and in due time I heard the martins twittering over my clearing, though it

had not seemed that the township contained so many that it could afford
me any, and I fancied that they were peculiarly of the ancient race
that dwelt in hollow trees ere white men came. In almost all climes the
tortoise and the frog are among the precursors and heralds of this
season, and birds fly with song and glancing plumage, and plants
spring and bloom, and winds blow, to correct this slight oscillation of
the poles and preserve the equilibrium of Nature.

As every season seems best to us in its turn, so the coming in of
spring is like the creation of Cosmos out of Chaos and the realization
of the Golden Age. —

> "Eurus ad Auroram, Nabathacaque regna recessit,
>   Persidaque, et radiis juga subdita matutinis."

> "The East-Wind withdrew to Aurora and the Nabathæan kingdom,
> And the Persian, and the ridges placed under the morning rays.
> .   .   .   .
> Man was born. Whether that Artificer of things,
> The origin of a better world, made him from the divine seed;
> Or the earth being recent and lately sundered from the high
> Ether, retained some seeds of cognate heaven."

A single gentle rain makes the grass many shades greener. So our
prospects brighten on the influx of better thoughts. We should be
blessed if we lived in the present always, and took advantage of every
accident that befell us, like the grass which confesses the influence of
the slightest dew that falls on it; and did not spend our time in atoning
for the neglect of past opportunities, which we call doing our duty.
We loiter in winter while it is already spring. In a pleasant spring
morning all men's sins are forgiven. Such a day is a truce to vice.
While such a sun holds out to burn, the vilest sinner may return.
Through our own recovered innocence we discern the innocence of
our neighbors. You may have known your neighbor yesterday for a
thief, a drunkard, or a sensualist, and merely pitied or despised him,
and despaired of the world; but the sun shines bright and warm this
first spring morning, recreating the world, and you meet him at some
serene work, and see how his exhausted and debauched veins expand
with still joy and bless the new day, feel the spring influence with the
innocence of infancy, and all his faults are forgotten. There is not
only an atmosphere of good will about him, but even a savor of holiness groping for expression, blindly and ineffectually perhaps, like a
new-born instinct, and for a short hour the south hill-side echoes to no

vulgar jest. You see some innocent fair shoots preparing to burst from his gnarled rind and try another year's life, tender and fresh as the youngest plant. Even he has entered into the joy of his Lord. Why the jailer does not leave open his prison doors, — why the judge does not dismiss his case, — why the preacher does not dismiss his congregation! It is because they do not obey the hint which God gives them, nor accept the pardon which he freely offers to all.

"A return to goodness produced each day in the tranquil and beneficent breath of the morning, causes that in respect to the love of virtue and the hatred of vice, one approaches a little the primitive nature of man, as the sprouts of the forest which has been felled. In like manner the evil which one does in the interval of a day prevents the germs of virtues which began to spring up again from developing themselves and destroys them.

"After the germs of virtue have thus been prevented many times from developing themselves, then the beneficent breath of evening does not suffice to preserve them. As soon as the breath of evening does not suffice longer to preserve them, then the nature of man does not differ much from that of the brute. Men seeing the nature of this man like that of the brute, think that he has never possessed the innate faculty of reason. Are those the true and natural sentiments of man?"

> "The Golden Age was first created, which without any avenger
> Spontaneously without law cherished fidelity and rectitude.
> Punishment and fear were not; nor were threatening words read
> On suspended brass; nor did the suppliant crowd fear
> The words of their judge; but were safe without an avenger.
> Not yet the pine felled on its mountains had descended
> To the liquid waves that it might see a foreign world,
> And mortals knew no shores but their own.
>
> . . . .
>
> There was eternal spring, and placid zephyrs with warm
> Blasts soothed the flowers born without seed."

On the 29th of April, as I was fishing from the bank of the river near the Nine-Acre-Corner bridge, standing on the quaking grass and willow roots, where the muskrats lurk, I heard a singular rattling sound, somewhat like that of the sticks which boys play with their fingers, when, looking up, I observed a very slight and graceful hawk, like a night-hawk, alternately soaring like a ripple and tumbling a rod or two over and over, showing the underside of its wings, which gleamed like a satin ribbon in the sun, or like the pearly inside of a shell. This sight reminded me of falconry and what nobleness and poetry are associated with that sport. The Merlin it seemed to me it might be called: but I care not for its name. It was the most ethereal flight I had ever witnessed. It did not simply flutter like a butterfly, nor soar like the larger hawks, but it sported with proud reliance in the fields of air; mounting again and again with its strange chuckle, it repeated its free and beautiful fall, turning over and over like a kite, and then recovering from its lofty tumbling, as if it had never set its foot on *terra firma*. It appeared to have no companion in the universe, — sporting there alone, — and to need none but the morning and the ether with which it played. It was not lonely, but made all the earth lonely beneath it. Where was the parent which hatched it, its kindred, and its father in the heavens? The tenant of the air, it seemed related to the earth but by an egg hatched some time in the crevice of a crag; — or was its native nest made in the angle of a cloud, woven of the rainbow's trimmings and the sunset sky, and lined with some soft midsummer haze caught up from earth? Its eyry now some cliffy cloud.

Beside this I got a rare mess of golden and silver and bright cupreous fishes, which looked like a string of jewels. Ah! I have penetrated to those meadows on the morning of many a first spring day, jumping from hummock to hummock, from willow root to willow root, when the wild river valley and the woods were bathed in so pure and bright a light as would have waked the dead, if they had been slumbering in their graves, as some suppose. There needs no stronger proof of immortality. All things must live in such a light. O Death, where was thy sting? O Grave, where was thy victory, then?

Our village life would stagnate if it were not for the unexplored forests and meadows which surround it. We need the tonic of wildness, — to wade sometimes in marshes where the bittern and the meadow-hen lurk, and hear the booming of the snipe; to smell the whispering sedge where only some wilder and more solitary fowl builds her nest, and the mink crawls with its belly close to the ground. At the same time that we are earnest to explore and learn all things, we require that all things be mysterious and unexplorable, that land and sea be infinitely wild, unsurveyed and unfathomed by us because unfathomable. We can never have enough of Nature. We must be refreshed by the sight of inexhaustible vigor, vast and Titanic features, the sea-coast with its wrecks, the wilderness with its living and its decaying trees, the thunder cloud, and the rain which lasts three

weeks and produces freshets.[1] We need to witness our own limits
transgressed, and some life pasturing freely where we never wander.
We are cheered when we observe the vulture feeding on the carrion,
which disgusts and disheartens us, and deriving health and strength
from the repast. There was a dead horse in the hollow by the path
to my house, which compelled me sometimes to go out of my way,
especially in the night when the air was heavy, but the assurance it
gave me of the strong appetite and inviolable health of Nature was my
compensation for this. I love to see that Nature is so rife with life
that myriads can be afforded to be sacrificed and suffered to prey on
one another; that tender organizations can be so serenely squashed out
of existence like pulp, — tadpoles which herons gobble up, and tortoises and toads run over in the road; and that sometimes it has rained
flesh and blood! With the liability to accident, we must see how little
account is to be made of it. The impression made on a wise man is
that of universal innocence. Poison is not poisonous after all, nor are
any wounds fatal. Compassion is a very untenable ground. It must
be expeditious. Its pleadings will not bear to be stereotyped.

Early in May, the oaks, hickories, maples, and other trees, just
putting out amidst the pine woods around the pond, imparted a brightness like sunshine to the landscape, especially in cloudy days, as if the
sun were breaking through mists and shining faintly on the hill-sides
here and there. On the third or fourth of May I saw a loon in the
pond, and during the first week of the month I heard the whippoorwill,
the brown-thrasher, the veery, the wood-pewee, the chewink, and
other birds. I had heard the wood-thrush long before. The phœbe
had already come once more and looked in at my door and window, to
see if my house was cavern-like enough for her, sustaining herself on
humming wings with clinched talons, as if she held by the air, while
she surveyed the premises. The sulphur-like pollen of the pitch-pine
soon covered the pond and the stones and rotten wood along the shore,
so that you could have collected a barrel-ful. This is the "sulphur
showers" we hear of. Even in Calidas' drama of Sacontala, we read
of "rills dyed yellow with the golden dust of the lotus." And so the
seasons went rolling on into summer, as one rambles into higher and
higher grass.

[1] Thoreau did not learn this at Walden but on his trips to the Maine woods and
Cape Cod. The value of the wild as "the preservation of the World" became one
of the dominant themes of his last years; the spoliation of the landscape showed him
the need for parks and forest-preserves.

Thus was my first year's life in the woods completed; and the second year was similar to it. I finally left Walden September 6th, 1847.

XVIII. CONCLUSION

To the sick the doctors wisely recommend a change of air and scenery. Thank Heaven, here is not all the world. The buck-eye does not grow in New England, and the mocking-bird is rarely heard here. The wild-goose is more of a cosmopolite than we; he breaks his fast in Canada, takes a luncheon in the Ohio, and plumes himself for the night in a southern bayou. Even the bison, to some extent, keeps pace with the seasons, cropping the pastures of the Colorado only till a greener and sweeter grass awaits him by the Yellowstone. Yet we think that if rail-fences are pulled down, and stone-walls piled up on our farms, bounds are henceforth set to our lives and our fates decided. If you are chosen town-clerk, forsooth, you cannot go to Tierra del Fuego this summer: but you may go to the land of infernal fire never--theless. The universe is wider than our views of it.

Yet we should oftener look over the tafferel of our craft, like curious passengers, and not make the voyage like stupid sailors picking oakum. The other side of the globe is but the home of our correspondent. Our voyaging is only great-circle sailing, and the doctors prescribe for diseases of the skin merely. One hastens to Southern Africa to chase the giraffe; but surely that is not the game he would be after. How long, pray, would a man hunt giraffes if he could? Snipes and wood-cocks also may afford rare sport; but I trust it would be nobler game to shoot one's self. —

> "Direct your eye right inward, and you'll find
> A thousand regions in your mind
> Yet undiscovered. Travel them, and be
> Expert in home-cosmography."

What does Africa, — what does the West stand for? Is not our own interior white on the chart? black though it may prove, like the coast when discovered. Is it the source of the Nile, or the Niger, or the

Mississippi, or a North-West Passage around this continent, that we would find? Are these the problems which most concern mankind? Is Franklin the only man who is lost, that his wife should be so earnest to find him? Does Mr. Grinnell know where he himself is? Be rather the Mungo Park, the Lewis and Clarke and Frobisher, of your own streams and oceans; explore your own higher latitudes, — with shiploads of preserved meats to support you, if they be necessary; and pile the empty cans sky-high for a sign. Were preserved meats invented to preserve meat merely? Nay, be a Columbus to whole new continents and worlds within you, opening new channels, not of trade, but of thought. Every man is the lord of a realm beside which the earthly empire of the Czar is but a petty state, a hummock left by the ice. Yet some can be patriotic who have no *self*-respect, and sacrifice the greater to the less. They love the soil which makes their graves, but have no sympathy with the spirit which may still animate their clay. Patriotism is a maggot in their heads. What was the meaning of that South-Sea Exploring Expedition, with all its parade and expense, but an indirect recognition of the fact, that there are continents and seas in the moral world, to which every man is an isthmus or an inlet, yet unexplored by him, but that it is easier to sail many thousand miles through cold and storm and cannibals, in a government ship, with five hundred men and boys to assist one, than it is to explore the private sea, the Atlantic and Pacific Ocean of one's being alone. —

> "Erret, et extremos alter scrutetur Iberos.
> Plus habet hic vitæ, plus habet ille viæ."

> Let them wander and scrutinize the outlandish Australians.
> I have more of God, they more of the road.

It is not worth the while to go round the world to count the cats in Zanzibar. Yet do this even till you can do better, and you may perhaps find some "Symmes' Hole" by which to get at the inside at last. England and France, Spain and Portugal, Gold Coast and Slave Coast, all front on this private sea; but no bark from them has ventured out of sight of land, though it is without doubt the direct way to India. If you would learn to speak all tongues and conform to the customs of all nations, if you would travel farther than all travellers, be naturalized in all climes, and cause the Sphinx to dash her head against a stone, even obey the precept of the old philosopher, and Explore thyself. Herein are demanded the eye and the nerve. Only the defeated and deserters go to the wars, cowards that run away and enlist. Start now on that farthest western way, which does not pause at the Mississippi or the Pacific, nor conduct toward a wornout China or Japan, but leads on direct a tangent to this sphere, summer and winter, day and night, sun down, moon down, and at last earth down too.

It is said that Mirabeau took to highway robbery "to ascertain what degree of resolution was necessary in order to place one's self in formal opposition to the most sacred laws of society." He declared that "a soldier who fights in the ranks does not require half so much courage as a foot-pad," — "that honor and religion have never stood in the way of a well-considered and a firm resolve." This was manly, as the world goes; and yet it was idle, if not desperate. A saner man would have found himself often enough "in formal opposition" to what are deemed "the most sacred laws of society," through obedience to yet more sacred laws, and so have tested his resolution without going out of his way. It is not for a man to put himself in such an attitude to society, but to maintain himself in whatever attitude he find himself through obedience to the laws of his being which will never be one of opposition to a just government, if he should chance to meet with such.

I left the woods for as good a reason as I went there. Perhaps it seemed to me that I had several more lives to live, and could not spare any more time for that one. It is remarkable how easily and insensibly we fall into a particular route, and make a beaten track for ourselves. I had not lived there a week before my feet wore a path from my door to the pond-side; and though it is five or six years since I trod it, it is still quite distinct. It is true, I fear that others may have fallen into it, and so helped to keep it open. The surface of the earth is soft and impressible by the feet of men; and so with the paths which the mind travels. How worn and dusty, then, must be the highways of the world, how deep the ruts of tradition and conformity! I did not wish to take a cabin passage, but rather to go before the mast and on the deck of the world, for there I could best see the moonlight amid the mountains. I do not wish to go below now.

I learned this, at least, by my experiment; that if one advances confidently in the direction of his dreams, and endeavors to live the life which he has imagined, he will meet with a success unexpected in common hours. He will put some things behind, will pass an invisible boundary; new, universal, and more liberal laws will begin to establish themselves around and within him; or the old laws be expanded, and interpreted in his favor in a more liberal sense, and he will live with

the license of a higher order of beings. In proportion as he simplifies
his life, the laws of the universe will appear less complex, and solitude
will not be solitude, nor poverty poverty, nor weakness weakness.
If you have built castles in the air, your work need not be lost; that is
where they should be. Now put the foundations under them.

It is a ridiculous demand which England and America make, that
you shall speak so that they can understand you. Neither men nor
toad-stools grow so. As if that were important, and there were not
enough to understand you without them. As if Nature could support
but one order of understandings, could not sustain birds as well as
quadrupeds, flying as well as creeping things, and *hush* and *who*, which
Bright can understand, were the best English. As if there were safety
in stupidity alone. I fear chiefly lest my expression may not be *extra-
vagant* enough, may not wander far enough beyond the narrow limits
of my daily experience, so as to be adequate to the truth of which
I have been convinced. *Extra vagance!* it depends on how you are
yarded. The migrating buffalo, who seeks new pastures in another
latitude, is not extravagant like the cow which kicks over the pail,
leaps the cowyard fence, and runs after her calf, in milking time. I
desire to speak somewhere *without* bounds; like a man in a waking
moment, to men in their waking moments; for I am convinced that I
cannot exaggerate enough even to lay the foundation of a true expression. Who that has heard a strain of music feared then lest he should
speak extravagantly any more forever? In view of the future or possible, we should live quite laxly and undefined in front, our outlines
dim and misty on that side; as our shadows reveal an insensible perspiration toward the sun. The volatile truth of our words should
continually betray the inadequacy of the residual statement. Their
truth is instantly *translated*; its literal monument alone remains. The
words which express our faith and piety are not definite; yet they are
significant and fragrant like frankincense to superior natures.

Why level downward to our dullest perception always, and praise
that as common sense? The commonest sense is the sense of men
asleep, which they express by snoring. Sometimes we are inclined to
class those who are-once-and-a-half witted with the half-witted, because we appreciate only a third part of their wit. Some would find
fault with the morning-red, if they ever got up early enough. "They
pretend," as I hear, "that the verses of Kabir have four different
senses; illusion, spirit, intellect, and the exoteric doctrine of the
Vedas;" but in this part of the world it is considered a ground for com-

plaint if a man's writings admit of more than one interpretation. While
England endeavors to cure the potato-rot, will not any endeavor to
cure the brain-rot, which prevails so much more widely and fatally?

I do not suppose that I have attained to obscurity, but I should be
proud if no more fatal fault were found with my pages on this score
than was found with the Walden ice. Southern customers objected to
its blue color, which is the evidence of its purity, as if it were muddy,
and preferred the Cambridge ice, which is white, but tastes of weeds.
The purity men love is like the mists which envelop the earth, and not
like the azure ether beyond.

Some are dinning in our ears that we Americans, and moderns generally, are intellectual dwarfs compared with the ancients, or even the
Elizabethan men. But what is that to the purpose? A living dog is
better than a dead lion. Shall a man go and hang himself because he
belongs to the race of pygmies, and not be the biggest pygmy that he
can? Let every one mind his own business, and endeavor to be what
he was made.

Why should we be in such desperate haste to succeed and in such
desperate enterprises? If a man does not keep pace with his companions, perhaps it is because he hears a different drummer. Let him step
to the music which he hears, however measured or far away. It is not
important that he should mature as soon as an apple-tree or an oak.
Shall he turn his spring into summer? If the condition of things which
we were made for is not yet, what were any reality which we can substitute? We will not be shipwrecked on a vain reality. Shall we with
pains erect a heaven of blue glass over ourselves, though when it is
done we shall be sure to gaze still at the true ethereal heaven far above,
as if the former were not?

There was an artist in the city of Kouroo who was disposed to strive
after perfection. One day it came into his mind to make a staff. Having considered that in an imperfect work time is an ingredient, but into
a perfect work time does not enter, he said to himself, It shall be perfect in all respects, though I should do nothing else in my life. He proceeded instantly to the forest for wood, being resolved that it should
not be made of unsuitable material; and as he searched for and rejected
stick after stick, his friends gradually deserted him, for they grew old
in their works and died, but he grew not older by a moment. His
singleness of purpose and resolution, and his elevated piety, endowed
him, without his knowledge, with perennial youth. As he made no
compromise with Time, Time kept out of his way, and only sighed at

a distance because he could not overcome him. Before he had found a stock in all respects suitable the city of Kouroo was a hoary ruin, and he sat on one of its mounds to peel the stick. Before he had given it the proper shape the dynasty of the Candahars was at an end, and with the point of the stick he wrote the name of the last of that race in the sand, and then resumed his work. By the time he had smoothed and polished the staff Kalpa was no longer the pole-star; and ere he had put on the ferule and the head adorned with precious stones, Brahma had awoke and slumbered many times. But why do I stay to mention these things? When the finishing stroke was put to his work, it suddenly expanded before the eyes of the astonished artist into the fairest of all the creations of Brahma. He had made a new system in making a staff, a world with full and fair proportions; in which, though the old cities and dynasties had passed away, fairer and more glorious ones had taken their places. And now he saw by the heap of shavings still fresh at his feet, that, for him and his work, the former lapse of time had been an illusion, and that no more time had elapsed than is required for a single scintillation from the brain of Brahma to fall on and inflame the tinder of a mortal brain. The material was pure, and his art was pure; how could the result be other than wonderful? [1]

No face which we can give to a matter will stead us so well at last as the truth. This alone wears well. For the most part, we are not where we are, but in a false position. Through an infirmity of our natures, we suppose a case, and put ourselves into it, and hence are in two cases at the same time, and it is doubly difficult to get out. In sane moments we regard only the facts, the case that is. Say what you have to say, not what you ought. Any truth is better than make-believe. Tom Hyde, the tinker, standing on the gallows, was asked if he had anything to say. "Tell the tailors," said he, "to remember to make a knot in their thread before they take the first stitch." His companion's prayer is forgotten.

However mean your life is, meet it and live it; do not shun it and call it hard names. It is not so bad as you are. It looks poorest when you are richest. The fault-finder will find faults even in paradise. Love your life, poor as it is. You may perhaps have some pleasant, thrilling, glorious hours, even in a poor-house. The setting sun is

---

[1] The parable was obviously Thoreau's own work. It had been much revised in manuscript, and the personal allusions as well as his characteristic puns ("lapse" and "elapsed"), make this clear. "Kouroo" is Thoreau's spelling for Kuru, Kooroo, or Curu, the nation that fought the Pandoos in the *Mahabharata*, the sacred land that Arjuna was assigned to protect in the *Bhagavad-Gita*.

reflected from the windows of the alms-house as brightly as from the rich man's abode; the snow melts before its door as early in the spring. I do not see but a quiet mind may live as contentedly there, and have as cheering thoughts, as in a palace. The town's poor seem to me often to live the most independent lives of any. May be they are simply great enough to receive without misgiving. Most think that they are above being supported by the town; but it oftener happens that they are not above supporting themselves by dishonest means, which should be more disreputable. Cultivate poverty like a garden herb, like sage. Do not trouble yourself much to get new things, whether clothes or friends. Turn the old; return to them. Things do not change; we change. Sell your clothes and keep your thoughts. God will see that you do not want society. If I were confined to a corner of a garret all my days, like a spider, the world would be just as large to me while I had my thoughts about me. The philosopher said: "From an army of three divisions one can take away its general, and put it in disorder; from the man the most abject and vulgar one cannot take away his thought." Do not seek so anxiously to be developed, to subject your-self to many influences to be played on; it is all dissipation. Humility like darkness reveals the heavenly lights. The shadows of poverty and meanness gather around us, "and lo! creation widens to our view." We are often reminded that if there were bestowed on us the wealth of Crœsus, our aims must still be the same, and our means essentially the same. Moreover, if you are restricted in your range by poverty, if you cannot buy books and newspapers, for instance, you are but confined to the most significant and vital experiences; you are com-pelled to deal with the material which yields the most sugar and the most starch. It is life near the bone where it is sweetest. You are de-fended from being a trifler. No man loses ever on a lower level by magnanimity on a higher. Superfluous wealth can buy superfluities only. Money is not required to buy one necessary of the soul.

I live in the angle of a leaden wall, into whose composition was poured a little alloy of bell metal. Often, in the repose of my mid-day, there reaches my ears a confused *tintinnabulum* from without. It is the noise of my contemporaries. My neighbors tell me of their adventures with famous gentlemen and ladies, what notabilities they met at the dinner-table; but I am no more interested in such things than in the contents of the Daily Times. The interest and the conversation are about costume and manners chiefly; but a goose is a goose still, dress it as you will. They tell me of California and Texas, of England

and the Indies, of the Hon. Mr. —— of Georgia or of Massachusetts, all transient and fleeting phenomena, till I am ready to leap from their court-yard like the Mameluke bey. I delight to come to my bearings, — not walk in procession with pomp and parade, in a conspicuous place, but to walk even with the Builder of the universe, if I may, — not to live in this restless, nervous, bustling, trivial Nineteenth Century, but stand or sit thoughtfully while it goes by. What are men celebrating? They are all on a committee of arrangements, and hourly expect a speech from somebody. God is only the president of the day, and Webster is his orator. I love to weigh, to settle, to gravitate toward that which most strongly and rightfully attracts me; — not hang by the beam of the scale and try to weigh less, — not suppose a case, but take the case that is; to travel the only path I can, and that on which no power can resist me. It affords me no satisfaction to commence to spring an arch before I have got a solid foundation. Let us not play at kittlybenders. There is a solid bottom everywhere. We read that the traveller asked the boy if the swamp before him had a hard bottom. The boy replied that it had. But presently the traveller's horse sank in up to the girths, and he observed to the boy, "I thought you said that this bog had a hard bottom." "So it has," answered the latter, "but you have not got half way to it yet." So it is with the bogs and quicksands of society; but he is an old boy that knows it. Only what is thought, said, or done at a certain rare coincidence is good. I would not be one of those who will foolishly drive a nail into mere lath and plastering; such a deed would keep me awake nights. Give me a hammer, and let me feel for the furrowing. Do not depend on the putty. Drive a nail home and clinch it so faithfully that you can wake up in the night and think of your work with satisfaction, — a work at which you would not be ashamed to invoke the Muse. So will help you God, and so only. Every nail driven should be as another rivet in the machine of the universe, you carrying on the work.

Rather than love, than money, than fame, give me truth. I sat at a table where were rich food and wine in abundance, and obsequious attendance, but sincerity and truth were not; and I went away hungry from the inhospitable board. The hospitality was as cold as the ices. I thought that there was no need of ice to freeze them. They talked to me of the age of the wine and the fame of the vintage; but I thought of an older, a newer, and purer wine, of a more glorious vintage, which they had not got, and could not buy. The style, the house and grounds and "entertainment" pass for nothing with me. I called on the king, but he made me wait in his hall, and conducted like a man incapacitated for hospitality. There was a man in my neighborhood who lived in a hollow tree. His manners were truly regal. I should have done better had I called on him.

How long shall we sit in our porticoes practising idle and musty virtues, which any work would make impertinent? As if one were to begin the day with long-suffering, and hire a man to hoe his potatoes, and in the afternoon go forth to practise Christian meekness and charity with goodness aforethought! Consider the China pride and stagnant self-complacency of mankind. This generation inclines a little to congratulate itself on being the last of an illustrious line; and in Boston and London and Paris and Rome, thinking of its long descent, it speaks of its progress in art and science and literature with satisfaction. There are the Records of the Philosophical Societies, and the public Eulogies of *Great Men!* It is the good Adam contemplating his own virtue. "Yes, we have done great deeds, and sung divine songs, which shall never die," — that is, as long as *we* can remember them. The learned societies and great men of Assyria, — where are they? What youthful philosophers and experimentalists we are! There is not one of my readers who has yet lived a whole human life. These may be but the spring months in the life of the race. If we have had the seven-years' itch, we have not seen the seventeen-year locust yet in Concord. We are acquainted with a mere pellicle of the globe on which we live. Most have not delved six feet beneath the surface, nor leaped as many above it. We know not where we are. Beside, we are sound asleep nearly half our time. Yet we esteem ourselves wise, and have an established order on the surface. Truly, we are deep thinkers, we are ambitious spirits! As I stand over the insect crawling amid the pine needles on the forest floor, and endeavoring to conceal itself from my sight, and ask myself why it will cherish those humble thoughts, and hide its head from me who might, perhaps, be its benefactor, and impart to its race some cheering information, I am reminded of the greater Benefactor and Intelligence that stands over me the human insect.

There is an incessant influx of novelty into the world, and yet we tolerate incredible dulness. I need only suggest what kind of sermons are still listened to in the most enlightened countries. There are such words as joy and sorrow, but they are only the burden of a psalm, sung with a nasal twang, while we believe in the ordinary and mean. We think that we can change our clothes only. It is said that the British Empire is very large and respectable, and that the United States are a first-rate power. We do not believe that a tide rises and falls behind every man which can float the British Empire like a chip, if he should ever harbor it in his mind. Who knows what sort of seventeen-year locust will next come out of the ground? The government of the world I live in was not framed, like that of Britain, in after-dinner conversations over the wine.

The life in us is like the water in the river. It may rise this year higher than man has ever known it, and flood the parched uplands; even this may be the eventful year, which will drown out all our musk-rats. It was not always dry land where we dwell. I see far inland the banks which the stream anciently washed, before science began to record its freshets. Every one has heard the story which has gone the rounds of New England, of a strong and beautiful bug which came out of the dry leaf of an old table of apple-tree wood, which had stood in a farmer's kitchen for sixty years, first in Connecticut, and afterward in Massachusetts, — from an egg deposited in the living tree many years earlier still, as appeared by counting the annual layers beyond it; which was heard gnawing out for several weeks, hatched perchance by the heat of an urn. Who does not feel his faith in a resurrection and immortality strengthened by hearing of this? Who knows what beautiful and winged life, whose egg has been buried for ages under many concentric layers of woodenness in the dead dry life of society, deposited at first in the alburnum of the green and living tree, which has been gradually converted into the semblance of its well-seasoned tomb, — heard perchance gnawing out now for years by the aston-ished family of man, as they sat round the festive board, — may unexpectedly come forth from amidst society's most trivial and hand-selled furniture, to enjoy its perfect summer life at last!

I do not say that John or Jonathan will realize all this; but such is the character of that morrow which mere lapse of time can never make to dawn. The light which puts out our eyes is darkness to us. Only that day dawns to which we are awake. There is more day to dawn. The sun is but a morning-star.

CIVIL DISOBEDIENCE

[Mrs. Bronson Alcott recorded in her journal on January 17, 1843:

A day of some excitement, as Mr. Alcott has refused to pay his town tax and they had gone through the form of taking him to jail. After waiting some time to be committed, he was told it was paid by a friend. Thus we were spared the affliction of his absence and he the triumph of suffering for his principles.

Thoreau, too, had refused to pay the poll tax as early as 1842; but it was not until late July 1846 that Sam Staples, the town jailer who would have had to pay the tax he could not collect, interrupted Thoreau's life at Walden Pond by taking him to jail. Though Thoreau, at least, had a night in jail before someone paid his tax — probably his Aunt Maria, not Emerson who thought Thoreau's refusal "mean and skulking, and in bad taste" — he was unwilling to lose the value of suffering for his principles. In *A Week on the Concord and Merrimack Rivers*, which he was then composing at the pond, he considered the rights and duties of the individual in relation to government. Early in 1848 he lectured twice on civil disobedience at the Concord Lyceum, and in the next year he published his essay in Elizabeth Peabody's *Aesthetic Papers*. Even in *Walden* he made point of his refusal to recognize the authority of "the State which buys and sells men, women, and children, like cattle at the door of its senate-house."

Thoreau was forced to write so extensively about his civil disobedience because whoever paid his tax had robbed him of the chance of bringing the tax to a test. Such a test would have dramatized the issue, and so educated public opinion; without it, he had to become his own publicist. To be successful his action had to arouse attention, for though it may have satisfied his personal need to live out his principles, it did not satisfy his desire to raise the issue — to bring conscience to bear on political action. Going to jail and lecturing on the principles that had prompted this act were examples of what John Jay Chapman called "practical agitation." They were individual gestures with no immediate or programmatic reforms in view; they were valuable only to the end of educating the public. For politics was education. "Use every issue," Chapman said, "as a symbol . . . . Act first — explain afterwards. That is the way to get heard." For, like Thoreau, who may have influenced him (Chapman wrote an essay on "The Doctrine of Non-Resistance") he had learned that "what you condone, you support; what you neglect, you confirm." After a decade of organized reform effort he had learned that the impulse of principle is dissipated in the compromises made to gain temporary political victories; that, if you wish to serve the State with your conscience, you must eventually rely, as Thoreau said, on "the vitality and force of a single living man . . . ." Such practical agitation calls for courage and for the "urgent conscience" which Henry James attributed in fullest measure to the New Englander. Thoreau approved the heroism of such action in John Brown's desperate raid; bloodshed did not alter for him the fact that Brown had enacted principle. He could speak eloquently for Brown, where others lamented his folly, because he recognized his consanguinity.

Apathy, complacency, passivity, moral cowardice — these were the social results of the expedient materialism against which the Transcendentalists unfurled the banner of moral law. In the *Week*, Thoreau noted that most men live with "too passive a regard for the moral laws," and he related those scenes in *Antigone* in which Antigone refuses to obey the laws of Creon because she heeds "the unwritten and immovable laws of the gods." Antigone's behavior defines Thoreau's: man's primary allegiance is not to the State, but to the universal laws. "Only the absolutely right," he claimed, "is expedient for all." Man is not bound to a State that legislates injustice; conscience is superior to the expedients of majority rule. This is not to say that Thoreau repudiated government, but only that he would serve it when its ends were moral. He considers the State an instrument of good, a positive moral agency; its end is to forward human rights, not merely property rights, and to this end it must respect the "wise minority." Where government furthered the social welfare — in highways, schools, conservation — Thoreau was willing to pay his tax and, as he said, "but too ready to conform. . . . "

But what remedy did an individual have when government was not coordinate with justice, when it made one the unwilling partner in its evils? In the *Week* Thoreau acknowledged that where evil was concerned he could not follow the passivity advocated in the Hindu scriptures; too practically Western, Thoreau preferred to courageously assault evil rather than to starve it out. Not the Brahmin who "never thought to be a brother of mankind," but Christ, he said, was "the prince of Reformers and Radicals." Christ — from whose example Chapman had also learned — Christ who had said, "Resist not evil; but overcome evil with good." Expedience will not rout expedience; the proper weapon is conscience; only conscience will leaven "the whole lump" of society. If, as Raleigh said, a corporation has no soul, the individual must give it one.

Civil disobedience is not passive. Its immediate end is to clog the machinery of the State; it is counter-friction. Its ultimate end, however, is to undermine expediency by introducing a standard higher than social right and authority — the moral law. Where the moral law becomes the fulcrum even the individual lever is an instrument of incalculable force. Thoreau's refusal to pay his tax was probably futile, but the explanation of his purposes and principles in "Civil Disobedience" had consequences which he could not foresee — in the British Labor Movement, in Gandhi's *Satyagraha*, in resistance to tyranny everywhere. Not only did he think wisely about the ends of government, he provided a ready weapon for keeping it just. It is perhaps fitting that "Civil Disobedience" is the essay by which Thoreau is best known throughout the world.]

CIVIL DISOBEDIENCE

I HEARTILY ACCEPT the motto, "That government is best which governs least;" and I should like to see it acted up to more rapidly and systematically. Carried out, it finally amounts to this, which also I believe — "That government is best which governs not at all;" and when men are prepared for it, that will be the kind of government which they will have. Government is at best but an expedient; but most governments are usually, and all governments are sometimes, inexpedient. The objections which have been brought against a standing army, and they are many and weighty, and deserve to prevail, may also at last be brought against a standing government. The standing army is only an arm of the standing government. The government itself, which is only the mode which the people have chosen to execute their will, is equally liable to be abused and perverted before the people can act through it. Witness the present Mexican war, the work of comparatively a few individuals using the standing government as their tool; for, in the outset, the people would not have consented to this measure.

This American government — what is it but a tradition, though a recent one, endeavoring to transmit itself unimpaired to posterity, but each instant losing some of its integrity? It has not the vitality and force of a single living man; for a single man can bend it to his will. It is a sort of wooden gun to the people themselves. But it is not the less necessary for this; for the people must have some complicated machinery or other, and hear its din, to satisfy that idea of government which they have. Governments show thus how successfully men can be imposed on, even impose on themselves, for their own advantage. It is excellent, we must all allow. Yet this government never of itself furthered any enterprise, but by the alacrity with which it got out of its way. *It* does not keep the country free. *It* does not settle the West. *It* does not educate. The character inherent in the American people has done all that has been accomplished; and it would have done somewhat more, if the government had not sometimes got in its way. For government is an expedient by which men would fain succeed in letting one another alone; and, as has been said, when it is most expedient, the governed are most let alone by it. Trade and commerce, if they were not made of india-rubber, would never manage to bounce over the obstacles which legislators are continually putting in their way; and, if one were to judge these men wholly by the effects of their actions and not partly by their intentions, they would deserve to be classed and punished with those mischievous persons who put obstructions on the railroads.

But, to speak practically and as a citizen, unlike those who call themselves no-government men, I ask for, not at once no government, but *at once* a better government. Let every man make known what kind of government would command his respect, and that will be one step toward obtaining it.

After all, the practical reason why, when the power is once in the hands of the people, a majority are permitted, and for a long period continue, to rule is not because they are most likely to be in the right, nor because this seems fairest to the minority, but because they are physically the strongest. But a government in which the majority rule in all cases cannot be based on justice, even as far as men understand it. Can there not be a government in which majorities do not virtually decide right and wrong, but conscience? — in which majorities decide only those questions to which the rule of expediency is applicable? Must the citizen ever for a moment, or in the least degree, resign his conscience to the legislator? Why has every man a conscience, then? I think that we should be men first, and subjects afterwards. It is not desirable to cultivate a respect for the law, so much as for the right. The only obligation which I have a right to assume is to do at any time what I think right. It is truly enough said that a corporation has no conscience; but a corporation of conscientious men is a corporation *with* a conscience. Law never made men a whit more just; and, by means of their respect for it, even the well-disposed are daily made the agents of injustice. A common and natural result of an undue respect for law is, that you may see a file of soldiers, colonel, captain, corporal, privates, powder-monkeys, and all, marching in admirable order over hill

and dale to the wars, against their wills, ay, against their common sense and consciences, which makes it very steep marching indeed, and produces a palpitation of the heart. They have no doubt that it is a damnable business in which they are concerned; they are all peaceably inclined. Now, what are they? Men at all? or small movable forts and magazines, at the service of some unscrupulous man in power? Visit the Navy-Yard, and behold a marine, such a man as an American government can make, or such as it can make a man with its black arts — a mere shadow and reminiscence of humanity, a man laid out alive and standing, and already, as one may say, buried under arms with funeral accompaniments, though it may be, —

> "Not a drum was heard, not a funeral note,
>   As his corse to the rampart we hurried;
> Not a soldier discharged his farewell shot
>   O'er the grave where our hero was buried." [1]

The mass of men serve the state thus, not as men mainly, but as machines, with their bodies. They are the standing army, and the militia, jailers, constables, *posse comitatus*, etc. In most cases there is no free exercise whatever of the judgment or of the moral sense; but they put themselves on a level with wood and earth and stones; and wooden men can perhaps be manufactured that will serve the purpose as well. Such command no more respect than men of straw or a lump of dirt. They have the same sort of worth only as horses and dogs. Yet such as these even are commonly esteemed good citizens. Others — as most legislators, politicians, lawyers, ministers, and office-holders — serve the state chiefly with their heads; and, as they rarely make any moral distinctions, they are as likely to serve the devil, without *intending* it, as God. A very few — as heroes, patriots, martyrs, reformers in the great sense, and *men* — serve the state with their consciences also, and so necessarily resist it for the most part; and they are commonly treated as enemies by it. A wise man will only be useful as a man, and will not submit to be "clay," and "stop a hole to keep the wind away," [2] but leave that office to his dust at least: —

[1] Charles Wolfe, "Burial of Sir John Moore at Corunna" (1817).
[2] *Hamlet*, V, i, ll. 236–237.

> "I am too high-born to be propertied,
> To be a secondary at control,
> Or useful serving-man and instrument
> To any sovereign state throughout the world." [3]

He who gives himself entirely to his fellow-men appears to them useless and selfish; but he who gives himself partially to them is pronounced a benefactor and philanthropist.

How does it become a man to behave toward this American government today? I answer, that he cannot without disgrace be associated with it. I cannot for an instant recognize that political organization as *my* government which is the *slave's* government also.

All men recognize the right of revolution; that is, the right to refuse allegiance to, and to resist, the government, when its tyranny or its inefficiency are great and unendurable. But almost all say that such is not the case now. But such was the case, they think, in the Revolution of '75. If one were to tell me that this was a bad government because it taxed certain foreign commodities brought to its ports, it is most probable that I should not make an ado about it, for I can do without them. All machines have their friction; and possibly this does enough good to counterbalance the evil. At any rate, it is a great evil to make a stir about it. But when the friction comes to have its machine, and oppression and robbery are organized, I say, let us not have such a machine any longer. In other words, when a sixth of the population of a nation which has undertaken to be the refuge of liberty are slaves, and a whole country is unjustly overrun and conquered by a foreign army, and subjected to military law, I think that it is not too soon for honest men to rebel and revolutionize. What makes this duty the more urgent is the fact that the country so overrun is not our own, but ours is the invading army.

Paley,[4] a common authority with many on moral questions, in his chapter on the "Duty of Submission to Civil Government," resolves all civil obligation into expediency; and he proceeds to say that "so long as the interest of the whole society requires it, that is, so long as the established government cannot be resisted

[3] *King John*, V, ii, ll. 79–82.
[4] Rev. William Paley, *Principles of Moral and Political Philosophy* (1785), a text Thoreau is known to have studied at Harvard College.

or changed without public inconveniency, it is the will of God . . . that the established government be obeyed — and no longer. This principle being admitted, the justice of every particular case of resistance is reduced to a computation of the quantity of the danger and grievance on the one side, and of the probability and expense of redressing it on the other." Of this, he says, every man shall judge for himself. But Paley appears never to have contemplated those cases to which the rule of expediency does not apply, in which a people, as well as an individual, must do justice, cost what it may. If I have unjustly wrested a plank from a drowning man, I must restore it to him though I drown myself.[5] This, according to Paley, would be inconvenient. But he that would save his life, in such a case, shall lose it.[6] This people must cease to hold slaves, and to make war on Mexico, though it cost them their existence as a people.

In their practice, nations agree with Paley; but does any one think that Massachusetts does exactly what is right at the present crisis?

"A drab of state, a cloth-o'-silver slut,
  To have her train borne up, and her soul trail in the dirt."

Practically speaking, the opponents to a reform in Massachusetts are not a hundred thousand politicians at the South, but a hundred thousand merchants and farmers here, who are more interested in commerce and agriculture than they are in humanity, and are not prepared to do justice to the slave and to Mexico, *cost what it may*. I quarrel not with far-off foes, but with those who, near at home, coöperate with, and do the bidding of, those far away, and without whom the latter would be harmless. We are accustomed to say, that the mass of men are unprepared; but improvement is slow, because the few are not materially wiser or better than the many. It is not so important that many should be as good as you, as that there be some absolute goodness somewhere; for that will leaven the whole lump.[7] There are thousands who are *in opinion* opposed to slavery and to the war, who yet in effect do nothing to put an end to them; who, esteem-

[5] Cited by Cicero, *De Officiis*, III, a text Thoreau knew at college.
[6] Luke IX: 24; Matthew X: 39.
[7] I Corinthians V: 6.

ing themselves children of Washington and Franklin, sit down
with their hands in their pockets, and say that they know not
what to do, and do nothing; who even postpone the question of
freedom to the question of free trade, and quietly read the prices-
current along with the latest advices from Mexico, after dinner,
and, it may be, fall asleep over them both. What is the price-
current of an honest man and patriot today? They hesitate, and
they regret, and sometimes they petition; but they do nothing
in earnest and with effect. They will wait, well disposed, for
others to remedy the evil, that they may no longer have it to
regret. At most, they give only a cheap vote, and a feeble
countenance and God-speed, to the right, as it goes by them.
There are nine hundred and ninety-nine patrons of virtue to one
virtuous man. But it is easier to deal with the real possessor of a
thing than with the temporary guardian of it.

All voting is a sort of gaming, like checkers or backgammon,
with a slight moral tinge to it, a playing with right and wrong,
with moral questions; and betting naturally accompanies it. The
character of the voters is not staked. I cast my vote, perchance,
as I think right; but I am not vitally concerned that that right
should prevail. I am willing to leave it to the majority. Its obligation, therefore, never exceeds that of expediency. Even voting
for the right is *doing* nothing for it. It is only expressing to men
feebly your desire that it should prevail. A wise man will not
leave the right to the mercy of chance, nor wish it to prevail
through the power of the majority. There is but little virtue in
the action of masses of men. When the majority shall at length
vote for the abolition of slavery, it will be because they are
indifferent to slavery, or because thère is but little slavery left
to be abolished by their vote. *They* will then be the only slaves.
Only *his* vote can hasten the abolition of slavery who asserts
his own freedom by his vote.

I hear of a convention to be held at Baltimore, or elsewhere,
for the selection of a candidate for the Presidency, made up
chiefly of editors, and men who are politicians by profession; but
I think, what is it to any independent, intelligent, and respectable
man what decision they may come to? Shall we not have the
advantage of his wisdom and honesty, nevertheless? Can we
not count upon some independent votes? Are there not many

individuals in the country who do not attend conventions? But no: I find that the respectable man, so called, has immediately drifted from his position, and despairs of his country, when his country has more reason to despair of him. He forthwith adopts one of the candidates thus selected as the only *available* one, thus proving that he is himself *available* for any purposes of the demagogue. His vote is of no more worth than that of any unprincipled foreigner or hireling native, who may have been bought. O for a man who is a *man,* and, as my neighbor says, has a bone in his back which you cannot pass your hand through! Our statistics are at fault: the population has been returned too large. How many *men* are there to a square thousand miles in this country? Hardly one. Does not America offer any inducement for men to settle here? The American has dwindled into an Odd Fellow — one who may be known by the development of his organ of gregariousness, and a manifest lack of intellect and cheerful self-reliance; whose first and chief concern, on coming into the world, is to see that the almshouses are in good repair; and, before yet he has lawfully donned the virile garb, to collect a fund for the support of the widows and orphans that may be; who, in short, ventures to live only by the aid of the Mutual Insurance company, which has promised to bury him decently.

It is not a man's duty, as a matter of course, to devote himself to the eradication of any, even the most enormous, wrong; he may still properly have other concerns to engage him; but it is his duty, at least, to wash his hands of it, and, if he gives it no thought longer, not to give it practically his support. If I devote myself to other pursuits and contemplations, I must first see, at least, that I do not pursue them sitting upon another man's shoulders. I must get off him first, that he may pursue his contemplations too. See what gross inconsistency is tolerated. I have heard some of my townsmen say, "I should like to have them order me out to help put down an insurrection of the slaves, or to march to Mexico; — see if I would go"; and yet these very men have each, directly by their allegiance, and so indirectly, at least, by their money, furnished a substitute. The soldier is applauded who refuses to serve in an unjust war by those who do not refuse to sustain the unjust government which makes the war; is applauded by those whose own act and authority

he disregards and sets at naught; as if the state were penitent to
that degree that it hired one to scourge it while it sinned, but
not to that degree that it left off sinning for a moment. Thus,
under the name of Order and Civil Government, we are all made
at last to pay homage to and support our own meanness. After
the first blush of sin comes its indifference; and from immoral
it becomes, as it were, *un*moral, and not quite unnecessary to
that life which we have made.

The broadest and most prevalent error requires the most
disinterested virtue to sustain it. The slight reproach to which
the virtue of patriotism is commonly liable, the noble are most
likely to incur. Those who, while they disapprove of the character and measures of a government, yield to it their allegiance
and support are undoubtedly its most conscientious supporters,
and so frequently the most serious obstacles to reform. Some
are petitioning the State to dissolve the Union, to disregard the
requisitions of the President. Why do they not dissolve it themselves — the union between themselves and the State — and refuse to pay their quota into its treasury? Do not they stand in
the same relation to the State that the State does to the Union?
And have not the same reasons prevented the State from resisting
the Union which have prevented them from resisting the State?

How can a man be satisfied to entertain an opinion merely, and
enjoy *it?* Is there any enjoyment in it, if his opinion is that he
is aggrieved? If you are cheated out of a single dollar by your
neighbor, you do not rest satisfied with knowing that you are
cheated, or with saying that you are cheated, or even with
petitioning him to pay you your due; but you take effectual
steps at once to obtain the full amount, and see that you are
never cheated again. Action from principle, the perception and
the performance of right, changes things and relations; it is
essentially revolutionary, and does not consist wholly with anything which was. It not only divides States and churches, it
divides families; ay, it divides the *individual*, separating the
diabolical in him from the divine.

Unjust laws exist: shall we be content to obey them, or shall
we endeavor to amend them, and obey them until we have succeeded, or shall we transgress them at once? Men generally, under
such a government as this, think that they ought to wait until

they have persuaded the majority to alter them. They think that, if they should resist, the remedy would be worse than the evil. But it is the fault of the government itself that the remedy *is* worse than the evil. *It* makes it worse. Why is it not more apt to anticipate and provide for reform? Why does it not cherish its wise minority? Why does it cry and resist before it is hurt? Why does it not encourage its citizens to be on the alert to point out its faults, and *do* better than it would have them? Why does it always crucify Christ, and excommunicate Copernicus and Luther, and pronounce Washington and Franklin rebels?

One would think, that a deliberate and practical denial of its authority was the only offence never contemplated by government; else, why has it not assigned its definite, its suitable and proportionate, penalty? If a man who has no property refuses but once to earn nine shillings for the State, he is put in prison for a period unlimited by any law that I know, and determined only by the discretion of those who placed him there; but if he should steal ninety times nine shillings from the State, he is soon permitted to go at large again.

If the injustice is part of the necessary friction of the machine of government, let it go, let it go: perchance it will wear smooth — certainly the machine will wear out. If the injustice has a spring, or a pulley, or a rope, or a crank, exclusively for itself, then perhaps you may consider whether the remedy will not be worse than the evil; but if it is of such a nature that it requires you to be the agent of injustice to another, then, I say, break the law. Let your life be a counter friction to stop the machine. What I have to do is to see, at any rate, that I do not lend myself to the wrong which I condemn.

As for adopting the ways which the State has provided for remedying the evil, I know not of such ways. They take too much time, and a man's life will be gone. I have other affairs to attend to. I came into this world, not chiefly to make this a good place to live in, but to live in it, be it good or bad. A man has not everything to do, but something; and because he cannot do *everything*, it is not necessary that he should do *something* wrong. It is not my business to be petitioning the Governor or the Legislature any more than it is theirs to petition me; and if they should not hear my petition, what should I do then? But

in this case the State has provided no way: its very Constitution
is the evil. This may seem to be harsh and stubborn and uncon-
ciliatory; but it is to treat with the utmost kindness and consideration the only spirit that can appreciate or deserves it. So
is all change for the better, like birth and death, which convulse
the body.

I do not hesitate to say, that those who call themselves Aboli-
tionists should at once effectually withdraw their support, both
in person and property, from the government of Massachusetts,
and not wait till they constitute a majority of one, before they
suffer the right to prevail through them. I think that it is enough
if they have God on their side, without waiting for that other one.
Moreover, any man more right than his neighbors constitutes a
majority of one already.

I meet this American government, or its representative, the
State government, directly, and face to face, once a year — no
more — in the person of its tax-gatherer; this is the only mode
in which a man situated as I am necessarily meets it; and it then
says distinctly, Recognize me; and the simplest, the most effectual,
and, in the present posture of affairs, the indispensablest mode
of treating with it on this head, of expressing your little satisfaction with and love for it, is to deny it then. My civil neighbor,
the tax-gatherer, is the very man I have to deal with — for it is,
after all, with men and not with parchment that I quarrel — and
he has voluntarily chosen to be an agent of the government.
How shall he ever know well what he is and does as an officer of
the government, or as a man, until he is obliged to consider
whether he shall treat me, his neighbor, for whom he has respect,
as a neighbor and well-disposed man, or as a maniac and dis-
turber of the peace, and see if he can get over this obstruction
to his neighborliness without a ruder and more impetuous
thought or speech corresponding with his action. I know this
well, that if one thousand, if one hundred, if ten men whom I
could name — if ten *honest* men only — ay, if *one* HONEST man, in
this State of Massachusetts, *ceasing to hold slaves*, were actually
to withdraw from this copartnership, and be locked up in the
county jail therefor, it would be the abolition of slavery in
America. For it matters not how small the beginning may seem
to be: what is once well done is done forever. But we love

better to talk about it: that we say is our mission. Reform keeps many scores of newspapers in its service, but not one man. If my esteemed neighbor, the State's ambassador,[8] who will devote his days to the settlement of the question of human rights in the Council Chamber, instead of being threatened with the prisons of Carolina, were to sit down the prisoner of Massachusetts, that State which is so anxious to foist the sin of slavery upon her sister — though at present she can discover only an act of in-hospitality to be the ground of a quarrel with her — the Legislature would not wholly waive the subject the following winter.

Under a government which imprisons any unjustly, the true place for a just man is also a prison. The proper place to-day, the only place which Massachusetts has provided for her freer and less desponding spirits, is in her prisons, to be put out and locked out of the State by her own act, as they have already put themselves out by their principles. It is there that the fugitive slave, and the Mexican prisoner on parole, and the Indian come to plead the wrongs of his race should find them; on that separate, but more free and honorable, ground, where the State places those who are not *with* her, but *against* her — the only house in a slave State in which a free man can abide with honor. If any think that their influence would be lost there, and their voices no longer afflict the ear of the State, that they would not be as an enemy within its walls, they do not know by how much truth is stronger than error, nor how much more eloquently and effec-tively he can combat injustice who has experienced a little in his own person. Cast your whole vote, not a strip of paper merely, but your whole influence. A minority is powerless while it conforms to the majority; it is not even a minority then; but it is irresistible when it clogs by its whole weight. If the alterna-tive is to keep all just men in prison, or give up war and slavery, the State will not hesitate which to choose. If a thousand men were not to pay their tax-bills this year, that would not be a violent and bloody measure, as it would be to pay them, and enable the State to commit violence and shed innocent blood.

[8] In 1844, Samuel Hoar, the statesman of Concord, was sent to Charleston, South Carolina, on behalf of Negro seamen from Massachusetts threatened with arrest and slavery on entering the port, and was rudely expelled from Charleston.

This is, in fact, the definition of a peaceable revolution, if any such is possible. If the tax-gatherer, or any other public officer, asks me, as one has done, "But what shall I do?" my answer is, "If you really wish to do anything, resign your office." When the subject has refused allegiance, and the officer has resigned his office, then the revolution is accomplished. But even suppose blood should flow. Is there not a sort of blood shed when the conscience is wounded? Through this wound a man's real manhood and immortality flow out, and he bleeds to an everlasting death. I see this blood flowing now.

I have contemplated the imprisonment of the offender, rather than the seizure of his goods — though both will serve the same purpose — because they who assert the purest right, and consequently are most dangerous to a corrupt State, commonly have not spent much time in accumulating property. To such the State renders comparatively small service, and a slight tax is wont to appear exorbitant, particularly if they are obliged to earn it by special labor with their hands. If there were one who lived wholly without the use of money, the State itself would hesitate to demand it of him. But the rich man — not to make any invidious comparison — is always sold to the institution which makes him rich. Absolutely speaking, the more money, the less virtue; for money comes between a man and his objects, and obtains them for him; and it was certainly no great virtue to obtain it. It puts to rest many questions which he would otherwise be taxed to answer; while the only new question which it puts is the hard but superfluous one, how to spend it. Thus his moral ground is taken from under his feet. The opportunities of living are diminished in proportion as what are called the "means" are increased. The best thing a man can do for his culture when he is rich is to endeavor to carry out those schemes which he entertained when he was poor. Christ answered the Herodians according to their condition. "Show me the tribute-money," said he; — and one took a penny out of his pocket; — if you use money which has the image of Cæsar on it, and which he has made current and valuable, that is, *if you are men of the State*, and gladly enjoy the advantages of Cæsar's government, then pay him back some of his own when he demands it. "Render therefore to Cæsar that which is Cæsar's, and to God those things which are God's" — leaving them no wiser than before as to which was which; for they did not wish to know.

When I converse with the freest of my neighbors, I perceive that, whatever they may say about the magnitude and seriousness of the question, and their regard for the public tranquillity, the long and the short of the matter is, that they cannot spare the protection of the existing government, and they dread the consequences to their property and families of disobedience to it. For my own part, I should not like to think that I ever rely on the protection of the State. But, if I deny the authority of the State when it presents its tax-bill, it will soon take and waste all my property, and so harass me and my children without end. This is hard. This makes it impossible for a man to live honestly, and at the same time comfortably, in outward respects. It will not be worth the while to accumulate property; that would be sure to go again. You must hire or squat somewhere, and raise but a small crop, and eat that soon. You must live within yourself, and depend upon yourself always tucked up and ready for a start, and not have many affairs. A man may grow rich in Turkey even, if he will be in all respects a good subject of the Turkish government. Confucius said: "If a state is governed by the principles of reason, poverty and misery are subjects of shame; if a state is not governed by the principles of reason, riches and honors are the subjects of shame." No: until I want the protection of Massachusetts to be extended to me in some distant Southern port, where my liberty is endangered, or until I am bent solely on building up an estate at home by peaceful enterprise, I can afford to refuse allegiance to Massachusetts, and her right to my property and life. It costs me less in every sense to incur the penalty of disobedience to the State than it would to obey. I should feel as if I were worth less in that case.

Some years ago, the State met me in behalf of the Church, and commanded me to pay a certain sum toward the support of a clergyman whose preaching my father attended, but never I myself. "Pay," it said, "or be locked up in the jail." I declined to pay.[9] But, unfortunately, another man saw fit to pay it. I did not see why the schoolmaster should be taxed to support the

---

[9] Thoreau's first act on returning to Concord after leaving college was to "sign off" from the Church.

priest, and not the priest the schoolmaster; for I was not the State's schoolmaster, but I supported myself by voluntary subscription. I did not see why the lyceum should not present its tax-bill, and have the State to back its demand, as well as the Church. However, at the request of the selectmen, I condescended to make some such statement as this in writing: — "Know all men by these presents, that I, Henry Thoreau, do not wish to be regarded as a member of any incorporated society which I have not joined." This I gave to the town clerk; and he has it. The State, having thus learned that I did not wish to be regarded as a member of that church, has never made a like demand on me since; though it said that it must adhere to its original presumption that time. If I had known how to name them, I should then have signed off in detail from all the societies which I never signed on to; but I did not know where to find a complete list.

I have paid no poll-tax for six years. I was put into a jail once on this account, for one night; and, as I stood considering the walls of solid stone, two or three feet thick, the door of wood and iron, a foot thick, and the iron grating which strained the light, I could not help being struck with the foolishness of that institution which treated me as if I were mere flesh and blood and bones to be locked up. I wondered that it should have concluded at length that this was the best use it could put me to, and had never thought to avail itself of my services in some way. I saw that, if there was a wall of stone between me and my townsmen, there was a still more difficult one to climb or break through before they could get to be as free as I was. I did not for a moment feel confined, and the walls seemed a great waste of stone and mortar. I felt as if I alone of all my townsmen had paid my tax. They plainly did not know how to treat me, but behaved like persons who are underbred. In every threat and in every compliment there was a blunder; for they thought that my chief desire was to stand the other side of that stone wall. I could not but smile to see how industriously they locked the door on my meditations, which followed them out again without let or hindrance, and *they* were really all that was dangerous. As they could not reach me, they had resolved to punish my body; just as boys, of they cannot come at some person against whom they have a spite, will abuse his dog. I saw that the State was half-witted, that it was timid as a lone woman with her silver spoons, and that it did not know its friends from its foes, and I lost all my remaining respect for it, and pitied it.

Thus the State never intentionally confronts a man's sense, intellectual or moral, but only his body, his senses. It is not armed with superior wit or honesty, but with superior physical strength. I was not born to be forced. I will breathe after my own fashion. Let us see who is the strongest. What force has a multitude? They only can force me who obey a higher law than I. They force me to become like themselves. I do not hear of *men* being *forced* to live this way or that by masses of men. What sort of life were that to live? When I meet a government which says to me, "Your money or your life," why should I be in haste to give it my money? It may be in a great strait, and not know what to do: I cannot help that. It must help itself; do as I do. It is not worth the while to snivel about it. I am not responsible for the successful working of the machinery of society. I am not the son of the engineer. I perceive that, when an acorn and a chestnut fall side by side, the one does not remain inert to make way for the other, but both obey their own laws, and spring and grow and flourish as best they can, till one, perchance, overshadows and destroys the other. If a plant cannot live according to its nature, it dies; and so a man.

The night in prison was novel and interesting enough. The prisoners in their shirt-sleeves were enjoying a chat and the evening air in the doorway, when I entered. But the jailer said, "Come, boys, it is time to lock up"; and so they dispersed, and I heard the sound of their steps returning into the hollow apartments. My room-mate was introduced to me by the jailer as "a first-rate fellow and a clever man." When the door was locked, he showed me where to hang my hat, and how he managed matters there. The rooms were whitewashed once a month; and this one, at least, was the whitest, most simply furnished, and probably the neatest apartment in the town. He naturally wanted to know where I came from, and what brought me there; and, when I had told him, I asked him in my turn how he came there, presuming him to be an honest man, of course; and, as the world goes, I believe he was. "Why," said he, "they accuse me of burning a barn; but I never did it." As near as I could discover, he had probably gone to bed in a barn when drunk, and smoked his pipe there; and so a barn was burnt. He had the reputation of being a clever man, had been there some three months waiting for his trial to come on, and would have to wait as much longer; but he was quite domesticated and contented, since he got his board for nothing, and thought that he was well treated.

He occupied one window, and I the other; and I saw that if one stayed there long, his principal business would be to look out the window. I had soon read all the tracts that were left there, and examined where former prisoners had broken out, and where a grate had been sawed off, and heard the history of the various occupants of that room; for I found that even here there was a history and a gossip which never circulated beyond the walls of the jail. Probably this is the only house in the town where verses are composed, which are afterward printed in a circular form, but not published. I was shown quite a long list of verses which were composed by some young men who had been detected in an attempt to escape, who avenged themselves by singing them.

I pumped my fellow-prisoner as dry as I could, for fear I should never see him again; but at length he showed me which was my bed, and left me to blow out the lamp.

It was like travelling into a far country, such as I had never expected to behold, to lie there for one night. It seemed to me that I never had heard the town clock strike before, nor the evening sounds of the village; for we slept with the windows open, which were inside the grating. It was to see my native village in the light of the Middle Ages, and our Concord was turned into a Rhine stream, and visions of knights and castles passed before me. They were the voices of old burghers that I heard in the streets. I was an involuntary spectator and auditor of whatever was done and said in the kitchen of the adjacent village inn — a wholly new and rare experience to me. It was a closer view of my native town. I was fairly inside of it. I never had seen its institutions before. This is one of its peculiar institutions; for it is a shire town. I began to comprehend what its inhabitants were about.

In the morning, our breakfasts were put through the hole in

the door, in small oblong-square tin pans, made to fit, and holding a pint of chocolate, with brown bread, and an iron spoon. When they called for the vessels again, I was green enough to return what bread I had left; but my comrade seized it, and said that I should lay that up for lunch or dinner. Soon after he was let out to work at haying in a neighboring field, whither he went every day, and would not be back till noon; so he bade me good-day, saying that he doubted if he should see me again.

When I came out of prison — for some one interfered, and paid that tax — I did not perceive that great changes had taken place on the common, such as he observed who went in a youth and emerged a tottering and gray-headed man; and yet a change had to my eyes come over the scene — the town, and State, and country — greater than any that mere time could effect. I saw yet more distinctly the State in which I lived. I saw to what extent the people among whom I lived could be trusted as good neighbors and friends; that their friendship was for summer weather only; that they did not greatly propose to do right; that they were a distinct race from me by their prejudices and super-stitions, as the Chinamen and Malays are; that in their sacrifices to humanity they ran no risks, not even to their property; that after all they were not so noble but they treated the thief as he had treated them, and hoped, by a certain outward observance and a few prayers, and by walking in a particular straight though useless path from time to time, to save their souls. This may be to judge my neighbors harshly; for I believe that many of them are not aware that they have such an institution as the jail in their village.

It was formerly the custom in our village, when a poor debtor came out of jail, for his acquaintances to salute him, looking through their fingers, which were crossed to represent the grat-ing of a jail window," How do ye do?" My neighbors did not thus salute me, but first looked at me, and then at one another, as if I had returned from a long journey. I was put into jail as I was going to the shoemaker's to get a shoe which was mended. When I was let out the next morning, I preceeded to finish my errand, and, having put on my mended shoe, joined a huckle-berry party, who were impatient to put themselves under my conduct; and in half an hour — for the horse was soon tackled —

was in the midst of a huckleberry field, on one of our highest
hills, two miles off, and then the State was nowhere to be seen.
This is the whole history of "My Prisons."

I have never declined paying the highway tax, because I am
as desirous of being a good neighbor as I am of being a bad subject; and as for supporting schools, I am doing my part to educate my fellow-countrymen now. It is for no particular item
in the tax-bill that I refuse to pay it. I simply wish to refuse
allegiance to the State, to withdraw and stand aloof from it effectually. I do not care to trace the course of my dollar, if I
could, till it buys a man or a musket to shoot one with — the
dollar is innocent — but I am concerned to trace the effects of
my allegiance. In fact, I quietly declare war with the State,
after my fashion, though I will still make what use and get what
advantage of her I can, as is usual in such cases.

If others pay the tax which is demanded of me, from a sympathy with the State, they do but what they have already done
in their own case, or rather they abet injustice to a greater extent than the State requires. If they pay the tax from a mistaken
interest in the individual taxed, to save his property, or prevent
his going to jail, it is because they have not considered wisely
how far they let their private feelings interfere with the public
good.

This, then, is my position at present. But one cannot be too
much on his guard in such a case, lest his action be biased by
obstinacy or an undue regard for the opinions of men. Let him
see that he does only what belongs to himself an to the hour.

I think sometimes, Why, this people mean well, they are only
ignorant; they would do better if they knew how: why give
your neighbors this pain to treat you as they are not inclined
to? But I think again, This is no reason why I should do as they
do, or permit others to suffer much greater pain of a different
kind. Again, I sometimes say to myself, When many millions of
men, without heat, without ill will, without personal feeling of
any kind, demand of you a few shillings only, without the possibility, such is their constitution, of retracting or altering their
present demand, and without the possibility, on your side, of appeal to any other millions, why expose yourself to this over-

whelming brute force? You do not resist cold and hunger, the winds and the waves, thus obstinately; you quietly submit to a thousand similar necessities. You do not put your head into the fire. But just in proportion as I regard this as not wholly a brute force, but partly a human force, and consider that I have relations to those millions as to so many millions of men, and not of mere brute or inanimate things, I see that appeal is possible, first and instantaneously, from them to the Maker of them, and, secondly, from them to themselves. But if I put my head deliberately into the fire, there is no appeal to fire or to the Maker of fire, and I have only myself to blame. If I could convince myself that I have any right to be satisfied with men as they are, and to treat them accordingly, and not according, in some respects, to my requisitions and expectations of what they and I ought to be, then, like a good Mussulman and fatalist, I should endeavor to be satisfied with things as they are, and say it is the will of God. And, above all, there is this difference between resisting this and a purely brute or natural force, that I can resist this with some effect; but I cannot expect, like Orpheus, to change the nature of the rocks and trees and beasts.

I do not wish to quarrel with any man or nation. I do not wish to split hairs, to make fine distinctions, or set myself up as better than my neighbors. I seek rather, I may say, even an excuse for conforming the laws of the land. I am but too ready to conform to them. Indeed, I have reason to suspect myself on this head; and each year, as the tax-gatherer comes round, I find myself disposed to review the acts and positions of the general and State governments, and the spirit of the people, to discover a pretext for conformity.

> "We must affect our country as our parents,
>   And if at any time we alienate
>   Our love or industry from doing it honor,
>   We must respect effects and teach the soul
>   Matter of conscience and religion,
>   And not desire of rule or benefit."

I believe that the State will soon be able to take all my work of this sort out of my hands, and then I shall be no better a patriot than my fellow-countrymen. Seen from a lower point of view, the Constitution, with all its faults, is very good; the law and the courts are very respectable; even this State and this American government are, in many respects, very admirable, and rare things, to be thankful for, such as a great many have described them; but seen from a point of view a little higher, they are what I have described them; seen from a higher still, and the highest, who shall say what they are, or that they are worth looking at or thinking of at all?

However, the government does not concern me much, and I shall bestow the fewest possible thoughts on it. It is not many moments that I live under a government, even in this world. If a man is thought-free, fancy-free, imagination-free, that which *is not* never for a long time appearing *to be* to him, unwise rulers or reformers cannot fatally interrupt him.

I know that most men think differently from myself; but those whose lives are by profession devoted to the study of these or kindred subjects content me as little as any. Statesmen and legislators, standing so completely within the institution, never distinctly and nakedly behold it. They speak of moving society, but have no resting-place without it. They may be men of a certain experience and discrimination, and have no doubt invented ingenious and even useful systems, for which we sincerely thank them; but all their wit and usefulness lie within certain not very wide limits. They are wont to forget that the world is not governed by policy and expediency. Webster never goes behind government, and so cannot speak with authority about it. His words are wisdom to those legislators who contemplate no essential reform in the existing government; but for thinkers, and those who legislate for all time, he never once glances at the subject. I know of those whose serene and wise speculations on this theme would soon reveal the limits of his mind's range and hospitality. Yet, compared with the cheap professions of most reformers, and the still cheaper wisdom and eloquence of politicians in general, his are almost the only sensible and valuable words, and we thank Heaven for him. Comparatively, he is always strong, original, and, above all, practical. Still, his quality is not wisdom, but prudence. The lawyer's truth is not Truth, but consistency or a consistent expediency. Truth is always in harmony with herself, and is not concerned chiefly to reveal the justice that may consist with wrong-doing. He well deserves to be called, as he has been called, the Defender of the Constitution. There are really no blows to be given by him but defensive ones. He is not a leader, but a follower. His leaders are the men of '87. "I have never made an effort," he says, "and never propose to make an effort; I have never countenanced an effort, and never mean to countenance an effort, to disturb the arrangement as originally made, by which the various States came into the Union." Still thinking of the sanction which the Constitution gives to slavery, he says, "Because it was a part of the original compact — let it stand." Notwithstanding his special acuteness and ability, he is unable to take a fact out of its merely political relations, and behold it as it lies absolutely to be disposed of by the intellect — what, for instance, it behooves a man to do here in America today with regard to slavery — but ventures, or is driven, to make some such desperate answer as the following, while professing to speak absolutely, and as a private man — from which what new and similar code of social duties might be inferred? "The manner," says he, "in which the governments of those States where slavery exists are to regulate it is for their own consideration, under their responsibility to their constituents, to the general laws of propriety, humanity, and justice, and to God. Associations formed elsewhere, springing from a feeling of humanity, or any other cause, have nothing whatever to do with it. They have never received any encouragement from me, and they never will." [10]

They who know of no purer sources of truth, who have traced up its steam no higher, stand, and wisely stand, by the Bible and the Constitution, and drink at it there with reverence and humility; but they who behold where it comes trickling into this lake or that pool, gird up their loins once more, and continue their pilgrimage toward its fountain-head.

No man with a genius for legislation has appeared in America. They are rare in the history of the world. There are orators, politicians, and eloquent men, by the thousand; but the speaker has not yet opened his mouth to speak who is capable of settling the much-vexed questions of the day. We love eloquence for its own sake, and not for any truth which it may utter, or any heroism it may inspire. Our legislators have not yet learned the

[10] These extracts have been inserted since the lecture was read. [Author's note.]

comparative value of free trade and of freedom, of union, and
of rectitude, to a nation. They have no genius or talent for comparatively humble questions of taxation and finance, commerce
and manufactures and agriculture. If we were left solely to the
wordy wit of legislators in Congress for our guidance, uncor-
rected by the seasonable experience and the effectual complaints
of the people, America would not long retain her rank among
the nations. For eighteen hundred years, though perchance I
have no right to say it, the New Testament has been written;
yet where is the legislator who has wisdom and practical talent
enough to avail himself of the light which it sheds on the science
of legislation?

The authority of government, even such as I am willing to
submit to — for I will cheerfully obey those who know and can
do better than I, and in many things even those who neither
know nor can do so well — is still an impure one: to be strictly
just, it must have the sanction and consent of the governed. It
can have no pure right over my person and property but what
I concede to it. The progress from an absolute to a limited
monarchy, from a limited monarchy to a democracy, is a progress toward a true respect for the individual. Even the Chinese
philosopher was wise enough to regard the individual as the
basis of the empire. Is a democracy, such is we know it, the
last improvement possible in government? Is it not possible to
take a step further towards recognizing and organizing the rights
of man? There will never be a really free and enlightened State
until the State comes to recognize the individual as a higher and
independent power, from which all its own power and authority
are derived, and treats him accordingly. I please myself with imagining a State at least which can afford to be just to all men, and
to treat the individual with respect as a neighbor; which even
would not think it inconsistent with its own repose if a few were
to live aloof from it, not meddling with it, nor embraced by it,
who fulfilled all the duties of neighbors and fellow-men. A
State which bore this kind of fruit, and suffered it to drop off
as fast as it ripened, would prepare the way for a still more
perfect and glorious State, which also I have imagined, but not
yet anywhere seen.

APPENDIX

LIFE IN THE WOODS

by Charles Lane

From *The Dial*, April, 1844

[Charles Lane, an English reformer, returned to Concord with Alcott in the fall of 1842 — a result Emerson, who had sent Alcott to England, hardly expected. In May, 1843, Lane purchased a farm at Harvard, Massachusetts, and in June he began the "Fruitlands" experiment with the Alcott family. By the end of the year, more as the result of Lane's ideas than of Alcott's alleged impracticality, the experiment ended in failure. Both Lane and Alcott were philosophers of the hearth and garden, reformers who proposed the regeneration of society by making the family the primary unit of nurture. Since Nature for them was spirit "lapsed," in need of redemption by the spiritualizing agency of man, they did not approve of Thoreau's outright love of Nature. Early in 1843, Mrs. Emerson reported a "conversation" by Alcott and Lane, in which the love of Nature was said to be a "refined idolatry" — "the most subtle and dangerous of sins. . . ." Thoreau, Mrs. Emerson said, "frankly affirmed to both the wise men that they were wholly deficient in the faculty in question, and therefore could not judge it." Alcott, however, had the last word, telling Thoreau that he went beyond the "mere material objects" with his "spiritual love and perception" — as Thoreau did not. Alcott later better appreciated Thoreau's study of Nature, but this early misunderstanding continued into Lane's article in *The Dial* (April, 1844). And though there were areas of disagreement in the transcendentalism of Alcott and Lane and that of Emerson, the article was general enough to express the commonly felt preference for life in village parlors that most transcendentalists really owned when faced with the choice of actually realizing their lives in Nature. Here, in fact, was one of the first signs of their commitment to society, of the difficulty those unaccustomed to wearing corduroy found in primitivism. Beyond the fact that *Walden* directly answered Lane's major charges — that, though "sylvan" rather than barbaric, the primitive life was not fit for the white man, that to undertake it would lead to an unsocial solitude and defeat the spiritual ends of life — there is no evidence that Thoreau took his subtitle from this article.]

LIFE IN THE WOODS

"Here shall he see
No enemy
But winter and rough weather."
SHAKESPEARE.

THAT must be a very pleasant life indeed, wherein no enemy shall appear who cannot be easily subdued by a strong arm and an axe. Yet it seems to have been an enemy no more potent which drove men from free life in the woods, to the shackles of a closer congregation. It is the fashion to speak of the woodland life, as savage, barbarous, and brutal; and of the housed life, either in feudal castle or trading city, as refined, polished, and elevated. It might not be altogether wasted time to inquire whether this conclusion stands upon a true foundation or not. So many errors pass current as truths, that one may be not illiberally induced to investigate such a question, though it be one that the stricter student will deem of minor morality. Of such small questions, much that is of mighty import is not unfrequently constructed.

That cosmogony which affirms for man the highest origin, represents him in his pristine creation as contravening his Creator's will, and in the very first generation, the very first vital act, as quarrelling with, and murdering his brother. If this be literally true of the external man, as it is now undoubtedly a true signature of operations in the human soul, the first wigwam was probably erected more as a defence from the assaults of man against his brother, than from the assaults of uncongenial weather. When peace reigns in every human bosom, the free man may wander for food and for repose to whatever latitude the season shall render propitious to his feelings and his wants. The thought of erecting a house grew not out of human necessity so much as out of human rapacity. The love of power in some assailant, rather than the love of art in some pacific being, forced on man the utility of a house for his protection, while in a state of repose. It at least defended him from too sudden a surprise, if it did not wholly protect him. The inclemency of a stronger brother, more than the inclemency of the weather, generated the thought of a stockade.

Passing over this consideration, let us contemplate the sylvan man in his native state, let us compare him with the civilian, and see to which the superiority must be awarded, both as respects nature and conditions. Behold, what it is difficult for us to imagine, an individual wholly free from the diseases consequent upon luxury and debauchery, and subject only to the little incidental ills of the exhilarating chase. Conceive of one to whom hereditary or chronic disease is unknown, to whom catarrh, and cough, and palsying apprehension of a cold never are disturbances. He walks erect, with elastic, almost bounding, step, expanded and uncovered chest, and limbs untrammelled by

the ligatures of fashion. Health, strength, and agility, combined with an un-
checked reliance on their continuance, are a living fund of joy, wonderfully
contrasting with the disease, weakness, and imbecility of modern refinement.

Every sense in the primitive forester's frame is integrally preserved. He
holds an immediate intercourse with nature herself, or at least by his unerring
senses and the undeviating objects in nature, he is enabled intuitively to read off
the living volume as it lies open and unpolluted before him. By mere sight
and smell, he is at once inducted into a knowledge of the essential properties of
plants, and can without experience, foretel their operations on the human
system, as unerringly as the native sheep can select its suitable food, or the
untamed wood-dove, can without schooling, essay a winged journey.

If *after* long labor and close study, the civic student knows something concerning nature from his books and pictures, the sylvan student knows much
of her and her laws *before* the record of book or graver was constructed.
He is as a mother who knows of maternity, and a mother's feelings in a living
and soul-participating manner, antecedent to all external observation, while
the college student is comparable to the obstetric physician, who compiles a
book from external observation only, and writes of feelings he never felt, and
of experiences he never did or can experience.

The sylvan is present at the very fountain head, living in and with the
works, productions, and operations which will, by and by, be recorded; the
civilian is acquainted only with the record. The one is witness to the vital
spring and birth of nature's offspring; the other's studies are comparable only
to a poring over the parish register.

It is the boast of modern experimental philosophy, that it has abandoned or
overturned the Aristotelian method of study by words, adopting that of
studying things. But it pursues its objects by means of crucibles, retorts, and
balances, as deceptive, vague, and unsatisfactory as the studies they have
superseded; for these, after all, stood as near the moral source as modern
science. Whereas the pure, unsophisticated human body, is a retort, a test,
far surpassing all the instruments which the highest science can boast. By the
sylvan man all nature is affectionately felt; by the civilized it is only intellectually scanned. The warmth of life is characteristic of one; the coldness of
death the distinguishing mark of the other. Chymical science, the great boast
and wonder worker of our enlightened age, cannot even discern those delicate
differences and lineaments in nature, which optics can reveal, and it can do
nothing in any department of nature, until the object is reduced to its mineral
state. In the grand and noble field of life it is powerless. Vegetables and
animals, as such, in their living beauty are fruitlessly presented to the chymist's
skill. He has weights and measures, but cannot compute living motion any
more than he can fathom moral emotion. He has testing apparatus, but no
taste. But our natural chymist only sees and knows such objects in life and
motion. With his unassisted eye, he perceives varieties which the chymist
never learns, and by an unvitiated palate, he detects in the living volume of

nature the occult essential qualities of plants, which the last analysis in the laboratory rarely or never can reveal. The forms, odors, statures of plants, as they simply stand before him, are types in the boundless volume of which the scientific student seems ever destined to peruse merely the title page. The eye, the nose, the palate, the touch, and every sense is an inlet direct from the book of nature, a first impression, which to the civilized student rarely comes otherwise than at second hand. He must refer to his printed authority, and his human classification, his encyclopedia, his constructed circle of circumferential science; while our nature-student has in himself the authority, knows truly the real author, and feels himself to be at the centre of science, of which the circumference lies about him. "The unity of the Sciences," the last pleasing thought of labored skill, the key-stone with which studious industry has at length crowned its self-wondrous arch, is no novelty to the free soul. He never felt knowledge otherwise than as a unity; nature or natural objects never were thus dissectively presented to him. He sees objects analytically without doubt, as well as synthetically; but always perhaps under both aspects at once, always in their individual existence as well as united to an antecedent unity, the parent of them all.

For all the purposes of life, for all the utilities of his life, the science of the forest man is complete. All the wants which in such a life are generated, in the immediate world about him, find their supplies. The pressure of hunger, the needful clothing, even the ornaments which he desires, with their tasteful forms, and superadded tints, he obtains without difficulty or danger to himself or fellow man. Not so is it with the wants and wishes generated in civic life. These know no bounds, but expand with every gratification; their victims at once boasting over their expansion, and groaning over their denial. No sea or land is unexplored to create new wants, or to supply excited and extraneous appetites, and carrying with him to the innocent and pure, disease and vice of the cruellest kind, civilized man boasts the extension of his domain, the multiplication of his likeness.

A darker age presumes upon its false illumination, to call antecedent ages dark. A busy, wandering, restless civilization ventures from the point of its own worthless activity, to pronounce the contented child of nature savage and barbarous. Literally, perhaps, these epithets are justly applied. If savage means a dweller in the wood, and barbarian one who does not denude his chin of hair; if the terms be taken to mean no more than these, there would be clearly no greater injustice or condemnation in them, than in calling one a civilian who dwells in a city. But the design in using these words is to affirm that the heights of mind, elevation of thought, purity in sentiment are denied to man in one condition of life, and granted in the other.

That those who are most ready to use these allusions aspersively ever think about the matter, or are capable of thinking very profoundly, may, until they feel more benignly, very charitably be doubted. But there is sufficient evidence on record to prove that the sublimest conceptions have not been withheld from the mind of the North American native, any more than from the highly taught sons of civilization. A narrative not unworthy of Swedenborg, or even of Plato, is reported in David Brainerd's Diary, kept while he was a missionary among the natives of New Jersey, about one hundred years ago. Of its correctness there is very little room to doubt; since the recorder mourns over it in every aspect, and that the seer could have acquired it from any other person, there is no ground whatever to suspect. It is given in these words: —

"What increases the aversion of the Indians to Christianity, is the influence their *powwows* have upon them. These are supposed to have a power of foretelling future events, of recovering the sick, and of charming persons to death. And their *Spirit*, in its various operations, seems to be a Satanical imitation of the spirit of prophecy, that the church in early ages was favored with.

"I have labored to gain some acquaintance with this affair, and have for that end consulted the man mentioned in my journal, of the 9th of May, who since his conversion to Christianity has endeavored to give me the best intelligence he could of this matter. But it seems to be such a mystery of iniquity, that I cannot well understand it, and so far as I can learn, he himself has not any clear notions of the thing, now his spirit of divination is gone from him. However, the manner in which he says he obtained this spirit, was, he was admitted into the presence of a great man who informed him that he loved, pitied, and desired to do him good. It was not in this world that he saw the great man, but in a world above at a vast distance from this. The great man, he says, was clothed with the day; yea, with the brightest day he ever saw, a day of many years, yea of everlasting continuance! This whole world, he says, was drawn upon him, so that in him the earth and all things in it might be seen. I asked him if rocks, mountains, and seas were drawn upon, or appeared in him. He replied, that every thing that was beautiful and lovely in the earth was upon him, and might be seen by looking on him, as well as if one was on the earth to take a view of them there. By the side of the great man, he said, stood his shadow or spirit. This shadow, he says, was as lovely as the man himself, and filled all places, and was most agreeable as well as wonderful to him.

"Here, he says, he tarried some time, and was unspeakably entertained and delighted with a view of the great man, of his shadow or spirit, and of all things in him. And what is most of all astonishing, he imagined all this to have passed before he was born. He never had been, he says, in this world at that time. And what confirms him in the belief of this, is, that the great man told him he must come down to earth, be born of such a woman, meet with such and such things, and in particular, that he should once in his life be guilty of murder. At this he was displeased, and told the great man he would never murder. But the great man replied, 'I have said it, and it shall be so.' Which has accordingly happened. At this time, he says, the great man asked him what he would choose in life. He replied, first to be a hunter, and afterwards to be a powwow or diviner. Whereupon the great man told him he should have what he desired, and that his shadow should go along with him down to earth, and be with him forever. There were, he says, all this time no words spoken between them. The conference was not carried on by any human language, but they had a kind of mental intelligence of each other's thoughts. After this, he says, he saw the great man no more; but supposes he came down to earth to be born, but the spirit or shadow of the great man still attended him, and ever after continued to appear to him in dreams, and other ways, until he felt the power of God's word upon his heart, since which it has entirely left him.

"There were some times when this spirit came upon him in a special manner, and he was full of what he saw in the great man; and then, he says, he was all light, and not only light himself, but it was light all around him, so that he could see through men, and know the thoughts of their hearts. These depths of Satan I leave to others to fathom, and do not know what ideas to affix to such terms, nor can guess what conceptions of things these creatures have at the times when they call themselves all light." — p. 204.

So similar are some of these sentiments, and so like are some of these words to those of Swedenborg and Wordsworth, that in the obscurity of time they might be attributed to these sources. But as our record is dated three fourths of a century before one, and many years before the other authority, such hypothesis is manifestly untenable; but the converse is rather to be maintained. In a previous passage the zealous Brainerd remarks.

"I find that in antient times, before the coming of the white people, some supposed there were four invisible powers, who presided over the four corners of the earth. Others imagined the Sun to be the only deity, and that all things were made by him. Others at the same time having a confused notion of a certain body or fountain of deity, somewhat like the *anima mundi;* so frequently mentioned by the more learned antient heathens, diffusing itself to various animals, and even to inanimate things, making them the immediate authors of good to certain persons."

When we find so unwilling a witness bearing satisfactory testimony to the spontaneous generation of the most profound and subtile thoughts, which have ever entered the human soul, filling, in so vivid a manner, that of the unschooled savage, how can we deny the presence of that mental life and quickness, which as polished and civilized beings we delight to boast. To these red men, and to all the white who came into connexion with them, the names and works and thoughts of Behmen the profound, or of Plato the elegant, were alike unknown. To these wilds their renown had not then travelled, and even now they are unpopular and obscure authors. Had it indeed been otherwise, and could it be proved that such sentiments were the results of outward lessons, it would prove no less satisfactorily to what subtlety of thought the native mind could ascend; even beyond that of the missionary teacher having St. John's mystic gospel in his hand. For I must not suppose that those whom I now address, like Brainerd, "cannot even guess what conceptions these creatures have at the time they call themselves all light," seeing that we know there "is a true light, which lighteth every man who cometh into the world."

No wonder need be then excited in our minds, when we occasionally hear of the young spirit, to whom the costliest education has been afforded, and before whom the whole world invitingly lies as a beautiful unexplored garden, every path free to his foot, turning, after a little experience, his course from the city towards the woods. The experiment of a true wilderness life by a white person must, however, be very rare. He is not born for it; he is not natured for it. He lacks the essential qualities as well as the physical substance for such a life, and the notion of entering on it must be considered merely an interesting dream. Some amalgamation may, however, be possible; and to unite the advantages of the two modes has doubtless been the aim of many. Even now we hear of some individuals, on whom the world might hopefully rely to become eminent even amongst the worthy, betaking themselves from the busy haunts of men to a more select and secluded life.

But will they succeed in wrestling against their increased natural needs, and their remaining civic wants, diminished as these may be? On trial, as on due consideration, it will be found that this is not a very promising course. By the time the hut is built, the rudest furniture constructed, the wood chopped, the fire burning, the bread grown and prepared, the whole time will be exhausted, and no interval remain for comfortably clothing the body, for expansion in art, or for recreation by the book or pen. This but faintly promises to be the mode, by which the simple and pure in heart shall escape the pressures and burdens, which prevent the full and happy development of the soul.

Of those who have sought a recluse life on a religious basis, it has been remarked that solitude is a state suitable only to the best or the worst. The average cast of humanity cannot be much benefitted by it. It is not a condition in which human beings can be brought into the world, and it is rarely a condition in which they should attempt to remain in it. The austerities pertaining to silence and solitude may improve the very bad; they may leave uninjured the very good; but such as are in the process of improvement, an association of some kind seems more suitable, as it is evidently more natural. It is natural, not only in the sense of harmony with the humane affections, which out of social intimacy must painfully wither, but also it is natural to the interior or spirit life. The highest virtue can be promoted by friendship and fellowship. If even God himself may have a favorite disciple upon whose bosom he can recline; the spiritually minded surely cannot commit a very great error in adopting the aid of co-support, when they are so fortunate as to find it, or still more fortunate to be able to bestow it.

No mistake could be more evident than that of assuming that the child of nature lives an isolate life. On the contrary, he moves in a circle much more social than modern cities can boast. The tribe is a better type of the universal family than the city, where the inhabitants of the same street are frequently unknown to each other after dwelling many years side by side. Again, so little of the love-destroying notion of property enters into this free man's scheme, that the universal idea is not erased. He is not an isolated but a dispersive being. He lives not alone; he merely occupies a large space. He does not estimate his strength, his value, or his happiness by the density of the population, but rather by its rarity. In the spare civic statistics of forty persons to the square mile, he is oppressed by the crowd. He requires abundant supplies of vital air, and the atmosphere is corrupted for him long before the white man's neighborhood arrives at a comfortable point. The pure oxygen which the Creator provides is suitable to the red man, while the white is only happy in steam, or some other self-generated atmosphere. By union of numbers, by condensation into a phalanx, the white man conquers the red, whom singly he could never subdue. By a new and superior phalanx, constructed altogether on a different basis, it is probably destined that the present civilized institutions shall be superseded, and the new and superior nature in man receive a new and superior development.

This is in fact the point to which all our endeavors must converge. Poetic wanderings will not more rectify us than trading conversations. And on calm consideration, unswayed by those paradoxes which ingenious men have from time to time constructed concerning the beautiful liberty of the sylvan life, and to which imaginations we have on this occasion perhaps too strongly tended, have we not to confess that one is as distant from true life as the other? They both lie on the same circumference. They are but segments of one circle, struck by the compasses of human selfishness at too great a distance from the true centre. There does not appear to have been any true inward progress by the change from the woods to the town; if indeed men ever were so changed, and it be not the fact that these two lives belong to two distinct races, each severally fitted by organization for its respective mode of life; which seems the truer hypothesis.

Conceding civilization to be some *improvement* in social arrangements, while we assert that it secures no vital *progress* to the soul, we have to conclude that it is our business and our duty to look in some other, some new direction. It is evidently not by a new circumferential disposition of humanity, that it will be brought into new vital relations. The outward conditions may be more or less favorable to the placing of each individual soul in a position to receive the higher influences, and to live the higher life; but such conditions are scarcely within the scope of any scientific predictions. They seem to be in all cases as immediately within the hands of the highest source of good, as the good itself of which the human soul is by such conditions brought to be the recipient. Or, if there be any conditioning required, it is not to be sought in persons, events, or things without and about man, so much as *in* himself. The critical event in the career of any human soul, which shall open it to the highest consciousness, and subject it to the highest, and tenderest, and loveliest graces can never be foretold. The uninitiate spectator can scarcely believe the importance of the occasion when it is affirmed. Actions of the most ordinary kind, but performed by some particular person; events of apparently the lightest character, yet administered by providence through some delicate human relationship, often suffice to produce that sacred effect, which results from the feeling that every door of human sympathy is closed against us. It is in this sad hour; it is in such sacred mood of mind; that the holy flame descends upon the altar of the human bosom; after which the outward conditions of life in very deed become a matter of light importance. Thenceforward riches or poverty, cities or woods, association or isolation or dispersion, nay even health and sickness dwindle into films and shadows, scarcely noticeable by the regenerate soul.

To view all things as male and female is a favorite habit of many acute minds; and to such it may appear, that the forest and civilized lives are the male and female, from whose marriage an offspring shall result more conducive to human bliss. But it is difficult to conceive how corrupt parents shall have pure progeny, until their own corruption be annulled. They are rather to be estimated both as males. And, as in the olden history, the tiller of the ground is again destined to destroy the keeper of sheep, the hunter of deer.

C. L.

EJ62

RIVERSIDE EDITIONS

* In preparation